UK Cheese Producers Map

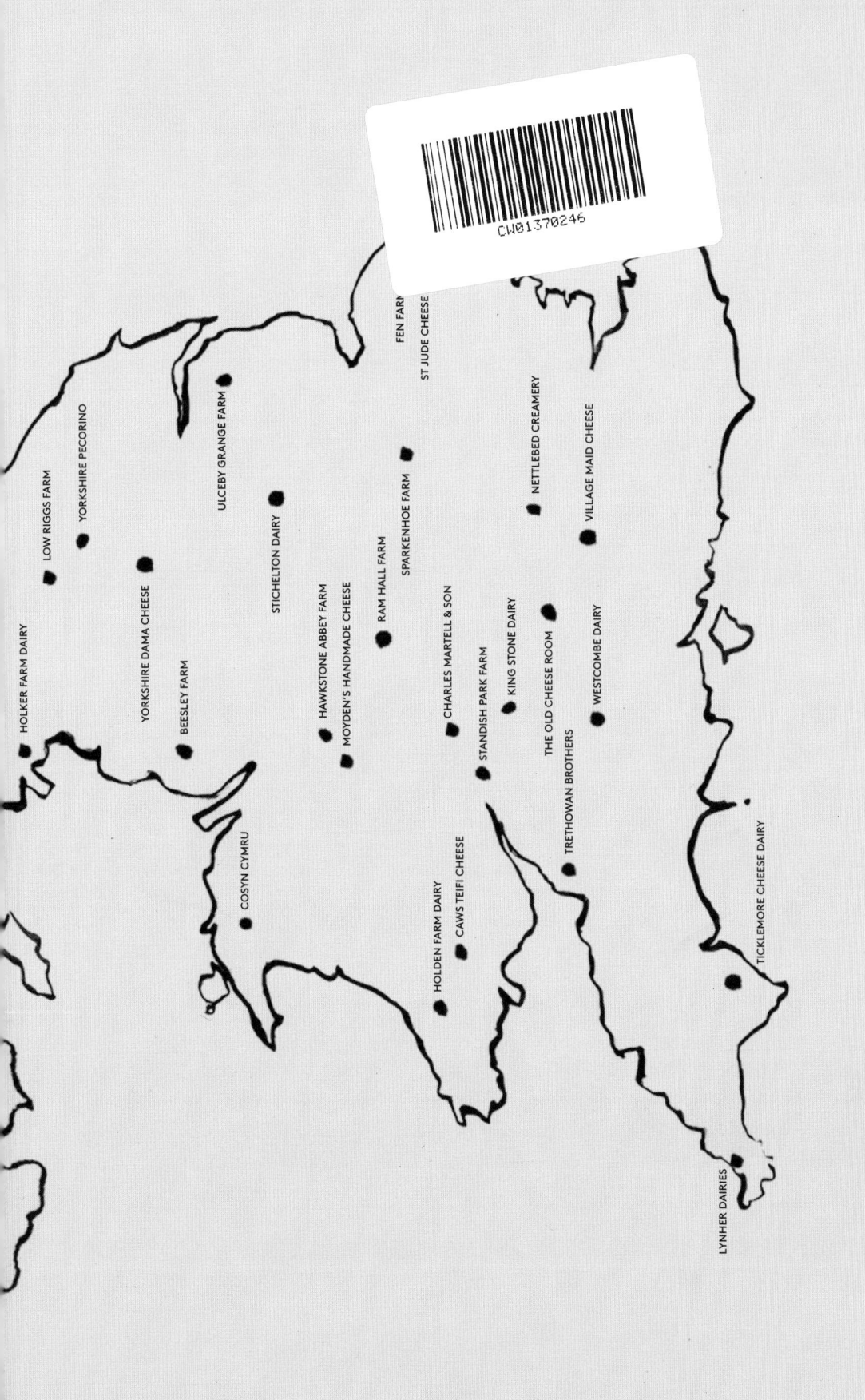

- HOLKER FARM DAIRY
- LOW RIGGS FARM
- YORKSHIRE PECORINO
- YORKSHIRE DAMA CHEESE
- BEESLEY FARM
- ULCEBY GRANGE FARM
- STICHELTON DAIRY
- HAWKSTONE ABBEY FARM
- MOYDEN'S HANDMADE CHEESE
- RAM HALL FARM
- SPARKENHOE FARM
- FEN FARM
- ST JUDE CHEESE
- CHARLES MARTELL & SON
- STANDISH PARK FARM
- KING STONE DAIRY
- NETTLEBED CREAMERY
- VILLAGE MAID CHEESE
- THE OLD CHEESE ROOM
- WESTCOMBE DAIRY
- COSYN CYMRU
- HOLDEN FARM DAIRY
- CAWS TEIFI CHEESE
- TRETHOWAN BROTHERS
- TICKLEMORE CHEESE DAIRY
- LYNHER DAIRIES

Stinking Bishop

Hafod

Caws Teifi

Stichelton

Baron Bigod

Jersey Curd

Shropshire Blue

Rollright

Kirkham's Lancashire

St Jude

Appleby's Cheshire

Witheridge

Doddington

Maida Vale

Leeds Blue

A PORTRAIT OF BRITISH CHEESE

A Celebration of Artistry, Regionality and Recipes

Angus D. Birditt

Hardie Grant
QUADRILLE

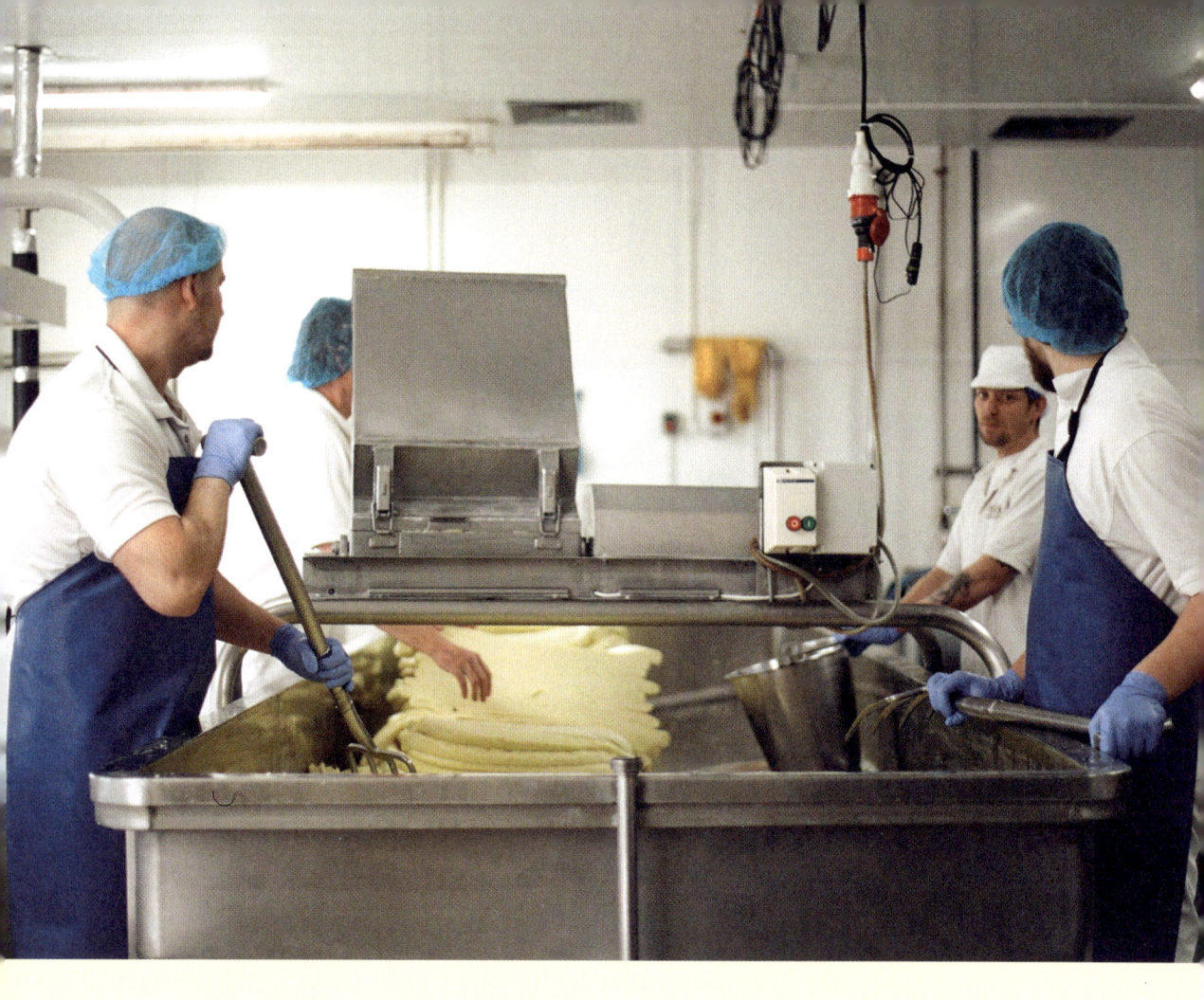

Above: The team of cheesemakers at Westcombe Dairy.

4	INTRODUCTION
10	STRUCTURE OF THE BOOK
16	FOOD PROVENANCE
20	HISTORY OF BRITISH CHEESE
26	HOW CHEESE IS MADE
50	IN SUPPORT OF BRITISH CHEESE
51	MAKING THE RECIPES
256	THE LAST VIEW
258	GLOSSARY
260	WHERE TO BUY ARTISAN CHEESE
266	FARMERS AND PRODUCERS
267	REFERENCES
268	INDEX
271	ACKNOWLEDGEMENTS

THE CHEESES

54   Appleby's Cheshire / Hawkstone Abbey Farm, Shropshire

62   Baron Bigod / Fen Farm Dairy, Suffolk

70   Berkswell / Ram Hall Farm, West Midlands

76   Cornish Yarg / Lynher Dairies, Cornwall

82   Doddington / North Doddington Farm, Northumberland

90   Gorwydd Caerphilly / Trethowan Brothers, Somerset

96   Harbourne Blue / Ticklemore Cheese Dairy, Devon

102 Jersey Curd / The Old Cheese Room, Wiltshire

108 Kirkham's Lancashire / Beesley Farm, Lancashire

114 Leeds Blue / Yorkshire Pecorino, West Yorkshire

120 Lincolnshire Poacher / Ulceby Grange Farm, Lincolnshire

126 Maida Vale / Village Maid Cheese, Berkshire

132 Rollright / King Stone Dairy, Gloucestershire

138 St James / Holker Farm, Cumbria

144 St Jude / St Jude Cheese, Suffolk

150 Shropshire Blue / Sparkenhoe Farm, Warwickshire

156 Single Gloucester / Standish Park Farm, Gloucestershire

164 Stichelton / Stichelton Dairy, Nottinghamshire

172 Stinking Bishop / Charles Martell & Son, Gloucestershire

178 Stonebeck / Low Riggs Farm, North Yorkshire

184 Westcombe Cheddar / Westcombe Dairy, Somerset

190 Witheridge / Nettlebed Creamery, Oxfordshire

198 Wrekin White / Moyden's Handmade Cheese, Shropshire

206 Yorkshire Squeaky / Yorkshire Dama Cheese, West Yorkshire

212 Brefu Bach / Cosyn Cymru, Gwynedd

220 Celtic Promise / Caws Teifi Cheese, Ceredigion

228 Hafod / Holden Farm Dairy, Ceredigion

234 Elrick Log / Errington Cheese, South Lanarkshire

242 Isle of Mull / Isle of Mull Cheese, Isle of Mull

248 Young Buck / Mike's Fancy Cheese, County Down

INTRODUCTION

Left: One of the finest views in all of Wales: the Snowdonia National Park where, nestled within the mountains, lies the dairy where Carrie makes her Brefu Bach.

Right: Gary Gray has made Appleby's Cheshire for over thirty years at Hawkstone Abbey Farm in Shropshire.

Can there be anything more blissful than savouring a sizeable chunk of artisan cheese, one that has been made lovingly by hand using traditional methods and with completely natural, full-fat creamy milk from happy cows that have grazed on diverse pasture? Sampling cheese is often seen as a refined pastime, to be conducted in an appropriate setting – but for me, to make the most of it, I prefer to pick a spot somewhere deep within the countryside, on a riverbank or in a meadow, underneath an oak or willow tree and watch any wildlife that happens to pass by. All that's needed is a slice of fresh bread or a cracker, smothered in a thick layer of salted butter, with the cheese placed carefully on top.

The monumental sight of thousands of cheeses stacked high in the maturing rooms at Ulceby Grange Farm in Lincolnshire, where they splash water on the floor to maintain humidity and the correct temperature.

I try to replicate this experience whenever possible, and when I do, I find that everything around me stops. My mind and body are soaking in the rural setting while my taste buds drown in cheesy euphoria.

For as long as I can remember, cheese has been a rich source of pleasure and indulgence, fully endorsed by my mother, who regarded it as a sort of elixir of life: 'Did you know that your great-grandmother Eva enjoyed a large slice of Irish blue cheese and a half pint of stout every night for her tea, and she lived until she was ninety-four years old!' So, of course, hearing that, I just assumed it was in my blood to eat copious amounts of the stuff and that it would do me nothing but good.

However prevalent cheese may have been on our family table, it was never there for very long and, being the youngest of three brothers, I invariably had to fight for it. Picture three boys at suppertime in our small nook of a kitchen, tussling over the grater, the last sliver of Parmesan, and a huge mound of steaming spaghetti, which all needed to be portioned equally to prevent all-out war from erupting. Often it did, ignited by one brother taking one too many sprinklings of grated cheese and with the other two fuming in righteous indignation at the unfairness of it.

Growing up in the Cambridgeshire countryside, I spent most days exploring the surrounding fields with my head full of dreams and make-believe, and always fuelled by some sort of cheese. As my teens turned into my twenties, my adventures grew longer and evolved from fantasy into fact-finding and quiet observation, and always with a cheese sandwich of some sort to keep me going. Guided by my trusty copy of Richard Mabey's *Food for Free*, I could now augment my cheese sandwiches with fresh sprigs of wild garlic or bitter dandelion.

After university, I moved to Wales, swapping the vast arable fields and open skies of East Anglia for steep mountains and long winding rivers with kingfishers, dippers and otters, and along the banks, grazing happily, cows and sheep – all rarely seen in Cambridgeshire. The cheeses changed too. After devouring Suffolk classics and Norfolk staples, I was now peeling the wax off Welsh Black Bombers, sampling Snowdonian raw ewe's milk cheese (see page 212) and trying authentic Cheshire made by the Appleby family just over the border in Shropshire (see page 54).

It has got to the point, since researching this book, that I now feel a little lost on a walk if my bag isn't weighed down with a hefty ration of cheese. To make the most of any expedition, whether pleasure- or work-related, I now try to plan my journey via a village with a shop or, better still, a cheesemonger where I can stop and indulge my dairy addiction.

Wherever I am in the countryside, I always try to connect with the land, whether by learning about the history of a particular place, identifying the local flora and fauna or by following the seasons – each bringing a bounty of different wild foods – or simply trying to raise awareness about the natural world and all its wonders.

Over the years, I have discovered that the best way to learn about such things is to find the people whose lives are deeply interwoven with the natural environment, whose knowledge and skills are perfectly adapted to its cycles, who know how to value its wildlife, harness its elements or harvest the plenty of its soil and coastline. And if the harvest is mouth-wateringly good, well, I am all the keener to learn!

My enthusiasm to learn from such individuals has led me all over the British Isles, from catching eels and crayfish under the open skies of East Anglia with the last traditional eel fisherman in the country, to foraging for dodgy-looking mushrooms in the rainforests of Snowdonia with the unofficial master of fungi. But it was the artisan cheesemaker whose quiet sense of belonging and intimate relationship with the natural environment that fascinated me the most. Maybe it was their savoury, unctuous creations that tipped the balance, but with each cheesemaker I met, I delved further and further into the extraordinarily complex and varied world of artisan cheese – the product of a magical symbiosis between land, livestock and producer.

If you came to me at the start of writing this book a couple of years ago, you would find me just touching the surface of artisan cheese – skimming the milk, if you will! Looking back, I had absolutely no idea how much I would learn about it; now it is a subject about which it seems I can never learn enough. But as I have travelled to what seems like every corner of the British Isles – clocking up thousands of miles in my old midnight-blue Saab estate packed full of cameras, raincoats, wellies, hats, shorts, books, a pair of binoculars, an old wooden wine box full of apples, beetroot juice and half-nibbled cheeses to keep me going, and regularly dragging around my other half, Lilly, or my mother, Serena – to meet the best makers in the business, nagging them to tell me everything they know, I have become spellbound by the range and complexity of British artisan cheese. It is a marvel of our isles, and one that I would like to share with you all.

The exact origin of my love of artisan cheese, besides that of my blue-cheese-loving great-grandmother, is rather blurred – the downside of having a useless memory! But what I do remember are certain events that had me swimming in dairy delight. One of my first memories is of summer holidays with my family in North Norfolk, where we would walk through the countryside and along the sweeping sands of Holkham Bay and Burnham Overy Staithe. On every walk we would stop for a picnic, laid out by my mother on a green and blue tartan blanket, which would always include a hefty slice of cheese, several baguettes and wafer-thin layers of Wiltshire ham, all masterfully constructed into sandwiches with the aid of her miniature Swiss army knife.

Another, perhaps less nostalgic, memory was of my time at university when Lilly and I worked part-time as waiters at one of the Oxford colleges. For several nights of the week, we would serve the dinner guests – the dons, fellows, guest speakers and lucky students. Each person would be served a three-course meal, and each table a crate of red, white and dessert wines, followed by a vast platter of cheese. The wine was demolished, of course, but more often than not, the cheese was never touched. So, at the end of each meal, when the guests had left, the leftover cheese was at our disposal – I will be forever grateful to Karl, the catering manager, for our weekly cornucopia of free cheese. Taking full advantage, we wrapped in baking parchment as much cheese as we could hold in our hands and balance on our bikes. Thick, melting slices of British blue and semi-soft cheeses, alongside plenty of French varieties, from Comté to Reblochon, were devoured in the wee hours of the morning, vital fuel to power us through the next day's lectures.

Although I have visited several of the best artisan and farmhouse cheesemakers in the British Isles over the course of making this book, and made cheese with a large number of them, I cannot profess to being your typical cheese expert, holding forth upon the complexities of cheese or what would go best with a full-bodied burgundy. I am more adept at putting away kilos of the stuff. I must admit with a heavy heart – or more appropriately, with a bulging stomach – that a lot of cheese was harmed in the making of this book, repeatedly ripped, sliced, gnawed and melted, mainly owing to my own self-indulgence, but all heartily enjoyed and none of it wasted.

Where I do have a smattering of experience, however, is in simple storytelling. For me, it is all about capturing the rural environment I have visited, cherishing the nature I have seen and experienced, evoking a remarkable individual I have met or community I have been among, all of whom are deeply entwined with the rural landscape and its heritage. With a background in history of art and being an artisan food producer myself, I have always been fascinated by the origins of things, the meaning of heritage and the importance of tradition. This is what Our Isles encompasses, the platform I established online to celebrate and try to conserve the wonders of the rural environment for everyone to enjoy now and in the future. This book is part of that celebration and effort at conservation – my attempt to create something both informative and beautiful, offering a glimpse into the fascinating and flavoursome world of British artisan cheese.

Structure of the book

With *A Portrait of British Cheese*, I wanted to celebrate the excellence of cheese in the British Isles. Through a selection of thirty cheesemakers and their cheeses, I hope to show how British artisan cheese is profoundly connected to the land, farm animals and people involved in making it. The book shines a light on the industry's rich heritage, community and, above all, its cheesemakers, looking at how, through a mixture of knowledge and intuition, science and artistry, they create their cheese. It also goes behind the scenes, looking at aspects of the industry and cheesemaking process that are often unsung or unseen, to show what makes each cheese unique.

The portrait I've presented in the book is a selective but, I hope, representative one, based on thirty small-scale cheesemakers in the British Isles, each chapter focusing on one of their cheeses, with an introduction to the cheese, followed by a recipe. In the introduction to the cheese, I've noted the type of landscape where the cheese is made, the farm and farming methods used to produce the milk to make the cheese – or, where the milk is collected from a local farmer, the source of the milk. I've described the types and breeds of animals – cows, sheep and goats – the distinctive milk they produce, how the cheese is made and matured, and, of course, the cheesemakers themselves. Each chapter highlights one particular cheese, though I also list other cheeses made by the same cheesemaker.

In every chapter, I've included a selection of photographs that I took during my trip, to evoke the unique environment in which each cheese is produced: the landscape, the farm and source of milk, the animals, the method, and the cheesemakers themselves. I wanted the photographs to convey an authentic portrait of British artisan cheese, evoking a sense of place and the character and dedication of the people involved, as well as highlighting the importance of farming in the production of the cheese.

Each chapter includes a recipe inspired by the particular cheese. Artisan cheese is, of course, best appreciated on its own or with a little something to enhance the flavour, such as a glass of wine, a bottle of cider, a fruit paste, and so on. Yet, the thought behind the thirty recipes included in this book was to show how the cheesemakers themselves like to enjoy their cheese, from using it in traditional, regional dishes or family favourites, to eating it with the best seasonal produce or simply enjoying it with one or two other local ingredients or products. Sometimes I have created the recipe myself, often incorporating seasonal and foraged foods that I particularly enjoy.

Angus taking photographs of cheesemakers in the field.

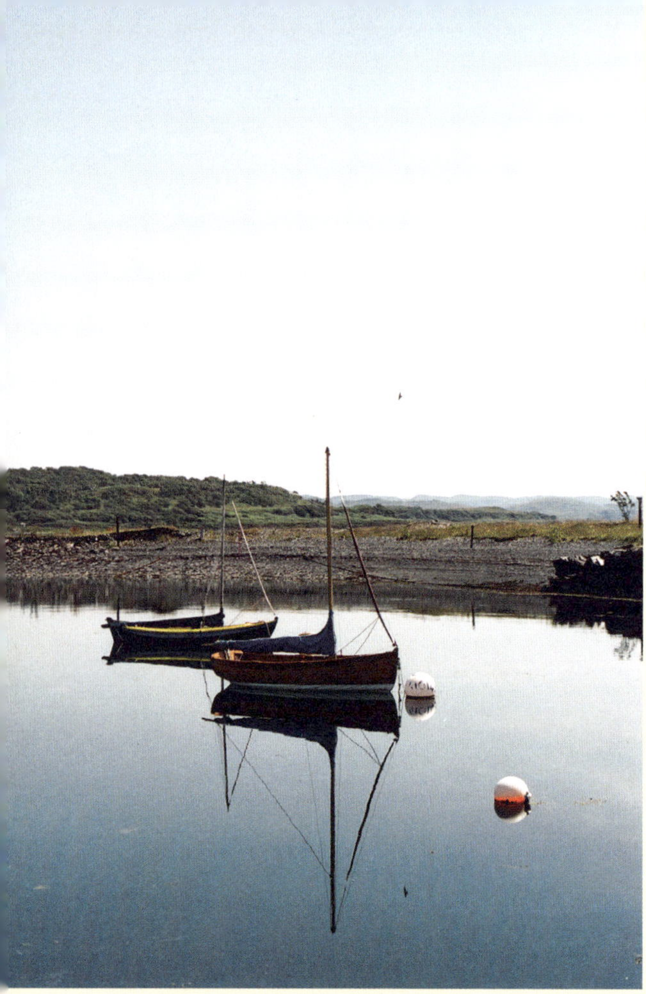

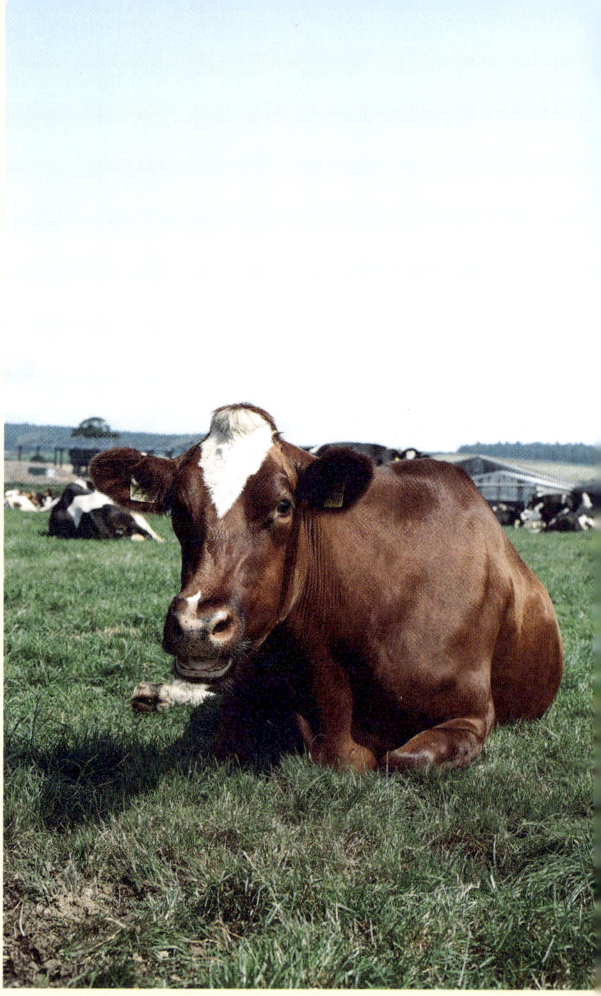

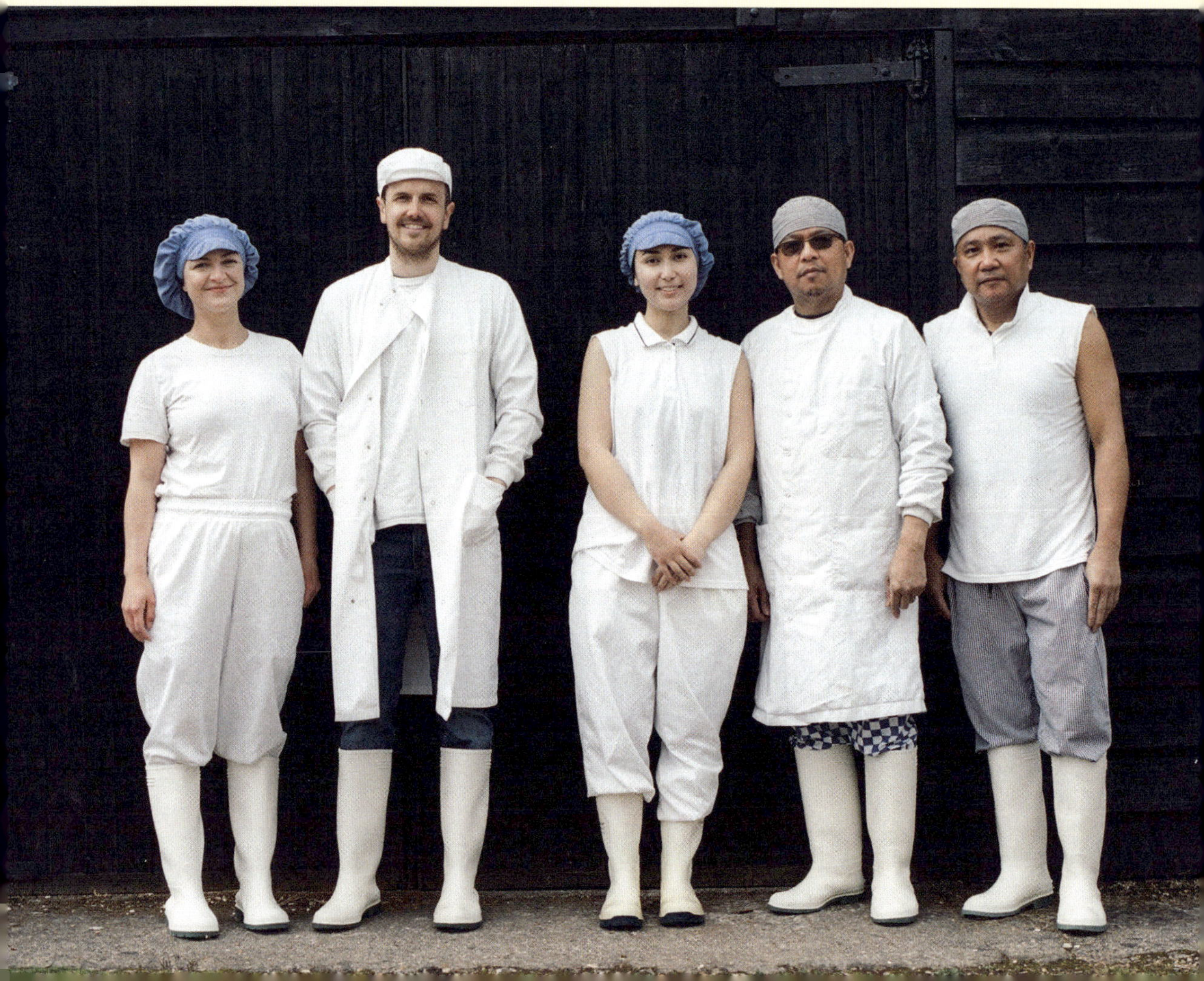

SELECTION OF CHEESES

I have tried to present a broad range of styles and flavours, locations and terrains in the British Isles, types and treatments of milk, and methods of making and maturing. I have also tried to choose cheeses that are made from milk that has been responsibly sourced from farms working to the highest standards with regard to food, farming and the environment. The majority of the cheeses are unique and, as you will discover, plenty have taken on characteristics of other cheeses, made using methods borrowed from other makers. Lincolnshire Poacher, for example (see page 120), which combines both traditional Cheddar and Alpine characteristics, is made by Simon Jones, who learned cheesemaking from the late Dougal Campbell, who in turn acquired his cheesemaking skills in the French Alps. There are cheeses, such as Kirkham's Lancashire (see page 108), made using methods that have been handed down from generation to generation, old recipes that have been reproduced, or those that have been influenced by other regions, such as Brefu Bach, a French-style soft lactic cow's milk cheese, made by Carrie Rimes using Welsh ewe's milk (see page 212).

While the book's title, *A Portrait of British Cheese*, refers to the selection of artisan cheese being made in Britain, many of the cheeses have connections to the wider world. For instance, Julianna Sedli (see page 102) makes cheese in Wiltshire that is influenced by her Hungarian heritage and American training; Mario Olianas (see page 114) makes cheese in Leeds that is inspired by his Sardinian upbringing; and Razan Alsous (see page 206) makes Syrian-style cheeses in Yorkshire.

When choosing which cheeses and cheesemakers to focus on for this book, I was truly spoilt for choice, and although I have selected only thirty cheesemakers, I would like to highlight that there are hundreds of other brilliant artisan cheeses in the British Isles, all made with dedication and passion. I hope that reading this book will inspire you to support all those other artisan cheesemakers throughout the British Isles by buying their unique and delicious cheeses.

LANDSCAPE

This book also tries to portray the diversity of the British countryside. From the cosy confines of the Lincolnshire Wolds to the vast Suffolk skies and the rocky terrain of the Inner Hebrides, I hope to capture the stunning pastoral scenery and breathtaking landscapes of the British Isles. In the introduction to each recipe, I include a few details of my visit to that particular cheesemaker, in which I talk about the day, a bit like a diary entry, noting any highlights and special memories.

Top left: Isle of Mull, Scotland.
Top right: A British Friesian-Swiss Red Holstein cross cow.
Bottom: The cheesemakers at Village Maid Cheese standing in line outside the dairy in Berkshire. From left to right: Kayleigh, Jake, Lisa, Ferdy and Ramil.

ANIMALS

The various types and breeds of animals that are used in the industry will also be acknowledged and celebrated. On these islands a range of livestock – cows, sheep, goats and buffaloes – are milked to make cheese. Britain boasts an astonishing array of breeds for each animal, including rare breeds that cheesemakers are rearing to help increase their populations and make distinctive cheeses. For example, Andrew and Sally Hattan (see page 178) make Stonebeck in Yorkshire using the cows' milk from their herd of Northern Dairy Shorthorns. In so doing, they are helping to save a rare breed of cattle that is native to Yorkshire and the surrounding counties.

COMMUNITY

With each chapter, I hope to convey that there is a wonderful, altruistic community in the artisan cheese industry – one that is enriched by its makers and fellow cheese lovers of all ages, whose passion unites all who wish to learn about and delight in the subject of cheese.

You will meet multiple generations of one family making cheese together from the same recipe as their great-great-grandmother, or newcomers to the industry producing a brand new cheese. You will come across farmers employing some of the most regenerative and sustainable agricultural methods in the UK: implementing systems to enhance soil health and structure; increasing biodiversity through hedgelaying, coppicing and planting native tree species; and improving animal welfare to enhance the quality of their milk. Some cheesemakers may use the latest technologies to make their cheese, while others rely on producing it by hand. They also almost always have some sort of charming illustration on the packaging for their cheeses, inspired by their history, whether long or short. All those involved in British cheese do it for no other reason than because it is a way of life, as far removed as possible from a conventional nine-to-five job. None of them, I can tell you, are in it to make money or to find fame; they just want to make distinctive, great-tasting cheese with a complexity of flavour that people can revel in.

CHEESEMAKERS

That brings us neatly to the cheesemakers themselves, individuals worthy of celebration, each with a fascinating story to tell. These are our lords and ladies of the land, students of the soil, herders of herbivores, masters of metamorphosing milk, whose products embody the land in all its pastoral glory.

These cheesemakers are incredibly proud of what they do, food producers that are at the top of their game, professionals in their industry. What their work entails is impressive, to say the least, not to mention exhausting: not only do they have to make the cheese, they also have to run a business; fill in copious amounts of paperwork; follow legislation and hygiene regulations; manage a team and often keep livestock too; be mindful of looking after the land; deliver their cheeses; write newsletters, and post on social media most days. Many of them have families as well, so there isn't much time to relax – hence why you'll find many a son or daughter helping out in the dairy!

Under those mesh hairnets and cotton hats are minds imbued with know-how that combines both artistry and science, with all the precise details of timings, temperature and ageing (cheese, that is), and a work ethic that demands long hours and back-breaking labour. They are among only a handful of food producers that continue to be directly inspired by the practices of our earliest forebears.

The majority of the cheesemakers portrayed in this book are also farmers, who, as well as producing cheese, tend to their animals and farm the soil. As touched on previously, many of these farmers-cum-cheesemakers represent some of the most progressive minds in the rural sphere, valuing permaculture on their farms and consciously working with the natural environment, effectively trying to mimic nature.

For all of their extra toil and dedication, and for their commitment to farming in ways that hone their milk to produce the most distinctive and delectable cheese, these cheesemakers deserve the highest praise. I have dedicated the following pages to the farming stage in the cheesemaking process in the hope of highlighting its vital importance.

Food provenance

One of the reasons for creating this book was to draw attention to artisan cheese – and particularly farmhouse cheese, produced using milk collected on the same farm – as a good example of food provenance. But what is food provenance exactly, and how do we define it? The answers to those questions would probably fill a whole book, though 'provenance' can be simply defined as 'place of origin', and is arguably the word in English that is closest in sense to the French term *terroir* – itself roughly translated as 'character of the land'.

Applied to food, provenance identifies something as the product of a specific environment, embodying its qualities and, at a wider level, connecting us directly to the land and soil, where it all begins. Like the best single malt whiskies, made with home-grown malted barley soaked in local spring water and flavoured with native peat, or raw honey tasting of the flowers from which the bees gathered nectar, or cider made with local varieties of apple and fermented naturally, farmhouse cheese is absolutely the product of a specific environment. The idea is that the climate affects the land, the land (the soil, that is) feeds the grass, the herd eats the grass and produces milk, and the milk makes the cheese, each aspect coming together to create the wonder that is farmhouse cheese and this true sense of food provenance.

The significance of food provenance is changing, for both the consumer and producer. With the urgent need to reverse climate change and improve the health of our planet, consumers are increasingly questioning where their food comes from and what impact it has on the environment. For food producers and retailers, especially supermarkets, there is mounting pressure to be completely transparent in every stage of the production process, sourcing environmentally friendly ingredients and products made using renewable methods of production that don't guzzle copious amounts of fossil fuel.

Now this may sound all hunky-dory, but in reality it's more aspiration than action, and products appearing to adhere to such ideals can be promoted by marketing magic that hides the true farming facts. You only have to observe what has happened over recent decades, where the idea of food provenance has been blurred with phrases like 'quality-sourced' and 'grass-fed', with made-up farm names and five stars on packaging all painting a picture that is often more fiction than fact.

I have been mingling with the food industry long enough to realise that many producers, however large or small, misrepresent their practices as 'sustainable' or, more recently, 'regenerative'. You will be surprised at how many will spin a fairy-tale yarn or use beguiling packaging adorned with funky fonts and earthy green hues to deflect the consumer's attention from the true means of production. Don't get me wrong – they should win every design award going – but these buzz-words and marketing puff leave us none the wiser about the traceability of ingredients, transparency of production or the welfare of the animals and people involved.

Inside 'Mike's Fancy Cheese', the cheese shop Mike runs in the Cathedral Quarter of Belfast, where you'll find a splendid array of British and Irish cheeses.

It would be more to their credit, and to the benefit of the environment, if food producers were to say instead something along the lines of 'we are working towards being sustainable' or 'we use X amount of sustainable ingredients' to be a little more transparent and precise. Many producers I have come across call their products 'sustainable' when they are using only, say, 10 per cent of sustainable ingredients in the product, the other 90 per cent being anyone's guess. There are, however, many producers with products that are genuinely sustainable, genuinely regenerative, and for the integrity of the industry, I believe we should congratulate them and not let other, less scrupulous producers set up camp beneath the same flag. This begs a couple of questions: do we need to monitor producers hiding behind such trendy buzzwords, and should there be a set framework to measure sustainability? I agree with those who ask for better, more informed labelling on products on supermarket shelves and similar large stores where you cannot ask the producer directly about the source of their product. Take buying a leg of lamb, for example. In an ideal world, you should be able to know how and where the animal was raised, what it was fed throughout its entire life, how it was slaughtered and the nutritional value of the meat.

Returning to cheese, we can see the concept of food provenance being manipulated even as far back as post-war Britain. Factories and large creameries that made cheese at sites far from the places that farmed the animals misused the term 'farmhouse cheese', devastating the already-declining farmhouse-cheese industry, which was told to label its cheese as 'traditional'. Even now, I ask myself what the difference is between a small factory and a large specialist cheesemaker using bought-in milk.

Thankfully, there are now many different ways provenance can be defined and protected; for example, through registering certain unique or 'origin' qualities, either officially through the 'geographical indication' (GI) schemes: Protected Designation of Origin (PDO), Protected Geographical Indication (PGI) and Traditional Speciality Guaranteed (TSG) that protect products sold in the UK and the EU, or even unofficially, such as signalling the use of natural starters or raw milk.

An interesting example of food provenance can been seen at Hawkstone Abbey Farm, where the Applebys make their cheese in the part of Shropshire that lies in the Cheshire Basin. As a traditional indicator of provenance, it is said that a true Cheshire cheese must be made using the milk from cows that graze solely within this region. An ancient landform dating back to the Triassic period, the Cheshire Basin was once repeatedly flooded by seawater, each time evaporating in the hot, dry climate of the period to leave layer upon layer of salt. It is on this land of ancient salt beds that the Applebys' cows now graze, which gives their milk, and hence Appleby's Cheshire, its salty, mineral notes.

Having originally bought artisan cheese just to savour its complexity, many consumers are now asking about the entire journey of the cheese: from the sustainability of the farming methods used and the standards of animal welfare to the quality of the milk being produced and the handling of the milk in the cheesemaking process. And as Patrick Holden – farmer, cheesemaker and the founder of the Sustainable Food Trust – rightly says, the key to good cheesemaking lies in being both a good cheesemaker and a good farmer, or at least a cheesemaker who uses quality milk from good farmers who pride themselves on working to the highest standards of agriculture and animal welfare. That is to say, fresh delicious milk comes from healthy livestock grazing on healthy and diverse pasture. It's as simple as that. This movement towards farming and producing food in harmony with the environment is quite rightly being promoted and celebrated, something that I also hope to encourage through this book, and which I will go into more depth later (see pages 26–33).

Britain now has a rich and varied selection of cheeses. Yet, only a hundred years ago or so, we had a much greater number of farmhouse cheesemakers in the British Isles, as we shall see.

History of British cheese

While the exact origins of cheese are unknown, I like to think it was a couple of lucky Neolithic nomads who, one hot summer's day, having just milked their small herd of recently domesticated goats, found that the milk they'd collected a few hours earlier, rather than being liquid, had turned to what looked like cottage cheese (or the Neolithic equivalent). That could be complete nonsense, but who knows, it could well be completely true!

Yet, what we do know about the history of cheese in Britain is rather compelling – a rich chapter in our food history that is steeped in rural charm and tradition, not to mention its fair share of adversity. The countryside we see today in the British Isles, the west in particular, has largely been shaped by the dairy industry.

The history of British cheese stretches back through time. We find it in the lunchboxes of Roman legions, in purpose-built Cistercian cellars and in the markets of the medieval period, adorning the stalls of recently established towns, all connected, via new roads and bridges, to the countryside where it was made. After Henry VIII dissolved the monasteries, their cheesemaking skills were transferred to enterprising farmers, who were able to learn from the displaced monks how to make their own varieties of cheese.

In the succeeding centuries, we begin to find well-known cheeses like Gloucester, Stilton, Cheshire and the once-popular Wiltshire – if not the notoriously inedible Suffolk Bang – making their way to the British cheeseboard. Up until the nineteenth century, many villages in Britain were self-sufficient. As well as the miller, the baker and the brewer, there would be the smallholder – with a few open fields, along with chickens, geese, pigs, goats, sheep and a couple of native-breed cows – who would produce small batches of farmhouse cheese from their milk and would sell their produce straight from the farm gate. Cheese-making at this time was normally done by the farmer's wife or dairymaid, in addition to all the other jobs around the farm, such as feeding the chickens and pigs, making bread and preparing meals. The fact that cheesemaking had to fit around the farming routine perhaps explains why there were so many different varieties of cheese, even within a single parish or village.

The nineteenth century saw the railways expand across Britain, significantly affecting the cheese industry. Now milk could be transported more easily and further away, from the rural areas to the growing towns and cities of Victorian Britain. This change, more than anything, marked the beginning of the decline of the farmhouse cheese industry, as cheesemakers made the logical business decision to sell their fresh milk for quick and reliable cash, to be made into cheese elsewhere, rather than perform the back-breaking work of processing the milk themselves. The most recent and indelible transformation, not only for farmhouse cheese but the countryside as a whole, came during the Second World War, when the traditional layout of fields and hedgerows was effectively redrawn and

The farmhouse kitchen at Standish Park Farm. Here Annabelle Crump makes delicious meals for her family and a range of preserves, from greengage compote to pickled beetroot.

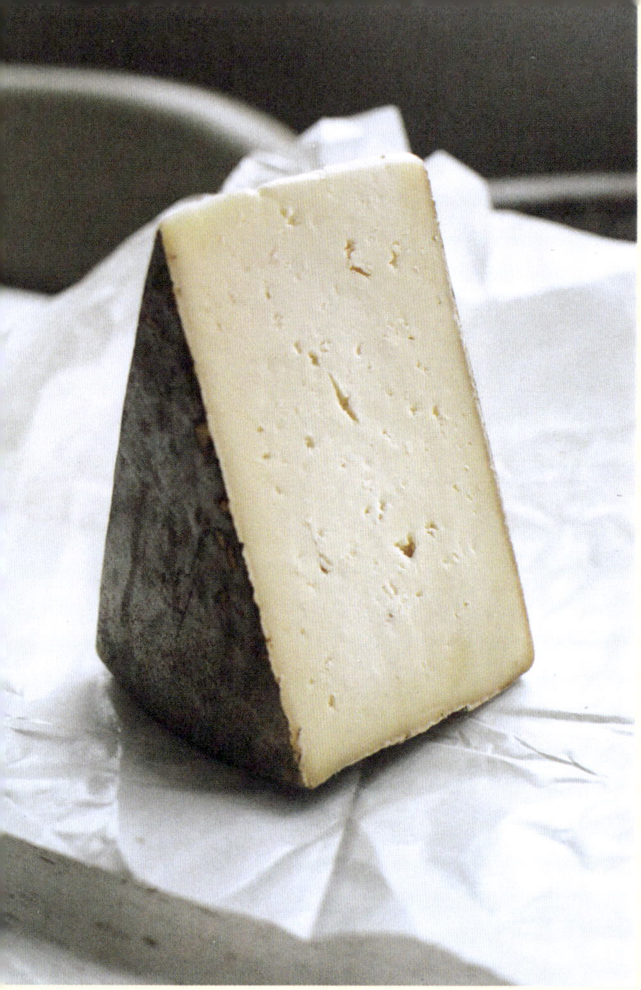
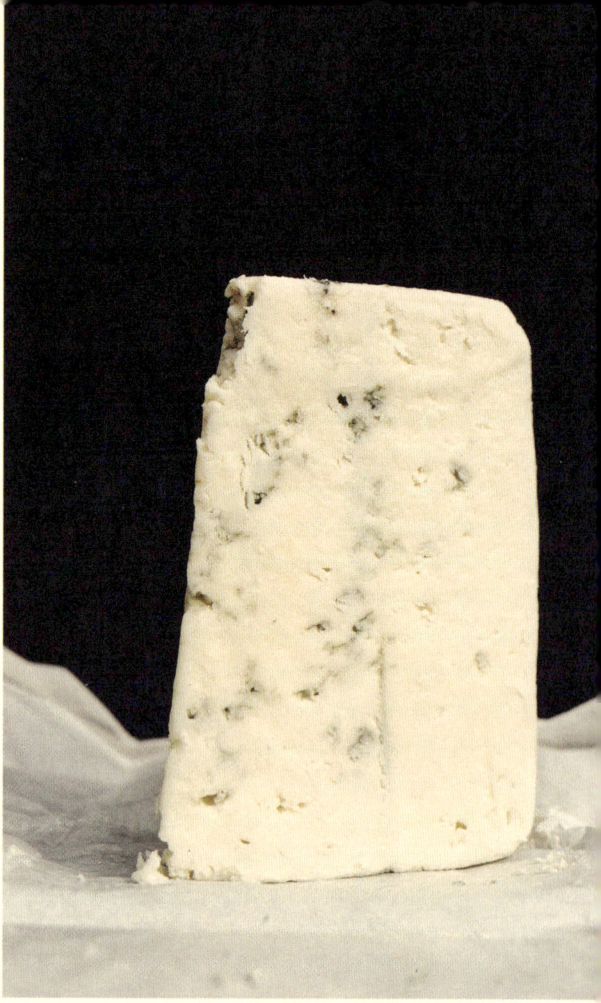
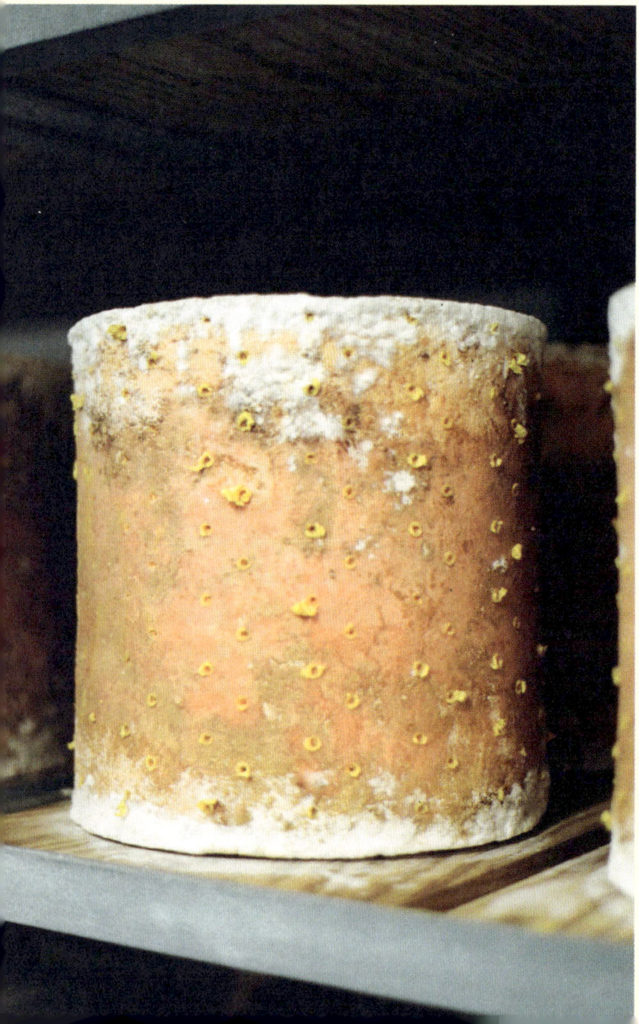
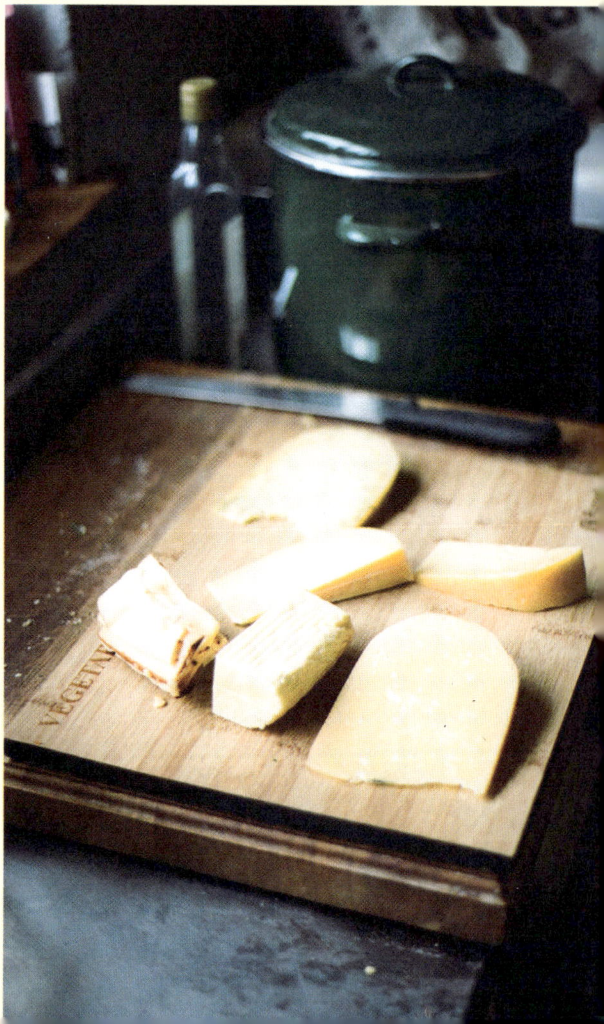

agriculture was streamlined to increase productivity to supply food for a hungry nation at war. By then, the Great War had come and gone, the Great Depression had sunk the global economy in the ensuing years, and already a huge number of farmhouse cheeses had been lost.

Another blow to the farmhouse industry in particular was the establishment in the early 1930s of the Milk Marketing Board, which, with the best of intentions, gave struggling farmers a guaranteed price for their milk, but at the same time made them more disinclined to bother with the hassle of making cheese. To make matters worse, during the Second World War many farmhouse cheesemakers were ordered to send their milk to larger, newly built production facilities to make a more uniform cheese. One particular example, nicknamed 'Government Cheddar', was a harder and more durable cheese that could last for months – perfect to transport and easy to divide up for rationing. This decision to consolidate milk production and make only a small range of hard cheeses caused a further loss to softer farmhouse varieties that didn't meet the criteria for a wartime cheese. Containing too much moisture or with too short a shelf life, they were deemed simply too inefficient to feed a nation that needed to win a war.

Over the couple of decades following the Second World War, the number of cheesemakers continued to fall, with fixed pricing of milk continuing and cooperatives and factories making a monoculture of hard-style cheeses that was generally preferred, and with the introduction of supermarkets that, according to Patrick Rance in *The Great British Cheese Book*, changed the nation's buying habits in a 'tidal wave of concrete [that] swept over the life, charm and traditional trades of many town centres'. Buying from a supermarket transformed the customer's experience from asking the cheesemonger, who knew about the cheeses, to cut the cheese to size, to helping themselves to prepacked blocks. This was a complete novelty for customers at the time, people like my mother, who remember the original white marble slabs on which the cheeses were cut, only to be replaced with bland shelves of pre-cut wrapped slabs of cheese with no one there to advise you what to buy.

A new demand grew for consistency in food that farmhouse cheese just couldn't provide. At the turn of the 1970s, there were still some small-scale producers of cheeses such as Cheddar and Cheshire, but they didn't have a premium and were too localised to make much impact. To make matters worse, supermarkets were opting to buy mass-produced block cheeses that tasted the same with each batch and were easy to sell – far easier, it seems, than small-batch farmhouse cheeses that were far more variable in taste and, in some cases, challenging to the palate. According to Patrick Rance, many food critics at the time said that the character

Clockwise from top left: Duckett's Aged Caerphilly.
A chunk of Beenleigh Blue.
Slices of Caws Teifi.
A wheel of Shropshire Blue.

of cheese was being lost when you couldn't tell the difference between a Double Gloucester and a Red Leicester. Britons as a nation were becoming increasingly disconnected from where their food originated and expected cheese to look and taste quite bland and homogeneous – very different, in short, from the artisan cheese that we enjoy today.

It was the brilliantly named Patrick Lowry Cole Holwell Rance who, in the latter part of the twentieth century, saw the time was ripe for a resurgence in artisan cheese and whose seminal book I refer to on the previous page. Together with the revival's protagonist were other stalwarts in the industry, such as Mary Holbrook (championing goat's cheese), James Aldridge (washed-rind cheese), Humphrey Errington (ewe's milk cheese), Robin Congdon (blue cheese), Dougal Campbell (organic production), Lucy and Lance Appleby (Cheshire cheese) and Charles Martell (rare Gloucester cows). In addition to these individuals were Neal's Yard Dairy (established in the summer of 1979) and Paxton & Whitfield (in business since 1797), who all worked together to entice the nation to eat more artisan cheese and, in doing so, saved many varieties from extinction.

Another key figure is Randolph Hodgson, who was instrumental in reinvigorating the production of cheese made from raw milk, having secured its survival after various attempts to ban it completely after a number of food scares in the late 1980s. On one celebrated occasion, Randolph rang in to make his case during a discussion on the topic on BBC Radio 4's *Today* programme. After listening to Randolph's plea to the nation to save raw milk cheese and with it a sizable portion of British culinary heritage, the presenter then asked, 'So, who are you representing?' to which Randolph replied, 'On behalf of the Specialist

Cheesemakers Association.' This discussion and resulting press actually lead to strengthening both food safety and the future of raw milk cheesemaking in the UK. There was no such organisation, in fact, but shortly afterwards, in 1989, Randolph set up the Specialist Cheesemakers Association to give farmhouse cheesemakers a platform. Now, overseen by its patron the Prince of Wales, the association supports cheesemakers, cheesemongers and others in the 'specialist' cheese sector. Since then, the emergence of a whole range of suppliers and other outlets – from cheesemongers, farm shops and delicatessens to farmers' markets, food festivals, food programmes and awards – all promoting the sale of artisan cheese, has been a lifeline for many cheesemakers, allowing them to stay in business and indeed flourish.

The coronavirus pandemic has been a major setback to the industry, however, especially at the beginning, when the vast majority of cheesemakers struggled with restaurant and wholesaler closures. Many were forced to halt production until they knew they could start selling again, a luxury that many farmhouse cheese producers who process their own milk could not afford. Farming, as we will hear later on, is a cycle, which simply cannot stop. Some artisan cheesemakers sadly had to cease production altogether, such as Innes Cheese at Highfields Farm in Staffordshire, well known for its raw-milk goat's cheeses. Cheesemakers who were able to adapt focused on producing harder cheeses, such as Martin Gott at Holker Farm in Cumbria (see page 138), who produced more of his harder cheese, Crookwheel, rather than his soft cheese, St James.

Throughout each lockdown, despite inconsistent supply and demand for their cheeses and multiple restrictions put in place, the cheesemakers slowly began to steady themselves, finally seeing the light at the end of a very long tunnel.

During this time, however, there was a silver lining. With the help of food writers, whether household names or simply cheese lovers, the artisan cheese community was able to encourage a locked-down nation to buy a growing mountain of cheese that had accumulated over the year, in the hope of saving and sustaining the nation's cheesemakers, which they did valiantly in their thousands. This huge surge of public support and interest undoubtedly saved a great number of suppliers from disappearing.

Over the year and successive lockdowns, the cheesemakers established or improved their online sales and direct delivery in order to survive. Many cheesemakers were forced to make new cheeses, both hard types for longer shelf life and soft varieties to expand their range. For example, David Jowett at King Stone Dairy in Gloucestershire (see page 132) created Ashcombe, a semi-hard cheese with a washed rind. Ashcombe enabled David to sell a cheese with a longer shelf life alongside his other softer cheeses, such as Rollright and Evenlode. Another great example is Lypiatt, a soft cheese with an ash-coated rind made by Julianna Sedli at The Old Cheese Room (see page 102); the cheese is named after one of their fields at Neston Park Home Farm in Wiltshire. Meanwhile, the team at Holker Farm made Holbrook, a hard goat's milk cheese named after the late Mary Holbrook.

How cheese is made

After seeing how the book is structured and how wonderful it is to be involved in the cheese community, and following a brief overview of the history of British cheese, it's now time to take a look at the whole, astonishingly complex process behind its production, which I have tried to encompass in three stages: farming, making and maturation.

I should mention that for the makers of farmhouse cheese, cheesemaking is often only one part of their farming activities, alongside participation in agri-environment programmes such as the Environmental Land Management (ELM) schemes, selling milk to wholesalers or direct from the farm gate, selling grain or rearing livestock for meat. It is also worth noting that each of the three stages involved in the production of cheese (farming, making and maturation) has a web of variables, some that overlap, many that are in constant flux and all of which affect the subsequent stage and the final flavour of the cheese – taste is another aspect I will touch on at the end. No single stage or variable is more important than another.

All the cheesemakers I have met unanimously agree that to make a good cheese you need to get every stage of the process right, and each stage is never one-dimensional. Not only is it about working with specific environmental conditions – even down to the weather on a particular day – and maintaining a high level of animal welfare to create good-quality milk, it is also about needing the skill and knowledge to tend to and manage the milk along every stage of the process that leads to the finished cheese. Cheesemaking is all about good practice and keeping it simple, which requires diligence in every aspect. It is a subject that many of the best cheesemakers, whose families have been making cheese for centuries, will say that they are still learning, every day. So let's look at the first of the three stages of cheesemaking: farming.

FARMING

Farming is the foundation of food provenance, and how food tastes is directly related to the quality of the soil and the land. This stage is effectively the start of the cheesemaking process, so it is up to the dairy farmer, farm manager or herdsman to implement a system using a range of techniques to produce milk whose taste and quality can be transferred to the cheese.

Any artisan cheesemaker will tell you that the quality of milk they are using is paramount, and it is the choice of system, the farming and husbandry methods employed that will help to determine the quality of milk. Other factors include the farm's unique ecosystem, the time of year, the animal type, breed and feed, even how the animal is milked – the treatment and condition of the udders, for example. It is the farmer or herdsman's job to work

Clockwise from top left: Field margins at Holden Farm Dairy.
Caws Teifi herding.
Friesland sheep at Berkswell.
Milking with Laura at Sparkenhoe Farm.

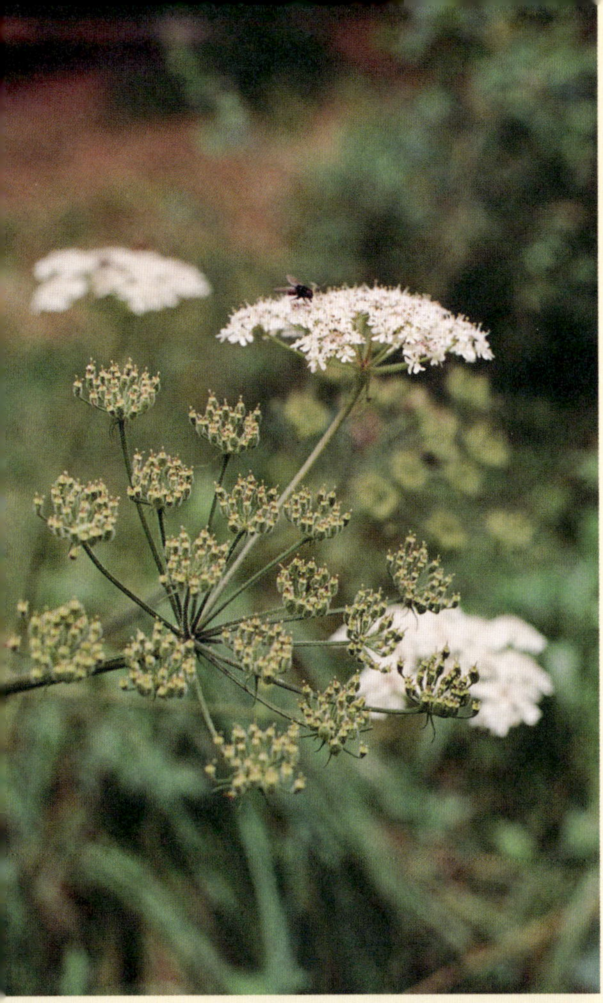
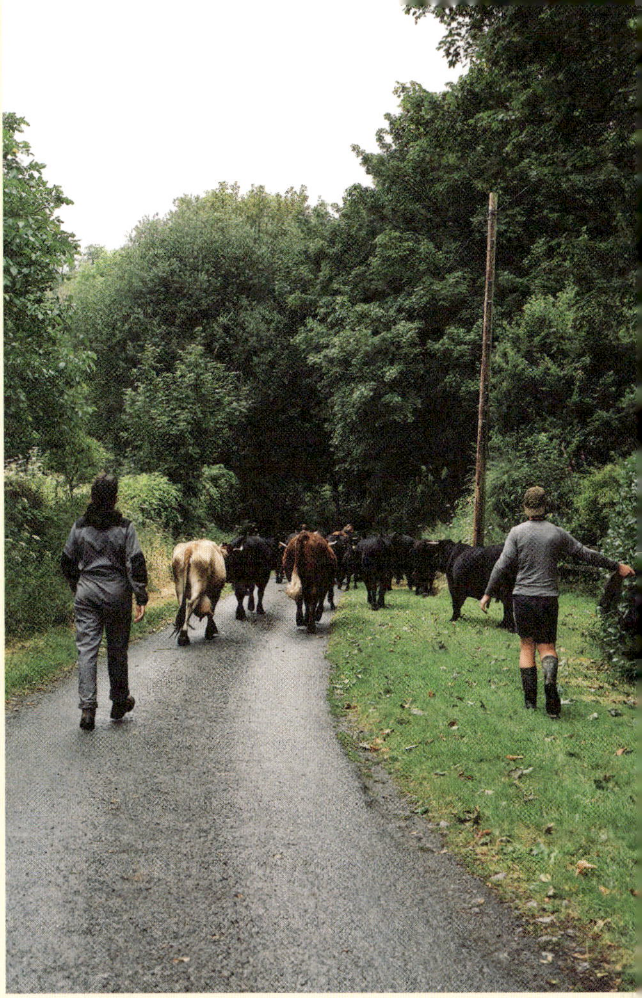
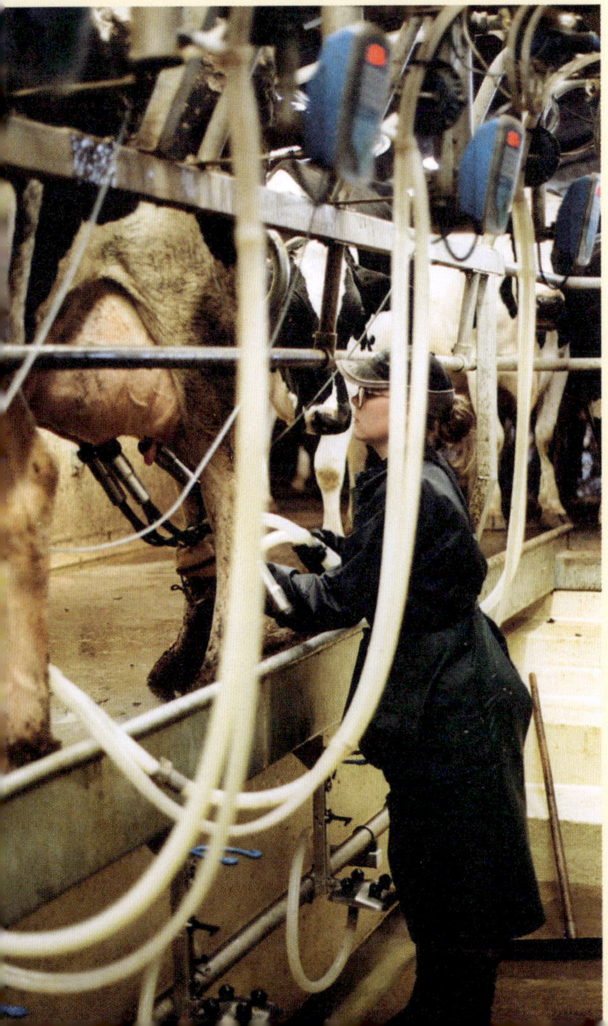
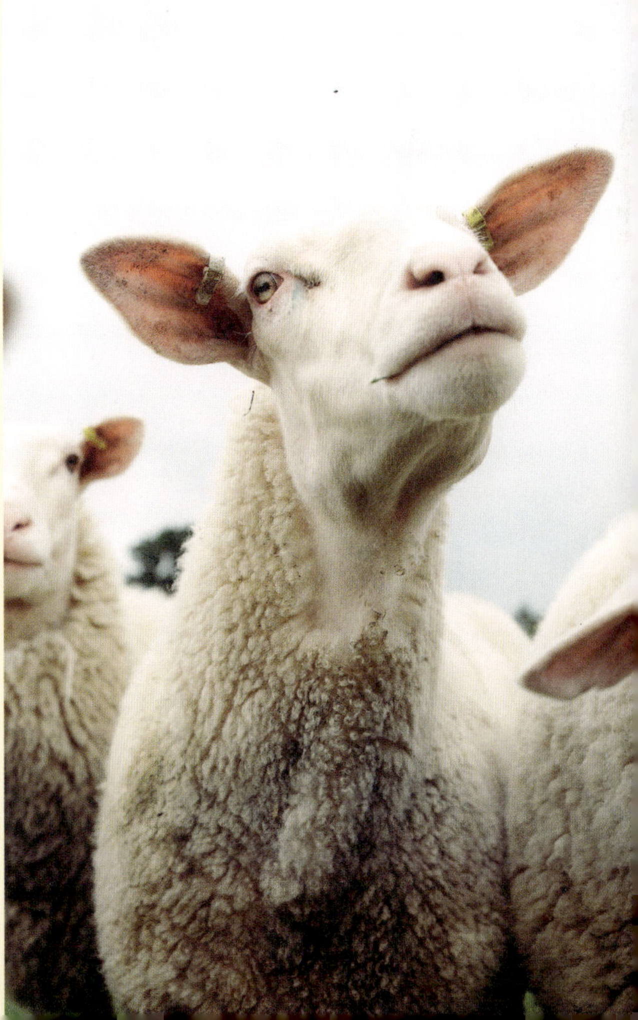

with those variables to produce the best possible milk at that time for cheesemaking.

In this book, I focused mainly on farmhouse cheesemakers who implement a regenerative farming system to produce their milk and who adhere to high standards of food production and farming, with nature and the environment uppermost in their minds. A number of these cheesemakers are certified organic, many choose to farm with rare species and several use raw milk to make their cheese, which involves following stricter regulations than for pasteurised milk. Being a farmhouse cheesemaker means that you have complete control over the milk used to make your cheese. In most cases, the milk is taken straight from the animal in the morning and in the afternoon, and channelled directly from the milking parlour to the cheese-making room.

The artisan cheesemakers in this book have been selected because they work closely with the farmers and herdsmen who provide them with their source of milk, many of whom are working to the highest standards of farming and food production. These cheesemakers collect milk or have it delivered from a local farm. By contrast, many artisan cheese-makers across the UK source their milk from larger cooperatives that take in milk from a number of farms.

Many of the farmhouse cheesemakers featured in the book are actively looking at ways to rejuvenate the land, particularly the health and structure of the soil, while feeding a nutritious diet to their animals to produce good-quality milk. These farmers are endeavouring to farm in harmony with the land and nature. An excellent example is Patrick and Becky Holden at Bwlchwernen Fawr (Holden Farm Dairy – see page 228), who make Hafod. Patrick has been farming organically at Bwlchwernen Fawr since 1973, which makes it the longest-serving registered organic dairy farm in Wales. Both Patrick and Becky believe that a farming system should be designed to produce not only high-quality, nutrient-dense food but also to improve the land, whether in relation to soil health, structure and fertility, to encourage greater biodiversity or to enhance carbon sequestration.

This leads me to regenerative agriculture – a system that aims to regenerate the productivity and diversity of the land (soil) and the wider environment (see below) – which I will touch on only briefly as it is such a vast topic and one that is still far from being defined, or perhaps, more accurately, it is me who has not fully grasped every aspect of it. But what is clear is that implementing a change to a farming system, whether intensive or conventional, to one that is regenerative doesn't happen overnight. It can take months, and even years, to see substantial improvement.

In some cases, you even have to adopt intensive measures initially to move towards being regenerative – taking one step back to take two steps forward. An example of this is when a farmer wants to plant a diverse herbal ley on which to feed their livestock – which I will explain in greater depth later. One farmhouse cheesemaker told me that to plant a diverse herbal ley, they would need to either plough up (breaking soil structure) or use a herbicide to remove the competitive perennial ryegrass. Which is better or, perhaps, which is worse? It can be simply a matter of choosing the lesser of two evils.

But how does one become a regenerative farmer or regenerative farmhouse cheesemaker? There are several farming methods that are seen to be regenerative, such as maximising crop diversity, growing companion crops and a move towards direct drilling, and minimum- or no-till farming. Although, as I mentioned, this is very hard to implement without use of herbicides, which have a negative impact on the fertility of the soil and therefore should be avoided if at all possible. One of the most popular methods is rotational or mob grazing, in which a large area of pasture is divided up by electric fences into smaller paddocks, each grazed on a rotational basis, allowing the vast majority of the pasture to rest.

In allowing pasture to rest, rotational grazing gives enough time for plants to grow above ground while establishing a more complex root system in the soil. This stronger, longer root system has so many benefits: it binds the soil together, reducing soil erosion; it improves soil fertility by tapping into mineral sources deeper in the soil; it improves water filtration in both droughts and floods owing to the longer roots; it improves soil health by encouraging micro-organisms to aerate the soil and create symbiotic interactions between the plants and the soil; and it draws down carbon in the environment. Allowing pasture to grow also creates a thick bed of organic matter above the ground, which is trampled by the livestock and gives the soil beneath a natural protective layer.

To increase the overall benefits of rotational grazing, farmers in both the meat and dairy industries are growing diverse herbal leys – a species-rich mixture of grasses, herbs and legumes. Each species is grown to do a particular job, from nitrogen-fixing plants such as clover, to plants with longer roots such as dandelion and lucerne that can draw up moisture from deeper in the ground. Growing mixed herbal leys also considerably lessens the need for artificial fertilisers and pesticides, reduces veterinary bills and gives animals a higher level of nutrients such as protein, for example, because of the inclusion of legumes in particular. Including legumes in pastures also enables the farmers to move away from their current dependency on nitrogen fertiliser, the use of which makes it very difficult for a wide range of wildflowers and herbs to coexist with nutrient-hungry and aggressive ryegrass.

Popular plant species being grown in diverse herbal leys include chicory, various types of fescue, three types of clover (alsike, red and white), bird's-foot trefoil, cocksfoot, burnet, plantain, timothy, sainfoin and yarrow, to name a handful. For the regenerative-minded dairy farmer, growing a diverse seed mixture provides a nutrient-rich diet for their livestock, and, for the cheesemaker, is thought to lead to a more complex milk to make cheese.

But it is important to note that every farm is different and will need to plant different species or tailor certain techniques to the specific terrain and conditions on the farm and in accordance with its own farming practices. I've visited many farmers over the years, and more and more of them are saying that observation is key, assessing what the livestock prefers and how the different plant species are faring. What I hear from many regenerative farmers is that, for both meat and dairy production, livestock management – using more native breeds and moving away from labour-intensive types such as Holstein-Friesians requiring higher volumes of feed – is essential for rejuvenating soil health and improving the wider environment.

In the livestock community, organisations such as the Pasture-Fed Livestock Association promote and support farmers using regenerative farming methods such as rotational grazing, as it increases grazing periods and, specific to the PFLA, promotes animals that are 100 per cent grass-fed, rather than reared partly on widely used feeds such as grain or soya. And going back to food provenance, the PFLA's 'Pasture for Life' certification can really help to clarify what we are eating.

A great example of a farmhouse cheesemaker looking at ways to become more regenerative is Westcombe Dairy in Somerset (see page 184). The farmers and herdsmen at Lower Westcombe Farm rotate their cattle on species-rich pasture, sectioning off their fields into smaller paddocks to enable part of the land to be grazed while the rest is allowed to grow and develop. They also grow wholecrop silage, including barley, peas and vetch (the two latter are both nitrogen-fixing), as well as cover crops that reduce soil erosion and improve structure, while they are phasing out their maize as it is a high-input monocrop with low resistance to disease or adverse weather and, compared to pasture, not a natural feed for livestock. Everything for the Westcombe team is at the experimental phase, though they hope to see that growing a diverse, healthy pasture will affect the final flavour of the cheese and result in happier cows able to graze outside for longer.

There are a small number of dairy farmers who produce milk entirely from grass-fed animals, but this requires a very high level of skill in pasture management and high-quality winter feed in the form of hay or silage, whereas it's not always possible to grow enough grass in the summer to feed a year-round calving herd – it is the British climate, after all! For Patrick and Becky at Holden Farm Dairy, the compromise is to feed their herd some home-grown organic grains and provide adequate nutrition during challenging periods of the year such as the autumn, when the nutritional quality of grass declines.

As we have seen, a species-rich sward is beneficial for the soil and the livestock, but it also encourages biodiversity. A diverse range of plant species helps to attract insects for pollination, and by allowing pasture to rest and grow, it will attract ground-nesting birds such as the curlew, lapwing or sandpiper, which are increasingly in danger of losing their habitats. Other ways farmers are encouraging biodiversity in their farms include planting native trees, more hedgerows and wildflower margins, which encourage invertebrates and larger wildlife to the area. Many farmers are also leaving areas on their farm to grow wild, or 'rewild', in the form of hedgerows, for instance, or by allowing shrubs to grow in fields to encourage the growth of oak trees and attract small mammals. Another way to promote biodiversity is to buy in fewer unsustainable inputs, such as artificial fertilisers and animal feed, and focus where possible on growing everything on the farm.

Farming is governed by a series of overlapping cycles: of the day, week, month and year; of the seasons and the phases of the moon; of plant rotation, animal lactation and grazing; of nutrients such as carbohydrates and chemical elements such as nitrogen; and of different generations of farmers and livestock. Each and every cycle has specific demands that determine when and what jobs need to be done on the farm and, in this case, to produce the best quality of milk for cheesemaking.

To understand this a little better, let's take a very brief look at each season throughout the farming year at Holden Farm Dairy in Wales, where Patrick and Becky make their Hafod Cheddar. Come spring, the warmer weather arrives after a long winter in west Wales. This means that the Holdens' beautiful herd of Ayrshires can be turned out to grass for the next seven months or longer, depending on the weather and particularly the rainfall, when there will be plenty of lush pasture to graze. Over the summer months, silage and hay are made, and the cows are still out munching on the species-rich pasture of grasses, legumes and herbs that includes three types of clover (alsike, red and white), bird's-foot trefoil, chicory and plantain. In the autumn, Patrick and Becky start to gradually bring in the cows for the night, feeding them on the species-rich silage grown on the farm in the previous months. When winter starts to close in, the barns are mucked out and straw bedding is laid down. Throughout these colder months, the cows are fed on feed that has been stored throughout the year – mostly silage and hay, but including oats and peas and whole-grain cereals, all organic and grown on the farm. Each day is different on the farm, determined by the aforementioned variables, all of which influence the taste and quality of the milk produced on that particular day.

Fundamentally, if everything during the farming stage is done to the highest possible standards – the soil is healthy and the pasture is diverse, the animals are well nourished and happy, and the milk being produced is consistent (many farmers calve year round to achieve this) – then, like a chef cooking with top-quality seasonal produce, the cheesemaker is already halfway to making a delicious cheese.

Farming has come under plenty of scrutiny in the last couple of decades, since the realisation that agricultural intensification is having a detrimental impact on climate change, soil health, biodiversity and the level of vital nutrients in our food. Yet, we cannot simply point the finger at the farmers growing our food. It is most important to question the demands and the policies from larger retailers and the government. It is obvious that our current agricultural policies need to

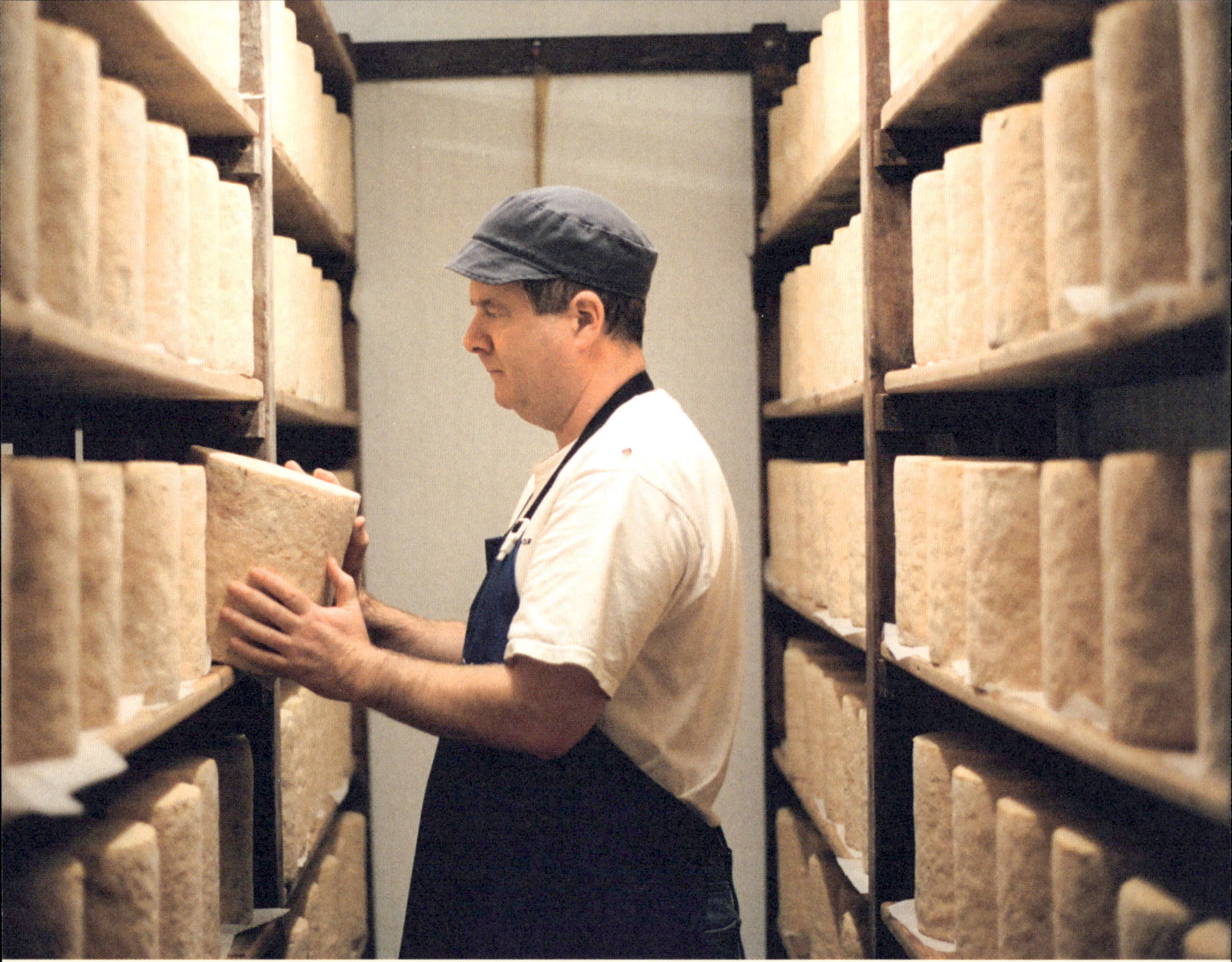
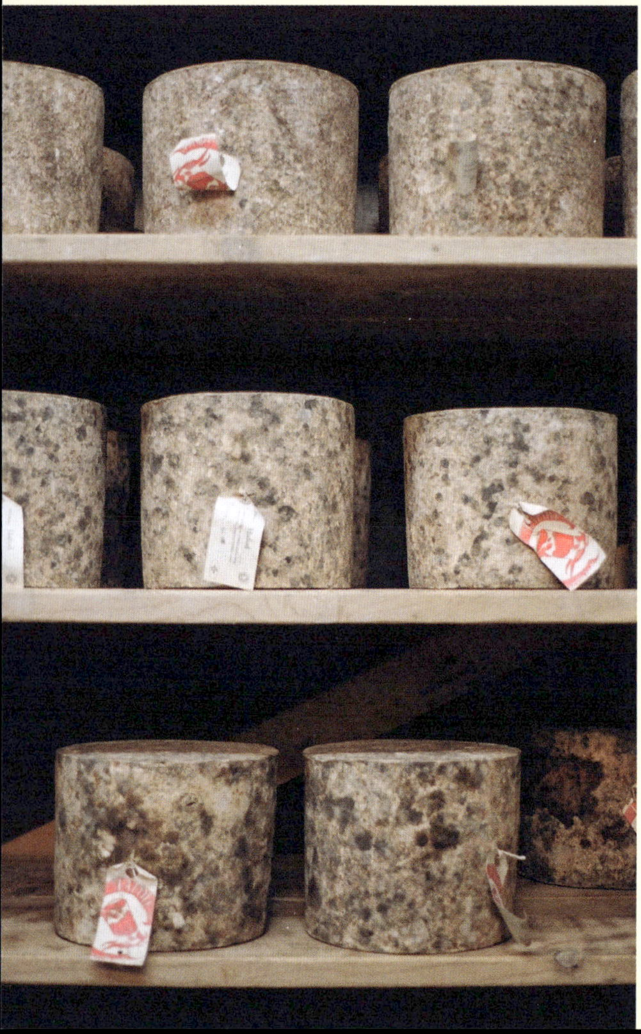
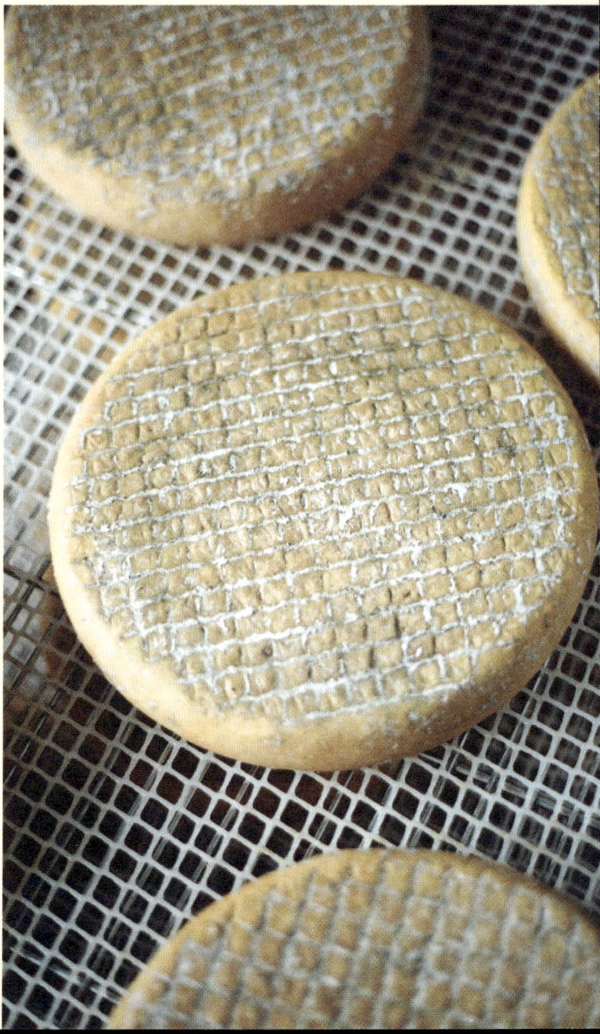

change – and they are improving, to some extent – but time is of the essence, and we need them to recognise and celebrate those that farm in a more regenerative way and work towards more sustainable food and farming systems.

It is important, however, to note that for the integrity and future of the industry it isn't dressed up as something it is not, and that others don't hide behind the relatively small number of farmers who are implementing good practices at the cutting edge of farming regeneratively and combating climate change. It should be highlighted also that too many so-called artisan and farmhouse cheeses are made using extremely intensive farming methods such as zero grazing, where the cows are kept indoors all year round, animals are fed on imported grain and soya, and the land is treated with artificial fertilisers. This book aims to support and celebrate those farmers and cheesemakers that are heading in a more positive direction to improve food and farming standards and the health of the environment.

Among the many farmhouse cheesemakers I've spoken to are a handful who are intent upon implementing past methods with new ideas and modern technologies to be as environmentally friendly as possible. An example of this is introducing – or more accurately, reintroducing – more native breeds into herds. These native breeds can be more easily managed, have longer grazing periods and can be fed on a species-rich crop that can be grown on the farm to produce high-quality milk for cheesemaking. This moves away from what many farmers have been doing over the last few decades, focusing on high-maintenance, high-costing breeds that need greater inputs of feed such as imported grain and soya, and demand intensive farming methods to produce high yields of milk, which is simply not sustainable. So while there is a move towards more sustainable farming methods, there are still many farmers who are not heading in this direction and who continue to use intensive farming systems.

The next phase is all about the making, the stage in which the cheesemaker uses his or her knowledge, skill and intuition, in a combination of artistry and science, to turn milk into cheese.

CHEESEMAKING

It's very early in the morning, the sun is just about up, and Paul Appleby and his farming hands have already milked the cows at Hawkstone Abbey Farm. I am in one of the cheesemaking rooms at the Applebys' farm, deep in rural Shropshire. In the room is a huge stainless-steel vat full of ivory-coloured milk, slowly sloshing as it is stirred by a mechanised paddle and shining in the natural light flooding in through the sash windows. The room is warm, and sharply scented with a sour yoghurt smell. Several cheesemakers are present, all tending to the vat in one way or another, treating the milk with both care and urgency as it starts to acidify. I have painted this picture to give you

Clockwise from top: Head Cheesemaker Joe Schneider in the maturing rooms at Stichelton Dairy.
St Helena at St Jude in Suffolk.
Hafod maturing room.

a rough idea of where I found myself most mornings when conducting research for this book – kitted out in the latest hygienic gear, and with my camera and notepad to hand, ready for the cheesemaking to begin!

There is no set rule to making cheese. It is all about the gentle acidification of milk, clotting it with rennet and tending to the curds to form the cheese. To make things a little clearer, I have noted down a few basic processes: heating the milk; adding starter culture and rennet; separation and set; cutting the curds and expelling the whey; salting, moulding and ageing the curds. I say 'basic', but really each step of the cheesemaking process has plenty of variables to it. 'The make', as it's called in the cheesemaking world, can be dependent on the conditions of the season, and even on a particular day, especially if you are working with raw milk.

Other variables include handling and temperature of the milk, timing, the amounts and type of starter culture and rennet, point of flocculation (when coagulation occurs and the solid curds begin to separate from the liquid whey), cutting and treatment of the curds, including salting, pressing and moulding, and even the size of the cheesemaker's hands. That's not to mention other factors such as the cheesemaker's own experience and intuition; the unique recipe they may be following, including the techniques used, whether traditional or modern; the location of the dairy and how it is set up, along with the particular equipment used in the making. I did say there were many variables!

At this first stage, it is all about the cheesemaker nurturing the milk, allowing it to develop its own character during the course of the process, which gives the final cheese its unique flavour and texture. As we have seen, milk differs throughout the year owing to the changing seasons and phases of the farming cycle. It is often said that the less intervention during the make, the better the cheese, reflecting the very essence of the milk collected straight from the animal.

From my experience of helping out at many farms and creameries around the British Isles, it is important to note that, in terms of hygiene, cheesemaking is perhaps one of the most highly regulated areas in the food industry, especially for those cheesemakers who use raw milk to make their cheese. Understandably, food safety is one of the most important aspects of the cheese industry. Simply walking into a cheesemaking room takes time because of the amount of cleaning and sanitising you have to do: signing in; washing hands and forearms (a cheesemaker's version of washing their hands); donning new boots or shoe covers, a coat and hair net.

Hygiene in cheesemaking, in terms of microbial activity, is almost a contradiction in terms, one could say. It is a delicate balancing act for cheesemakers, who are essentially nurturing both the souring process of milk and the decaying process of cheese (deliberately introducing 'good' bacteria) for the sake of flavour and texture while at the same time, of course, trying not to poison their customers (inadvertently introducing 'bad' bacteria, such as pathogens). But it would seem that, even at the microbial level, diversity may help. Many scientists and environmentalists believe that we are living in an environment that is becoming increasingly sterile, one that needs greater biodiversity in order to fight contamination naturally, and, with regard to cheese, simply reinstate the functioning of the microbiome – a fascinating subject that I will cover in more detail later. Others, meanwhile, believe that thorough sanitising to remove all microbial communities minimises the occurrence of pathogenic microorganisms that cause disease. This is a complex environmental, cultural and political issue that I won't delve into further here, though it is nonetheless an interesting and highly relevant topic.

So, as we all (I hope) know, cheesemaking starts with milk, and in the case of farmhouse cheese, it is taken straight from the animal and channelled from the milking parlour to the cheesemaking room, where it flows into a vat. How the milk is handled is incredibly important, with many farmhouse cheesemakers preferring to use the gentle pull of gravity to channel their milk into the vats. The concern is that, if the milk is pumped, too much pressure can cause 'shearing', which damages the fats in the milk. On this basis, many new dairies are designed so that the cheesemaking room is slightly lower than the milking parlour.

Depending on the preference of the cheesemaker, the style of cheese being made and the set-up in the dairy, the milk used in the cheesemaking process will either be just the morning's milk, or a mixture of the morning and evening's milk. If the cheesemaker is using only the morning's milk to make cheese, it is usually warm already, straight from the animal, and doesn't always need to be reheated, whereas if the cheesemaker is using the evening's milk as well (which will have been refrigerated overnight), it will need to be reheated to the desired temperature. Depending on the style of cheese being made, the milk is gently directed into the vat or vats and warmed for a specific length of time and to a specific temperature. As the milk is warmed, it is usually gently stirred at this point, either by hand or using a mechanised paddle, to prevent it from forming a skin and to keep it at an even temperature throughout the heating process.

Cheesemaking is essentially a process of fermentation, in which the lactose (sugar) in the milk is turned into lactic acid. To do this, a starter culture of 'friendly' bacteria is added to the warm milk, beginning what's called acidification or culturing of the milk, which also helps to prevent pathogens from gaining a foothold. Starter cultures are amazing things, and can either be imported in various forms or produced on the farm.

One form of starter culture, known as a 'pint starter', consists essentially of a pint of frozen milk that includes strains of bacteria that have been captured at a particular place and time. Many farmhouse cheesemakers use Barber's pint cultures – named after the Barber family who developed them initially when they began making Cheddar in Somerset from 1833 – that go back decades. The type of starter culture used will determine to some extent the flavour of the cheese being made. Some cheesemakers, such as the Trethowan Brothers (see page 90), even use a different strain of starter culture each day. So, for example, a Trethowan Brothers' Pitchfork Cheddar made on a Monday would be different from a Pitchfork Cheddar made the next day, on account of the different culture, not to mention all the other variables. Some artisan cheesemakers use freeze-dried cultures (pre-prepared freeze-dried powder cultures in a sachet) designed to be added directly to the vat. A handful of cheesemakers make their own starter cultures, as do the Applebys in Shropshire and Martin Gott at Holker Farm in Cumbria. I often think of a starter culture in cheesemaking as being like using a starter dough in baking, as in the recipe for a Sourdough Loaf on page 59.

Once the starter culture has been added, and the correct acidity level has been reached, rennet – either animal based (as is traditional, obtained from the stomach of a ruminant animal) or vegetarian – is also added to the milk to start the coagulation (clotting) process. Rennet is an enzyme that triggers the separation of the curds from the whey. The type and amount of rennet used, and length of coagulation, depends on what style of cheese is being made. Cardoon rennet, made from the vivid purple stamens of the cardoon thistle, has been used for many centuries as a vegetarian alternative. A great example of a cheese made using vegetarian rennet derived from the cardoon thistle is Sinodun Hill. Made by Fraser Norton and Rachel Yarrow in south Oxfordshire, this is a soft goat's milk cheese with a delicate, mousse-like texture and a flavour similar to that of fresh yoghurt.

Cutting the curds is the next stage, which varies according to the type of cheese being made. As the cheesemaker cuts the curds, liquid whey is expelled. The finer the cut, the more whey is expelled and less moisture is retained, resulting in a harder cheese.

Conversely, the coarser the cut, the less whey is expelled and the more moisture is retained in the curds, resulting in a softer cheese. For some soft cheeses, such as Brefu Bach in North Wales, the curds are not even cut, but simply scooped out and placed directly into moulds. I like to recreate this process at home when eating a crème brûlée, slowly diving the spoon into the creamy centre and using my mouth as the mould. When the curds are cut, it is normally done with a single blade (known as a cheese knife), often used in making a soft cheese, or a curd cutter – imagine a long thin harp-like device with a single handle and multiple blades/wires. You will often see a different style of cutter at every cheesemaker, either handed down the generations or, as at Holker Farm, handmade by the current cheesemaker. This stage is tremendously satisfying to watch. Once the cutting has been done, some makers of hard-style cheese 'scald' the curds, essentially heating and stirring the curds again, which removes more whey and tightens the curds. The curds are then normally left to 'pitch' (allowed to sink to the bottom of the vat) before the whey is drained.

The next stage is all about separating the curds and whey. For a fresh cheese, the whey is normally left in the vat, from which the curds are then carefully removed and placed in moulds to drain – remember the crème brûlée? For soft cheeses, some of the whey is taken from the top of the vat and, as before, the curds are gently ladled from the vat and left to drain on a drainage table or in moulds. The cheesemaking team at Stichelton Dairy in Nottinghamshire (see page 164) do this, scooping up the delicate curds from the vat and transferring them to the drainage table (a table that is perforated to allow whey to drain slowly).

For hard cheeses, the whey is drained completely, leaving a layer of curds at the bottom of the vat – they look like the biggest Rice Krispie slice you'll ever see. The curds are normally cut into blocks and often turned, then milled and salted before being placed into moulds. Many hard cheeses are also 'Cheddared', in which the curds are cut into large blocks and repeatedly stacked over the next few hours. This process increases the acidity of the curds, which is closely watched, and also encourages the proteins to come together, slowly squishing out moisture and transforming the large blocks into wide, flat sheets. I saw this being done at Westcombe Dairy. Robert Howard, the head cheesemaker, opened out one curd sheet and it looked like stringy dough or mozzarella when pulled apart – truly mouth-watering!

Another treatment is called 'texturing', very similar to 'Cheddaring', in which the curds are cut by hand into small cubes and gathered into a rough pile before being moulded. Soft and semi-soft cheeses are often salted after being moulded.

After being moulded, the curds start to resemble young cheeses. Soft cheese curds are usually left overnight to drain naturally and become more compact. To make a semi-hard or hard cheese, the curds are placed in presses and subjected to varying pressures. Many cheesemakers still use wonderful renovated cast-iron presses from the early nineteenth century, which would have been made by local blacksmiths.

As a by-product of cheesemaking, the whey can be used in a variety of ingenious ways, from making whey butter to feeding farm animals or spreading on the land as a natural fertiliser.

So now we have gone through the farming year and the making of cheese, it's time to take our young cheeses into the maturing phase, in which they are aged to develop their flavour and texture.

An important point to note here is that, when producing their cheese, the cheesemaker is very aware of forecasting – that is, working out when they should start making a batch of cheese, allowing time for it to age sufficiently before being sold to cheesemongers, wholesalers and online. They also need to keep up with trends and evolving preferences. Lynher Dairies and King Stone Dairy, for example, are making more than double the usual amount of smaller wheels to meet the demand among customers and cheesemongers for smaller sizes of cheese.

Overleaf: Maturing Kirkham's Lancashire

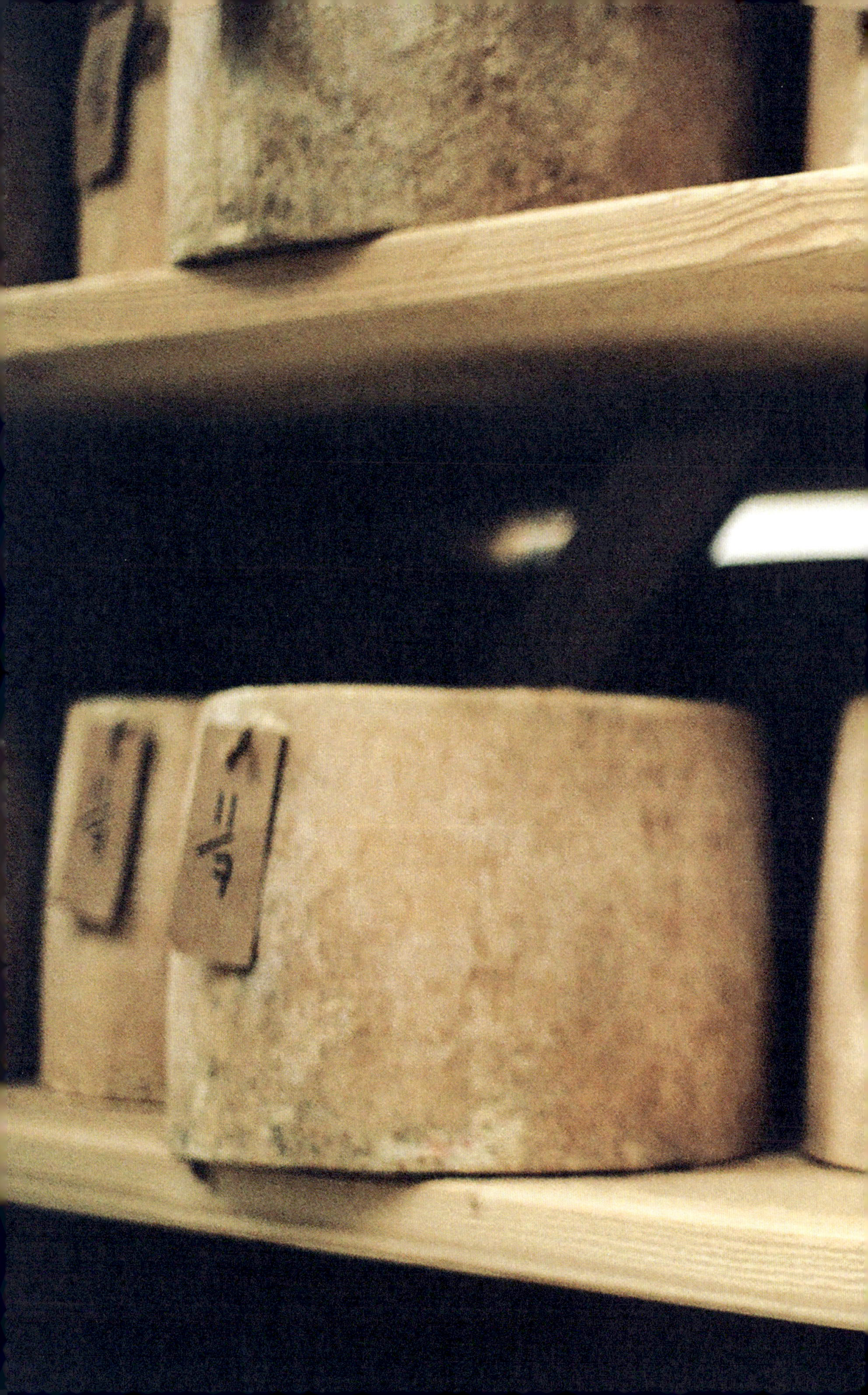

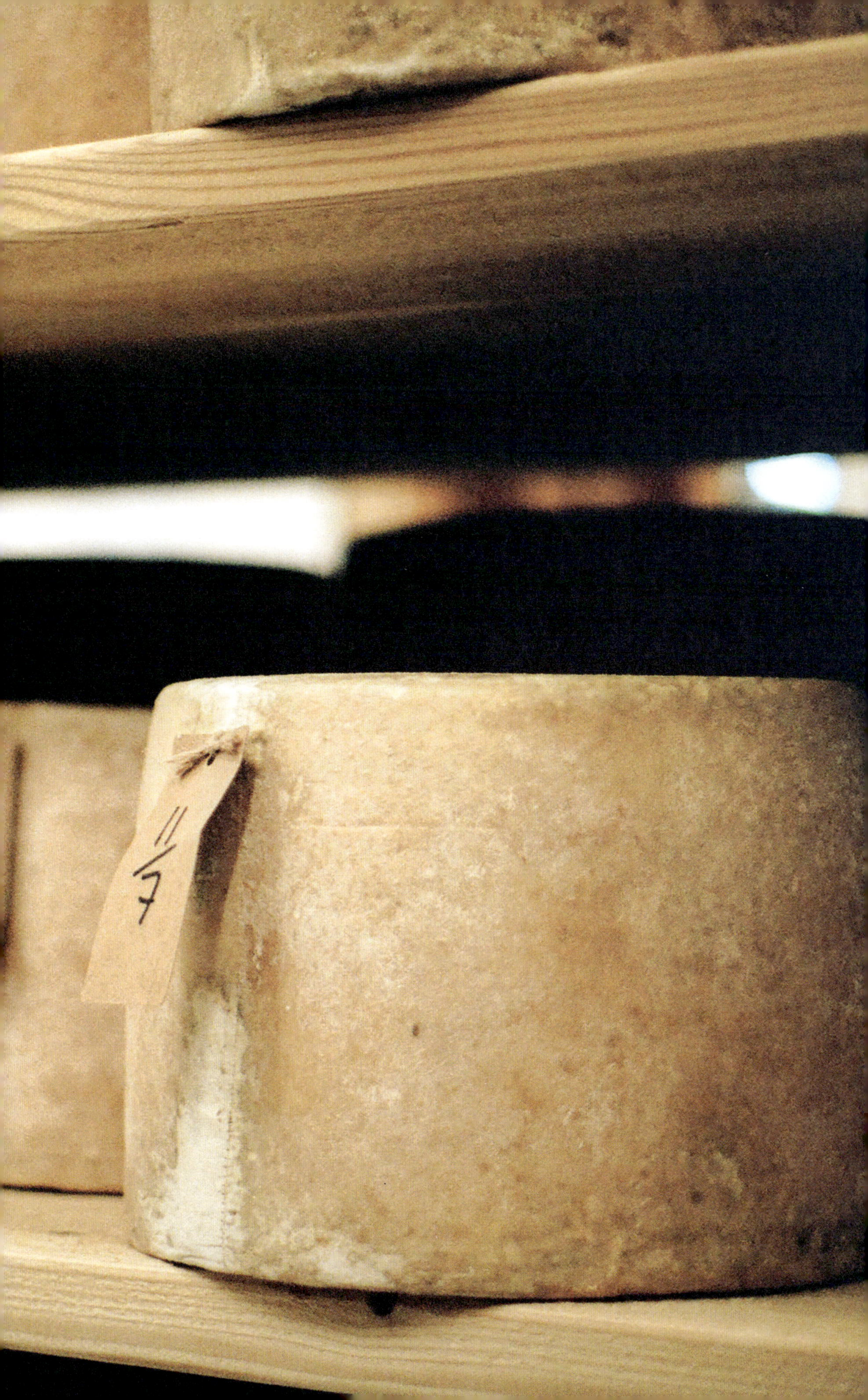
11/7

The microbiome

Microbial activity is an intrinsic yet invisible part of the cheesemaking process; it is completely fascinating, and still rather new in terms of what we know and what has been discovered so far. To introduce the subject of the microbiome, and try to understand what it all means, it may be helpful to talk first about raw milk – used by the majority of the thirty cheesemakers featured in this book – and how it is relates to the microbiome.

Known to contain an abundance of natural microbes, raw milk arguably makes for a more complex cheese. It is also interfered with less: this gives the cheese a closer connection to the source and a clearer food provenance. Now, I am no expert here, and I have to thank the micro-maestro that is Bronwen Percival, an expert in microbial activity in cheese and the buyer and technical manager at Neal's Yard Dairy, who enlightened me not only on the subject of the microbiome but also the complexities of the entire cheesemaking process. As she and co-author Francis Percival comment in *Reinventing the Wheel: Milk, Microbes and the Fight for Real Cheese*: 'Cheesemaking deploys the microbes that live within milk to preserve it and produce delicious flavours, and farms are natural reservoirs of microbial biodiversity.'

When it comes to cheesemaking, the microbiome – communities of multiple organisms (yeasts, bacteria and moulds) that coexist and often work together – is everywhere: in the soil, on the grass, in the atmosphere, in the animals, in the milk, in the cheesemaking rooms, on the cheesemaker and in the maturing rooms. In the cheese world, at least, the microbiome is broadly understood to be something magical – an invisible, undefined aspect of cheesemaking that affects the taste of the milk, and hence the flavour and texture of the cheese.

While our understanding of the microbiome is still at the entry level, our knowledge of food microbiology has expanded over the last twenty years. The more one learns about the microbiome, the more awe-inspiring it is – and how it works in cheese is a great way for us to try to understand it. We know that the microbiome has a direct impact on the complexity of flavour, and that the farmer, herdsman and cheesemaker are key partners in the shaping of the microbiome. Even the unique profile of the dairy and the equipment it uses becomes part and parcel of it. That is to say, the farming and cheesemaking process affect the microbiome of the cheese, and the conditions of the maturing rooms – mainly, their humidity and temperature – encourage or discourage the growth of particular strains of microbes (proliferating all the time) that are already on, or in, the cheese.

Take, for example, a cheese that is placed in a maturing room with its own particular conditions. In that unique environment, specific microbes will be encouraged to grow on and die inside the cheese. In each case, the microbes secrete enzymes that break down the proteins and the fats in the cheese from larger molecules into smaller ones associated with enhanced flavour. An example of this is when Baron Bigod (see page 62) is aged: microbial enzymes in the beautiful, thick rind start to break down the molecules in the cheese, oozing cheesy goodness and imparting the rich mushroom and umami flavours that are the hallmark of the cheese. Treatment of the cheese during maturation, which will be covered later, controls the growth of microbes and associated breakdown of molecules, affecting the final flavour of the cheese.

When Todd and Maugan Trethowan moved into their new dairy in Somerset, they felt they had to re-establish the microbiome that gave their cheeses unique character. To do this, the brothers took whey from their original dairy in Wales and splashed it around the cheesemaking rooms, before washing them down. They also brought their old Welsh wooden boards into the maturing rooms to encourage the original microbe community.

Natural rind of Sparkenhoe Blue.

MATURATION

If you ever find yourself needing a place to meditate, away from the stresses and strains of everyday life, a maturing room full of cheese would not be a bad place to start. Picture yourself in a large, dimly lit room in which only you and hundreds – sometimes thousands – of cheeses all sit in profound silence. Maturing rooms, especially those on a larger scale, such as the huge barns at Lincolnshire Poacher or the cave at Westcombe Dairy, are like cathedrals of cheese, with the same hushed and reverent atmosphere. Perhaps this is something new I've hit upon – cheese and mindfulness retreats, or even a new cheese religion?

From the farming to the making, we have now come to the maturing phase, which effectively starts as soon as the adolescent cheeses come out of their moulds. Transported from the cheesemaking rooms, or what was originally called the 'dairy house', the young cheeses are taken to the maturing rooms, or in some cases to a warmer 'hastener' or 'hastening room' to dry a little before being taken to a maturing room. These 'hastening rooms' can be found at blue-cheese makers like Stichelton Dairy in Nottinghamshire and Mike Thomson's dairy in Northern Ireland where he makes Young Buck (see page 248). As we saw earlier, no stage of the cheesemaking process is more important than another, and even at this late stage of maturation, a cheese can be spoilt if not handled sensitively.

The maturing process relies on variables – in this case, temperature, levels of humidity and salinity, airflow, the turning of the cheeses, the cheesemaker's intuition and treatment of the cheese, the length of maturation and, of course, microbial communities. The type of cheese is an important factor too, significantly affecting the length of maturation. Soft cheeses take only days to mature, semi-soft types a few weeks, semi-hard varieties a few months, and hard cheeses anything between several months and a year or even longer.

The reason for ageing cheese is mainly to develop its flavour and texture, but as recent studies have shown, placing the cheese in a maturing room in which certain conditions are present develops the aroma as well. New research carried out by Tufts University in Massachusetts has shown that this is all down to the microbiome. According to the researchers, those pungent smells that assail our nostrils so delightfully when we walk into a cheese room or maturing room, are, in fact, one aspect of the way that bacteria communicate with the fungi on rinds. As I mentioned above, there is still so much to learn about the microbiome, not only how it interrelates with cheese but with our own bodies – a hugely intriguing topic.

After the young cheeses have been allowed to drain naturally (soft cheeses), or have been pressed to remove the last drops of whey (hard cheeses), they are left to dry and mature, either on wire racks in a maturing room for soft and semi-soft cheeses, or on wooden shelves for hard cheeses – cue the towers of cheeses, stacked up in their hundreds, in a cavernous dark room. For fresh cheeses, maturing is generally non-existent, but they are still treated in various ways after being moulded.

For example, many are coated in an extra ingredient to add to their flavour and overall appearance, such as Perroche, a fresh goat's milk cheese made by Charlie Westhead at Neal's Yard Creamery, which is rolled in fresh herbs.

The maturing process is overseen by the cheesemaker, or an affineur in the case of a cheesemonger. What is remarkable is how a young cheese, matured in the same room, will turn out differently if its maturing is overseen by a different cheesemaker, even more so if the same cheese is aged in a different location, where the microbiome would come into play as well. This is all down to the specific techniques and treatments used by different cheesemakers when maturing the cheeses. In a competition run by the Academy of Cheese to find the best affineur, eight cheesemongers are put in charge of ageing a cheese from the same batch. The cheese with the most complex and interesting taste wins.

Many farms and cheesemongers will even mature a cheese to their customers' preference. Cheesemongers Andy and Kathy Swinscoe from The Courtyard Dairy in North Yorkshire, and Perry Wakeman from Rennet & Rind in Cambridgeshire, both have their own maturing rooms in which to store cheeses at a younger age so they can mature them according to their customers' wishes. The same is done at Neal's Yard Dairy, whose maturing rooms are nestled neatly beneath Victorian railway arches in Bermondsey, London. As well as Bronwen Percival at Neal's Yard Dairy, Andy Swinscoe at The Courtyard Dairy, alongside many other cheesemongers, help to sustain some of the best cheesemakers in the British Isles by early ordering and leaving cheeses to age in the shops' maturing rooms. Andy Swinscoe was also given a 'Cheese Maturing' award in 2010 by the Queen Elizabeth Scholarship Trust.

The maturation of cheese is a complex process, influenced by many factors, that all affect the development of the flavour and texture of the cheese and, as we are now discovering, aroma too. To recap, maturation mainly revolves around encouraging or discouraging the growth of moulds, yeasts and bacteria (the microbiome) that, on the whole, are already present in the cheese, both as the result of the farming and the cheesemaking phases. Only then, when the cheese is stored in a certain way in order to mature, do those particular conditions govern which moulds, yeasts and bacteria grow, producing enzymes to break down the protein and fat molecules in the cheese, and produce all those lovely multifaceted flavours.

As you will find throughout this book, maturing rooms come in all different shapes and sizes to accommodate the different cheeses, from huge, purpose-built caves to rooms the size of a cupboard. To ensure that their cheeses are being matured correctly, the cheesemaker or affineur is careful to monitor the room's temperature, levels of humidity and airflow. Using the appropriate equipment is also key to the maturing process. Many cheesemakers I have visited use wooden shelving to age their cheeses on, for example, which helps to retain moisture by providing a moisture reservoir that is at equilibrium with the rind. Each unique environment will create its own unique cheese; changing the environment will affect the finished cheese. Take David Jowett, for example, who has made his Rollright cheese at two different farms. Using slightly different milk at each farm, but exactly the same method of cheesemaking, David found that he was creating a completely different cheese at each location.

Along with the conditions in the maturing rooms, the way in which the cheese is treated is also important. Various treatments performed by the cheesemaker or affineur during the ageing process are used to control the growth of moulds, yeasts and bacteria to develop a cheese's flavour and texture. The resulting cheese generally falls into one of the following categories: mould-ripened, washed-rind and natural-rind cheeses.

Mould-ripened cheeses

For mould-ripened cheeses, one or more moulds are added to the milk during the cheesemaking process, as in the case of blue cheeses such as Stichelton and Young Buck, and/or sprayed on the surface of the cheese during the maturing phase. During the making of Stichelton, for instance, the cheesemakers inoculate the raw milk with a blue mould called *Penicillium roqueforti*, named after Roquefort cheese and used widely in other blue cheeses. As soon as the cheese is placed in the right conditions for the blue mould to thrive (i.e. in the maturing rooms), it gets to work specifically inside the cheese. Piercing the cheese with metal spikes during the maturing process encourages this breakdown by introducing more oxygen into the cheese, which helps the mould to grow. This produces that pungent, acidic – and what its maker Joe Schneider calls 'pointy' – taste that is so characteristic of a delightful blue.

Some cheesemakers add mould cultures to their milk, which then grow on the outside of their cheeses in the maturing rooms. Fen Farm Dairy in Suffolk, for example (see page 62), adds edible moulds including *Penicillium candidum* to Baron Bigod to produce a velvety, white bloom on the cheese that will slowly break down the rind to create that perfect outer ooze and firmer centre.

Others have even gone as far as cultivating their own unique mould in their local environment. The makers of Moyden's Handmade Cheese in Shropshire, for instance (see page 198), have worked on developing a specific mould based on samples taken from around the local farm that supplies their milk and from their own maturing rooms. Moyden's have been working with the University of Nottingham – who are looking into how mould ripens cheeses differently – to develop a unique 'Shropshire mould' to incorporate in the making of their Wrekin Blue.

Washed-rind cheeses

In another treatment used in the maturing process, the rind of the cheese may be washed with a brine solution and/or with an alcoholic drink, such as beer, perry or cider, or in the case of some Scottish cheeses, with single malt whisky. This changes the conditions on the outside of the cheese and consequently the make-up of its

Isle of Mull Cheese have a maze of cellars that are naturally cool, the perfect conditions for ageing their cheeses.

microbiome, which in turn affects the cheese's flavour, texture and aroma. Many makers of washed-rind cheese want to encourage particular bacteria, such as *Brevibacterium linens*, for example, which produces the familiar peachy, orange rind and strong aroma of cheeses such as Celtic Promise or Maida Vale (see pages 200 and 126). In some cases, washed-rind cheeses are supported with a thin collar of bark to keep their structural integrity, such as Stinking Bishop made by Charles Martell (see page 172), which has a beechwood collar, and Rollright from King Stone Dairy, which is banded with spruce bark to infuse the cheese with earthy flavours as well as support it.

Natural-rind cheeses
Many natural-rind cheeses, such as Westcombe Cheddar and Appleby's Cheshire, are clothbound to prevent mould from infiltrating the cheese and to increase shelf life. There are other treatments to note such as smoking the cheese or wrapping it in edible leaves, as in the case of Cornish Yarg (see page 76), to add to the flavour and help preserve it.

During the maturing stage, the cheese's development is monitored in various ways. Feeling the cheese, for example, may seem obvious, but it is a vital means of assessing the cheese's firmness and moisture level in order to see if anything needs to be adjusted. Turning the cheeses every so often is a good way to regulate their moisture level and structural form, although turning the cheeses by hand can be challenging.

I have turned a few sizeable Cheddars in my time and, I can tell you, it's unbelievably difficult, never mind turning 2,600 cheeses at 25kg each! That's what the team at the Trethowan Brothers in Somerset, who make Pitchfork Cheddar, have to contend with when it's time to turn the entire stock. Some cheesemakers have machines to turn their cheese. Not only does this help prevent back problems, it also reduces human error and frees up cheesemakers for other tasks. Westcombe Dairy has a turning machine called Tina (which I'll leave you to work out).

Another technique for monitoring the development of the cheese is to use a tool called an iron. Mainly used by makers of hard, semi-hard and blue cheeses, this is a long, hollow metal device that is inserted into the centre of the cheese and then withdrawn, extracting a neat cylinder of cheese in the process, which is then analysed to assess the structure and taste of the cheese. Makers of blue cheese normally do this to check on the growth of the blue mould inside the cheese wheel.

TASTING THE CHEESE

After their tireless efforts during the farming and milking (if they are a farmhouse cheesemaker), the cheesemaking and the maturing phases, it is now time for the cheesemakers to sample their creations. It is at this stage that the cheese, in all its glorious complexity, is finally revealed to the world. Artisan cheese produces a labyrinth of flavour and texture in the mouth. Whether the cheese is savoury, sweet, acidic, buttery, lactic or fruity, this is the chance for the cheesemakers to finally reap the rewards of what they have so painstakingly sown, and share their cheese with those who are eagerly awaiting it, as well as enticing new customers.

The flavour of a great cheese is never one-dimensional and, as we have seen, is down to an astonishing number of variables in the key stages of farming, making and maturation. Each batch of cheese is different, its flavour and texture developing over time and from season to season, even from one day to the next. Take St James, for example, made using raw milk from Holker Farm's flock of Lacaune sheep. One of the main determinants of the flavour is the quality of the milk being used at a certain time of year. In spring, the sheep are in early lactation, with milk production at its peak, which gives St James a zesty, yoghurt-like taste. Towards late summer and autumn, the sheep are in late lactation, producing less but richer milk with a higher percentage of protein and fat, which gives the cheese a meatier, heavier taste. A good cheesemonger will often be able to tell a customer how long a cheese has been matured and when it was made. It is also useful to note that cheeses, like St James, which are made using raw milk in particular, have a flavour that reflects the environment in which they were made, giving the cheese a greater complexity of taste.

Artisan cheese can be so variable that one wheel, or even a single slice, of cheese may have a number of different flavours. Take Stichelton again, for example, and its maker, Joe Schneider, who speaks eloquently about how the cheese has different taste points: from the fruitier areas around the rind where microbial activity is greater, the sharper flavour of the areas of blue mould, to the creamier, honey-tinged centre just beyond the blue mould. Another example is the Trethowan Brothers' Gorwydd Caerphilly, which is renowned for having three flavours in one cheese: the mushroom flavours of the rind; the creamy notes just beneath the rind; and the more lactic notes of the centre of the cheese. This variability of flavour can be experienced in many artisan cheeses, and if you haven't tried artisan or true farmhouse cheese yet, I implore you to give it a go – the length and complexity of flavour you'll experience is truly exceptional.

Wigmore, made by Village Maid Cheese in Berkshire, has a bloomy white rind.

Is the rind edible?

One of the questions I'm most frequently asked when offering around a vast cheeseboard to guests is whether the rind is edible. The answer is yes! Well, in most cases it is, except for wax- or paper-wrapped cheeses or if the rind is particularly hard, as in the case of Berkswell (see page 70). Those wonderful bloomy, mould-ripened rinds on Baron Bigod or St Jude are edible, as are washed rinds on a Celtic Promise or Maida Vale. Edible rinds will often give you a whole new taste experience, and in some cases offer a very different flavour to the inside of a cheese.

Many hard-style cheeses, such as Isle of Mull (see page 242) or Westcombe Cheddar, are bound in cheesecloth before being aged. While it's not the end of the world if you consume the cloth, it's advisable not to eat it. If you have bought the cheese from a trusted cheesemonger, they will have removed the cheesecloth before cutting the large wheel of cheese into manageable slices to sell in their shop, and the rind on the cheese you have bought – with the cheesecloth now taken off – will then be edible. In any case, for the thirty cheeses in this book, you'll see that I've indicated whether the rind is edible or not.

As I said, it's all pretty straightforward. If you really don't want to eat the rind on a cheese, it's best to simply cut it off in a thin sliver and discard it in the food bin. If you're lucky enough to have a trusted cheesemonger nearby, I'm sure they'll be very willing to answer all your cheese-and-rind-related questions.

How to store artisan cheese

While researching this book, I was often eating enough cheese a day to feed a family of five, generously! Much of the time I was given or bought sizeable chunks after my visit to a cheesemaker, which I then photographed, tasted and wrote about. Despite eating huge amounts of cheese each day, more often than not I had enough cheese left over to feed several others. What I needed was a solution to keep the leftovers fresh, so who better to call than the font-of-all-knowledge on cheese, Andy Swinscoe at The Courtyard Dairy, who explained how to store it correctly:

'What we [at The Courtyard Dairy] always tell people is to buy less cheese but more often, which makes for no leftovers and you're always eating cheese fresh, when it's at its best! I always say, "Cheese is like a bottle of wine." Once you open a bottle of wine, you want to drink all of it there and then. Many of the flavours in wine are volatile, just like artisan cheese, so once you open [a cheese], that's when you are going to get the best out of it.'

Andy tells me that if you do have leftover cheese, the best thing to do is to wrap it in waxed paper (so it doesn't sweat), place the wrapped cheese in a plastic container (with a lid) lined with kitchen paper at the bottom (to soak up any moisture), and place the whole thing in the fridge. You can freeze cheese but, again, it's best to eat it fresh, as freezing affects the flavour and texture.

Now, when I buy artisan cheese, I buy it to eat it on the same day or, if I can't finish it then, on the day after. A good guide for a cheeseboard, for a group of 3–4 people, would be to buy 3–4 cheeses, each weighing around 150–200g.

In support of British cheese

Viewed through the eyes of a producer, as I was, on a very small scale, the food industry pushes towards consistency, relentlessly aiming for perfection. But what if you are working with free-roaming animals or natural ingredients? Artisan cheesemakers do their utmost to keep their cheeses consistent through the seasons, but using such a delicate, variable ingredient as milk, especially raw milk, it is, in truth, impossible. Any inconsistency due to natural phenomena such as the changing seasons is, in my opinion, something that should be celebrated; it is part and parcel of the charm and attraction of artisan cheese.

Just like those promoting an appreciation of wonky fruit and vegetables or meat from a 100 per cent pasture-fed animal, the artisan cheese industry flies the flag for a product that is intrinsically variable and dependent upon the seasons, capable of expressing the freshness of spring grass or the rich essences of autumn, not to mention the complexity imparted by a particular day, the specific climate or soil, the animal's feed and lactation cycle and the skill of the individual cheesemaker in pulling it all together. We should be savouring the delights of its diversity and seasonal characteristics, supporting the fact that it is one of the leading areas of our food industry – one that works to the highest standards of food and farming, and increasingly with the environment, rather than against it, giving back to the soil and the land from which their essential ingredients are drawn.

More than just an industry, it is perhaps best described as a culture or community: these British cheesemakers aren't simply making cheese, but are also supporting a wide range of social, economic and environmental interests. These cheeses are helping the rural economy by creating careers, sustaining and building on heritage, skills and new flavour sensations, strengthening small-scale food systems, and encouraging an appreciation of the importance of food provenance.

Having travelled the length and breadth of the British Isles for the last couple of years, learning about and championing artisan cheese, meeting the people behind the scenes, and trying each and every cheese in this book along the way, my eyes have been opened to its magnificence and importance. I have realised that artisan cheese represents a rich and vital way of life here in our isles, maintaining an important tradition, part of our heritage, with hard work and ladlefuls of love and commitment.

I hope that this book encourages a broader audience to try these artisan British cheeses, to taste how complex and utterly delicious they can be, and to support and promote the recognition of the people who, with their steadfastness and dedication, devote their lives to making them.

Making the recipes

To accompany the cheeses in the recipes in this book, I have tried to give ingredients that are generally accessible to everyone, suggesting alternatives for any more unusual items. I recommend using ingredients that are locally sourced and seasonal, chosen for their nutritional value and from expert producers, though I understand with the pressures of everyday life that it is very difficult to buy everything from sustainable sources all the time. It's a good starting point, however, to have a cupboard full of essentials such as flours, beans and pulses, oils, salt and spices, to which you can add your fresh produce – meat, fish, fruit and veg. I always try to source food that is whole and nutritious and, as much as I can, vary my food choices from week to week.

I recommend buying free-range eggs and raw honey locally, if you can, along with bee-friendly oils, sustainably accredited seafood or meat sourced from farmers certified with the Pasture-Fed Livestock Association or the Soil Association or with a similar accreditation indicating that it is from animals reared to the highest standards (I actually eat very little meat, just better-quality when I can). If possible, buy sustainably grown and heritage grains, pulses and flours from suppliers such as Hodmedod's, Shipton Mill, Doves Farm or Gilchesters Organics. And in terms of what cheese to buy, well, I hope that this book gives you a good starting point. A number of the cheesemakers sell directly and/or through various retailers across the British Isles (see page 260).

Visit your local farmers and producers either at a farmers' market or at the farm gate (usually adorned with welcoming signs for such delights as raw milk or seasonal fruit and veg) and try to get to know them personally so that you can get a better sense of what is available on your own doorstep. (See page 260.) Perhaps most satisfying of all, try growing as much as you can if you have a garden, green space or even just a balcony. I have a small raised trug planter where I grow numerous fresh herbs, salad leaves and edible wildflowers.

It's also nice to support even smaller suppliers and producers where you can, either finding them on your travels or researching them. Felin Ganol Watermill in Wales, for instance, produce organic, UK-grown grains to make wholemeal stoneground flour. Wakelyns Bakery (*wakelyns.co.uk/bakery*) use diverse and sustainable grains including their 'YQ and Q Population Wheats' – a population of wheat being a number of different wheat species grown on the same field – to make their breads. The bakery is based at Wakelyns, an organic agroforestry farm in Suffolk.

Fan ovens
Oven temperatures in the recipes are based on using a standard electric oven. If you have a fan-assisted oven, simply reduce the temperature given in the recipe by 20°C/70°F.

THE CHEESES

From left to right: Stichelton, Stichelton Dairy
Isle of Mull, Isle of Mull Cheese
Sparkenhoe Red Leicester, Sparkenhoe Farm
Crookwheel, Holker Farm

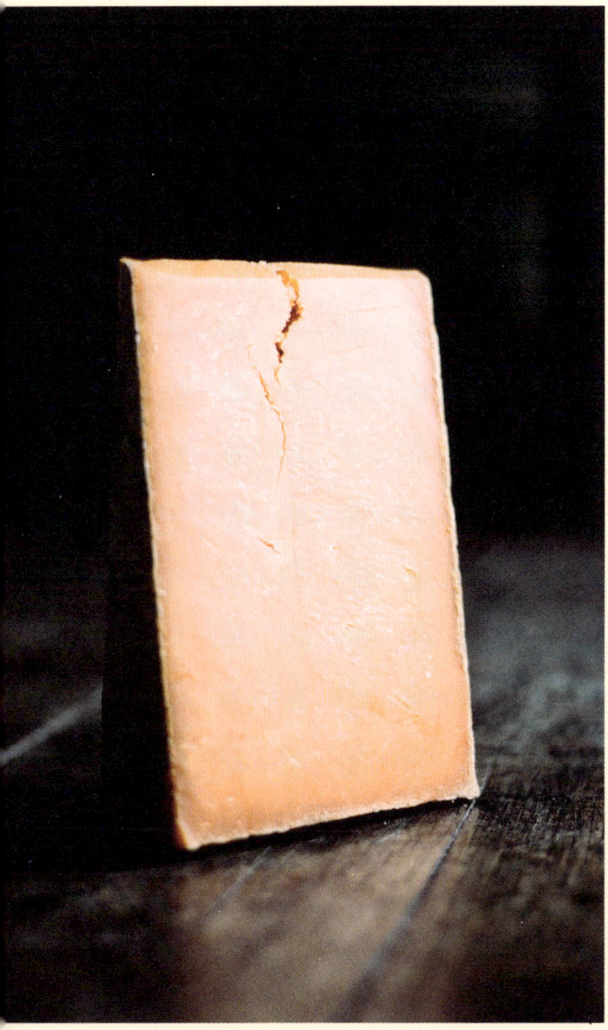

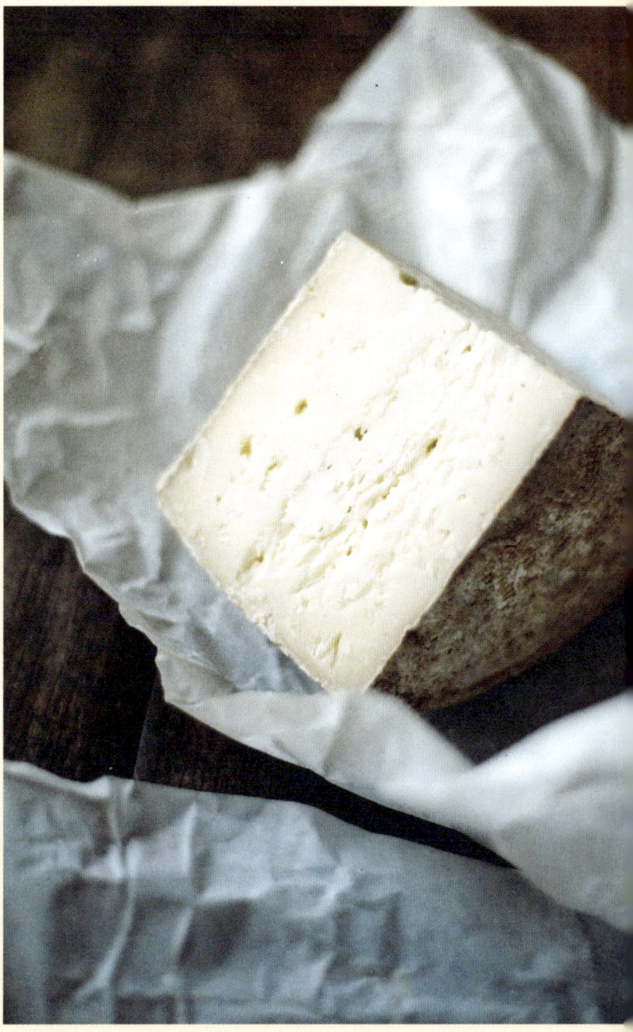

APPLEBY'S CHESHIRE

From left to right: Paul and Sarah Appleby are third-generation farmers and cheesemakers, here with Dorothy, one of their five children.

A British Friesian grazing the early-spring pasture, which the Applebys split into smaller paddocks as one of their ways of farming sustainably.

A full wheel of Appleby's Cheshire on an old milking stool at Hawkstone Abbey Farm in Shropshire.

Hawkstone Abbey Farm, Marchamley, Shropshire

Hawkstone Abbey Farm, in the heart of rural Shropshire, is home to the Appleby family, who make traditional farmhouse Cheshire. Paul and Sarah Appleby are third-generation farmers and cheesemakers who produce Cheshire using raw milk from their mixed herd of British Friesian, Ayrshire, Montbéliarde and Danish Red cows.

As with the majority of farmhouse cheeses, making the renowned Appleby's Cheshire starts with the land. The cattle at Hawkstone Abbey Farm graze the Shropshire countryside over land that crosses the Cheshire Basin. It is believed that an authentic Cheshire can only be made using the milk from cows that graze in this region of the British Isles that extends north towards Manchester and south into Shropshire. Dating back to the Triassic period, the basin is largely made up of salt beds – formed over thousands of years as shallow seawater repeatedly evaporated in the hot, dry climate of the time, leaving layer upon layer of salt – on which the Applebys' cows now graze, and is thought to add a salty, mineral flavour to their milk, which comes through in their Cheshire. The Applebys also grow diverse herbal leys, including three types of clover (red, white and alsike), chicory, plantain and yarrow, to enrich the cows' diet and fix nitrogen in the soil.

Appleby's Cheshire is made using a live starter culture, which gives a unique character to their cheese – a flavour of the farm, if you will. After the starter culture is added to the warm milk, the rennet is added to trigger coagulation. The familiar light golden colour of Appleby's Cheshire comes from the addition at this stage of annatto, a concentrated liquid, deep orange in colour, made from the seeds of the achiote tree. Once the milk has coagulated, the curds and whey are separated, the whey removed to make whey butter (and to feed the pigs), and the curds left in the vat to be hand cut, salted and milled in a peg mill (see page 259). The treated curds are then transferred into moulds and placed in presses locally made in Whitchurch to drain overnight.

The following day, the pressed cheeses are wrapped in cloth. Each wheel of young Cheshire is then taken to the adjoining barn, naturally cool inside, and aged for a few weeks. Here, the cheeses are rubbed regularly with a calico cloth, and turned on their wooden shelving to ensure that they ripen evenly.

The Appleby family also make a white Cheshire and Double Gloucester using the same raw cow's milk.

Appleby's Cheshire characteristics

Milk: Raw milk from the farm's mixed herd of British Friesian, Ayrshire, Montbéliarde and Danish Red cows

Rennet: Animal

Appearance: Hard and crumbly, clementine paste with an edible clothbound rind

Tasting notes: Fresh and zesty with a slightly mineral flavour, and a long finish in the mouth. Varies according to the season and length of maturation

The young pressed cheeses are carted from the cheesemaking rooms to the maturing rooms across the farmstead's courtyard.

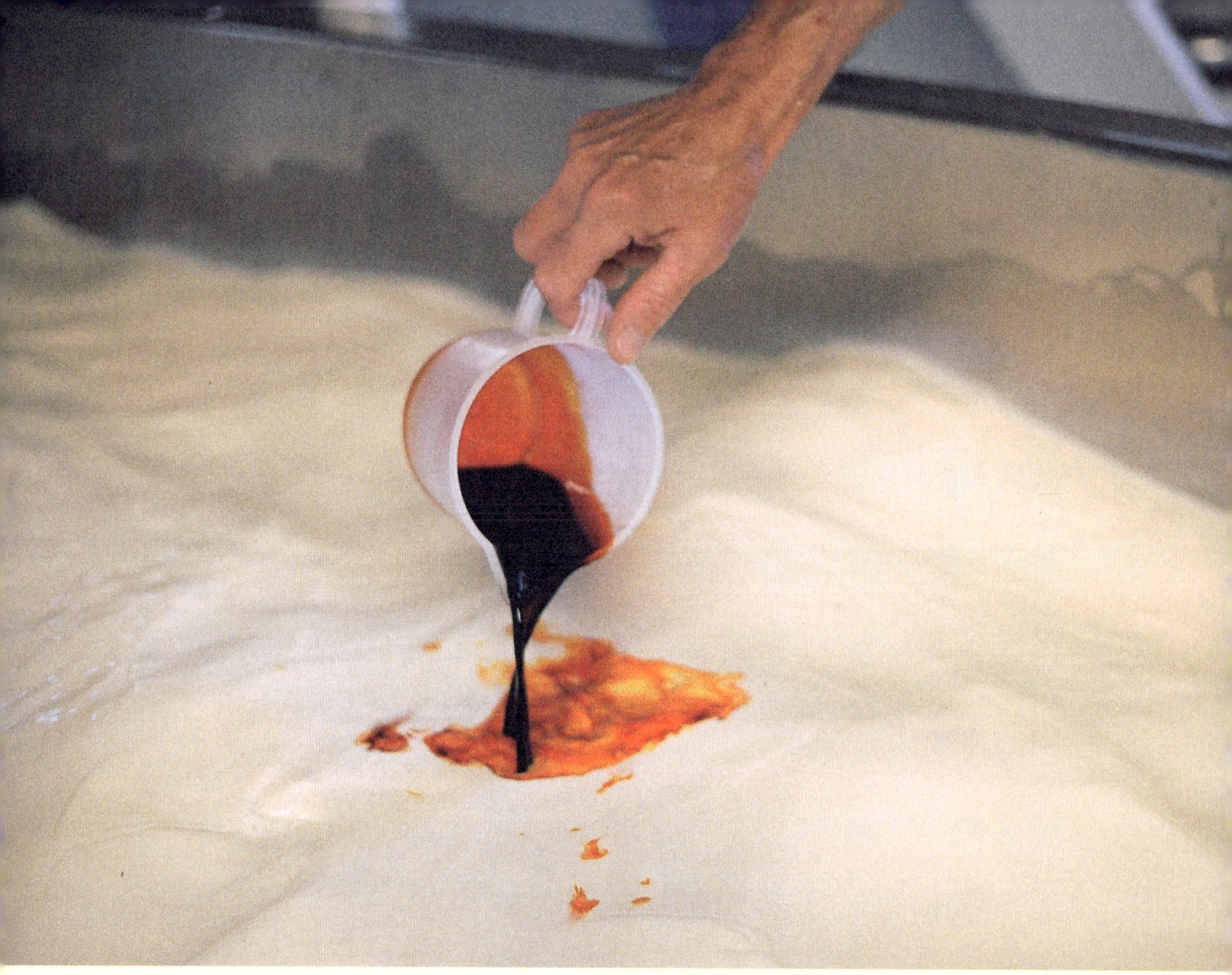
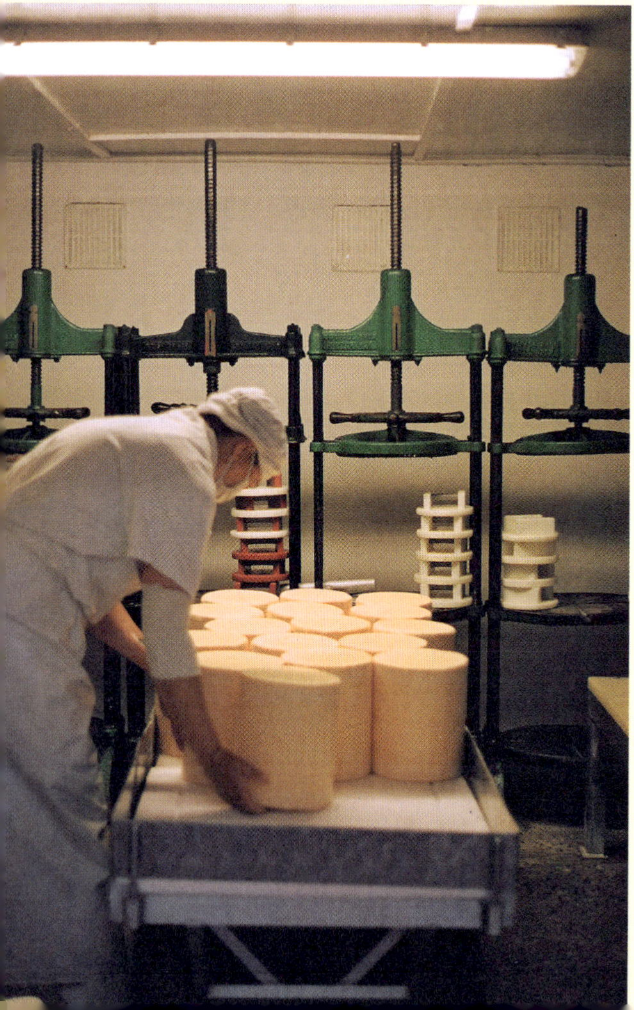
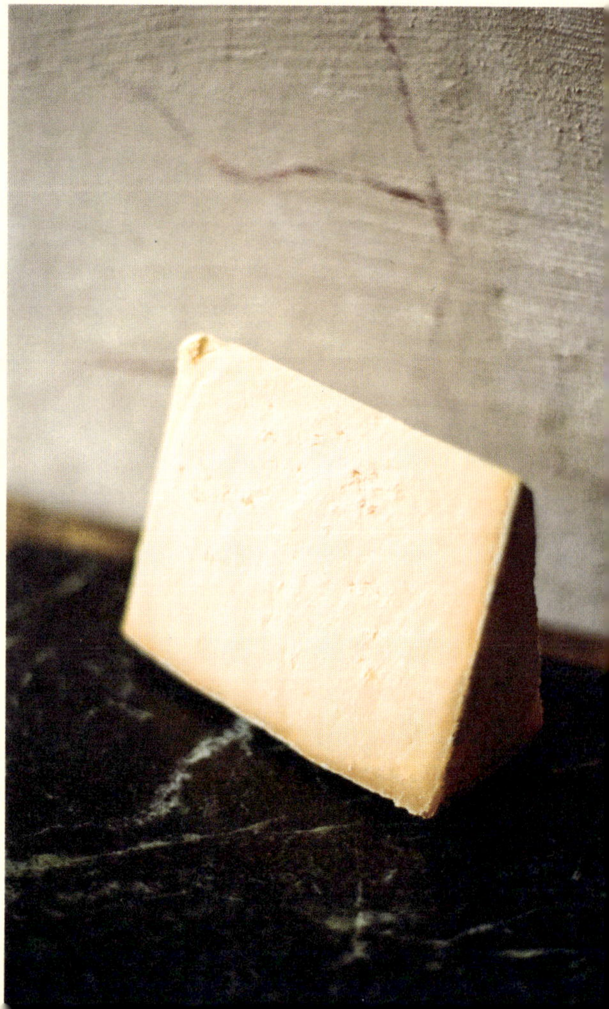

Toasted Cheshire cheese sandwich

A firm favourite with the Appleby family, this is perhaps one of the simplest recipes, especially if you use a ready-made loaf, but, as I am sure you will agree, it is one of the best. The Applebys have the most wonderful farmhouse kitchen in which to make their cheese toasties. Originally built as a folly in the 1700s for the large manor house on Hawkstone Hill, the farm consists of a charming cluster of red brick buildings and old wooden barns, typically teeming with farm animals, dogs, cats, children, farmers – not to mention swallows in the summer – all passing in and out of various doors and openings. Inside, the barns are naturally cool, hence perfect for maturing the Cheshire cheeses.

I have a cheese toastie most days for lunch using a good slab of any cheese going and with plenty of butter to make it extra gooey. For this toasted Cheshire cheese sandwich, I've made a medium-sized sourdough loaf from scratch to make it all that more lovely and indulgent, though you could speed things up, if you preferred, by using a good-quality shop-bought loaf instead.

MAKES 4 TOASTED SANDWICHES

SOURDOUGH STARTER
200g strong flour (white, rye or spelt)
200ml warm water

SOURDOUGH LOAF
125g sourdough starter
350ml warm water
500g strong white flour, plus extra for dusting
9g sea salt

TOASTED SANDWICHES
8 slices of sourdough bread
plenty of butter for spreading
400g Cheshire cheese, grated

SOURDOUGH STARTER
In a small bowl, mix together 50g of flour and 50ml of warm water into a smooth and runny paste, then cover and leave at room temperature for 24 hours. Repeat this process on each of the following three days, each time adding to the bowl and mixing an extra 50g of flour and 50ml of warm water. (You will have used 200g of flour and 200ml of warm water in total.)

On the fifth day, you should have an active starter that is bubbling away, ready for you to make your sourdough loaf. The starter can be kept in an airtight container in the fridge for 3–4 weeks. When using the starter, take as much as you need and just add flour and water in a proportion of 1:1, as before, to replenish the mixture and replace what you have removed.

I always leave the starter out overnight at room temperature if I am making the dough the next morning, by which time you will see it effervescing nicely. You can always check whether your starter is active by dropping a small spoonful into a glass of water. If the starter mixture floats to the surface of the water, then it's ready to use.

Method continues overleaf

Clockwise from the top: The familiar clementine-coloured paste of Appleby's Cheshire is produced by adding annatto to the milk during the cheesemaking.

A sizeable slice of Appleby's Cheshire showing the pale orange paste and slightly crumbly texture of the cheese.

After the curds have been ladled into moulds, they are pressed in old cast-iron presses that were made locally in the early twentieth century.

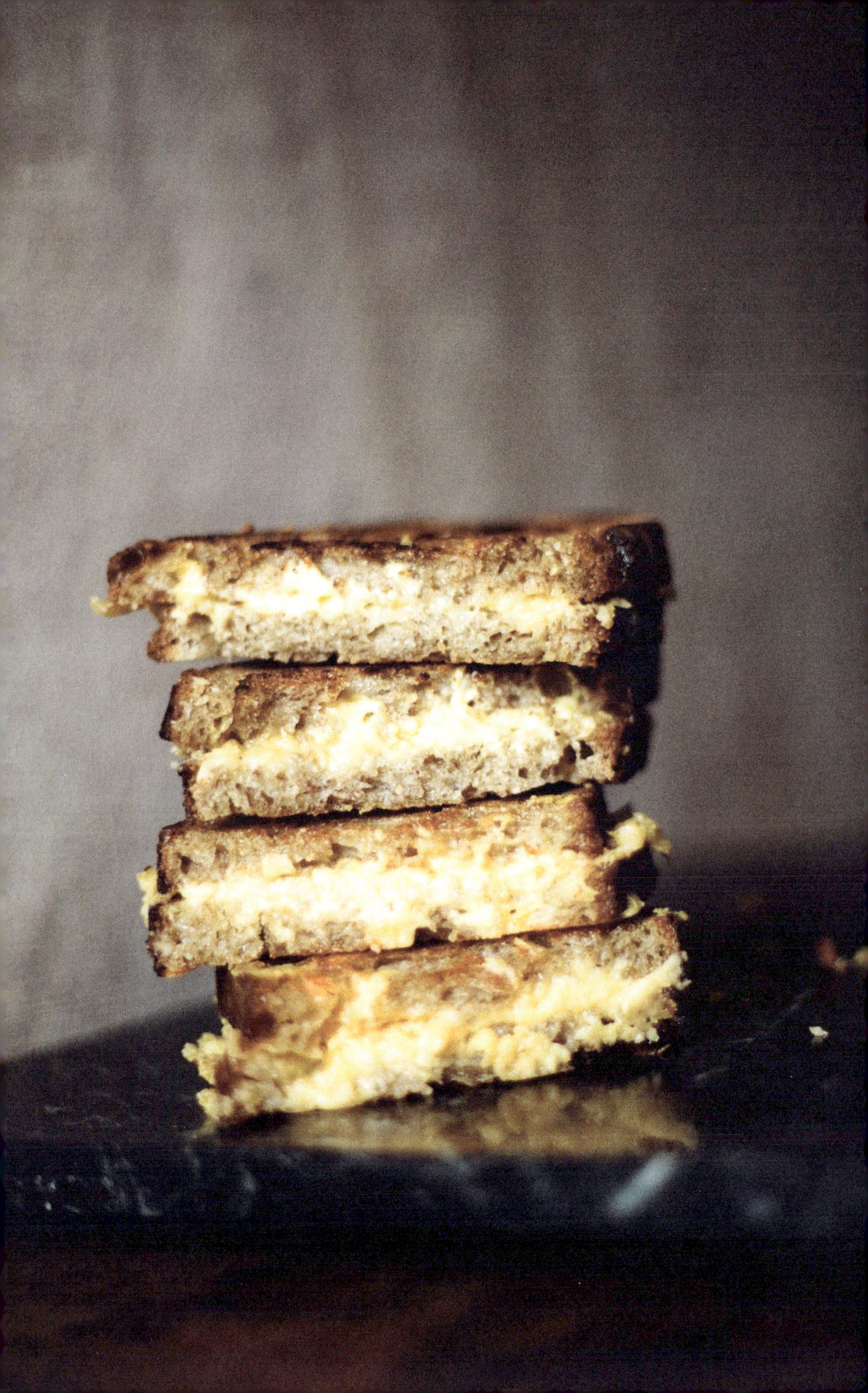

SOURDOUGH LOAF

Place the sourdough starter and warm water in a large bowl or jug and mix together well with two fingers.

Add the flour to a separate large bowl and then slowly pour in the runny starter mixture, working it for a couple of minutes to form a dough. Cover the bowl with a tea towel and leave in a warm place for an hour to allow the dough to rest and rise a little.

After the hour is up, sprinkle in the salt. Now it's time to stretch the dough. Take the side of the dough directly in front of you with a wet hand and stretch it up gently, as far as you can without breaking it, and then fold it back on itself. Give the bowl a quarter turn and repeat the process. Do this twice more, each time rotating the bowl by a quarter. I like to imagine a clock in which one turns the bowl first to 12 o'clock, then to quarter past, then half past and finally to quarter to 12. Cover the dough again and leave for a further hour.

You will need to repeat this step – stretching and folding the dough, turning it in the bowl, then covering and leaving to rest – another four times.

Now it's time to tip the dough out on to a lightly floured work surface to rest while you dust a proving basket (or banneton) with flour or line a mixing bowl with a clean tea towel and dust with flour. Then, using your hand or a dough scraper, gently shape the dough into a ball. Place it, seam side up, in the prepared basket or bowl. Dust the top well with flour and leave to rest, covered, for 3–4 hours at room temperature until the dough has doubled in size.

Twenty minutes or so before baking, preheat the oven to 230–240°C/450°–475°F/gas mark 8–9, and place a large round cast-iron casserole dish with a lid inside the oven to warm up. When the oven is up to temperature, take the lid off the dish using oven gloves. Flip the dough out of the basket or bowl and swiftly slide this into the hot dish, seam side down. Use the tip of a sharp knife to score the dough on top to create the characteristic sourdough fold or 'ear', which will form a lovely crust when baked. Place the lid on top of the dish and bake in the oven for 30 minutes.

After about 30 minutes, take the lid off the dish and bake for a further 10–15 minutes to crisp the top of the loaf. Once the loaf is nicely crisped on top, remove and place on a wire rack to cool down completely, then slice away.

TOASTED SANDWICHES

This is the easy bit. For each sandwich, butter two slices of bread on both sides, sprinkle a quarter of the grated Cheshire on one slice and sandwich together with the second slice of bread.

If you are using a cast-iron pan on the hob, wait until it gets hot before placing the cheese sandwich on top. Once one side is deliciously golden, flip it over and toast the other side. Alternatively, preheat the oven to 200°C/400°F/gas mark 6, place the four sandwiches on a baking sheet and bake for 10 minutes, until the tops are crispy and golden. Turn the sandwiches over to bake for another 10 minutes.

I love to have these toasted sandwiches with a tangy chutney (see page 183) or sharp-tasting pickled vegetables.

BARON BIGOD

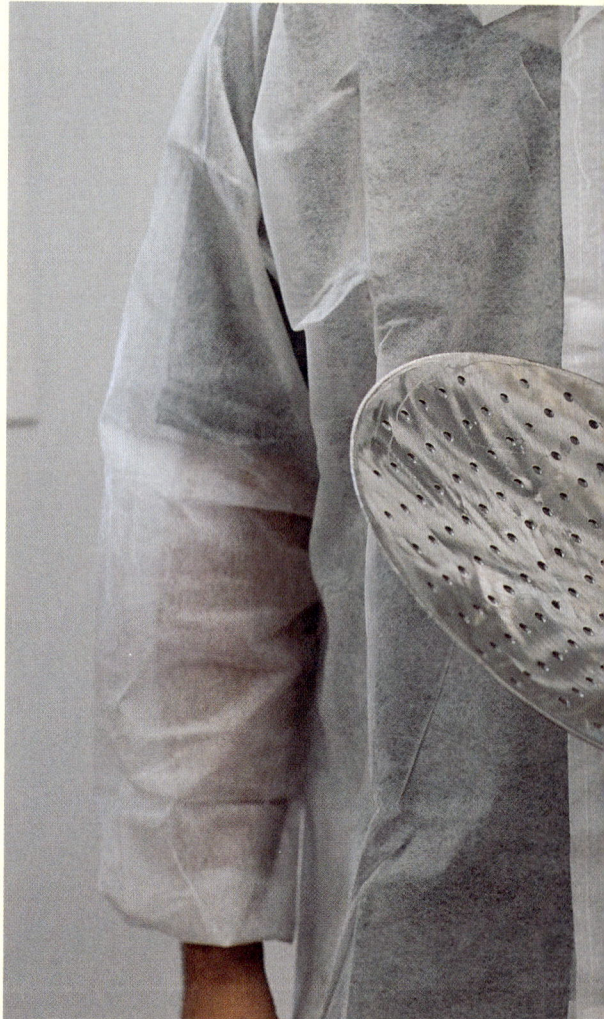

From left to right: The cut curds sitting nicely in their moulds are left overnight to drain any excess whey and to compress naturally into young cheeses.

A unique aspect in the process of making Baron Bigod is ladling the curds by hand with a *pelle à Brie*, used in making traditional Brie.

The satisfying, crumpled rind of a Baron Bigod. The bloomy mould-ripened rind breaks down when aged, resulting in delightful oozing.

Fen Farm Dairy, Bungay, Suffolk

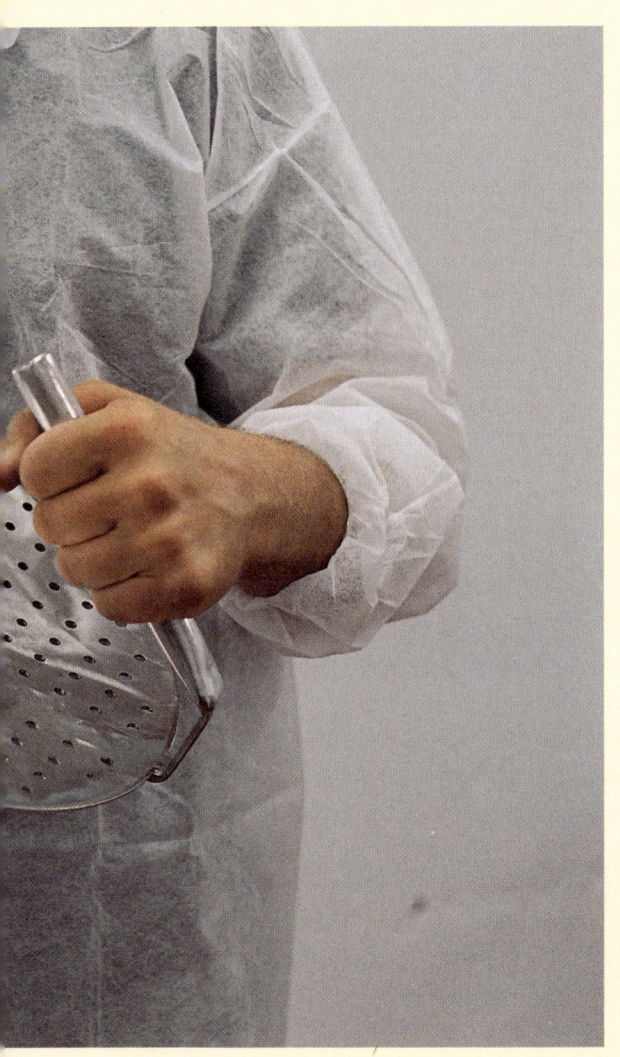

Situated in the Waveney Valley, between the parish of Flixton and the town of Bungay, is Fen Farm, home to the Crickmore family, who make Baron Bigod. Before diversifying into cheese in 2012, Jonny Crickmore, the head farmer and cheesemaker at Fen Farm, sold raw milk from the farm gate through an honesty-box scheme, each carton labelled 'cow–farmer–you'.

Baron Bigod uses raw milk from the farm's herd of Montbéliarde cows, milk that gives this Brie-style cheese its unique character. Handpicked by Jonny in the valleys of Jura, where the breed originates, Montbéliarde cows are renowned for producing milk that has a high percentage of protein and butterfat, both of which make for wonderfully rich and creamy cheese.

The make starts each morning when the warm milk is channelled into the cheesemaking rooms, straight from the cows. As the milking parlour is a little higher than the cheesemaking rooms, the milk is gently guided by gravity via a pipe

Jonny Crickmore, farmer and cheesemaker at Fen Farm Dairy, oversees everything on the farm, including the welfare of his beloved herd of cows.

connecting the two buildings. Once the vats are full of milk, Jonny and his team of cheesemakers heat it to the correct temperature. The starter culture and rennet go in, then a flocculation test is performed. As with any artisan cheese, the cutting and handling of the curds is incredibly important. To ensure the final cheese has the right amount of moisture, the curds are cut accordingly, and then very carefully ladled into moulds, or 'hoops', as they are otherwise known, using a shallow, dish-like receptacle called a *pelle à Brie* ('Brie shovel') – traditionally used in the making of Brie de Meaux.

Over the coming hours, in a temperature-controlled room, the curds are left to naturally expel whey and compress into a young cheese. Early the next morning, the young cheeses are salted according to their moisture content. Once transferred to the maturing rooms, the cheeses are aged for 5–7 weeks for a smaller cheese and 6–8 weeks for a larger one. The key to making a delicious Baron Bigod is to control the two fungi added during the making and encouraged during the maturing process: *Penicillium*, which forms a thick rind and imparts mushroom notes; and *Geotrichum*, which produces strong flavours in the finished cheese.

Throughout the seasons the consistency of milk on the farm changes, affecting the taste, texture, aroma and appearance of the cheese. At Fen Farm, spring brings with it lush grasses that, via the cows' milk, produce a slightly drier cheese. In the summer and autumn, the cows' milk has a higher fat content, which produces richer, more yeasty flavours, while in late winter the cheese becomes gooier.

Baron Bigod characteristics

Milk: Raw milk from the farm's herd of Montbéliarde cows

Rennet: Animal

Appearance: Ivory paste, gooey edges and chalky centre with a bloomy, mould-ripened, edible rind

Tasting notes: Creamy, buttery flavours with hints of mushroom and yeast. The centre has more lemony and slightly acidic notes. Varies according to the season and length of maturation

Baron Bigod potato pie

Jonny was one of the first cheesemakers I ever visited while I was getting to know farmhouse cheese and its brilliant community. It was Jonny who took me around Fen Farm years ago, explaining how in cheesemaking it all begins with healthy soil and happy cows. I even found myself helping to make Baron Bigod in the old cheesemaking rooms, which are now home to Julie Cheyney, who makes St Jude at the farm (see page 144), while Jonny has moved into new premises next door.

This recipe is based on a traditional potato pie. To give it extra depth, I have added foraged nettle tips (from the top of the plant) and parsley from the garden. If you can't get your (gloved) hands on any nettles, simply up the quantity of parsley or add a handful of chopped chives.

SERVES 6

PASTRY
225g wholemeal flour
100g butter, chilled and cut into cubes
2 tsp garlic powder
pinch of sea salt
3 tbsp cold water

FILLING
200ml whole milk
4 large potatoes, peeled and cut into small cubes
4 garlic cloves, peeled and finely chopped
160g Baron Bigod, sliced
handful of fresh parsley, finely chopped
handful of young nettle tips (or fresh parsley or chives), finely chopped
50g mature Cheddar, grated
sea salt and freshly ground black pepper

Preheat the oven to 200°C/400°F/gas mark 6.

To make the pastry, place the flour, butter, garlic powder and salt in a food processor, and blend until the mixture looks like breadcrumbs. Then add the water and blend until the mixture resembles damp breadcrumbs. For this recipe, there is no need to make a dough – simply tip the pastry mixture into a tart tin (I used a 20cm-diameter deep-sided tin with a removable base) and, with your fingertips, press and flatten it out to cover the base and sides of the tin. Refrigerate the pastry for 30 minutes; this will stop it shrinking during cooking.

After half an hour is up, blind bake the pastry for 15 minutes until lightly golden – no need to cover with baking parchment or add baking beans to keep the pastry down. Once cooked, set aside to cool while you make the filling.

Pour the milk into a large saucepan, add the potatoes, garlic, Baron Bigod and a good pinch of salt and some pepper. Set over a moderate heat and stir and combine for a few minutes until it comes together into a deliciously sticky mixture, then add your finely chopped parsley and nettles – the nettles can be blanched in boiling water for a couple of minutes first before chopping and adding.

Allow the mixture to cool slightly before tipping into the cooled cooked pastry case, and then sprinkle over the grated Cheddar. Bake in the oven for 30 minutes until crispy and golden on top.

A large slice of this pie is super served hot with a few spears of tenderstem broccoli and plenty of black pepper.

Overleaf: Over the winter, the pastures are often flooded, so the cows are kept inside for a short period, where they happily munch on home-grown silage.

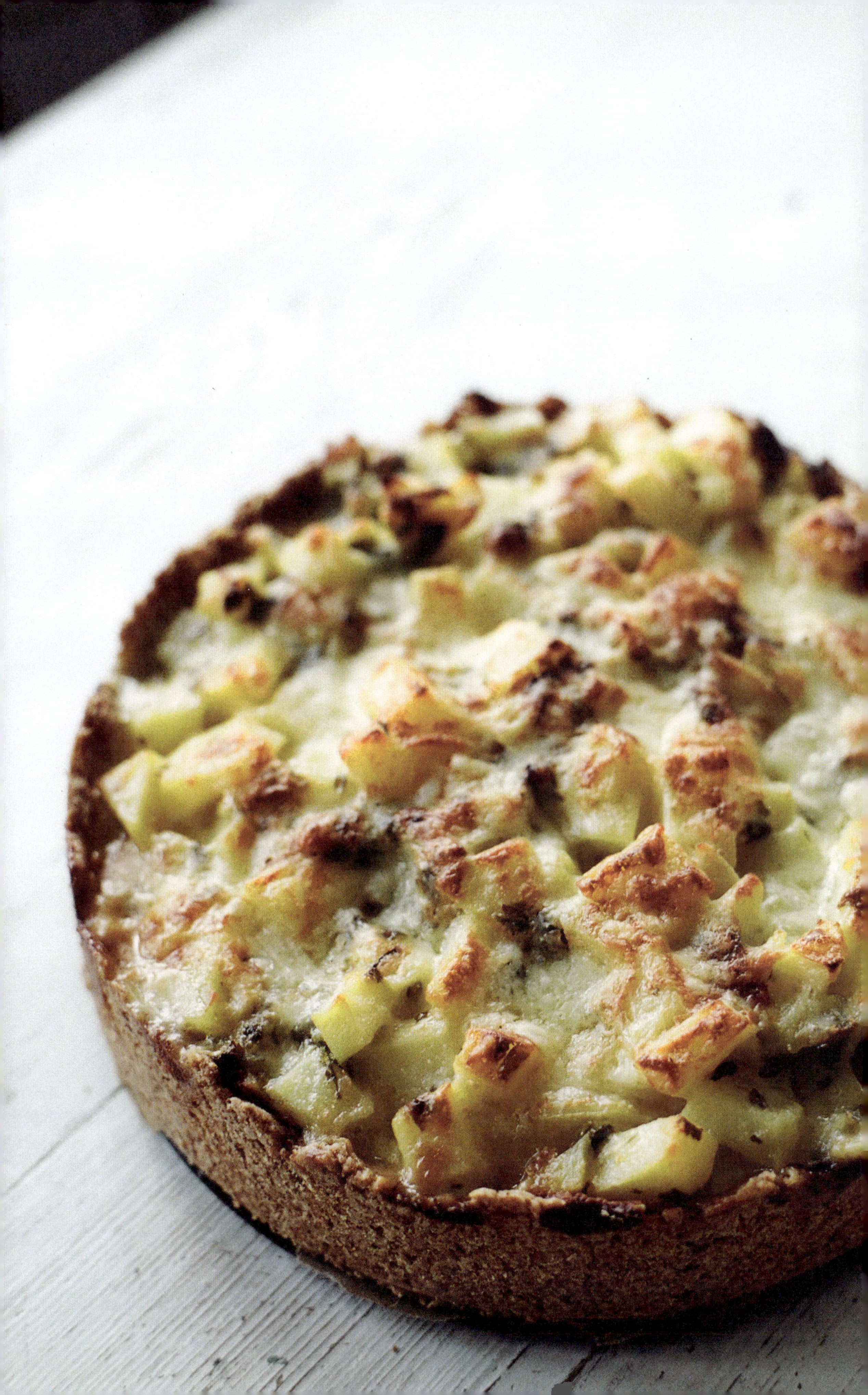

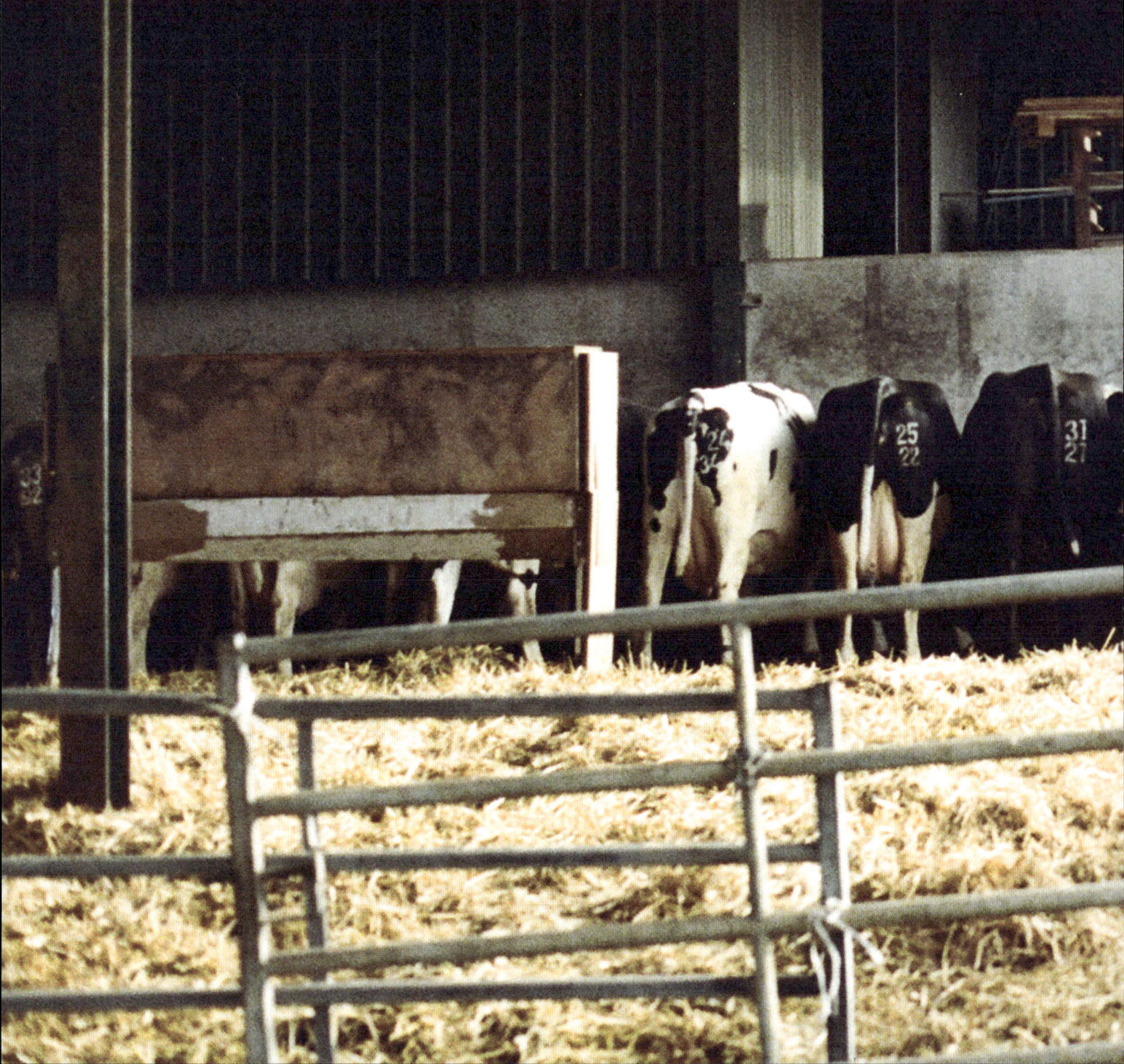
25
22
31
21

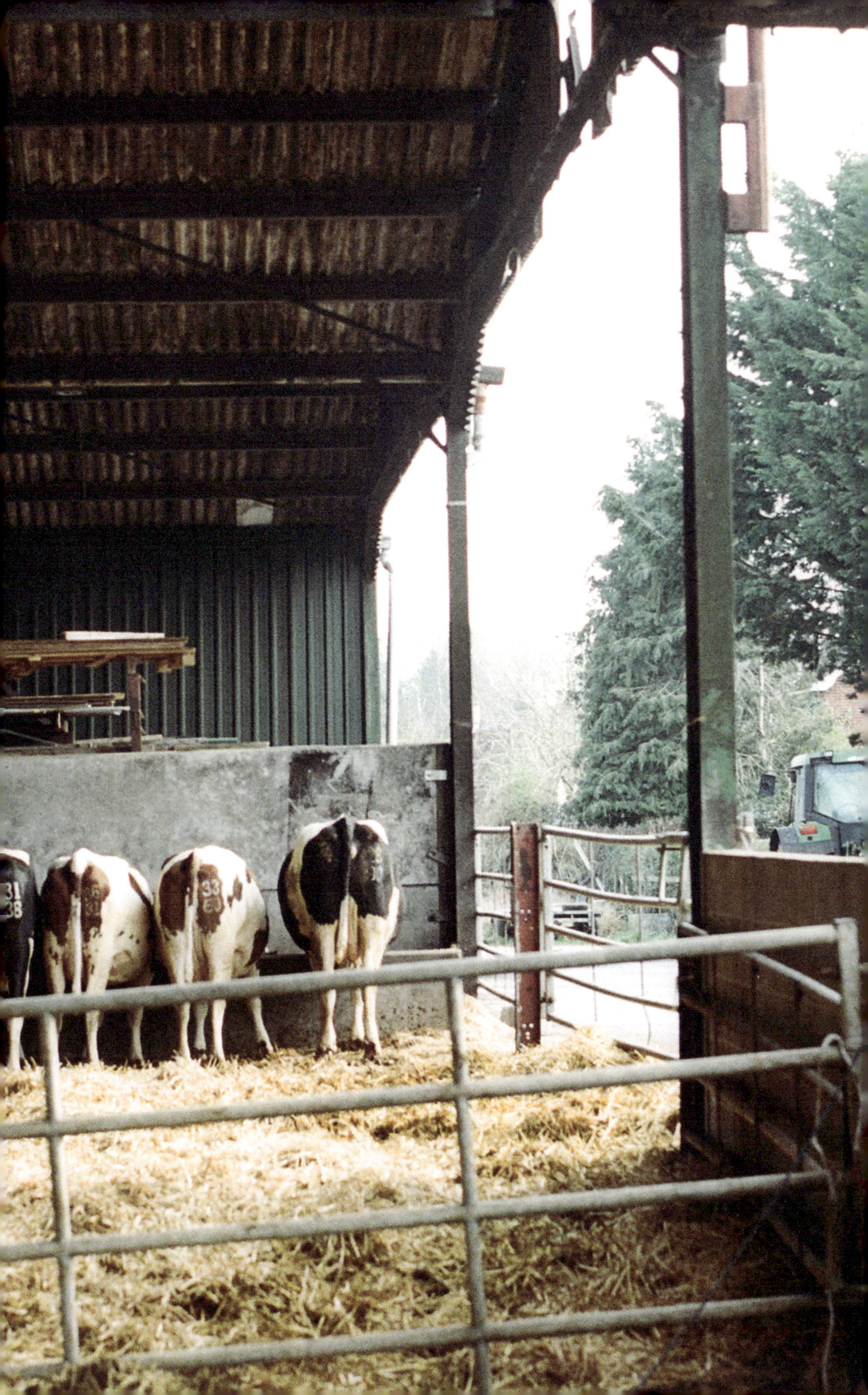

BERKSWELL

Left: Three generations of the Fletcher family in one photograph. From left to right: George (Stephen's son), Peter (Stephen's father) and Stephen.

Right: Stephen gazing out of his Land Rover at his rams at Ram Hall Farm. Stephen and his family are deeply rooted in the Berkswell community and its history.

Ram Hall Farm, Berkswell, West Midlands

Atop the sweeping hills of the Meriden Gap, with the distant cities of Birmingham on one side and Coventry on the other, is Ram Hall Farm, where Berkswell is produced. Named after the local village, Berkswell cheese is now made by the sixth generation of the Fletcher family to farm at Ram Hall. Berkswell is a hard-style cheese made using raw milk from the farm's mixed flock of Friesland and Lacaune ewes. Stephen Fletcher, who manages the business with his father Peter and son George, grows as much food as possible on the farm to feed the sheep during each season. This includes a diverse mixture of grass, cereals, beans and lucerne. Stephen and George are moving more towards farming with land

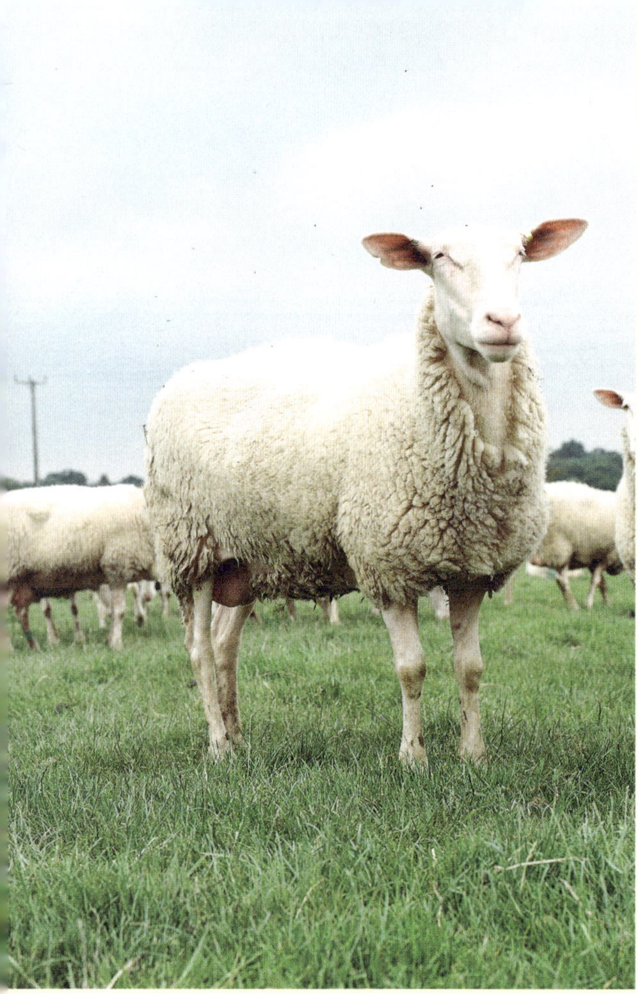
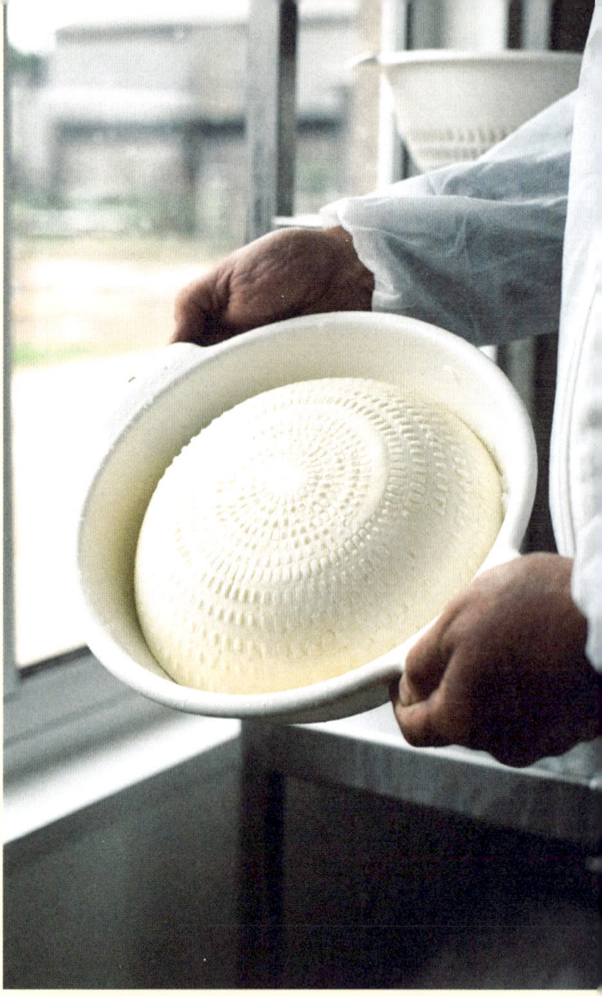
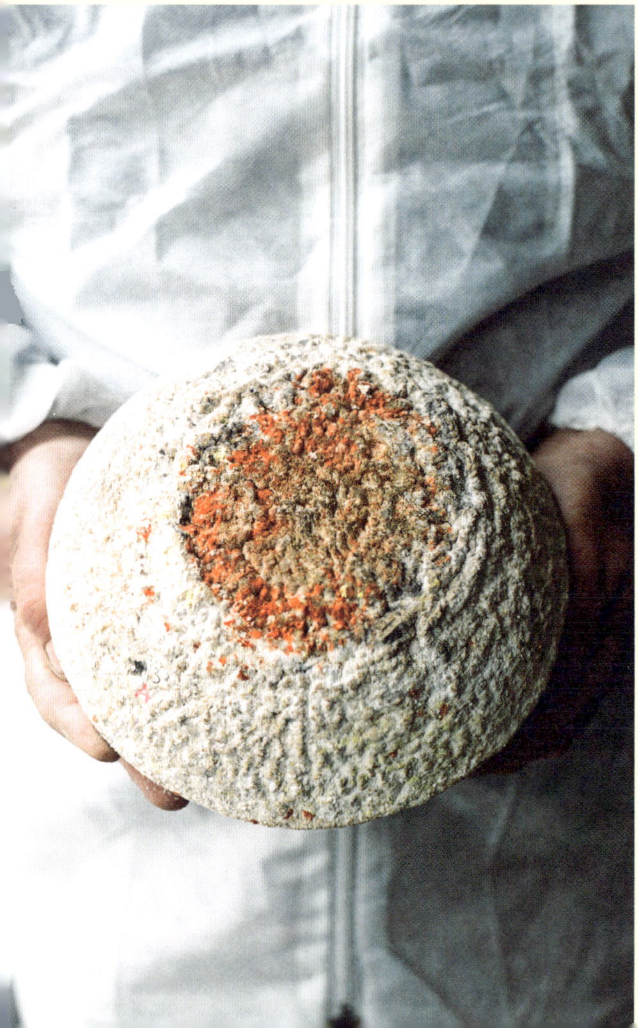
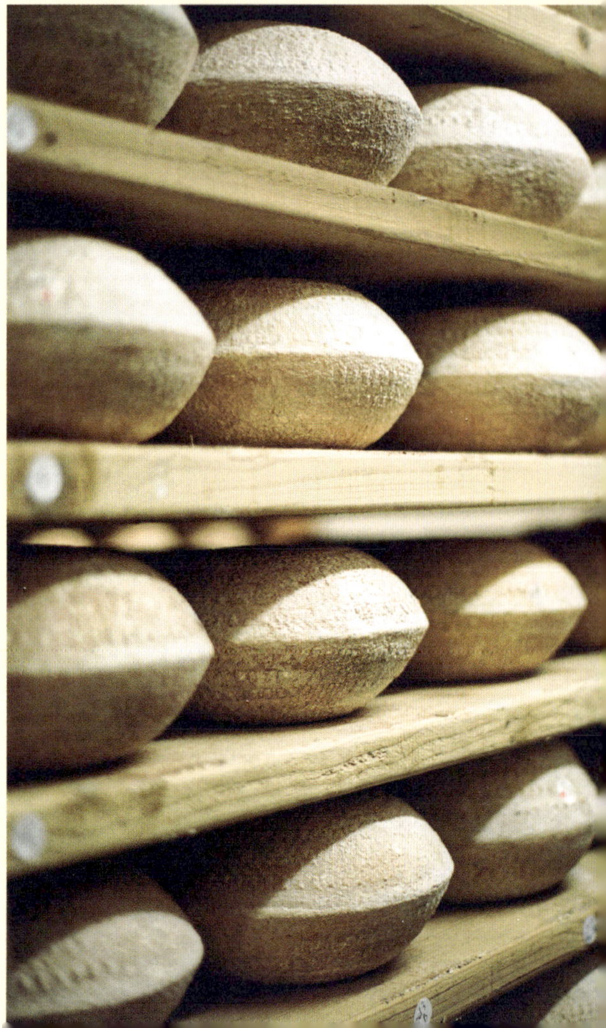

regeneration in mind, aiming to grow everything on the farm and planting new mixed herbal leys and heritage grains to enhance soil health and livestock feed. George is also making the farm more diverse by rearing a small drove of pasture-fed Tamworth pigs that are native to the area.

Berkswell has been made at Ram Hall Farm since the autumn of 1989, when the Fletcher family began the move from dairy cows to dairy sheep in response to what Stephen describes as 'an increasingly bleak outlook for small dairy herds'. The mixed flock they have now at the farm has been bred to produce the best possible milk for cheesemaking. The Friesland and Lacaune ewes are normally lambed from midwinter through to the early spring with the aim of maintaining consistency in their production of milk.

The head cheesemaker at Ram Hall Farm is Julie Hay who, alongside her helpers Sue and Beth, makes Berkswell four days a week. Julie and Sue have been making Berkswell for well over a decade. Making Berkswell is quick, a matter of hours, which helps to maintain the character of the milk. A wheel of Berkswell owes its unique flying-saucer appearance to the special colanders in which the young cheeses are matured, which also creates the distinctive lattice patterning on the rind. During the maturation, Berkswell is turned and brushed with a light saline solution every week for a minimum of four months.

The Fletcher family also make a year-old Berkswell with a Parmesan-like flavour and texture. The mould produced on the rind while ageing, mottled with a mixture of yellow *Chrysosporium sulphureum* and red *Sporendonema casei*, is another unique feature of Berkswell.

Berkswell characteristics

Milk: Raw milk from the farm's mixed flock of pure Friesland and Friesland crossed with Lacaune sheep

Rennet: Animal

Appearance: Firm ivory paste with a mottled, biscuit-coloured, tough inedible rind

Tasting notes: Rich, sweet nutty flavours with pineapple notes and a long finish in the mouth. Varies according to the season and length of maturation

Clockwise from top left: The regal bearing of a Friesland ewe in one of the fields at Ram Hall Farm in the West Midlands. The Friesland breed has a high yield of milk, ideal for cheesemaking.

A young Berkswell that has been left in its colander to drain any excess whey. Each cheese will then be labelled before being placed in the maturing rooms to age for several months.

Deep within the maturing rooms at Ram Hall Farm lie hundreds of wheels of Berkswell. A stunning sight to behold.

The remarkable mottled palette of an aged Berkswell, created by two moulds, *Chrysosporium sulphureum* (yellow patches) and *Sporendonema casei* (red patches).

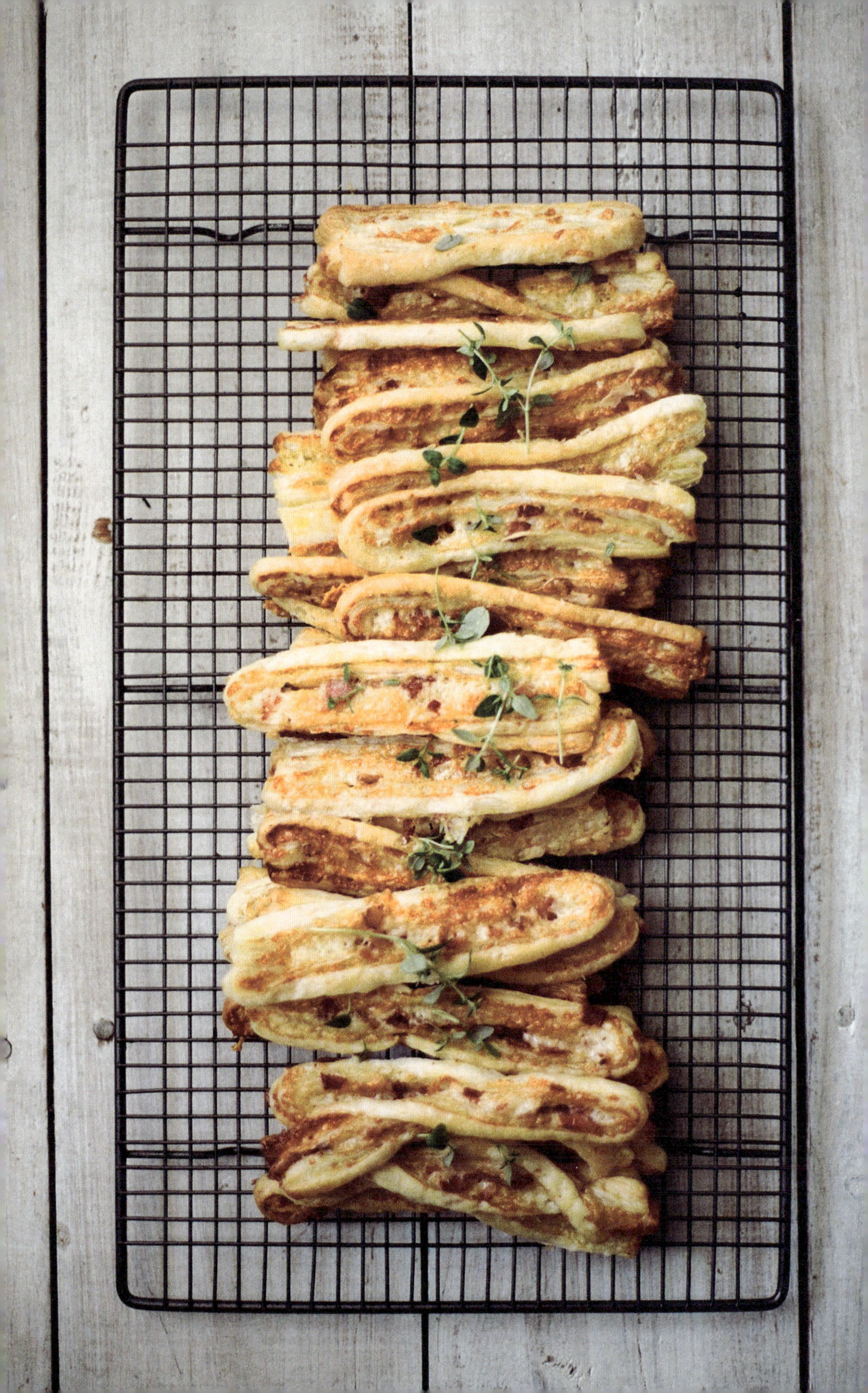

Berkswell and streaky bacon straws

Every time I visit a farmhouse cheesemaker, I am always struck by how wonderfully hospitable they are. The Fletcher family, who make Berkswell, are no different. I met George, who is the sixth generation of the family to farm at Ram Hall Farm, along with his father Stephen and grandfather Peter.

After a tour of the farm and the village of Berkswell, in which we took in the famous well, medieval church, historic stocks and hand-dug lake, it was clear to see how the Fletcher family are deeply rooted in the local community. One of the most memorable conversations I had was with Peter, who can remember seeing the Coventry Blitz reflected in his bedroom window at Ram Hall Farm as a boy.

To see firsthand all three generations of the Fletcher family working together to produce an award-winning farmhouse cheese is hugely inspiring. Even though each of them has learned how to steward the land in a very different way, they now work together, towards the same goals of high standards of animal welfare, land regeneration and self-sufficiency. George is especially keen on farming holistically, producing a farmhouse cheese in a manner that helps to improve the soil health and encourage wildlife. George has two sisters, one of whom loves to cook and make recipes using Berkswell cheese. Here is one recipe suggested by her: luxurious cheesy straws that make you want to eat one and then another and another…

MAKES 12–14 CHEESE STRAWS

100g rashers of smoked streaky bacon, cut into lardons
1 tbsp olive oil
1 x 320g sheet of ready-rolled all-butter puff pastry (about 35cm x 23cm)
flour, for dusting
2 tbsp Dijon mustard
200g Berkswell, grated

Preheat the oven to 200°C/400°F/gas mark 6 and line a baking tray with baking parchment.

Fry the lardons on a medium heat in the olive oil for a few minutes until slightly crispy. Drain any excess oil and set aside.

Unroll the puff pastry on a work surface lightly dusted in flour and spread half the mustard all over in a thin layer. Sprinkle over half the cheese and, using your fingertips, press the cheese into the pastry. Fold the pastry in half lengthways, and use a rolling pin to roll the pastry out into the same-sized rectangle that it was to begin with – don't worry if you can't get it back to exactly the same shape. It may help to dust the folded pastry and rolling pin with a little flour before rolling out.

Spread the rest of the mustard over the rolled-out pastry and add the rest of the cheese, pressing it in as before, then scatter over the bacon lardons before folding and rolling out as before – again dusting the pastry and rolling pin with flour to prevent them from sticking.

Cut the pastry widthways into 12–14 strips, each 2.5–3cm wide, and transfer them to the prepared baking tray. Bake for 15 minutes or until lightly golden brown, then remove from the oven and leave to cool down completely.

These cheesy fingers are perfect devoured with onion or asparagus soup.

CORNISH YARG

From left to right: Catherine Mead of Lynher Dairies, standing outside the dairy with a round of Cornish Yarg, and Binky, her wonderfully well-behaved spaniel.

Jonathan Hosken runs Gadles Farm, a 100-acre farm with around a hundred Ayrshire cows. The Ayrshire milk is mixed with milk from other local herds to make the Yarg.

Ruth Connolly, a 'nettler' and cheesemaker at Lynher Dairies, forages for nettles in the fields at Gadles Farm, where the dairy's pedigree herd of Ayrshire cows graze.

Ruth has been nettling for fifteen years at Lynher Dairies. Nettling may be an unusual profession, and as Ruth says, 'Try getting car insurance on it!'

Lynher Dairies, Truro, Cornwall

At the very top of the Kennall Valley in west Cornwall, surrounded by large woodlands of copper beech and oak, is Lynher Dairies, where Cornish Yarg is made. Based on a seventeenth-century recipe, Cornish Yarg was named after its creator, Alan Gray ('Yarg' being 'Gray' backwards), who originally made it in a dairy on the edge of the granite rocks of Bodmin Moor. Cornish Yarg is a semi-hard cheese now made by Lynher Dairies, headed by Catherine Mead, who, alongside her team of cheesemakers, produces it using milk sourced partly from a nearby pedigree herd of Ayrshire cows but mainly from other local herds of Holstein-Friesian cows via a cooperative.

The Ayrshire cows belong to Gadles Farm, only a couple of miles down the road. Gadles Farm is run by Jonathan Hosken, who focuses on maintaining a high standard of animal welfare and growing species-rich pasture for the cows to graze in order to produce the best possible milk for the cheesemaking. Jonathan's herd feeds on grass for most of the year and on silage, also grown on the farm, at other

The stunning nettle-wrapped rind of a Cornish Yarg. This wheel of Cornish Yarg weighs in at a hefty 3kg, but the cheese is also available in smaller rounds.

times. The cheesemakers at Lynher Dairies work closely with Jonathan, the former reporting on milk quality and the latter on how the animals are doing.

The making of Cornish Yarg, like all artisan cheese, is down to a combination of artistry and science, experience and intuition. The defining features of Cornish Yarg are the recipe, the milk used to produce the cheese and the nettles that are wrapped around it when the cheese is young. But before the nettle-wrapping begins, and just after the young cheeses have been placed in the moulds, they are pressed and left to rest for a few hours. The cheeses are then left in a tank of brine for eighteen hours to add flavour and to help preserve them. The following day, they are dried, ready to be wrapped in nettle leaves, which the cheesemakers add by hand, each using their own technique. The nettles are foraged, young and fresh, in the spring from local meadows and hedgerows, then frozen to last the year round.

Cornish Yarg is matured initially for 21–22 days, during which time a white bloomy mould develops. Each cheese is then packed in greaseproof paper and matured for a further few weeks; it is best eaten at 6–12 weeks. The dairy also makes Wild Garlic Yarg, made to the same recipe as Cornish Yarg but using wild garlic leaves in place of the nettles. Other cheeses Lynher Dairies makes include Cornish Kern, a Gouda-style cheese, and Stithians, essentially a 'Naked Yarg' without leaves and using purely Ayrshire milk.

Cornish Yarg characteristics

Milk: Pasteurised milk from a nearby herd of Ayrshire cows and local Holstein-Friesian herds

Rennet: Either animal or vegetarian

Appearance: Pale, creamy, crumbly paste wrapped in nettles with a white, bloomy edible rind

Tasting notes: Fresh lactic flavour with buttery and vegetal notes. Varies according to the season and length of maturation

Stuffed portobello mushrooms

Lynher Dairies sits high on the western side of Cornwall in a wooden-cladded building that looks rather attractive in the dappled shade of the surrounding beech trees. I visited the dairy on a glorious day in May, full Cornish sun shining down on me, deliberately timing my visit to avoid June and July and the hordes of seekers of sun and sand, who descend on the South West Peninsula every year. I met Catherine and her son Otto, who showed me around the whole set-up, including the large production rooms with their multiple gleaming vats, followed by the rooms for moulding, pressing and, that final magic touch, nettle-wrapping.

Ruth Connolly, a cheesemaker and 'nettler' at Lynher Dairies, was in charge of the nettle-wrapping that day. Ruth told me that she had been nettling for over fifteen years. With a pile of frozen leaves next to her, Ruth was effortlessly painting leaves, one by one, on to a young cheese. It was mesmerising to watch.

This recipe is delicious at any time of year, whether for a winter supper or a summer lunch. I've used portobello mushrooms here, but you could use any large mushrooms for the stuffing.

SERVES 3

6 extra-large portobello mushrooms
olive oil, for drizzling
2 spring onions, finely chopped
handful of fresh flat-leaf parsley, finely chopped
handful of fresh thyme, finely chopped
120g fresh breadcrumbs
250g Cornish Yarg, grated
a few gratings of nutmeg
1 large egg
sea salt and freshly ground black pepper

Preheat the oven to 200°C/400°F/gas mark 6.

Cut the stalks off the mushrooms to create a flat surface – keeping the stalks for later – and place, gill side up, in a deep baking tray. Drizzle a good glug of olive oil over the mushrooms and bake on the top shelf of the oven for 10 minutes. Remove the mushrooms, discarding any liquid that has collected in the bottom of the baking tray, and set aside, keeping the oven on.

Finely chop the mushroom stalks and add to a large bowl with the spring onions, fresh herbs, breadcrumbs and grated cheese. Season with 2 teaspoons of salt, some black pepper and a few gratings from a whole nutmeg, add the egg and combine everything together well.

Take a large handful of the mixture and, using your hands, pat it into a rough burger shape before placing it on top of one of the mushrooms in the baking tray. Repeat with the remaining mixture and mushrooms, so that all six mushrooms are stuffed with the cheesy herb mixture, then drizzle over another good glug of olive oil and bake on a low shelf in the oven for 20 minutes until golden and crisping on top.

These mushrooms would go well with a green-leaf salad or crispy kale.

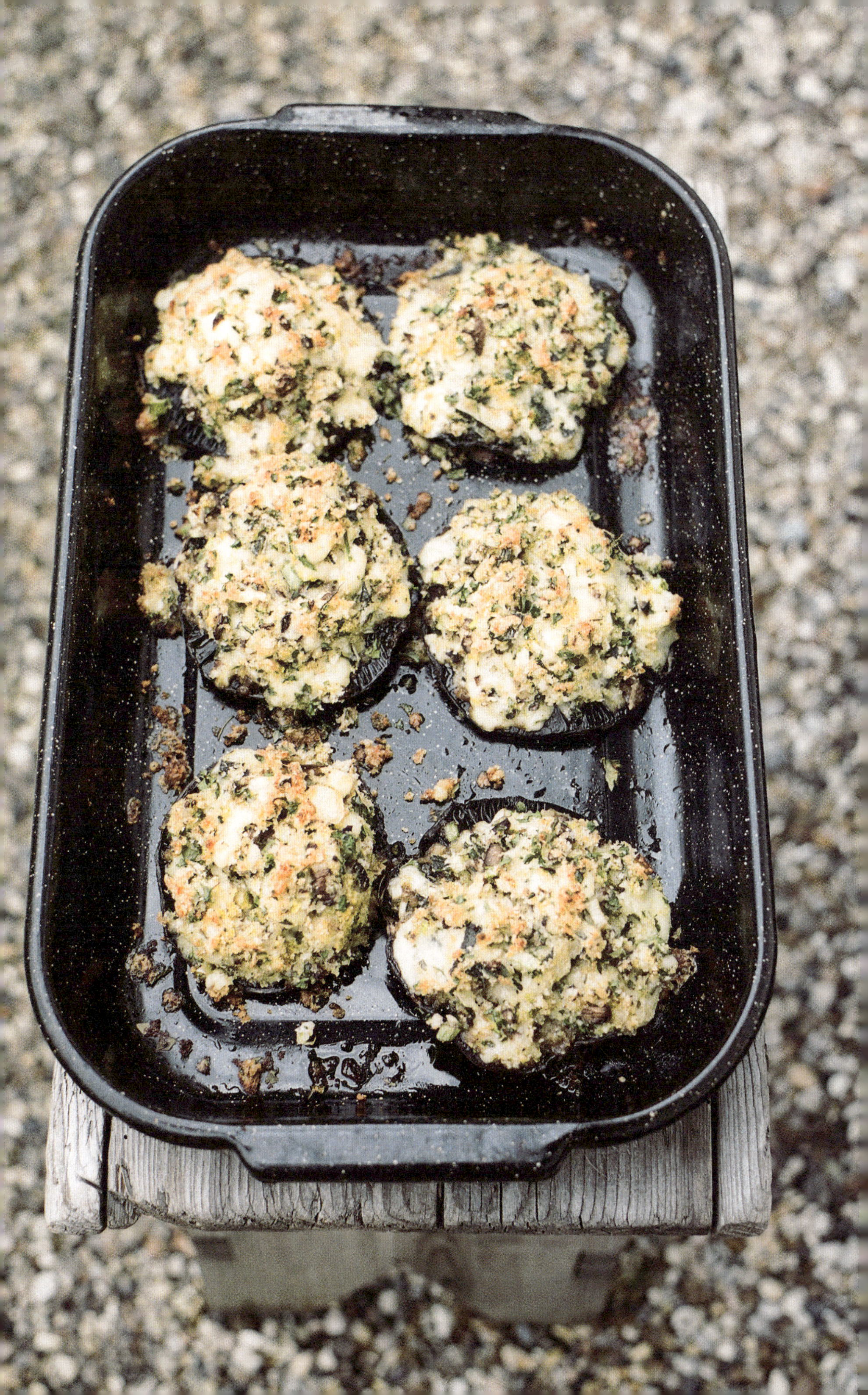

DODDINGTON

From left to right: The maturing rooms are bathed in a warm, ruddy light, mainly owing to the impressive red coating on the Doddington cheeses.

An inquisitive cow, Swedish Red crossed with British Friesian, part of the herd at North Doddington Farm with distant links to the Ayrshire breed.

The splendid view of North Doddington Farm with the Cheviot Hills beyond, marking the border between the North East of England and Scotland.

North Doddington Farm, Wooler, Northumberland

Situated in the Glendale Valley in Northumberland, within sight of the beautiful Cheviot Hills that mark the border between North East England and Scotland, is North Doddington Farm, where Doddington is made. Produced by the Maxwell family, Doddington is a hard-style cheese made using raw milk from the farm's mixed herd of British Friesian, Swedish Red and Montbéliarde cows.

The Maxwell family originally came from Dumfriesshire, where they had been dairy farming for generations. In the autumn of 1950, Malcolm Maxwell moved to Northumberland and they have been producing milk from their cows ever since, turning to cheesemaking in the late 1980s. Having travelled extensively to learn how to make cheese – from Scotland to Holland, France to the United States – the Maxwell family now use their experience to make their own cheese. Maggie Maxwell is in charge of making Doddington, while her brother Neill runs the farm.

The cows at North Doddington Farm graze outside for as long as possible, from April, when they are turned out to grass, until the end of the year – sometimes right up until Christmas. Neill grows complex herbal leys that include lots of wildflowers and plants such as bird's-foot trefoil, chicory, plantain, yarrow and timothy. This species-rich pasture provides the cattle with a nutritious diet, while attracting a huge variety of invertebrates to the fields. The diversity of plants also enhances soil health and structure, with each species contributing in different ways. One plant may have a longer root system than another, for instance, tapping the soil at a deeper level and absorbing different nutrients.

Like many farmhouse cheeses, what makes Doddington special is the quality of the milk produced at the farm. Originally based on a Leicester-type cheese recipe, Doddington has since evolved to encompass Cheddar-style qualities as well as characteristics of some continental-style cheeses. Doddington is always made using warm milk taken straight from the cows in the morning. This retains all the natural flora in the milk, said to give the cheese a sweeter, more complex flavour.

The starter culture is then added to the milk at the appropriate point, followed by the rennet for clotting it. The resulting curds are then cut into small pieces the size of wheat grains, and gradually heated again. This second stage of heating creates a slightly drier final cheese, which can be left to ripen for longer and develop more flavour. After the whey is drained, the curds are kept warm by piling them up, in a process very similar to 'Cheddaring'. Once the curds have been milled, and the right level of salt has been added, they are moulded, pressed – the pressing is done very gently and in stages so the salt is not pushed out, which aids preservation and improves flavour – and turned. The next morning, the young cheeses are coated in wax and placed in the maturing rooms. Doddington can be eaten from around a year old, but it is normally aged for 18–24 months or longer, to develop the full complexity of flavour.

Other cheeses made on the farm include Berwick Edge, Capability Brown, Darling Blue, Admiral Collingwood, Cuddy's Cave and Smoked Cuddy's Cave.

Doddington characteristics
Milk: Raw milk from the farm's mixed herd of British Friesian, Swedish Red and Montbéliarde cows

Rennet: Animal

Appearance: Light-golden buttery paste with an inedible, wax-coated burgundy rind

Tasting notes: Rich, sweet and nutty flavour with fruity, caramel notes. Varies according to the season and length of maturation

Maggie inspecting the farm's mixed herd of British Friesian, Swedish Red and Montbéliarde cows, grazing only a couple of hundred yards from the dairy.

Fish pie with flat-leaf parsley and sorrel

The region where Maggie and her family live and work – where the North East of England meets the Scottish Borders – is absolutely stunning. I hadn't visited the area before meeting Maggie, and I can safely say that I'll be visiting it again very soon. The journey through the Northumberland National Park was a memorable one, and one that I can imagine is best taken at a leisurely pace in a soft-top classic car or on a café racer, clipping the apexes on every juicy turn – when it's safe to do so, of course!

The landscape is beautifully varied, and in July, when I visited, it was festooned in the creams and purples of meadowsweet, oxeye daisy, rosebay willowherb and valerian. Travelling through the borderlands, you can just sense that the area is steeped in history, from bygone battles such as the Siege of Berwick or the Battle of Otterburn to the infamous reivers, the armed raiders who frequently crossed the border on either side to steal horses, sheep and cattle. Charming places to visit in the area are Wooler and Berwick-upon-Tweed in Northumberland, and Kelso and St Boswells in Scotland.

This recipe is a celebration of the two border regions, based on Maggie's Doddington cheese from Northumberland and local Eyemouth fish from across the Scottish border in Berwickshire, though you can use any white fish (haddock, cod or pollack) here. It is best served piping hot with fresh greens.

SERVES 3-4

TOPPING
- 400g peeled floury potatoes, cut into chunks
- 1 tsp sea salt
- 15g butter
- 140ml whole milk
- 160g Doddington, grated
- 1 egg yolk
- sea salt and freshly ground black pepper

Preheat the oven to 200°C/400°F/gas mark 6.

For the topping, place the potatoes in a saucepan, cover with cold water and add 1 teaspoon of salt, then bring to the boil and cook for about 10 minutes until the potatoes are tender. Drain the potatoes and leave to cool in a colander until the steam has evaporated.

While the potatoes are cooling, start making the filling (see ingredients on page 89). In a large frying pan over a medium heat, melt 15g of the butter and fry the shallots for 6–7 minutes until translucent and soft. Then add the fish, mussels and prawns, followed by the white wine. Simmer for about 5 minutes until the fish is cooked through and the white wine has reduced a little, then remove from the heat and set aside.

Ingredients and method continued on page 89

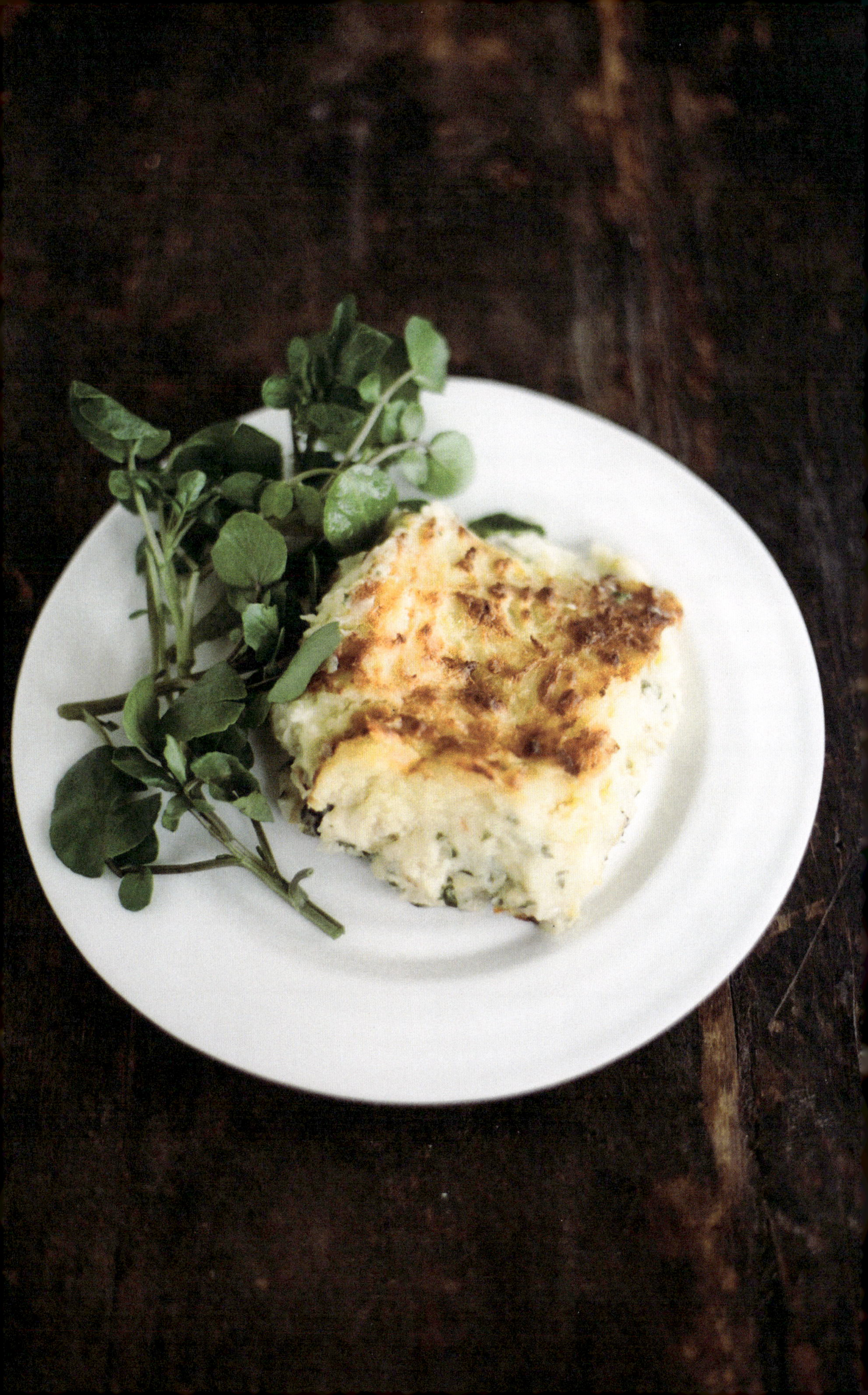

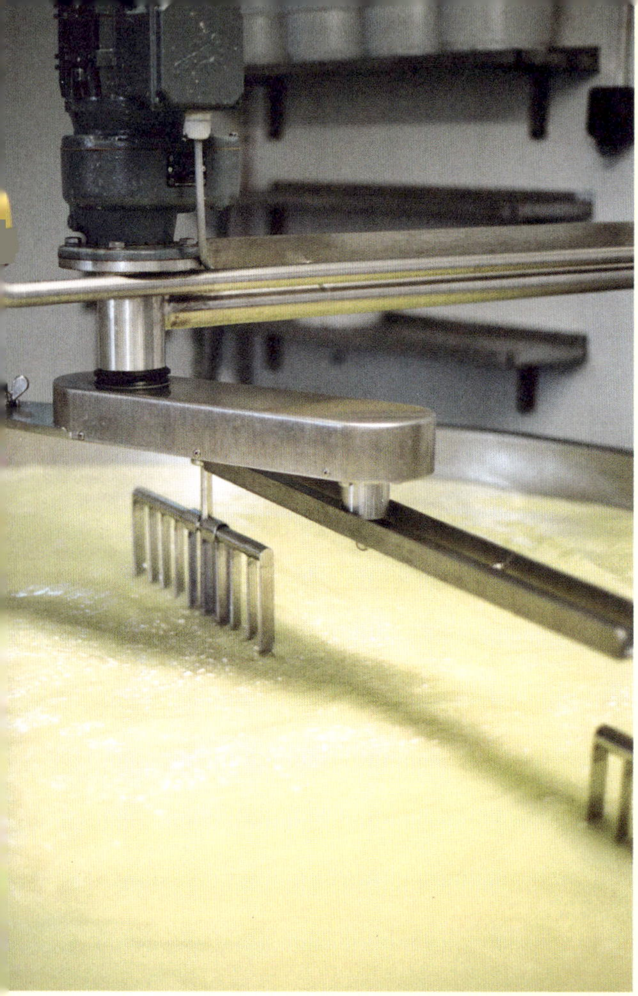
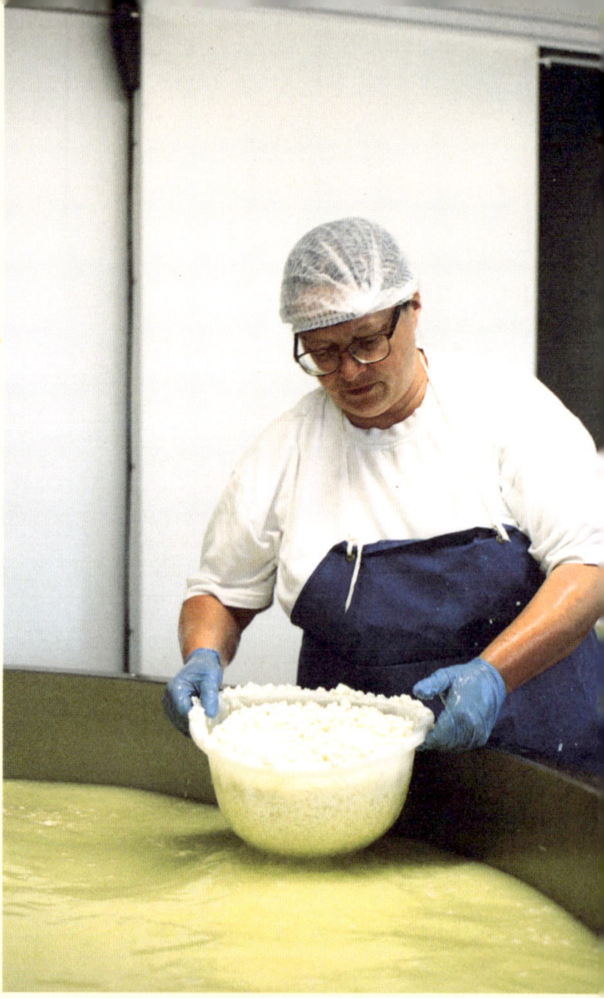
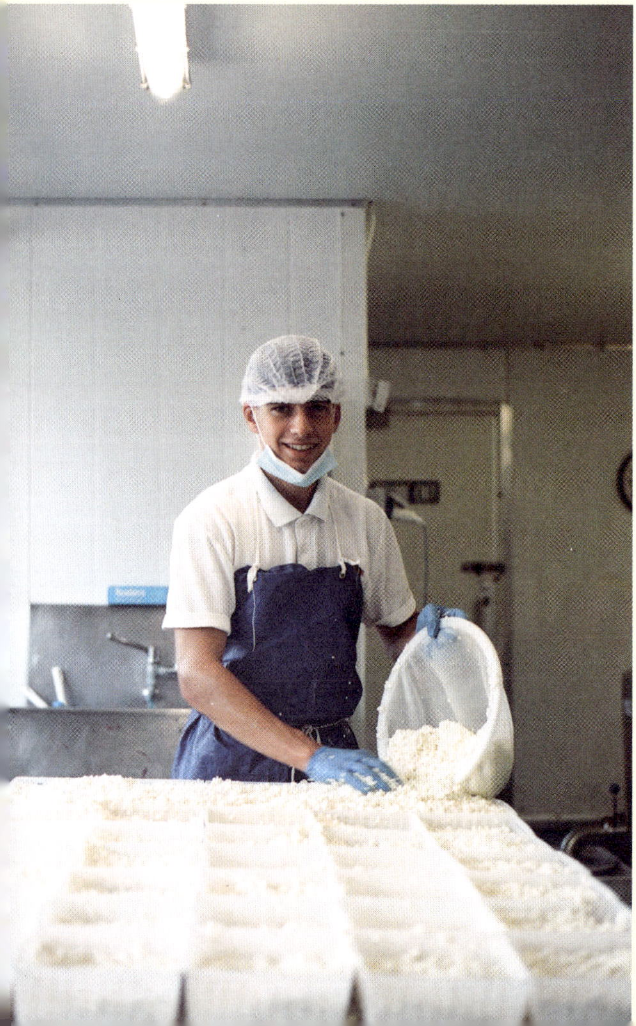
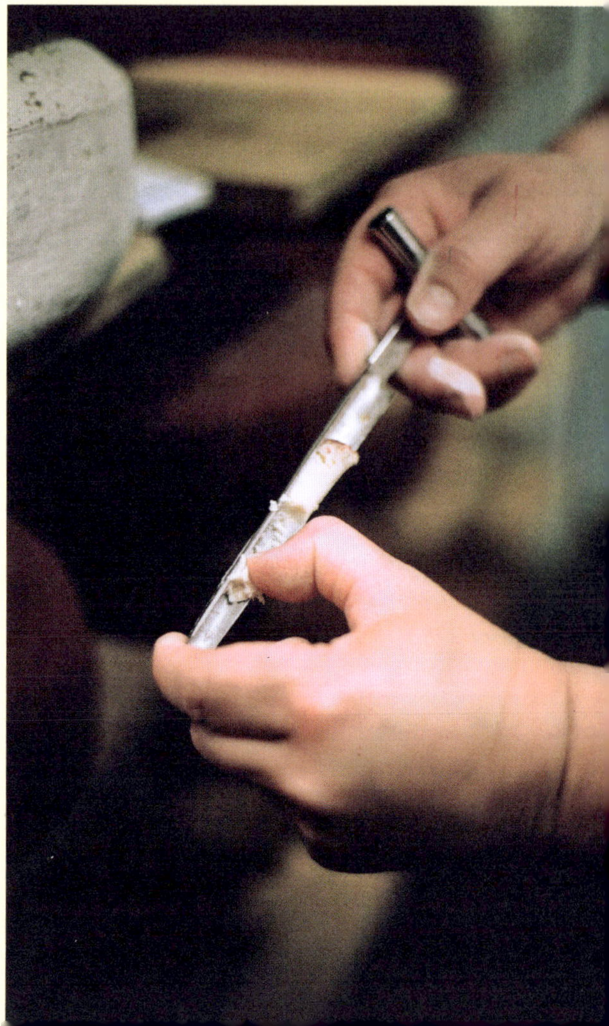

FILLING
75g butter
2 medium shallots, peeled and finely diced
300g skinless white fish fillet (haddock, cod or pollack), cut into 2.5cm pieces
100g shelled mussels
100g shelled prawns
50ml white wine
60g plain flour
300ml whole milk
handful of fresh flat-leaf parsley and sorrel (or just parsley), finely chopped

In a separate saucepan over a medium heat, melt the remaining 60g of butter and add the flour, whisking constantly to make a roux. Once all the flour has been added, continue to whisk as you gradually add the milk, stirring it in completely each time to prevent lumps from forming. Keep whisking until the sauce thickens, and then add 1 teaspoon of salt, a few grinds of pepper and the herbs. Add the fish mixture to the white sauce, stirring it in carefully in order not to break up the fish. Place in a small, deep-sided ovenproof dish, and set aside while you finish making the topping.

Return the potatoes to the first saucepan and mash until smooth. Beat in the butter and milk until the potato becomes smooth again, then add the grated cheese, followed by the egg yolk. Beat for another minute or two until the potato is smooth and glossy.

Spoon the mashed potato over the fish mixture, spreading it out in an even layer and running a fork over the top to create crispy ridges when cooked, then place in the oven to bake for 30–40 minutes and serve immediately.

Clockwise from top left: The metal curd cutters in the vat, doing exactly what their name suggests – cutting the curds into grain-sized particles before the whey is drained.

Maggie removing the small particles of curd from the whey. If you haven't tried whey before, it is incredibly sweet and rather delicious!

Tasting each batch of cheese is so important for any cheesemaker. Maggie does it frequently to check the flavour and structure of the cheese.

Back in the cheesemaking rooms, Maggie and assistant cheesemaker Joe mould Admiral Collingwood, a semi-soft raw-milk cheese, which is washed in Newcastle Brown Ale.

GORWYDD CAERPHILLY

Left: The profile of a beautiful Jersey cow at Puxton Court Farm, from which the brothers source the organic raw milk to make their cheeses.

Right: Todd, Maugan and the team of cheesemakers turn every single cheese in both the Gorwydd Caerphilly and Pitchfork maturing rooms once a week.

Trethowan Brothers, Weston-super-Mare, Somerset

Originally made at Gorwydd Farm in the Teifi Valley in West Wales, Gorwydd Caerphilly is now produced in the North Somerset Levels, five miles from Cheddar, with its low-lying, rich grassland and varied soils, a location selected by the Trethowan brothers, Todd and Maugan, with the aim of sourcing the best-quality milk to make their cheeses. Gorwydd Caerphilly, a semi-hard cheese, is made using organic, raw milk from the farm's mixed herd of Holstein-Friesian and Jersey cows. Working every day with the farmer and herdsman from Puxton Court Farm, the brothers and their team of cheesemakers headed by dairy manager Ben Ticehurst create Gorwydd Caerphilly and Pitchfork Cheddar.

Gorwydd Caerphilly starts with the morning's milk being gravity-fed gently into the vats via pipes from the milking parlour. Once the milk has been warmed, the natural starter culture is added. The brothers use traditional 'pint' starter cultures, each imparting its own distinctive flavour to the milk. Each day the cheesemakers use a different starter culture, so that each batch of resultant cheese will have a different flavour profile, aroma and texture. The rennet is then added and left for a coagulation process lasting about 45 minutes, again determining the final flavour. Once set, the curds are cut into large pieces and stirred gently by hand to prevent them from sinking in the whey and sticking together – the stirring also helps to solidify the curds. With the whey expelled and the curds now sitting at the bottom of the vat, four cheesemakers position themselves at each corner of the vat and cut the curds by hand, this time into small cubes. The cubed curds are then gathered into each corner and salted. This is known as 'texturing'. As they want to keep a creamier texture in the final cheese, the cheesemakers don't mill the curds.

The curds are then placed into special moulds. Normally, a wooden follower (board) would be placed between the moulds when stacking them, but Todd and Maugan prefer to allow the mould above to compress the mould beneath into a young cheese. This is a traditional Caerphilly pressing technique, visible in the prominent line around the outside of a wheel of cheese. The young cheeses are stacked into reclaimed Victorian cast-iron presses for the whey to drain overnight.

The next morning, the young cheeses are transferred from the presses to a brine tank, where they are turned and left to toughen up and for the rind to develop evenly. The maturation of Gorwydd Caerphilly takes around two months, during which time the cheeses are turned every day. Depending on the season, the cheesemakers like to see what they call a 'pie crust', or a lip around the top of the cheese, and an even, wrinkled texture to the whole rind.

Gorwydd Caerphilly characteristics

Milk: Organic, raw milk from a mixed herd of Holstein-Friesian and Jersey cows

Rennet: Animal

Appearance: Matt cream or pale yellow paste, softer edges and crumbly centre with a dark grey, mould-ripened edible rind

Tasting notes: Regarded as three cheeses in one: the rind with its mushroom flavours; the rind breakdown with creamy notes; and the middle of the cheese with a more lactic taste. Varies according to the season and length of maturation.

Clockwise from top left: The moist curds are cut and drained by hand in order to keep their soft structure.

The special moulds used for making Gorwydd Caerphilly. Each mould has an adjustable side that helps to create the prominent line around the outside of the cheese.

Todd and Maugan, the brothers who make Gorwydd Caerphilly and Pitchfork Cheddar.

Once the young Gorwydd Caerphilly cheeses have been moulded and pressed, they are placed in a brine bath to soak for twenty-four hours.

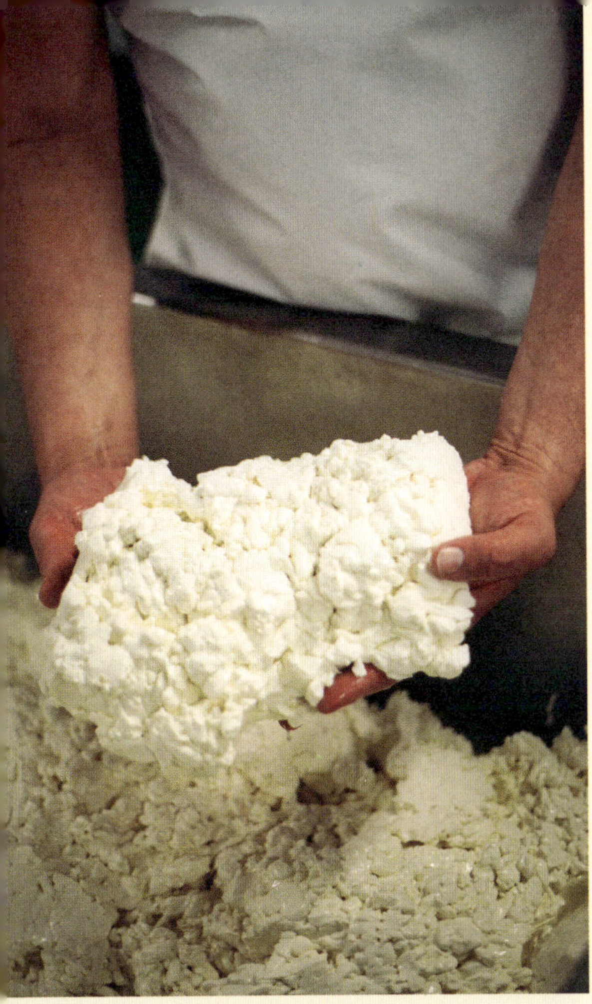
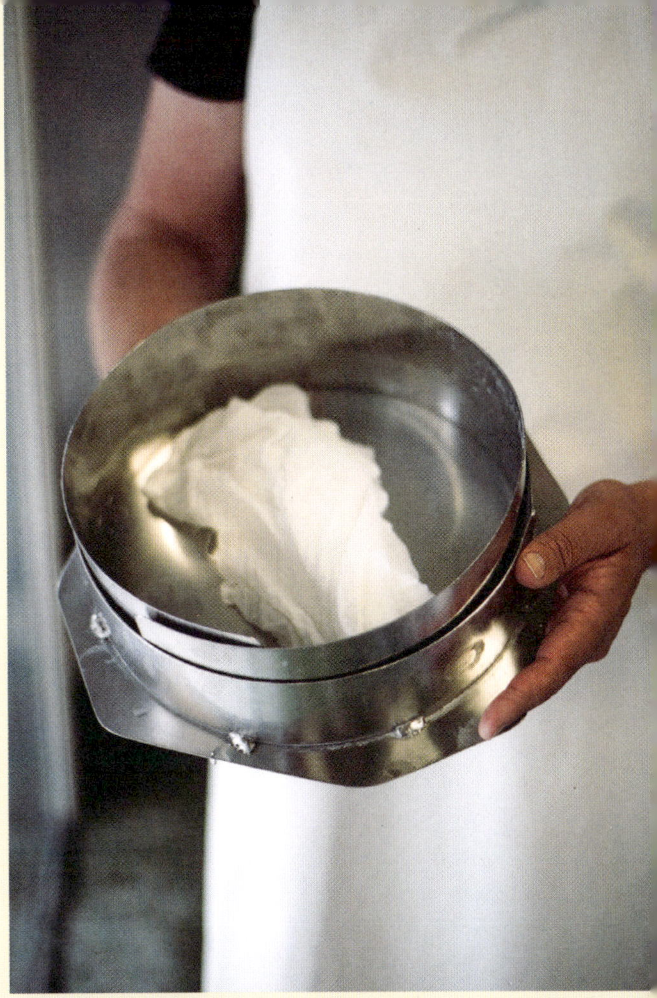
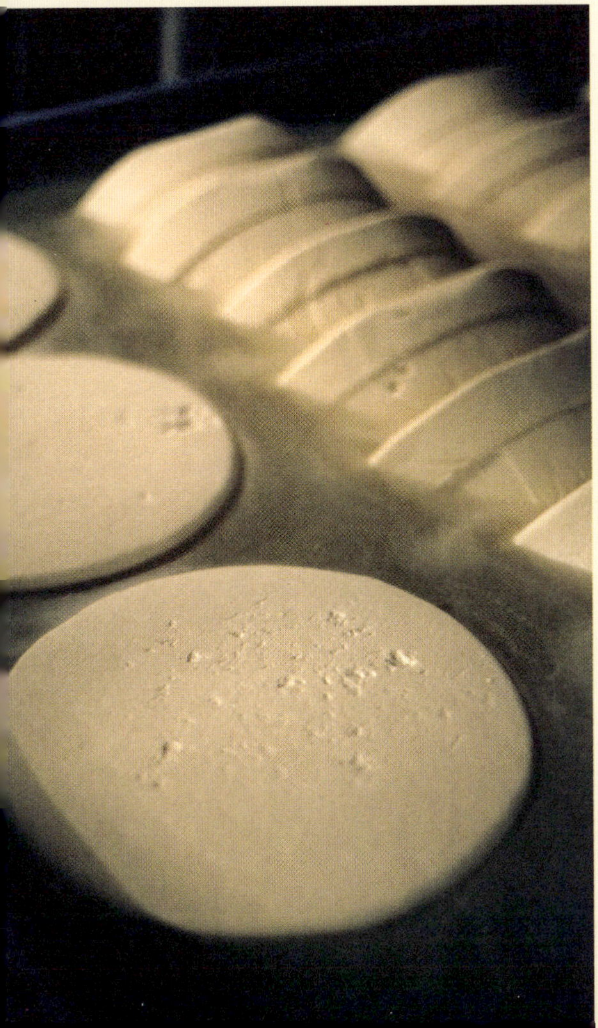
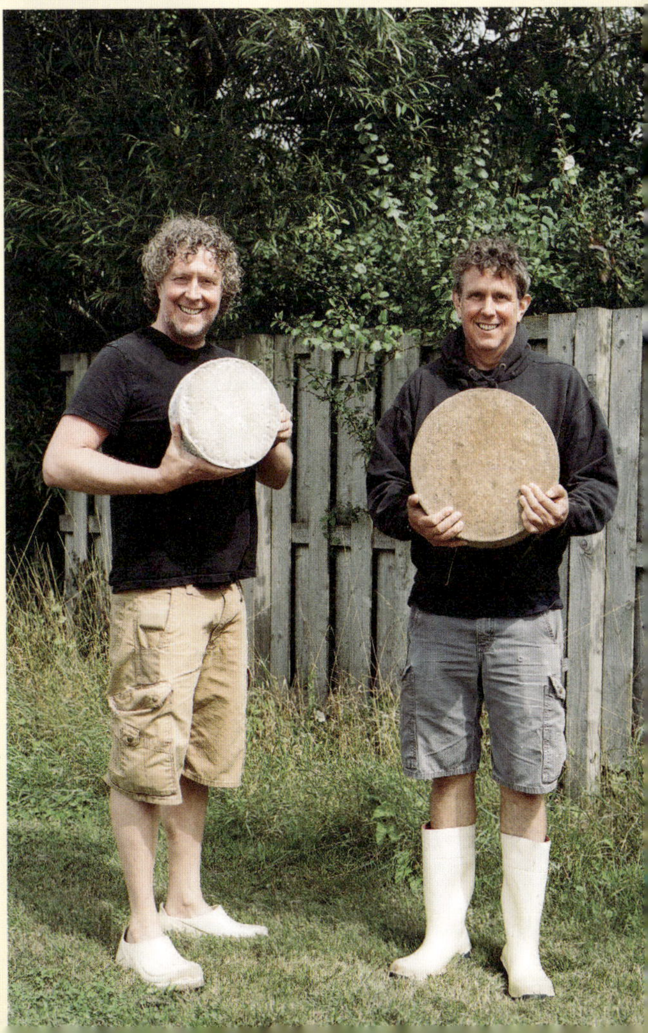

Purple-sprouting broccoli with creamy Gorwydd Caerphilly

Todd and Maugan built their dairy in Somerset in fewer than eight months, after eighteen months of searching for the right farm. By building their dairy from scratch, they could design everything themselves, from how the milk is channelled – gravity-fed to maintain the condition of the milk – to bespoke premises for their vats and moulding areas. And to build it all in under a year is certainly impressive!

Puxton Court Farm, next to the dairy, is part of an all-weather adventure park, where families can be taken around on a tractor-trailer to learn about the running of a farm, from watching the cows being milked in the afternoon, to meeting the calves in the adjoining barns.

As much as the eight-year-old in me yearned to go on the tractor-trailer, I resisted the temptation and instead was taken by the brothers on a brilliant tour of their impressive dairy and maturing rooms. Gorwydd Caerphilly and Pitchfork – their Cheddar-style cheese – are aged in separate maturing rooms. The Pitchfork maturing room is especially vast and, stacked full of cheese, has an intensely earthy smell. Maugan took me up on the dairy's cherry picker – normally used to turn the highest Pitchfork cheeses – to catch a glimpse from above of the entire maturing room and its regimented cheeses. The sight of hundreds of aged cheeses, all in perfect order and in an eerily quiet room, was really rather awe-inspiring and one that Maugan rightly said had a strange parallel with the Terracotta Army in China.

This recipe uses seasonal purple-sprouting broccoli in a dish that goes superbly well with sausages, chicken or new potatoes.

SERVES 4 AS A SIDE

400g tender-stem purple-sprouting broccoli
olive oil, for drizzling
200ml single cream
juice of ½ lemon
180g Gorwydd Caerphilly
sea salt and freshly ground black pepper

Preheat the oven to 200°C/400°F/gas mark 6.

Blanch the broccoli in boiling salted water for 3–4 minutes. Drain well and leave the broccoli spears in the colander until the steam has all but evaporated. Then cut each spear of broccoli in half lengthways and place in an ovenproof dish in a single layer.

Drizzle over a generous glug of olive oil, then add the cream, lemon juice, a pinch of salt and a good shower of black pepper. Finish by crumbling the Caerphilly over the entire dish, then bake in the oven for 12–15 minutes until nicely sizzling.

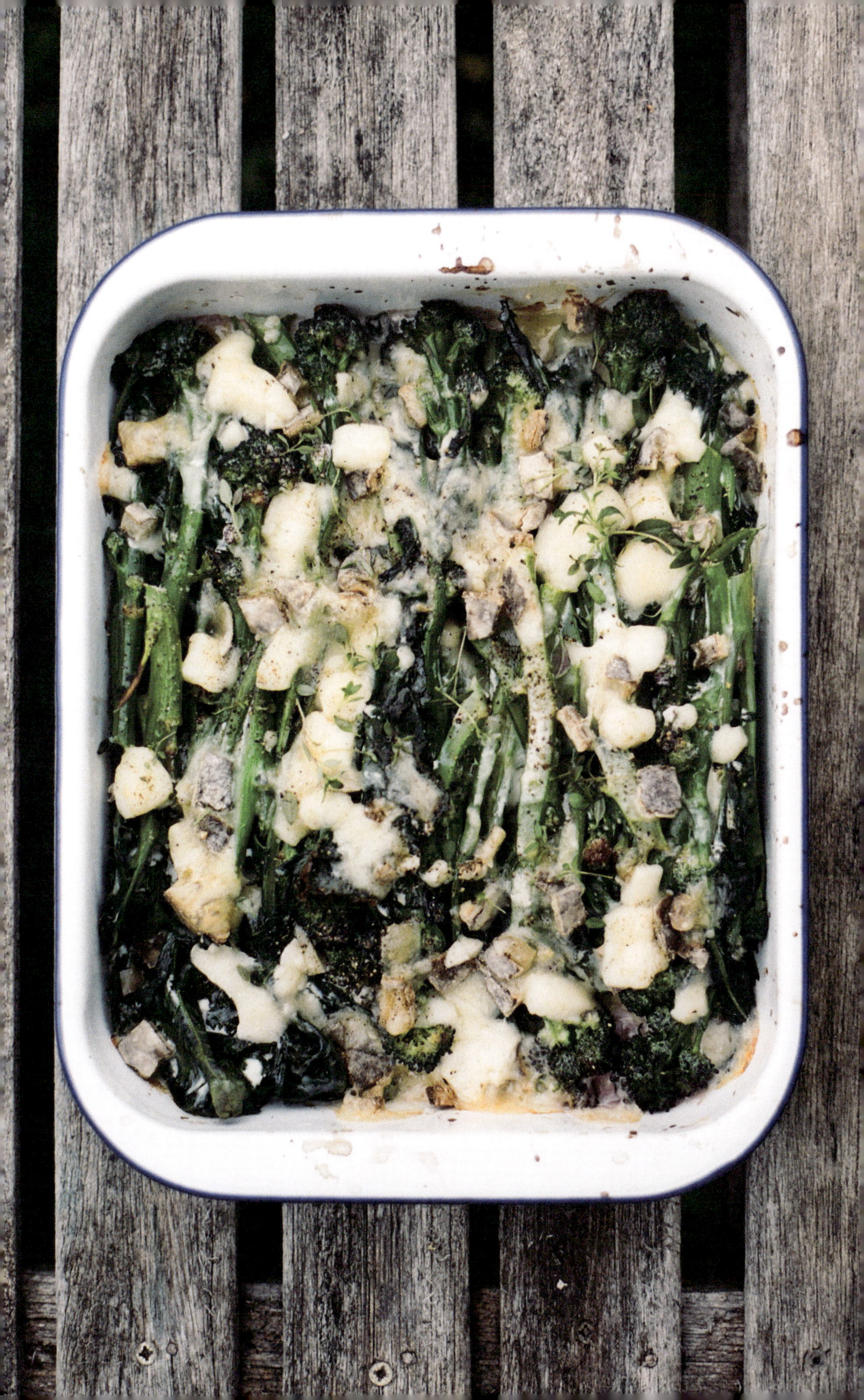

HARBOURNE BLUE

Left: The stippled blue mould and ivory paste of Harbourne Blue, made by Ben Harris in Devon using goat's milk from a local mixed herd.

Right: The delightful sight of sunbathing goats at the Lewis family farm in Devon. A Saanen (left, standing) and an Alpine (right, lying down).

Ticklemore Cheese Dairy, Totnes, Devon

On the north-eastern edge of the South Devon Area of Outstanding Natural Beauty lies Ticklemore Cheese Dairy, where Harbourne Blue is made. Named after the nearby Harbourne River, a tributary of the Dart, Harbourne Blue was originally created by Robin Congdon, a pioneer of farmhouse cheesemaking. Now, Ben Harris makes Harbourne Blue, a creamy Roquefort-style blue cheese, using milk from a local mixed herd of Saanen, Toggenburg, Alpine and Anglo-Nubian goats. The goats belong to the Lewis family at Burnhill Farm in deepest rural Devon, very near Wellington. The Lewis family – the father, David, and his two sons, Andrew and John – milk the goats twice a day, and deliver the milk directly to Ben.

The method of making Harbourne Blue is based on the dairy's recipe for Beenleigh Blue, itself based on a traditional Roquefort recipe but using goat's milk in place of ewe's. One of the unique aspects of the make is that the curds are cut twice (first slicing vertically and then in a figure of eight) and then stirred twice by hand using a technique known as coiffage, which causes a thin film to form on the curds, preventing them from sticking together and encouraging the blue mould to infiltrate the cheese during maturation. Once the curds have been ladled into moulds, they are left to compress into young cheeses. The cheeses are then turned several times, and placed into a hastening room to be dry-salted, which draws out moisture from the cheese. After being transferred to another, cooler room and salted again, the cheeses are finally taken to the maturing room, where they are pierced with metal spikes from top to bottom, to let in oxygen and encourage the blue mould to grow, then stored on their side. This piercing and storage technique is taken from the traditional Roquefort method of maturation, and is different from maturing Stilton, in which the cheese is pierced through the sides.

In the maturing room, Harbourne Blue is turned every few days and samples are taken from the cheese at three weeks old using a cheesemaker's iron to check the blue mould developing in the cheese. A constant airflow is maintained in the room to keep ammonia levels down and circulate the moisture. The cheeses are then wrapped in plastic film and aged for a minimum of three months. Harbourne Blue is best eaten at 5–6 months old.

Other cheeses Ticklemore Cheese Dairy makes include Devon Blue and Beenleigh Blue, which are both made to the same recipe as Harbourne Blue but using cow's and ewe's milk respectively.

Harbourne Blue characteristics

Milk: Pasteurised milk from a local mixed herd of Saanen, Toggenburg, Alpine and Anglo-Nubian goats

Rennet: Vegetarian

Appearance: Crumbly blue-veined white paste, with no rind as the cheese is wrapped in plastic film before ageing

Tasting notes: Floral, goaty flavour with fresh lemony notes. Varies according to the season and length of maturation

Ben Harris, in charge of Ticklemore Cheese Dairy and also the head cheesemaker, with Sarah Daligan, who first joined the dairy when she was sixteen.

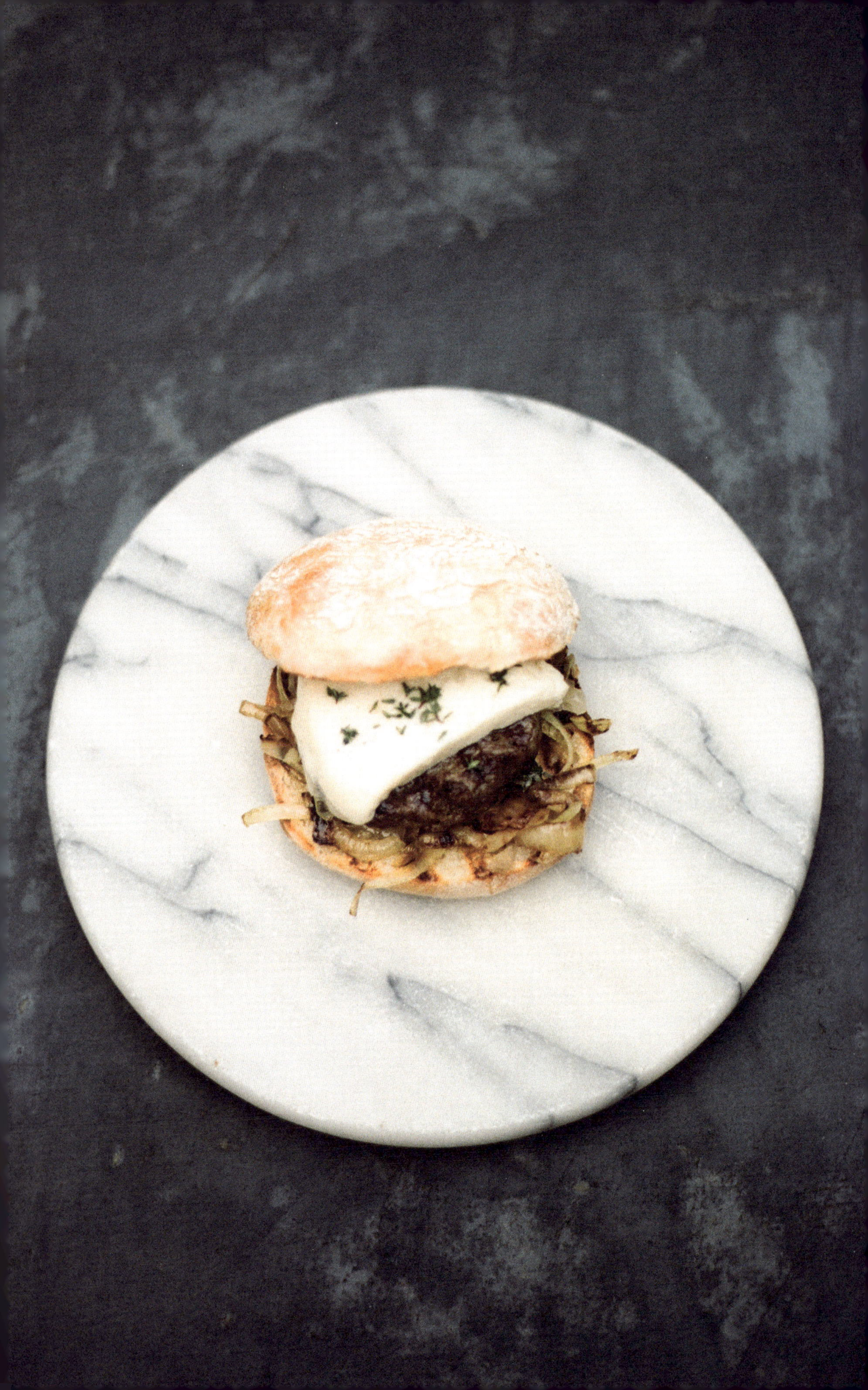

Harbourne Blue burgers

To see firsthand how Ben Harris makes his cheeses was impressive to say the least. When I arrived it was moulding time, and at this stage speed is of the essence. As I took photographs, Ben and his team of cheesemakers worked in such a wonderful, deft way. In a matter of seconds, a bowl full of curds was removed from the vat, taken to the drainage table to be fluffed and broken down, then ladled into an awaiting mould, before being left to naturally compress and age.

I visited Ben on a rainy afternoon in late May; the showers were unrelenting, with only the rare chink of warm sunshine. From Totnes, the dairy is down a series of long winding lanes overhung with large green or copper beeches and hedgerows full of delicate wildflowers. It was flowering season, so the verges were alight with fine white clusters of wild garlic, bluebells of every kind, red campion, stitchwort and, my personal favourite, cow parsley.

This recipe was inspired by my trip to Ticklemore, celebrating the area's local produce. Driving to the dairy, I passed Ben's Farm Shop in Staverton, Totnes, which sells organic meat alongside an array of other organic and free-range produce. It was here that I bought some wonderful local minced beef to make my four burgers. Marrying them with Harbourne Blue was a match made in heaven!

SERVES 4

1 tbsp sunflower oil, plus extra for brushing
1 large onion, peeled and finely sliced
200g Harbourne Blue, cut into 4 slices
4 ciabatta buns
butter, for spreading

BURGERS
500g minced beef
100g wild garlic leaves, finely chopped (or 2 tbsp dried herbs, such as oregano)
1 large egg, beaten
1 tsp sea salt
1 tsp freshly ground black pepper

Half an hour before cooking this recipe, take the minced beef out of the fridge to come to up to room temperature. This will make for a much tastier burger when cooked.

Preheat the oven to 180°C/350°F/gas mark 4.

Place the minced beef in a large bowl with all the other ingredients for the burgers and mix well. Divide the mixture into quarters, then shape into four patties and set aside.

Add the sunflower oil to an ovenproof frying pan on a medium heat, tip in the onions and cook for 7–10 minutes, stirring frequently, until well browned. Remove from the heat and place in the oven to keep warm.

Heat a ridged cast-iron griddle pan on the hob until it is very hot. Lightly brush oil on the pan, and cook the four beef burgers for 2–3 minutes on each side. Once the burgers are cooked, place a slice (50g) of blue cheese on top of each burger and place in the oven for 5 minutes for the cheese to melt.

Meanwhile, halve the buns and lightly butter each half. Place the ciabatta halves, buttered side down, on the hot griddle to cook for 5 minutes or until nicely charred. Remove the burgers and onions from the oven and assemble each burger. Top each bun half with a burger and a sprinkling of fried onions, then sandwich together with the other half of each bun.

JERSEY CURD

Left: A generous bowlful of Jersey Curd, made by Julianna Sedli and her husband Karim Niazy using organic Jersey milk.

Right: Jersey cows are wonderfully docile creatures. Here at Neston Park Home Farm, the cows graze the fresh spring pasture.

The Old Cheese Room, Neston Park Home Farm, Wiltshire

Located within the fine pastoral landscape of Neston Park, the estate's farm is where Julianna Sedli and her husband Karim Niazy make Jersey Curd. As well as other cheeses, Julianna and Karim make their Jersey Curd using organic milk from the farm's herd of Jersey cows. Julianna has had her fair share of experience in the farmhouse cheese industry, from making goat's cheese in the United States and working for Neal's Yard Dairy in London to making cheese with the late Mary Holbrook and with White Lake Cheese in Somerset, working with Wootton Organic Dairy in Devon and at The Fine Cheese Co. in Bath.

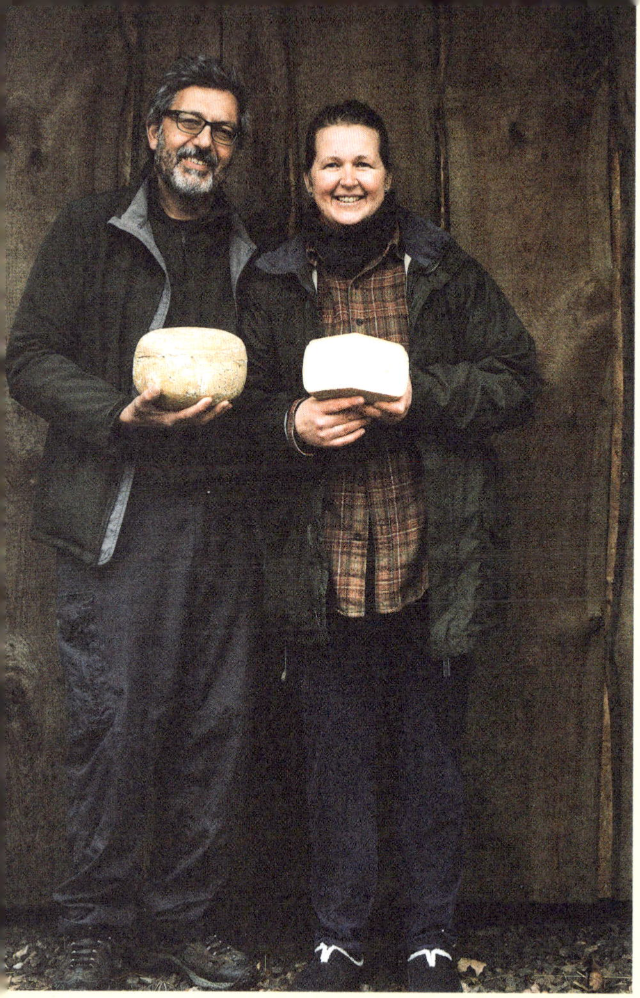
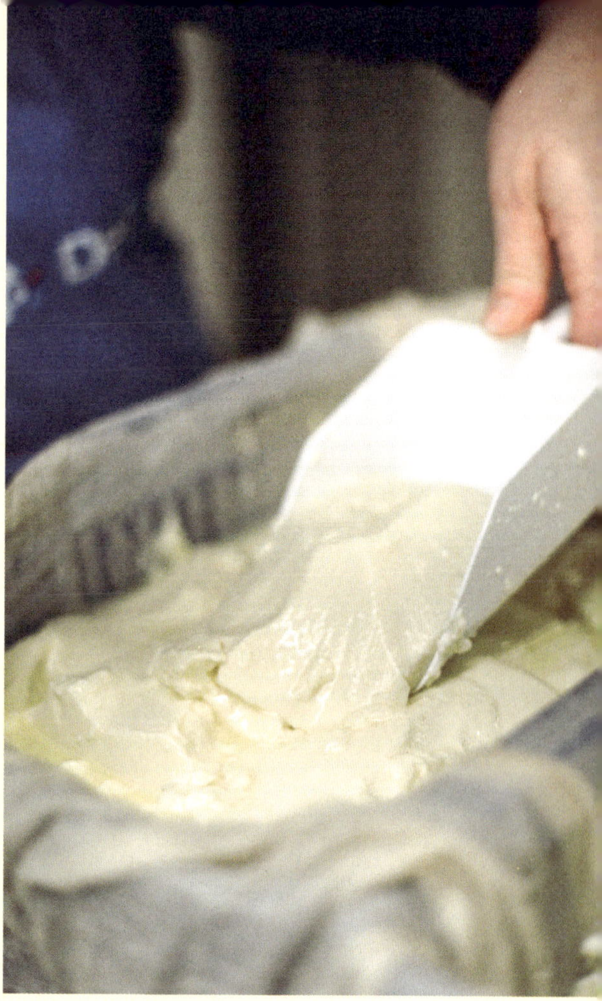
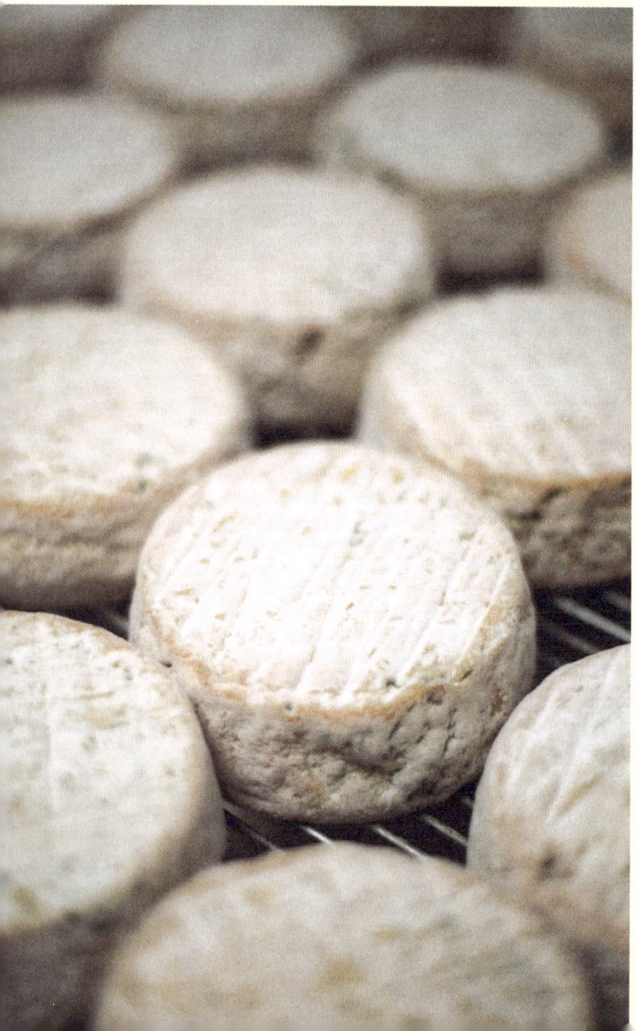
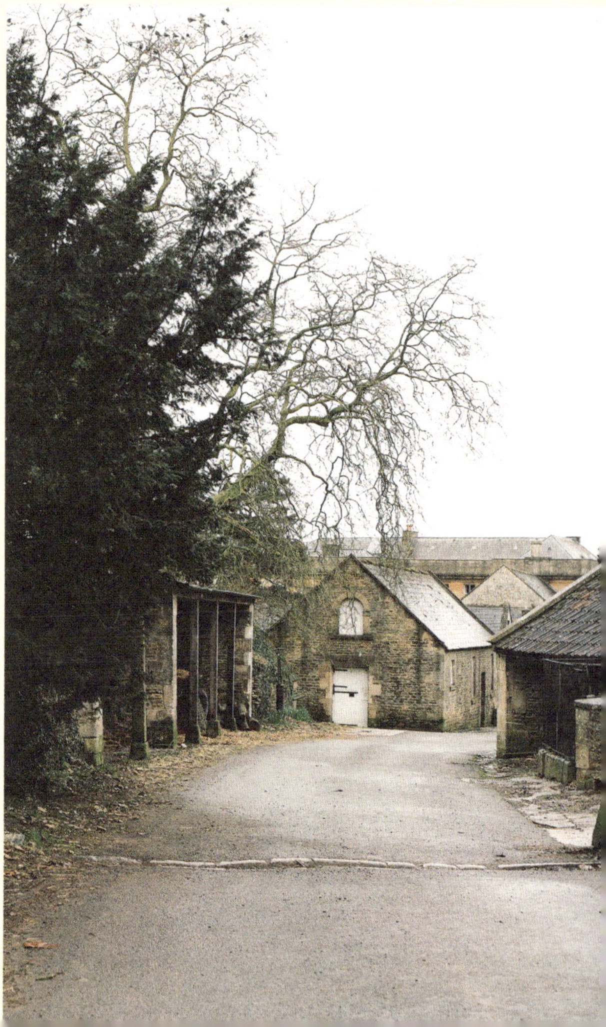

Coming from Hungary, Julianna is passionate about making curd as it's a common ingredient in many Hungarian dishes, both savoury and sweet. The method of making Jersey Curd follows a very traditional farmhouse-kitchen recipe. It starts with cooling the fresh milk down to a certain temperature, after which the starter culture is added. The milk is cooled further, then a small amount of rennet is added. It is then left to set overnight for 16–20 hours. The following morning, Julianna or Karim checks the acidity and temperature and tastes the curds to assess when to cut them. When they taste particularly citrusy, it is time to cut and ladle them, according to Julianna. Using a small scoop, Julianna carefully transfers the cut curds into baskets lined with cheesecloth, which, once filled, are hung up and then left to drain all day. The curds are then placed in a cold store, where they are salted by hand and hung up again to drain further overnight. The next morning, the resulting Jersey Curd is ready to be potted and eaten. Jersey milk is famously rich in butterfat, protein and calcium, making for a delectable curd.

Julianna and Karim named their cheese company The Old Cheese Room as their cheesemaking rooms are based in the original dairy shed at Neston Park Home Farm, where earlier farmers used to keep and milk their own small herd of native cows. The range of cheeses made by Julianna and Karim includes Baronet, Bybrook, Lypiatt, various flavours of Jersey Curd and, most recently, Culpeper. The name of each cheese has a story behind it. Culpeper, for example, was named after the seventeenth-century English botanist and herbalist Nicholas Culpeper. A small, round soft cheese rolled in fresh English herbs, Culpeper, as with all of their cheeses, is made with organic Jersey milk.

Jersey Curd characteristics
Milk: Organic, pasteurised milk from the farm's herd of Jersey cows
Rennet: Vegetarian
Appearance: Soft, silky paste with a typically light-golden Jersey hue
Tasting notes: Rich, delicate creamy flavour with light, zesty notes. Varies very slightly according to the season

Clockwise from top left: Julianna Sedli and Karim Niazy, who make a selection of cheeses using organic milk from the next-door farm's herd of Jersey cows.
Julianna ladling the delicate set curds into a basket lined with cheesecloth to be drained of excess whey.
Neston Park Farm, where Julianna and Karim make their cheese in the old cheesemaking rooms, hence the name of their company, The Old Cheese Room.
As well as Jersey Curd, Julianna and Karim make Baronet, a buttery washed-rind cheese based on a traditional French Reblochon recipe.

Pancakes with Jersey Curd

Julianna and Karim – like the majority of farmhouse cheesemakers – are wonderfully welcoming and generous, with a passion for their product running through their veins. Visiting them on a particularly stormy day in March, my dear mother and I gorged our way through their addictive truffle Jersey Curd smothered on toast. After seeing how the cheeses were made, we were taken on a tour by Sir James Fuller, the estate owner, who showed us the farm and the herd of Jersey cows. We even caught sight of a calf being born – a truly wonderful experience.

This recipe is inspired by Julianna's Hungarian culinary heritage, in which curd features prominently. Julianna, who comes from a farming family herself, has always loved to cook and makes these pancakes for her children most weeks.

MAKES 10–12 PANCAKES, SERVES 3–4

470g plain flour
2 tbsp icing sugar, plus extra for dusting
2 tsp baking powder
¼ tsp sea salt
1 large egg
200g Jersey Curd
290ml whole milk, plus extra if needed
2 tbsp vanilla extract
2 tbsp melted butter, plus extra butter for frying
grated zest of 1 lemon
whipped or pouring cream and/or maple syrup, to serve

Preheat the oven to 140°C/275°F/gas mark 1.

In a large bowl, sift together the flour, icing sugar, baking powder and salt. In a separate bowl, beat the egg with the Jersey Curd, milk and vanilla extract, then pour in the melted butter. Add this runny mixture to the flour mixture, mixing until the batter is smooth – don't worry too much about lumps. If the mixture is too thick, add a little more milk to loosen it.

Place a cast-iron or heavy-based frying pan on a medium heat to warm up. When it is hot, add a small knob of butter to melt. Place 2 tablespoons of the batter in the pan to form a pancake about 10cm in diameter and cook for around 1 minute. Once you see bubbles forming on top of the batter, it is ready to be flipped and cooked for the same amount of time on the other side. Transfer to a baking sheet and place in the oven to keep warm, then add another knob of butter and repeat until you have used all the batter. The mixture makes 10–12 pancakes in total; depending on the size of your pan, you may be able to cook 2–3 at a time.

To serve, dust a little icing sugar over each pancake and enjoy with a spoonful of cream or a glug of maple syrup, or both.

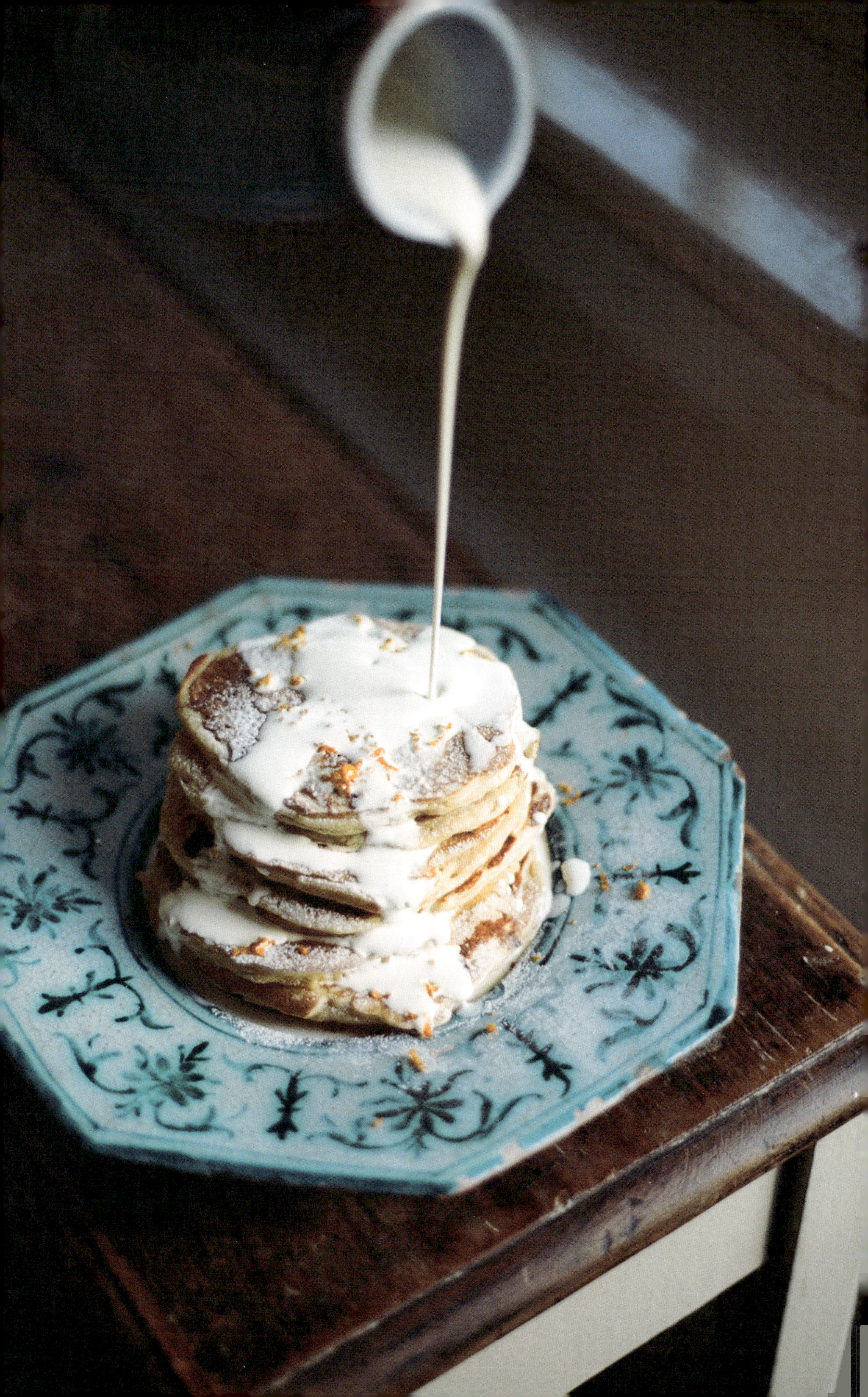

KIRKHAM'S LANCASHIRE

Left: Graham has a close working relationship with the farmer at Beesley Farm, knowing all about the health of the cows and the quality of their milk.

Right: A slice of ivory-white Lancashire made by the Kirkham family at Beesley Farm using raw milk from their herd of Holstein-Friesian cows.

Beesley Farm, Preston, Lancashire

A true Lancashire, it is said, is made within sight of Beacon Fell. Beesley Farm, where the Kirkham family make traditional farmhouse Lancashire, lies just south of the verdant valleys of the Forest of Bowland, and it is well within sight of the fell. The head cheesemaker at the farm, Graham Kirkham, and his team make Lancashire to a nineteenth-century recipe used by his grandmother, Ruth Townley. Graham originally learned how to make cheese from his mother, Ruth Kirkham.

Kirkham's Lancashire is a hard-style cheese made using raw milk from Beesley Farm's herd of Holstein-Friesian cows. At the farm they are slowly introducing

British Friesian cows into the herd because of their suitability to the British climate and grazing conditions. British Friesians are known to be very adaptable, more stable – or 'less leggy' – than the relatively tall Holstein-Friesians, and able to produce a good amount of milk based on a relatively simple grass-based diet. A British Friesian also has a longer average lifespan than that of a Holstein-Friesian. In addition, milk from a British Friesian has a higher percentage of fat and protein than milk from a Holstein-Friesian, making it better suited for cheesemaking.

Making Kirkham's Lancashire is a slow process, which focuses on using the morning's milk and a starter culture that includes strains of a culture going back to one used by Graham's grandmother.

One of the most unusual aspects of Kirkham's Lancashire is how the curds are treated during the cheesemaking process, a treatment that can take up to eleven hours each day, including rest periods. During the process, the curds are cut into blocks and given 'breaks', in which the curds are cut into small squares and gently broken by hand to keep the protein structure intact and allow the curds to dry slowly. After three 'breaks', the curds transform from a jelly-like consistency into a firmer texture.

The team uses what's referred to traditionally as a 'two-day curd' in the making of their cheese. When Graham makes cheese on a Wednesday, for instance, he uses the curd made on Monday and Tuesday.

Kirkham's Lancashire is aged from eight weeks, when it forms into a milky, soft Lancashire, up to a year, when it has become drier and firmer and with a more robust flavour. As Graham says about the whole cheesemaking process: 'Each piece of farmhouse cheese is a piece of history.'

Kirkham's Lancashire characteristics

Milk: Raw milk from the farm's herd of Holstein-Friesian and British Friesian cows

Rennet: Animal

Appearance: Crumbly, ivory paste with a rich, mottled, edible rind

Tasting notes: Rich, buttery flavour with light milky and acidic notes that live long in the mouth. Varies according to the season and length of maturation

Top: To analyse the taste and structure of the cheese, the cheesemaker or affineur (in the case of a cheesemonger) uses a hollow tool known as an iron to extract a cylinder of cheese from the centre.
Bottom: The infectious smiles of happy cheesemakers at Kirkham's Lancashire, whose passion and attention to detail is represented in their cheese.

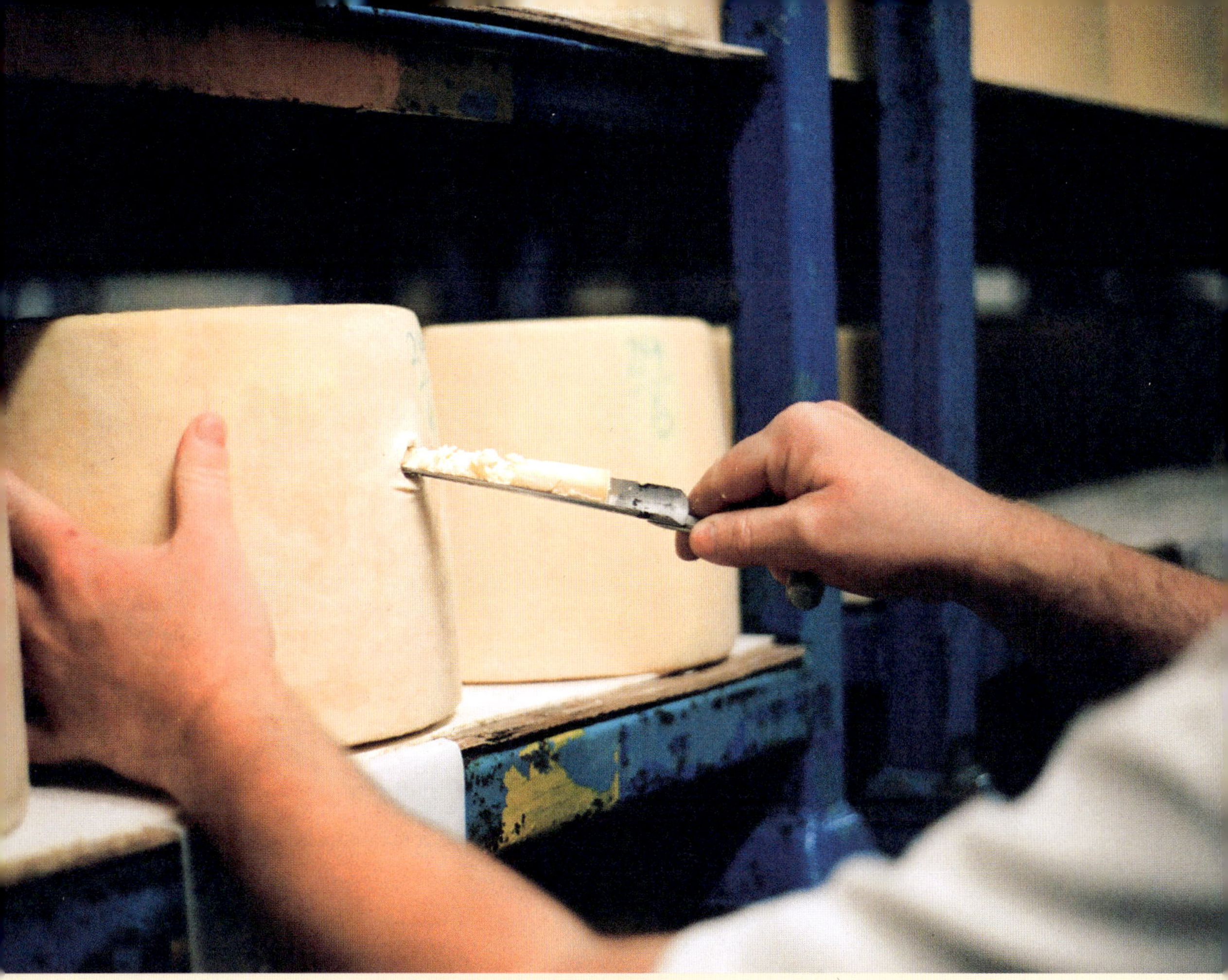

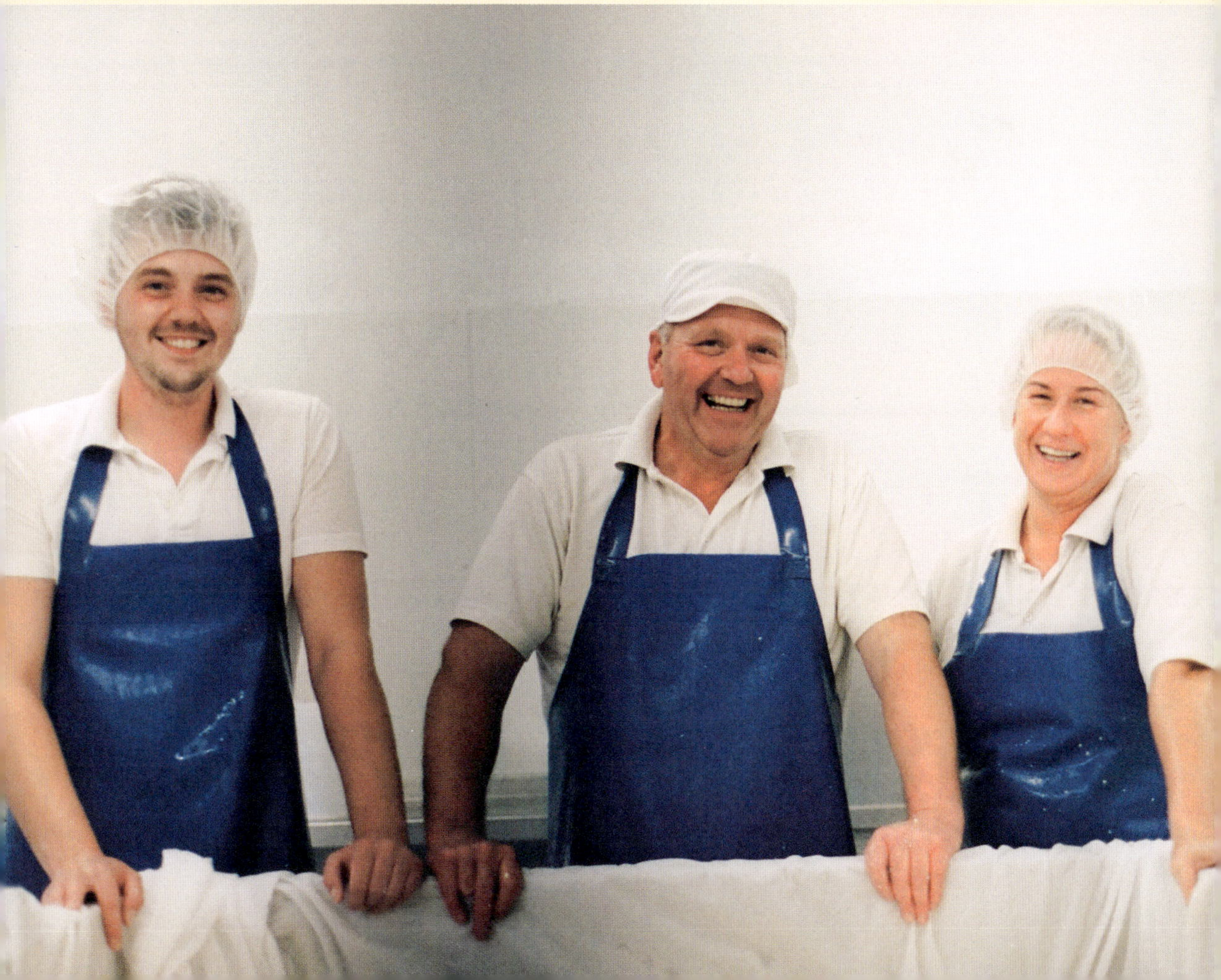

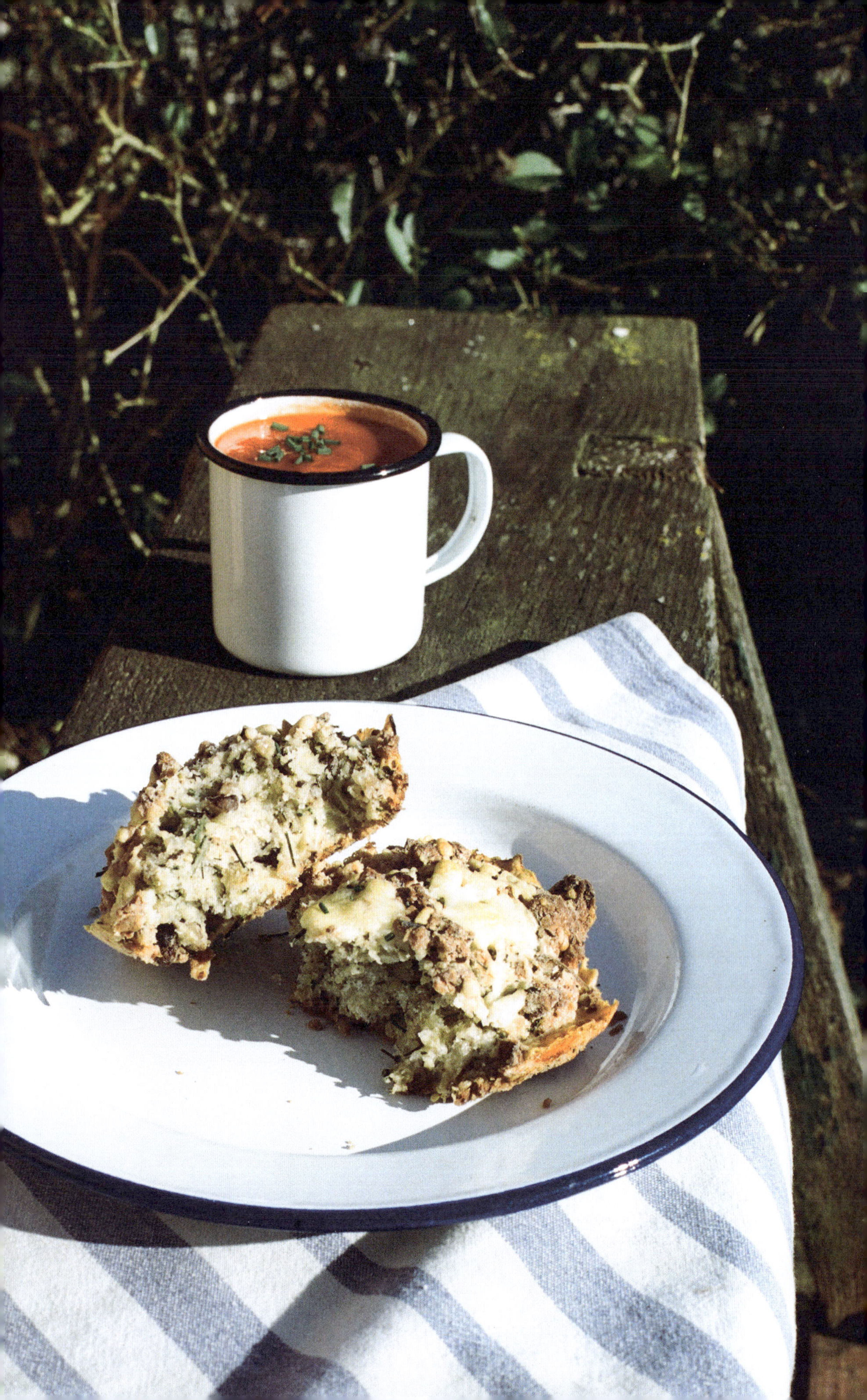

Kirkham's Lancashire loaf

I visited Graham and his lovely family in the summer when the cows were out grazing the lush Lancashire grass and the skies were a dark inky blue, though it was still clear enough to see Beacon Fell in the distance. Like many a farmhouse cheesemaker in the British Isles, Graham is wonderfully convivial, with a brilliant sense of humour. It's clear when you meet him that he loves his job, or 'just our way of life', as he would call it, making Lancashire cheese in exactly the same way his grandmother did many years before.

Over a brew, I sat with the Kirkham family, talking about the wonders of farmhouse cheese and its welcoming community, and how every year a bunch of Britain's best farmhouse cheesemakers travel to Cambridge for a long weekend and spend their days on the River Cam, invariably falling in as they try their hand at punting – something I'd love to see!

This loaf is effectively a large, savoury scone made with fresh chives, Kirkham's Lancashire and a handful of crunchy walnuts. I love to take slices of it on a long walk with a Thermos full of homemade soup, and savour it as I sit by the river or under the canopy of a large tree.

MAKES 2 SMALL LOAVES OR 1 MEDIUM LOAF

170g self-raising flour
handful of fresh chives, finely chopped
110g walnuts, finely chopped
170g Kirkham's Lancashire, grated
3 tbsp whole milk
1 large egg
sea salt and freshly ground black pepper

Preheat the oven to 180°C/350°F/gas mark 4 and line two small loaf tins with baking parchment (I used two white enamel oblong dishes at 16cm long). You can also use one large loaf tin – also lined with baking parchment – if you prefer having a larger loaf.

In both cases, combine the flour, chives, walnuts, 150g of the cheese, salt and pepper in a large bowl.

In a separate bowl, beat the milk and egg together. Gradually add the egg mixture to the flour and cheese mixture and stir together until all the flour has been combined well.

If using two small dishes, halve the dough mixture and roughly shape each half into a small loaf. Or if you are using one large dish, form the dough into a single loaf. In both cases, then scatter the rest of the cheese on top and bake in the oven for 25–30 minutes, until golden brown. Place the loaves (or large single loaf) on a wire rack to cool before slicing. Cut in to thick slices and spread with butter. I love serving this loaf with a sweet tomato or rich onion soup.

LEEDS BLUE

From left to right: When Leeds Blue comes of age at around thirty days, it is wrapped in foil to keep the mould and moisture in. A whole wheel weighs between 1.5kg and 2kg.

Mario Olianas outside his cheesemaking rooms in the Yorkshire sunshine. Mario holds a wheel of Leeds Blue at thirty days old.

Say 'cheese'! A very obliging member of the Lacaune flock whose milk is used for making Leeds Blue. These animals definitely know when their picture is being taken!

Yorkshire Pecorino, Otley, West Yorkshire

Located in the historic market town of Otley in Yorkshire, north of Leeds and right beside the River Wharfe on the very southern edge of the Nidderdale Area of Outstanding Natural Beauty, Yorkshire Pecorino is where you will find Mario and Sonia Olianas making Leeds Blue. Son of an Austrian mother and an Italian fisherman father, Mario grew up by the sea in Sardinia. It was here that Mario learned to appreciate good-quality, local produce, including the renowned pecorino sardo.

In 2001, Mario moved to Yorkshire, and in 2012 he started making small-batch cheeses with the idea of combining Italian techniques with top-quality Yorkshire ingredients. Mario now makes Leeds Blue, Pecorino Fresco, Pecorino Fiore, ricotta and mozzarella, all using milk from a local mixed flock of Lacaune and Friesland sheep that graze on the hills around Otley. Mario works closely with a nearby farmer, collecting milk every day to make the cheese. By working with such a local farm, Mario knows exactly how the animals are husbanded and how the milk varies from one day to the next.

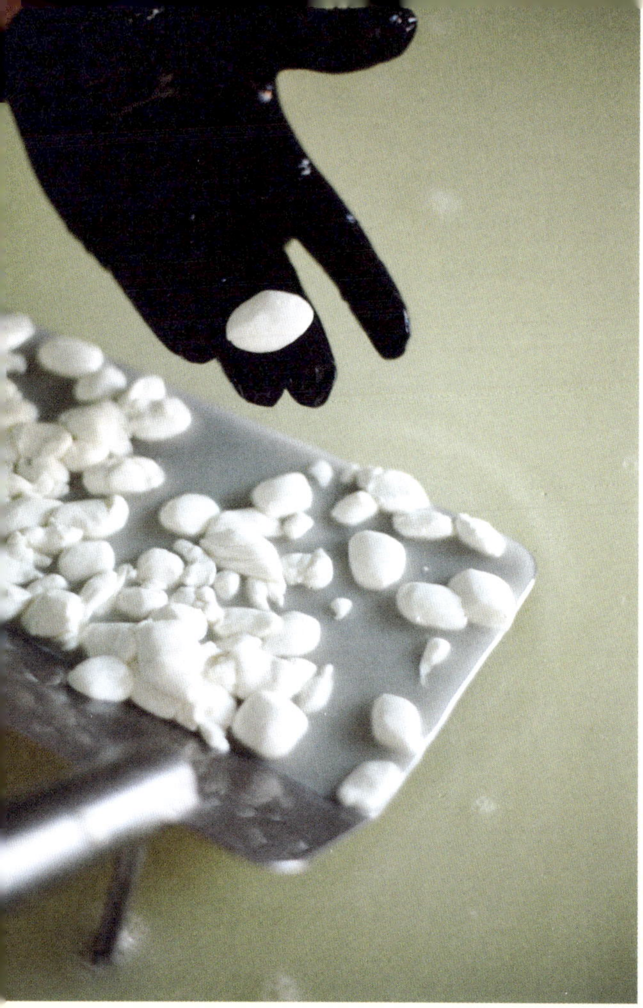
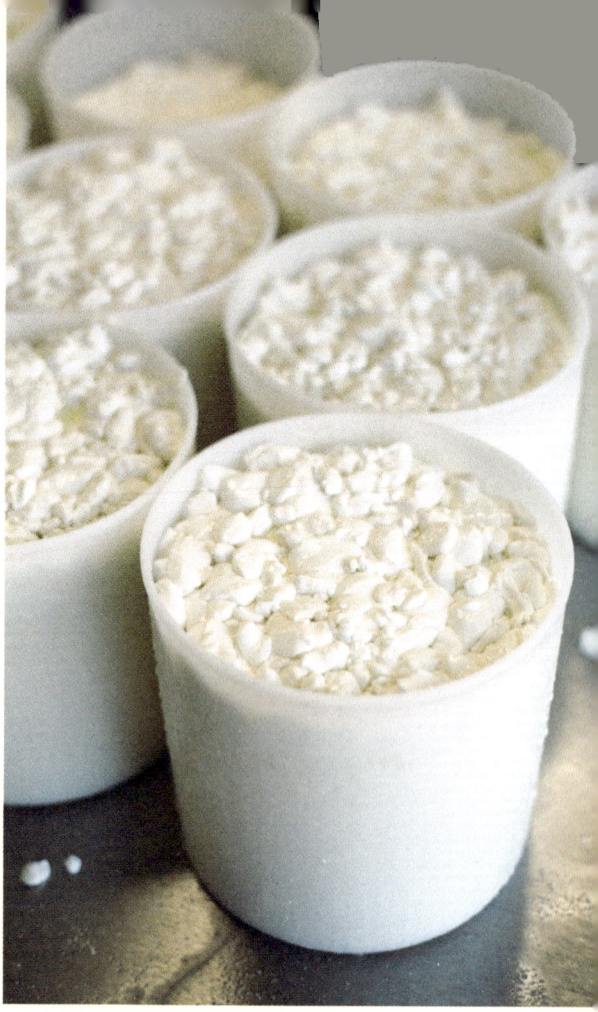
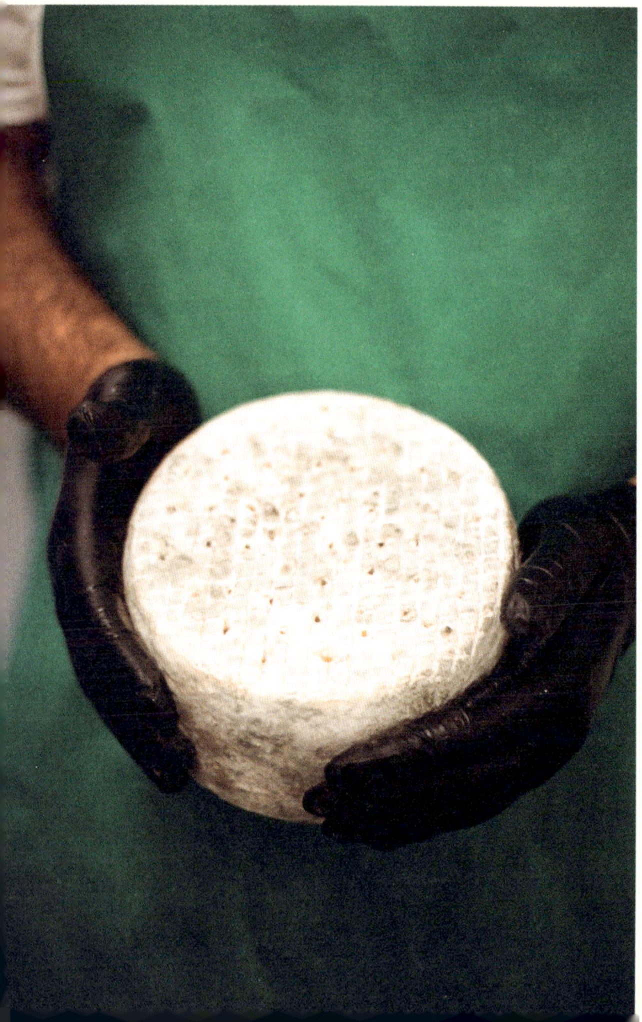
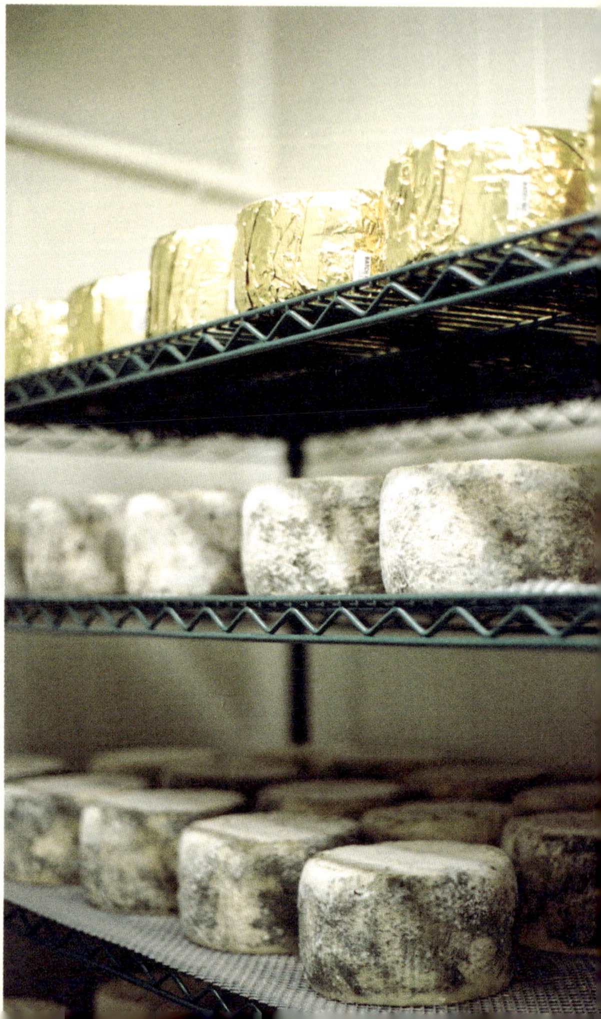

Between a light, creamy Gorgonzola and a salty Roquefort in style, Leeds Blue is made to a recipe that Mario has developed over the years. The level of acidity and length of acidification (the length of time the milk is left to acidify during the make), plus the treatment of the curds, are what give Leeds Blue its unique character. The make starts with warming the milk, before the starter culture is added and the milk is inoculated with a blue mould that will eventually create the distinctive blue veins in the cheese later on in the maturing phase.

After the starter culture has been poured in, animal rennet is added to start the separation process of the curds and whey. Once the curds have been cut, Mario stirs the curds in the whey, which he does very gently in order not to break them up too much but just enough to create small, cotton-bud-shaped curds that are very soft and delicate in texture. Only when the curds are exactly to Mario's liking are they then ladled straight into moulds, a knack that Mario has taken many years to acquire, having made the cheese on most days throughout the year and knowing the process like the back of his hand.

Mario deliberately overfills the moulds with the curds as they will eventually sink and naturally form into the young cheeses. These are then salted and left to age in the maturing rooms. After a week or so, the cheeses are pierced with metal spikes to let in oxygen to encourage the mould in the cheese to form those familiar blue veins. The maturation period for Leeds Blue is around thirty days, during which time it is turned every couple of days.

Leeds Blue characteristics

Milk: Pasteurised milk from a local mixed flock of Lacaune and Friesland sheep

Rennet: Animal

Appearance: Soft, creamy, blue-veined paste with a pale peach, edible rind dappled with dark blue

Tasting notes: Fresh umami flavour with lingering sour notes. Varies according to the season and length of maturation

Clockwise from top left: Mario in the cheesemaking rooms making Leeds Blue. Here he gently passes a metal stirrer through the curds and whey, moving it from one side of the vat to the other.

The moulds full of soft, delicate curds that Mario has been tending to for the last couple of hours. He deliberately overfills the moulds to allow the cheeses to compress naturally.

Leeds Blue in the maturing rooms at different stages of maturation. Mario spends a lot of time observing the progress of each wheel of cheese.

A wheel of Leeds Blue in the maturing rooms that has just been pierced to encourage the blue mould to grow, a technique that gives the finished cheese its familiar blue veins.

Mantecatura risotto with Leeds Blue

The aim of any artisan cheesemaker you meet is to make a unique and interesting-tasting cheese, something to savour with delight and discuss with pleasure. Mario's cheeses are certainly that, blending two cheesemaking cultures together to create a range of cheeses that are wonderfully distinctive. I could have picked any of his cheeses to focus on, all of which are inspired by his Sardinian heritage and using top-quality milk from Yorkshire.

Based on a popular Sardinian dish that is devoured across the island, Mario's recipe is one of his family's favourite dishes. The term mantecatura refers to the stage towards the end of cooking the risotto in which you stir in the final ingredients – the blue cheese in this case – to create a wonderfully creamy texture. Being a light, yoghurt-style blue cheese, Leeds Blue is perfect for this recipe as it doesn't make the dish too rich or heavy, as a Stilton-style cheese might. I've made this recipe multiple times since visiting Mario in Yorkshire, serving it up to family and friends for a summer's lunch outside or indoors on a cosy winter's evening. You can use any mushrooms you like. I cooked it once with a large fungus called 'chicken of the woods' that I foraged from an oak tree and which tastes just like delicious slow-cooked chicken. But be very careful when you are foraging for wild mushrooms as it can be tricky to identify the right one.

SERVES 2–3

50g butter
1 tbsp olive oil
375g mushrooms, roughly chopped
2 garlic cloves, peeled and chopped
pinch of dried thyme (or chopped fresh thyme leaves)
225g Arborio rice
125ml white wine
1 litre hot vegetable stock
100g Leeds Blue
sea salt and freshly ground black pepper
handful of fresh chives, finely chopped, to serve

Place the butter and oil in a large frying pan on a medium heat. When the butter has melted, add the mushrooms and sauté for 5–6 minutes until soft and golden edged. Then add the garlic, thyme and a pinch of salt.

Add the rice to the mushroom mixture and stir-fry for a minute until the rice is well coated and glossy. Next add the wine and cook until it has been completely absorbed.

Now it's time to add the vegetable stock – which should be hot – in stages to the rice and mushroom mixture. Start by pouring in 200ml of the stock, stirring constantly until it has been absorbed by the rice. Repeat this process four times, each time adding 200ml of the stock and stirring constantly. Cook for 20–25 minutes until the rice is tender and all the liquid has been absorbed.

Crumble in the cheese, grind over plenty of black pepper and stir until the cheese has melted. Divide between plates and serve sprinkled with the chopped chives.

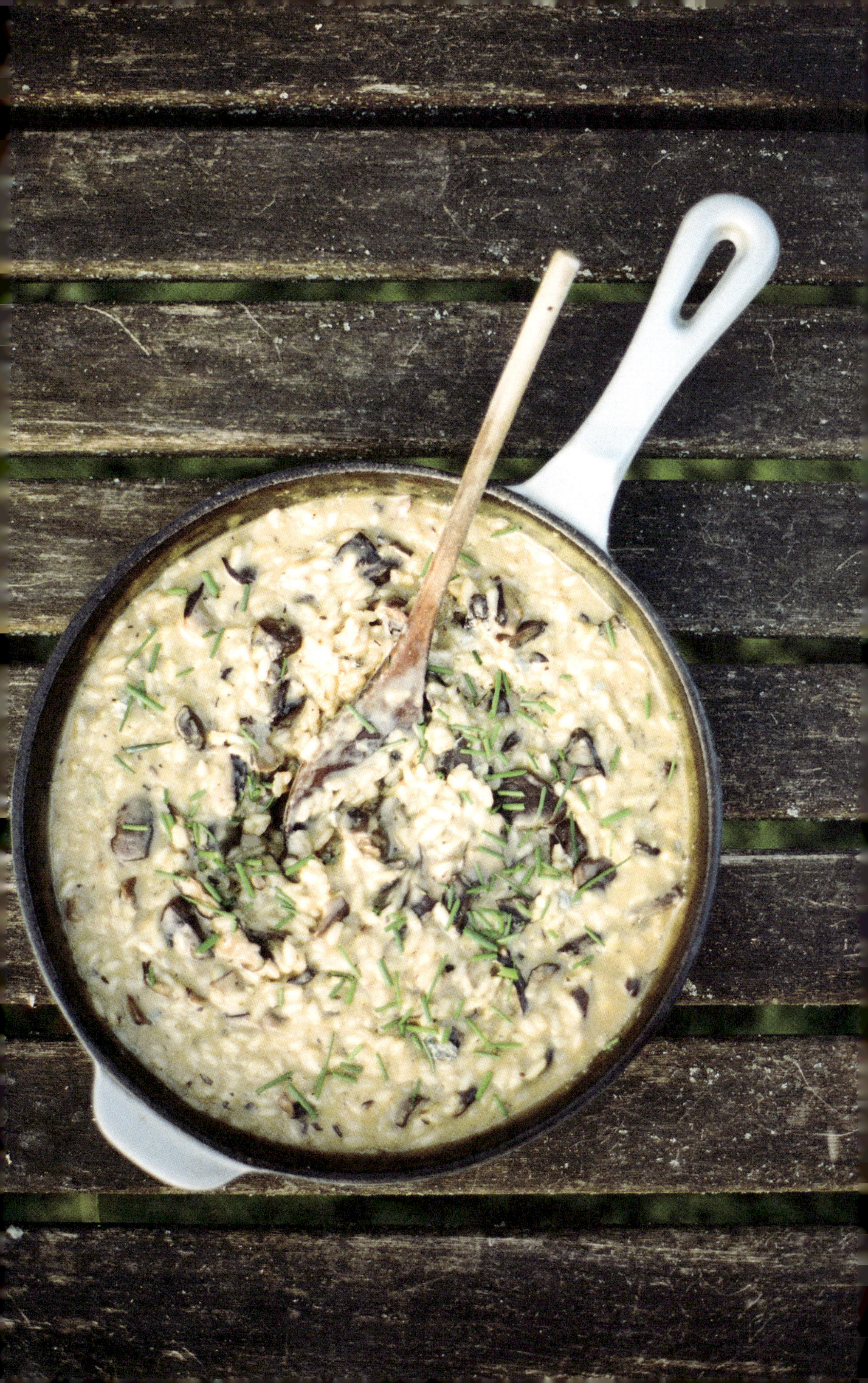

LINCOLNSHIRE POACHER

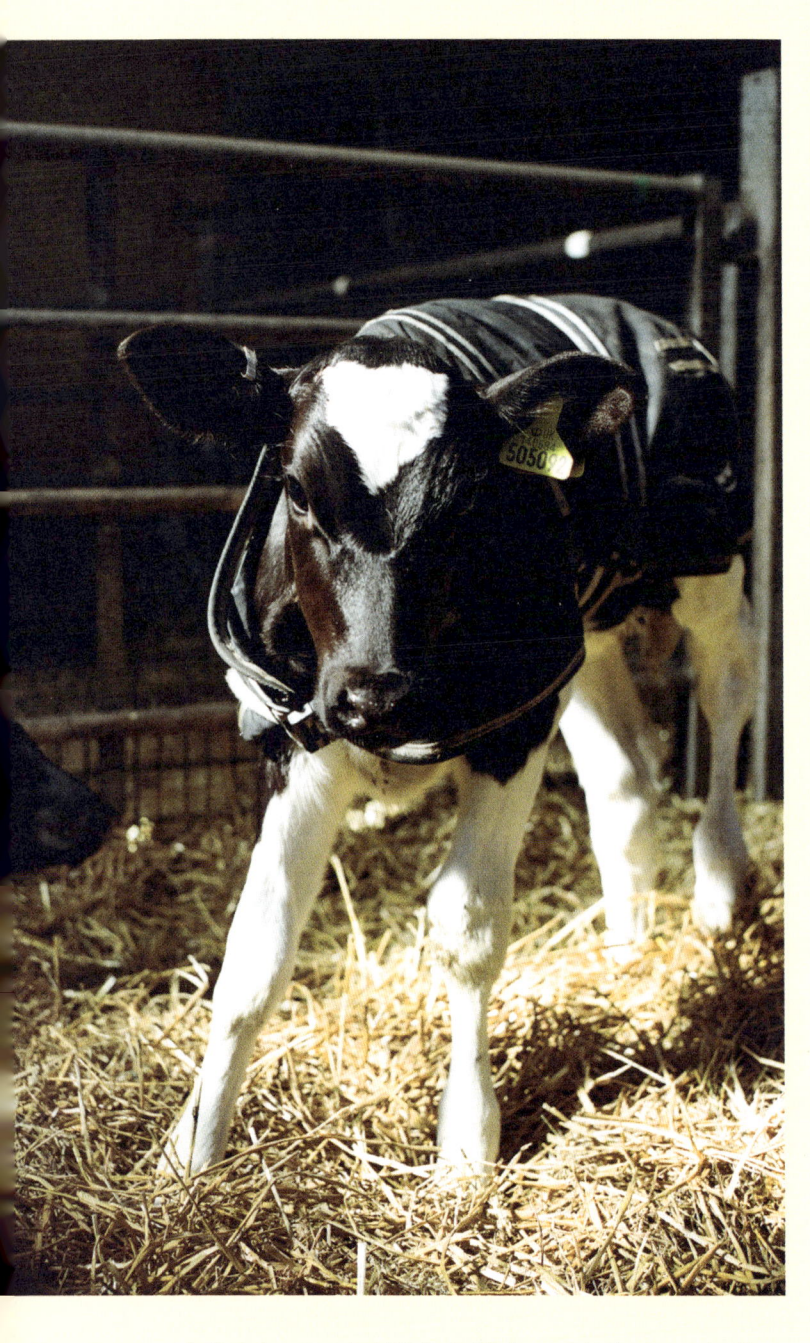

Left: A three-month-old Holstein-Friesian and Ayrshire crossed calf at Ulceby Grange Farm, warming up in the late winter sunshine in the Lincolnshire Wolds.

Right: The stunning speckled rind of a slice of Lincolnshire Poacher, twenty-two months old, from a whole wheel weighing in at 18kg.

Ulceby Grange Farm, Alford, Lincolnshire

Deep within the gentle rolling hills of the Lincolnshire Wolds, a few miles from the low-lying east coast, is Ulceby Grange Farm, where Lincolnshire Poacher is produced. Made using raw milk from the farm's mixed herd of Holstein-Friesian and Ayrshire cows, Lincolnshire Poacher is a cross between a traditional Cheddar and a continental Alpine cheese. Simon and Tim Jones and their team of cheesemakers use a recipe developed by Simon during his early career working in the French Alps and learning how to make traditional Alpine-style cheeses, alongside the late Dougal Campbell, founder of the first organic cheesemaking company in Britain, Welsh Organic Foods.

A defining feature of Lincolnshire Poacher is the very slow method with which it is made, with minimal intervention at each stage. Before that, it all starts with the quality of the raw ingredients, of course, from the grass on which the cows graze, which is left to grow naturally with as little intervention as possible to help produce the very best-quality milk. As the milk is channelled into the cheesemaking rooms, it is gently heated, with very little starter culture being added. The milk is already so fresh and alive that by adding only a small amount of starter culture, the true character of the milk is brought out, which will eventually develop into a more complex-flavoured cheese. Since the first production of Lincolnshire Poacher, when it was more Cheddar-like in style, the cheese has now shifted towards more of an Alpine style, all down to the use of relatively little starter culture and the slower method of making.

Lincolnshire Poacher is aged for 16–24 months, with some cheeses even being matured for up to three years – a variety called Poacher 50. As the milk changes according to the season, the maturing period of the cheese changes too, creating a different batch of cheese each time.

As with many cheesemakers across the British Isles, Simon and Tim are conscious about the environment, and have a number of projects on the go to lessen their impact upon it, including a woodchip boiler for warming the milk used for making their cheese. The cows graze on clover-rich pasture throughout most of the year, a plant that is both nitrogen-fixing and is believed to lead to a more multifaceted cheese. The hedges on the farm are also cut every few years, encouraging greater biodiversity with more bird species, such as linnets, yellowhammers and skylarks.

Other cheeses made at Ulceby Grange Farm include Smoked Lincolnshire Poacher and Lincolnshire Red.

Lincolnshire Poacher characteristics

Milk: Raw milk from the farm's mixed herd of Holstein-Friesian and Ayrshire cows

Rennet: Animal

Appearance: Firm, smooth paste with the odd fissure and a rust-coloured, mottled, tough inedible rind

Tasting notes: Savoury and fruity, sweet flavour with a long finish. Varies according to the season and length of maturation

Clockwise from top left: Tim walking through the fields at Ulceby Grange Farm towards the wind turbine that generates all the energy needed on the farm, and more.

The whole farming day comes down to this – around thirty wheels of Lincolnshire Poacher, newly stacked in the maturing rooms.

Simon and Tim Jones, who run Ulceby Grange Farm, where Lincolnshire Poacher is made using raw milk from their mixed herd of Holstein-Friesian and Ayrshire cows.

A close-up of wheels of Lincolnshire Poacher in the maturing rooms at Ulceby Grange Farm – a veritable cathedral of cheese that can hold up to 18,000 cheeses.

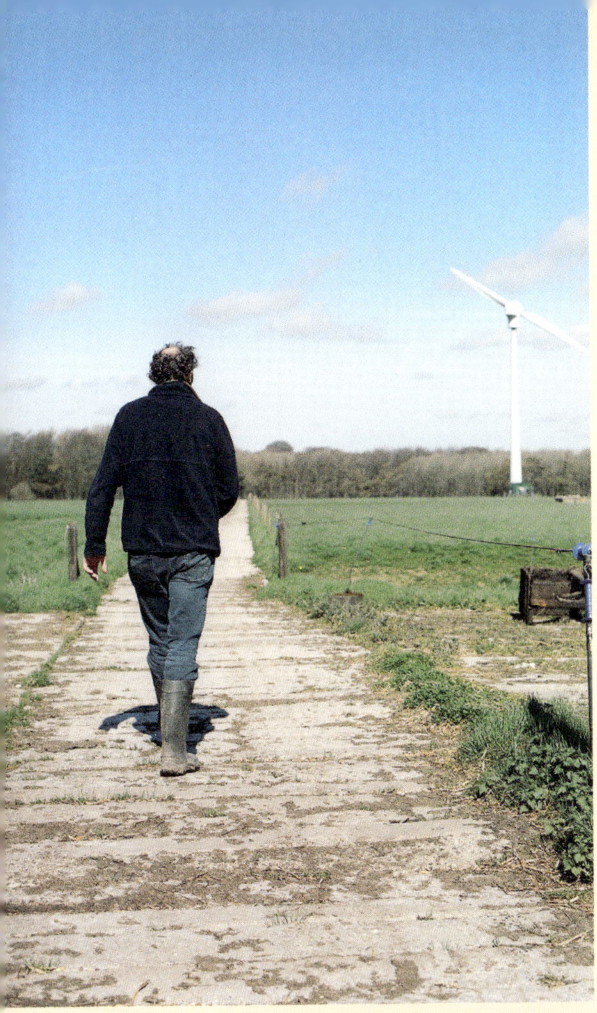
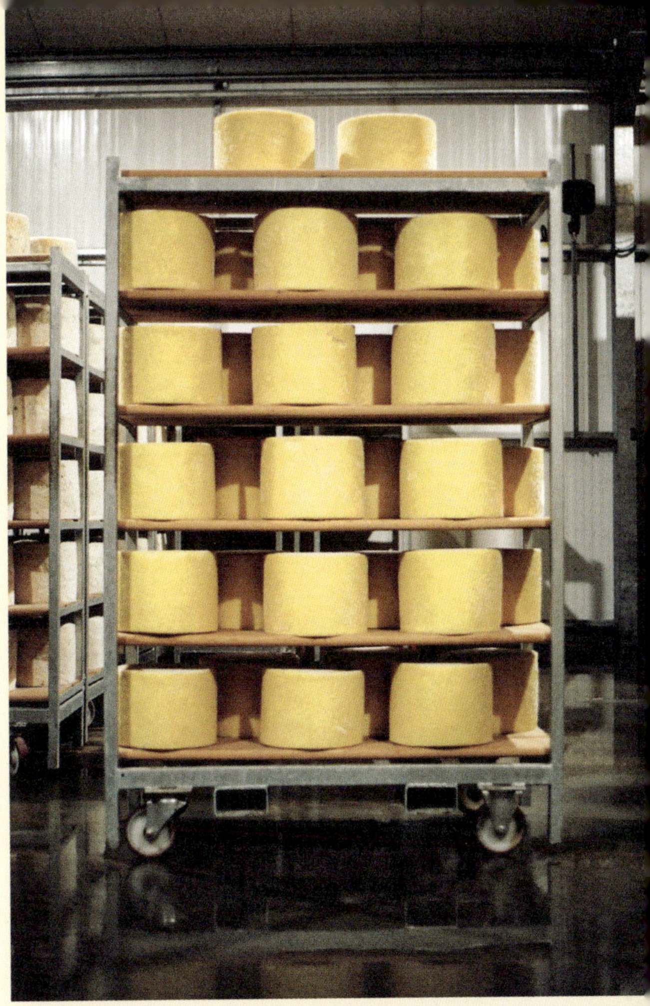
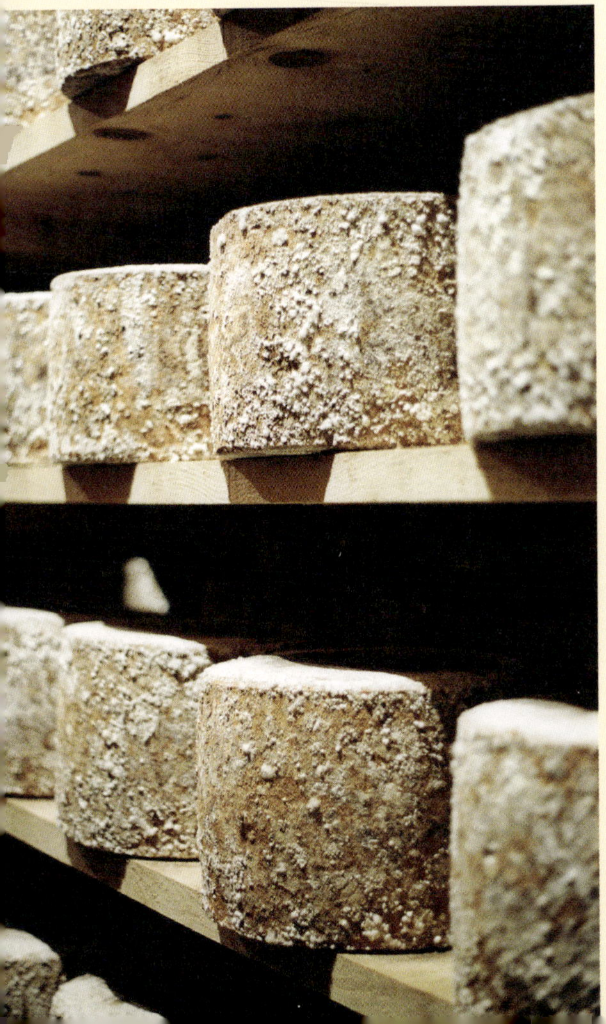
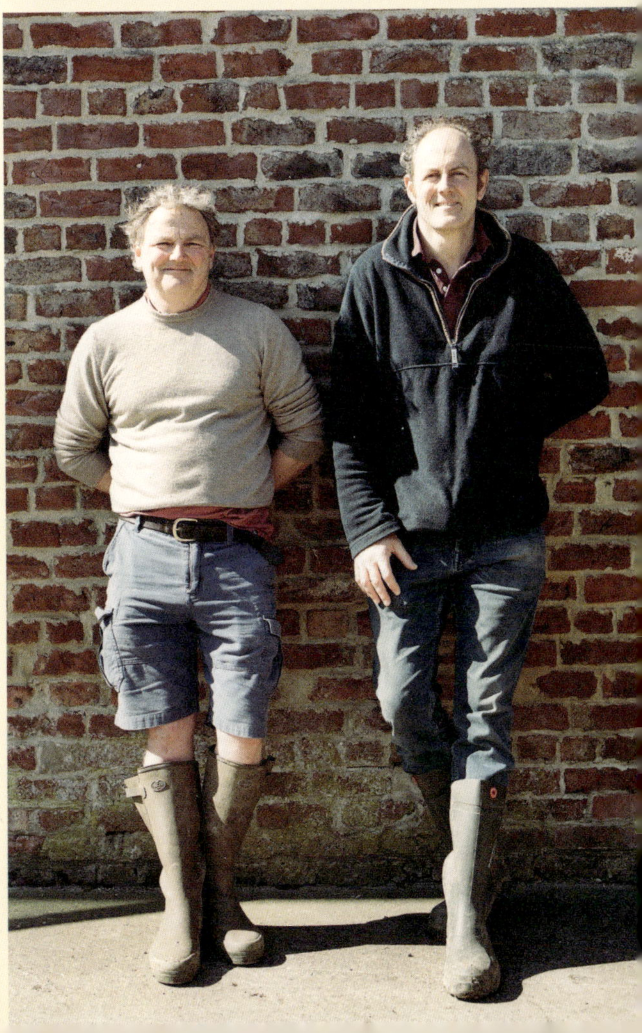

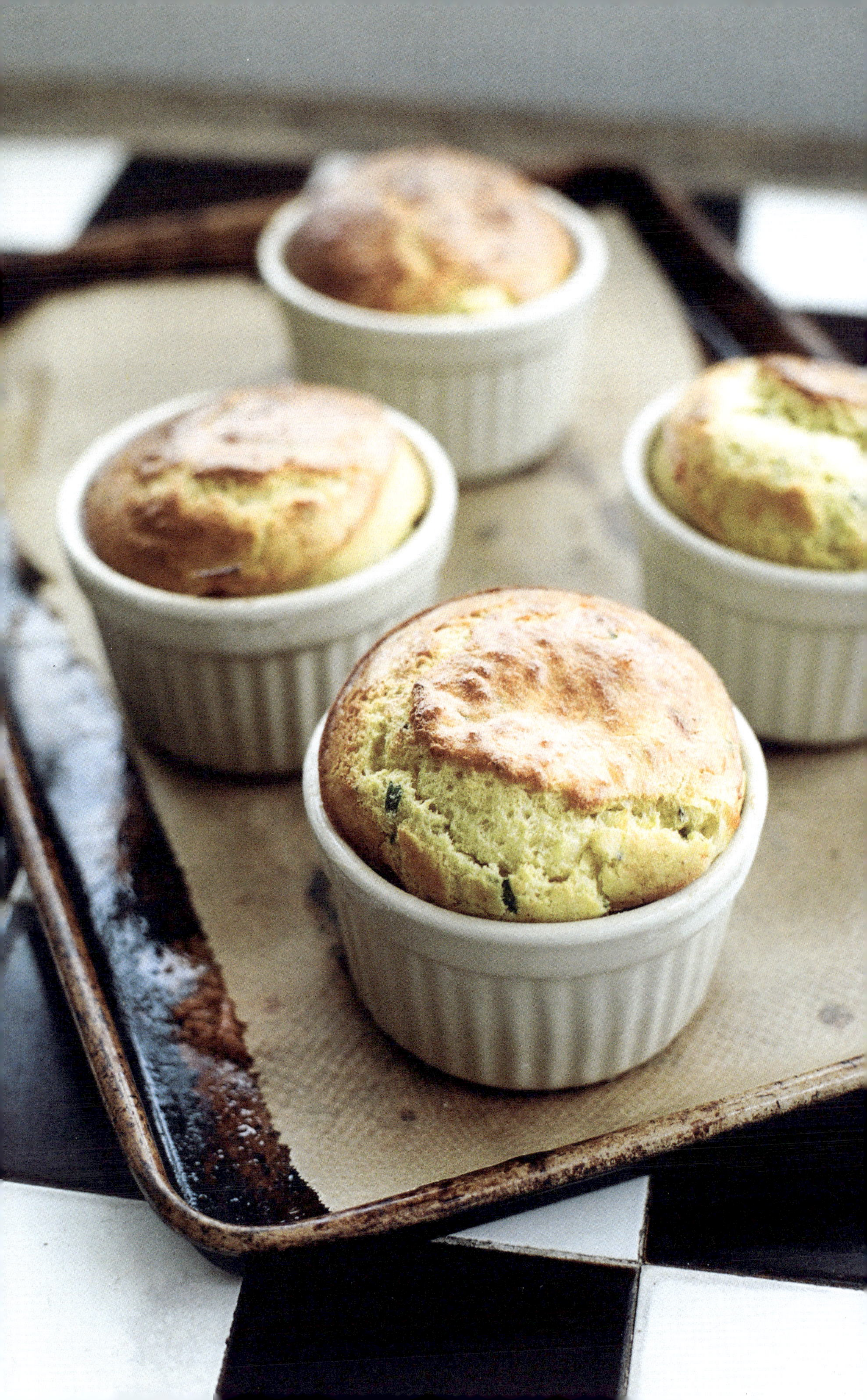

Lincolnshire Poacher soufflé

Simon and Tim are both salt of the earth, stewards of the land and advocates for real food. I visited the brothers on a fine spring day in the Lincolnshire Wolds, having driven from the south through the flat plains near Boston and up into the hills. Once at the top of the Wolds, you can see for miles until the horizon meets the North Sea – a band of brown stitched with tiny white turbines in a distant array.

On my visit, Simon and Tim took me around the farm, showing me the fields, the cows and the cheesemaking and maturing rooms. The maturing rooms at the farm can hold a whopping 18,000 wheels of Lincolnshire Poacher, a veritable cathedral of cheese. Walking around the enormous barn where the cheeses are kept is a surreal and almost meditative experience as you survey, all alone, the thousands of cheeses on their towering wooden shelving.

This scrumptious recipe is a staple in the culinary repertoire of Simon and Tim's mother. The brothers have had lunch with their mother every day on the farm for the past twenty years in a lovely family tradition.

MAKES 6 SMALL SOUFFLÉS

- 60g butter, plus extra for greasing
- 60g white spelt flour, plus extra for dusting
- 360ml whole milk
- 2 tsp sea salt
- 120g Lincolnshire Poacher, grated
- 2 tsp English mustard powder
- 2 tbsp finely chopped fresh chives
- 4 large eggs

Preheat the oven to 200°C/400°F/gas mark 6. Butter the sides and bottom of six small ramekins, or one large soufflé dish, and coat with a dusting of flour.

In a large saucepan on a medium heat, melt the butter and add the flour, constantly whisking to make a roux. Then add the milk in stages, still whisking to prevent lumps from forming. Keep whisking until the sauce thickens, and then add the salt, grated cheese, mustard powder and chives. Mix well, and take the pan off the heat to cool.

Separate the eggs, the whites going into a separate, clean bowl and the yolks going into the pan of cooled sauce. Stir the yolks into the sauce, then, in the separate bowl, whisk the egg whites to form stiff peaks. Using a large metal spoon, stir in one spoonful of the beaten egg whites into the sauce. In stages, gently fold in the rest of the egg whites. Fill the prepared ramekins or soufflé dish with the mixture, then place on a baking tray and bake in the oven for 15–20 minutes until well risen and a rich golden brown on top.

MAIDA VALE

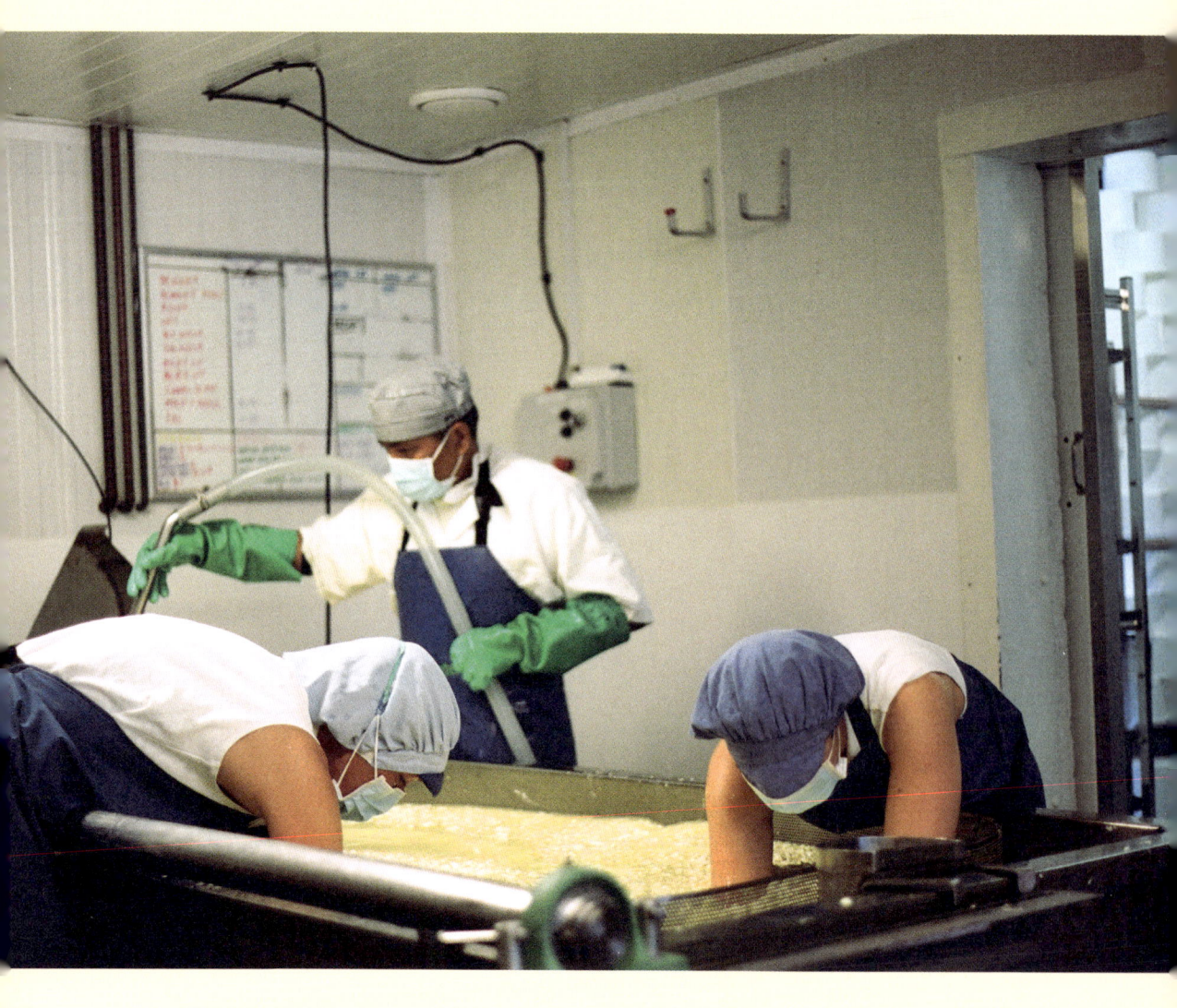

From left to right: An unusual aspect of making Maida Vale and Waterloo is washing the curds. Anne Wigmore was inspired by European cheesemakers, who use this technique to produce cheese with a mellower, milkier flavour.

Once the curds have been washed, they are ladled into either small or medium-sized moulds depending on whether they are to be made into little cheeses or standard-sized ones.

Jake Wigmore turning over a batch of Maida Vale cheeses of around 2–3 weeks old. A good airflow in any maturing room is essential to regulate the ageing process.

Village Maid Cheese, Riseley, Berkshire

Nestling between far-stretching fields on one side and dense deciduous woodland on the other is Village Maid Cheese in the heart of Berkshire, where Maida Vale is made. Founded in 1986 by Anne Wigmore, one of a handful of pioneering farmhouse cheesemakers in the 1980s, the dairy is now headed by her son, Jake. Maida Vale is a semi-soft, washed-rind cheese made using milk from a small local herd of Guernsey cows. Guernsey milk is wonderful for making rich cheese, owing to the high proportion of butterfat it contains compared to milk from other cattle breeds.

The cows belong to an organic farm less than two miles down the road. As Jake is in regular contact with Ian Constable-Dakeyne, the farm manager at Heckfield Home Farm, he knows exactly how the animals are raised and about the quality of the milk being produced. The cows graze on the meadows beside the River Whitewater and the fields that surround the farm. They feed on a rich herbal ley in the spring and summer months, and on silage in the winter, including species such

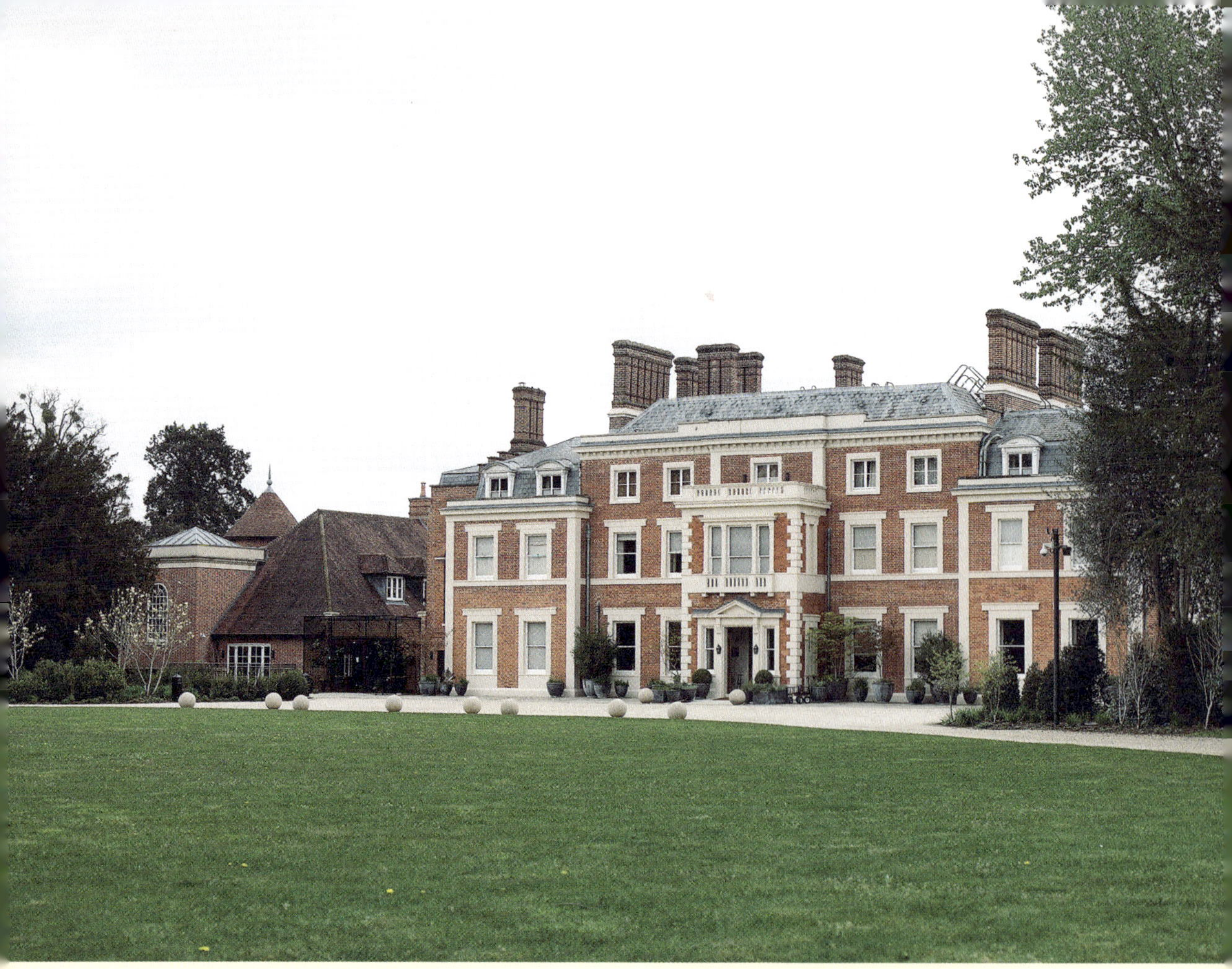

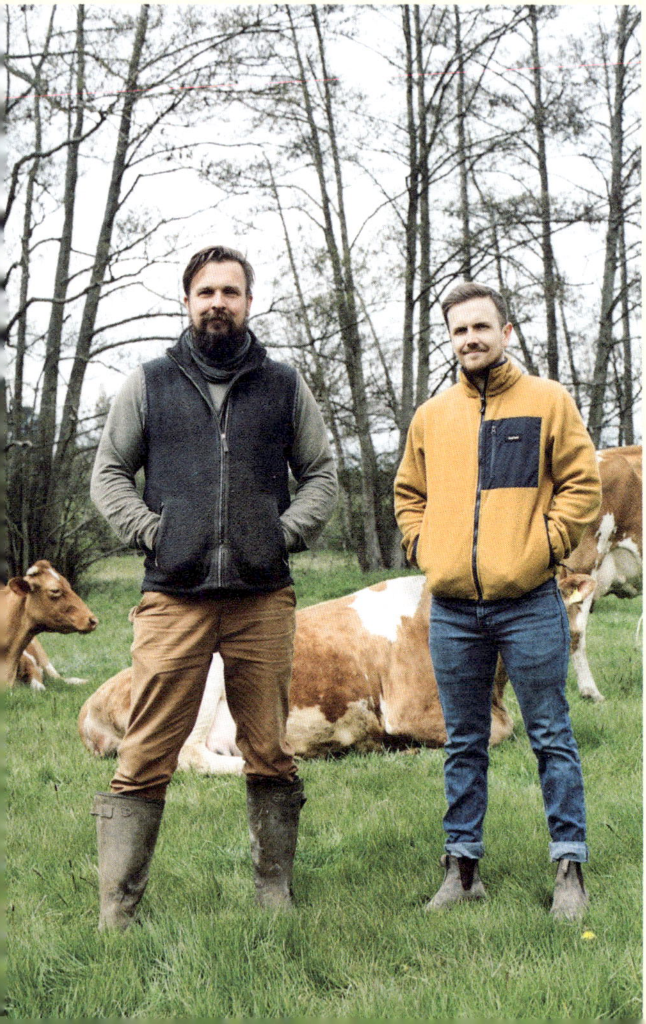

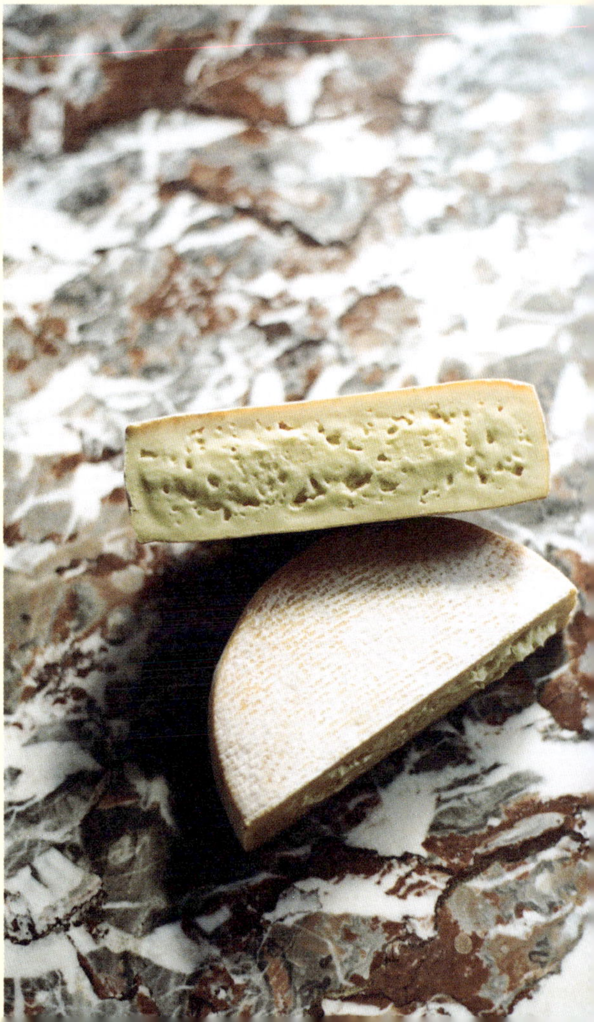

as ryegrass, fescues, red clover, white clover, chicory and plantain. Come winter, the cows are brought in to what is called a 'roundhouse' – an innovative circular barn that is open on all sides and roofed in weather-proof canvas – which is adjacent to a mixed fruit orchard that has 40–50 varieties of apple. The farm recently started replanting the historical hedgerows across the estates.

The method of making Maida Vale is similar to that of their Waterloo cheese, another semi-soft variety, the main difference being how the young cheeses are treated: Maida Vale is washed in ale while Waterloo is mould ripened. First, the milk is delivered from Heckfield Home Farm early in the morning and is 'thermised' at the dairy – warmed to 65°C and then rapidly cooled to around 16°C before being channelled into the vat. When the milk is at the right temperature, Kayleigh, Jake's wife and the head cheesemaker, adds the starter culture and rennet, and waits for the curds to set. An unusual aspect of the make is how the curds are treated. Once the curds have set and have been cut into small cubes, warm water is slowly added to the vat by the cheesemaker, stirring constantly by hand to replace part of the whey. This is done to remove sugar from the mixture to stop further acidification, a procedure that will contribute eventually to the flavour and semi-soft texture of the finished cheese. The soft curds are then ladled into moulds and left to drain overnight. The following day, the young cheeses are soaked in brine for a few hours. The number of cheeses made varies per batch, depending on what size is being made, either large (350g) or small (180g).

Over in the maturing rooms, each cheese is washed in local ale sourced from a microbrewery. The added moisture encourages the mould *Brevibacterium linens* to develop, endowing the rind with its distinctive deep orange colour and a markedly hoppy and citrusy flavour. Maida Vale is aged for 5–6 weeks, when it is best to eat.

Other cheeses Village Maid Cheese make include Wigmore, Spenwood, Waterloo, Heckfield and Swallowfield.

Maida Vale characteristics
Milk: Thermised milk from a local herd of Guernsey cows

Rennet: Vegetarian

Appearance: Vividly golden paste with an edible, bronze-coloured washed rind, flecked with white

Tasting notes: Rich, buttery flavour with tangy and yeasty notes. Varies according to the season and length of maturation

Clockwise from top: Heckfield Place, the heart of Home Farm's estate that champions its produce under the stewardship of Culinary Director Skye Gyngell.

The beautiful, dense round of a Maida Vale made by Village Maid Cheese. Maida Vale is washed in local ale when young, giving the rind its distinctive orange hue, flecked with white.

Ian Constable-Dakeyne, the farm manager at Heckfield Home Farm, with Jake Wigmore from Village Maid Cheese. The two work closely with one another to produce the best possible milk and cheese.

Maida Vale cauliflower cheese

I visited the cheesemaking team at Village Maid Cheese – consisting at the time of Jake, Kayleigh, Lisa, Ramil and Ferdy – when they were making Waterloo, Maida Vale and their Alpine-style cheese. Jake kindly showed me every aspect of the production process, explaining about thermised milk and letting me sample the local ale in which Maida Vale is washed before being left to mature. We also went down the road to the impressive Heckfield Home Farm to see the small herd of Guernsey cows whose milk is used to make Maida Vale, Waterloo and Heckfield – the latter named after the village where the farm is located, just over the border in Hampshire. Guernsey cows are an elegant and good-natured breed that produces rich, yellow milk. Ian, the farm manager, took us to where they graze beside the charming River Whitewater.

Cauliflower cheese was one of the top recommendations among all the cheesemakers I visited in the course of creating this book, and as Heckfield Home Farm also grows their own fruit and veg, I thought it appropriate to include the recipe here. Made with Maida Vale, this is possibly the most indulgent, delicious cauliflower cheese you'll have ever tasted!

SERVES 4 AS A SIDE

1 large cauliflower, broken into florets
2 tbsp olive oil
60g butter
4 tbsp plain flour
450ml whole milk
1 x 180g round of Maida Vale
sea salt and freshly ground black pepper

Preheat the oven to 200°C/400°F/gas mark 6.

In a deep-sided baking dish (I used a 30cm-diameter terracotta pot, but you could use a 40cm x 30cm deep-sided baking tray), toss the cauliflower florets in the olive oil and 2 teaspoons of salt, and roast in the oven for 25 minutes.

While the florets are cooking, make the cheese sauce. Start by melting the butter in a medium saucepan over a medium heat, then add the flour, whisking constantly until well combined. Gradually pour in the milk, adding about 50ml each time and whisking until you have a smooth, thick sauce. Keeping the sauce on the heat, add a teaspoon of salt and plenty of black pepper, followed by the cheese. Gently stir until the cheese has melted and is well combined.

Take the cauliflower out of the oven and allow to cool for 5 minutes. Then pour the cheese sauce over the florets and bake for a further 20–25 minutes until the top is golden brown.

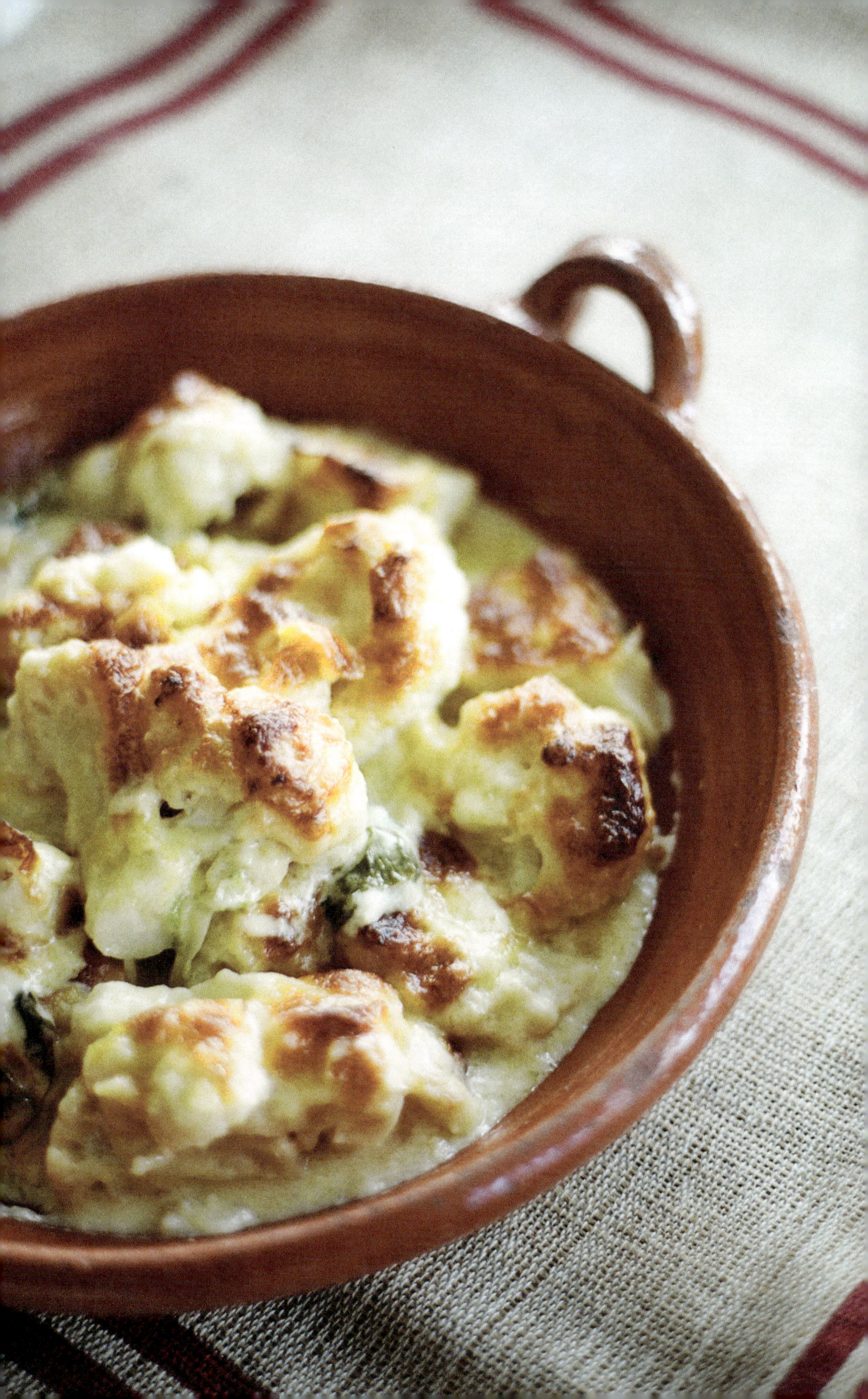

ROLLRIGHT

Left: A spruce-bound wheel of Rollright made at King Stone Dairy, using organic milk from a mixed herd of British Friesian and Dairy Shorthorn cows.

Right: The bands of spruce that give Rollright its distinctive appearance. These are normally sourced from France and come from the trunk of the tree.

King Stone Dairy, Chedworth, Gloucestershire

High up on the edge of the Cotswold escarpment, overlooking broad rolling hills and the beautiful river in the Coln Valley, is Manor Farm and King Stone Dairy, where Rollright is produced. Made by cheesemaker David Jowett, Rollright uses organic milk from the farm's mixed herd of British Friesian and Dairy Shorthorn cows. Named after the Oxfordshire parish where David first made the cheese, and after the ancient Rollright Stones, one of which, the 'King Stone', is located on the farm from which the milk originally came, Rollright is a celebration of the quality of milk currently used in its making and the progressive farming system in place at the 1,000-acre farm.

Manor Farm is owned by Jeannie Hamilton and run by the farm manager Toby Baxter, alongside the herdsman Dean Phillips, who work with David on a daily basis, discussing the condition of the animals, the consistency of the milk and how the cheese tastes. The farm started using regenerative farming methods a couple of decades ago to establish diverse herbal leys to improve the animals' diet and the soil health and structure. They also work to increase biodiversity on the farm, often hearing skylarks and barn owls as a result.

A rich, soft cheese taking inspiration from the French Vacherin du Haut-Doubs, Rollright is made in a process that, in David's words, is 'quite warm and quite quick in order to keep as much fat and moisture in the curds'. So the coagulation of the milk is speedy. Once the curds have been cut, they are moulded and then wrapped in a spruce strap that mainly serves a structural purpose but, during maturation, also infuses the cheese with earthy, resiny notes. The straps, known as sangles ('belts'), are made in France from spruce cambium (cambium is the thin layer of tissue found just beneath the tree's bark) cut by artisan sangliers ('belt makers') and shipped air-dried to King Stone Dairy. When David needs them, he boils the straps to make them flexible so they can be easily attached to each disc of Rollright.

Whereas the making of Rollright is quick, just a few hours, the maturation is a longer, slower process, during which time the cheeses will pass through a series of rooms with different temperatures and humidity levels. At first, the cheeses will go into a warm room with a high level of humidity to encourage the growth of fungi and yeasts (*Geotrichum*, *Debaryomyces* and *Kluyveromyces*) and bacteria (*Brevibacterium linens*). The cheeses are turned every day when they are young, and washed in a light brine solution every other day. They are then transferred into a cooler room before packing. The best time to eat Rollright is around week six.

Other cheeses King Stone Dairy makes include Evenlode, Moreton, Ashcombe and Chedworth.

Rollright characteristics

Milk: Organic, pasteurised milk from the farm's mixed herd of British Friesian and Dairy Shorthorn cows

Rennet: Animal

Appearance: Glossy light golden paste with an edible peachy washed rind (with inedible spruce straps)

Tasting notes: Rich savoury flavour with crème fraîche acidity, notes of bacon and resin. Varies according to the season and length of maturation

Top: A delightful example of a Dairy Shorthorn cow at Manor Farm. Originally from the North East of England, the Dairy Shorthorn was once a very popular breed of dairy cattle.

Bottom left: In addition to David, Joe and Alex also make cheese at King Stone Dairy. Here Joe is filling small moulds with curds to make Little Rollright.

Bottom right: David in the maturing rooms at King Stone Dairy, carefully assessing a batch of Rollright, each cheese wrapped in a band of spruce.

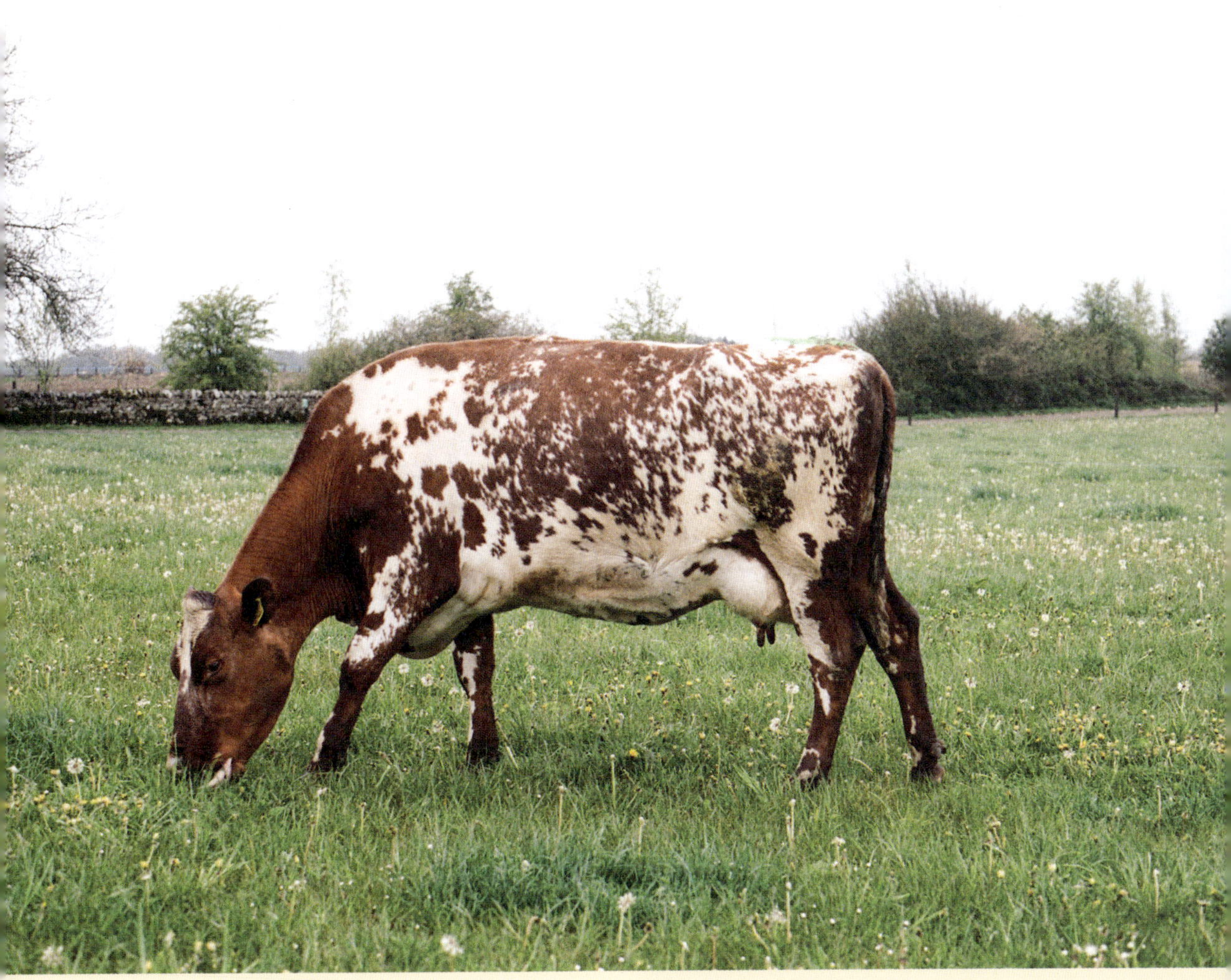

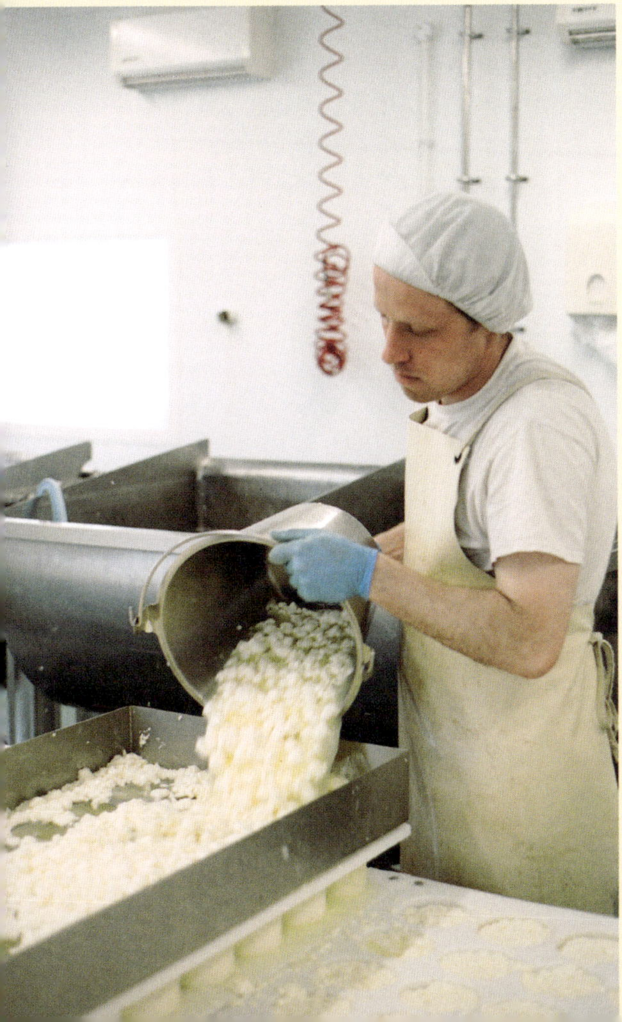

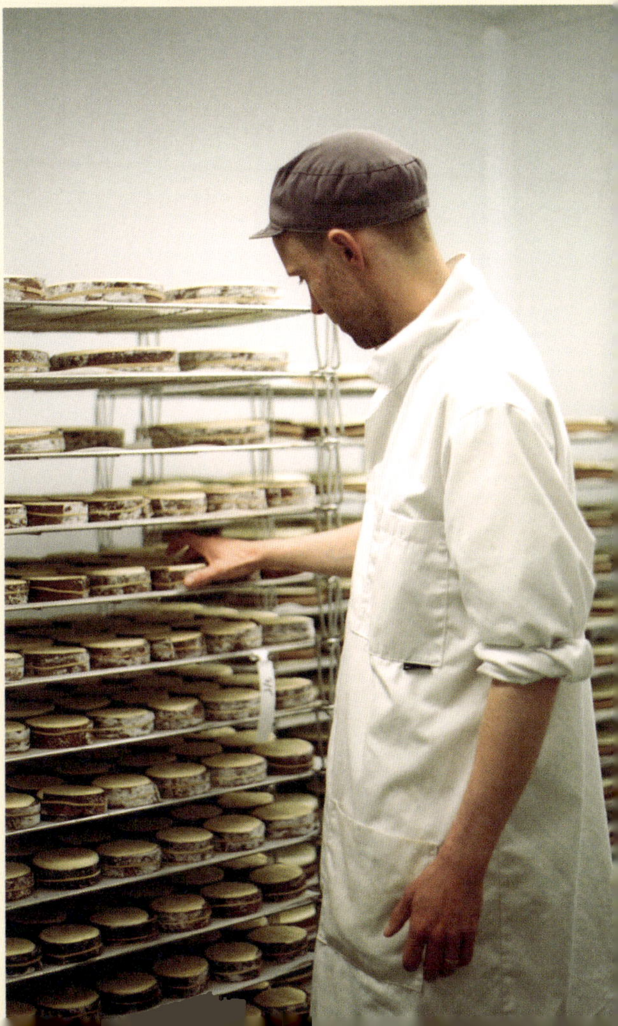

Baked Rollright

It was on a horrendously rainy day in May that I visited David Jowett at King Stone Dairy in the Cotswolds. It wasn't one of those wet days when it's throwing buckets and romantically atmospheric, but one with cold whipping winds and which gets you and your very temperamental camera equipment completely drenched. Nonetheless, it was a memorable day seeing David and his team, Alex and Joe, make their range of cheeses, and the hungry herd of British Friesian and Dairy Shorthorn cows munching the grass after just being milked in the parlour by Dean, the herdsman. The pasture (kept as grassland for successive years and therefore defined as permanent) was full of a diverse mix of dandelions, yarrow and clover, not to mention insects, the latter being dive-bombed by swallows whose wings brushed against my legs in their aerobatic displays.

David tells me how traditionally the Cotswolds was devoted to sheep farming, part of the thriving wool trade in the Middle Ages that made the area very wealthy, hence the name 'Cotswolds' – which, according to one theory, comes from 'cot' (sheep enclosure) and 'wolds' (range of hills) – and farming cattle was seen as rather unusual in the area. You'll also notice as you pass through the luscious green countryside into the Cotswolds that the border sign has a ram's head proudly emblazoned on it.

When I asked David for a recipe using Rollright, he was adamant that it had to be baked! This recipe of his uses a Little Rollright, which is perfect for two people, and can be served as an hors d'oeuvre or starter alongside a variety of savoury delights.

SERVES 2

1 whole Little Rollright
4 small sprigs of fresh rosemary
1 garlic clove, peeled and sliced
handful of asparagus spears, ends trimmed, to serve (optional)

Preheat the oven to 200°C/400°F/gas mark 6.

Score the top of the Rollright multiple times and, in each cut, place a sprig of rosemary and a slice of garlic. Place in a small ovenproof dish – keeping the spruce bark strap on the cheese – and bake in the oven for 10–15 minutes.

Once the baked Rollright is hot and oozing, you can serve it with a multitude of things, from crackers and crusty bread to olives, cornichons, cured meats, and even seasonal asparagus – simply charred on a hot griddle for 10 minutes, as I have done here. Pure heaven!

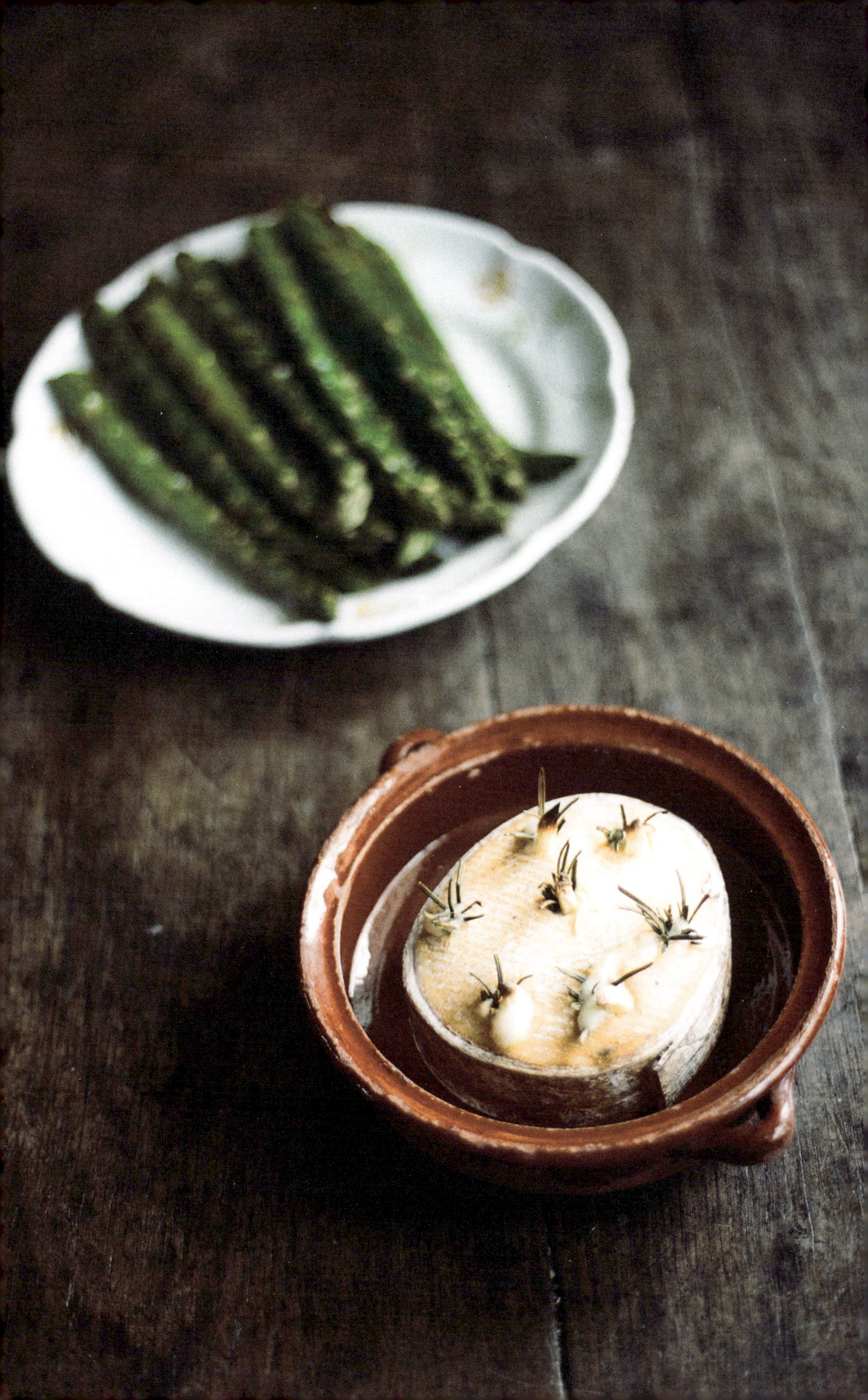

ST JAMES

Above, left to right: Cheesemakers Wing Mon Cheung and Niall Furlong with Martin Gott. Niall and Wing Mon enabled the purchase of the goats and developed all of the new cheeses as well as the St James recipe.

Right: The striking peachy-grey washed rind of St James, which is made using raw milk from Holker Farm's lovely flock of Lacaune sheep.

Holker Farm, Cark in Cartmel, Cumbria

Holker Farm, where St James cheese is made, is located between the rivers Leven and the Eea on the southern tip of Cartmel Peninsula in the Lake District. As you head south towards Morecambe Bay, the rustic landscape opens out into a glorious vista of lush pasture, distant mountains and sea views. Martin Gott and Nicola Robinson run Holker Farm, growing crops as well as raising livestock and producing a range of farmhouse cheeses. Standing on a mixture of limestone and peat, Holker Farm and the surrounding land is best suited for grazing sheep and other hardy ruminant animals, such as goats, which they keep along with a small herd of Belted Galloway cattle. St James is a semi-soft cheese

The flock of Lacaune sheep at Holker Farm, with their floppy ears and proud stance. The ewes produce milk that is perfect for cheesemaking.

made using raw milk from the farm's flock of Lacaune sheep, a French breed whose milk is most famously used for making Roquefort. Milked after the lambing season, the ewes produce a high-quality milk that is full of flavour and makes for a particularly rich, savoury cheese.

An unusual aspect of the making of St James is that the cheesemakers add a natural starter – essentially a fermented culture made on the farm using milk from their finest ewes – to the milk, which is still warm from the morning's milking. This makes for a truly distinctive cheese that evokes its provenance. Making St James is a fast and delicate process in order to retain the quality of the milk and allow the curds to drain before acidifying. The curd is left to set for just under an hour before being cut into small pieces using a long, harp-like wire cutter made by Martin himself – another unusual feature of the make – and gently ladled into moulds. Once the cheeses have set in their moulds, they are turned three times before being turned out and salted the following day.

Over the course of the next three weeks, each cheese is washed with brine every other day in order to develop the cheese's familiar peachy-coloured rind. St James is aged according to customer preference but is normally best eaten between two and three months. The older it gets, the gooier it becomes, as the breakdown of the rind develops. The flavours also become richer and more savoury. Each batch of St James is small and made seasonally, specifically between the months of March and October when the sheep start producing milk. During the winter months, the farm produces and sells its hard cheeses made from both sheep and goat's milk.

Martin and Nicola also make Crookwheel, Holbrook, Apatha, Lady Grey, Ingot and Goashee, while they constantly experiment with new recipes.

St James characteristics

Milk: Raw milk from the farm's flock of Lacaune sheep

Rennet: Animal

Appearance: Pale white paste that has a glossy edge and chalky centre, with an edible, peachy washed rind flecked with grey

Tasting notes: Unctuous, savoury flavour with zesty and bacon notes. Varies according to the season and length of maturation

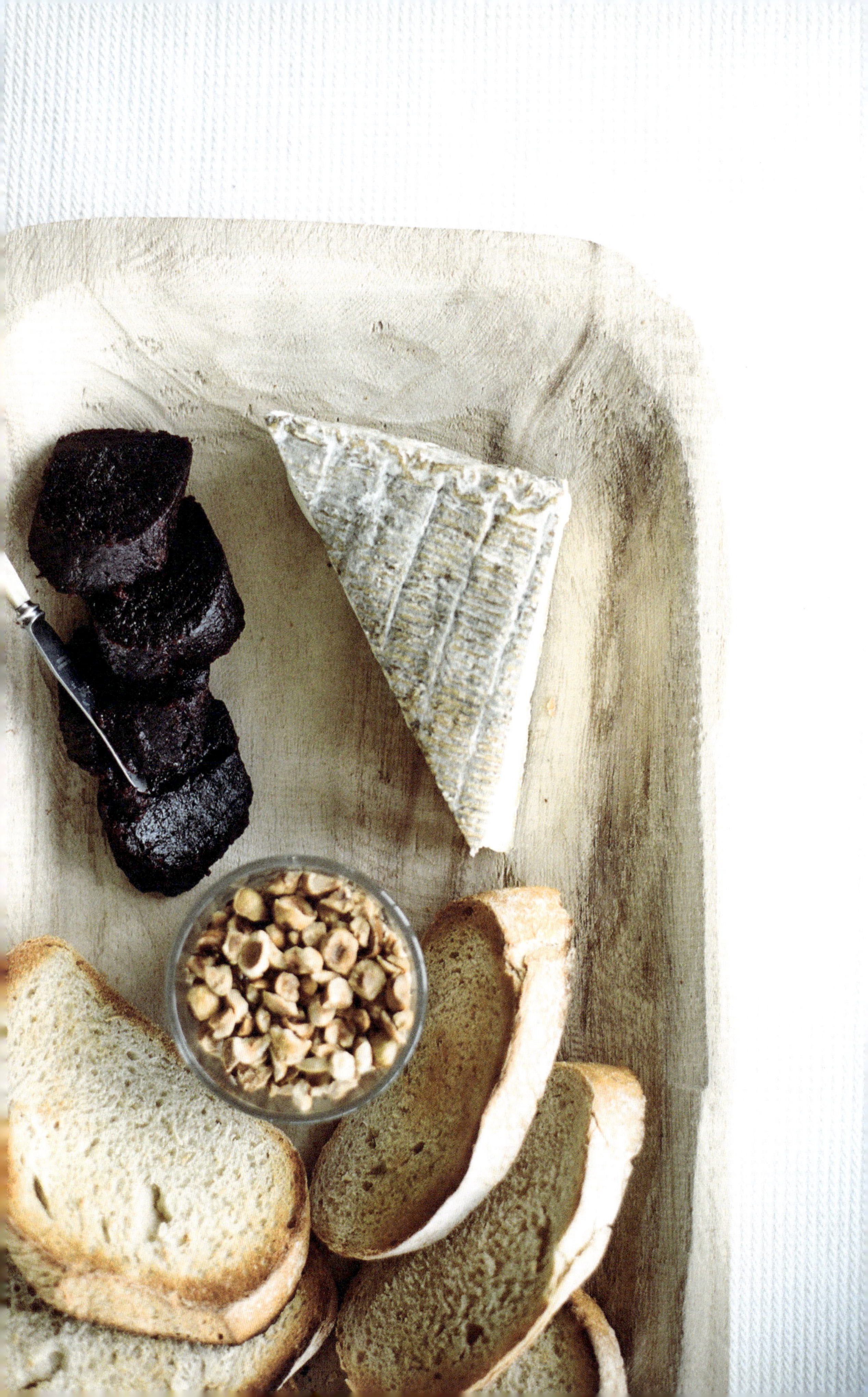

St James with damson cheese and toasted hazelnuts

Martin Gott and Nicola Robinson – alongside cheesemakers Niall Furlong and Wing Mon Cheung – make some of the most interesting cheeses in the British Isles, using natural starter cultures and raw milk from their ewes and goats. Everything here – from the farm to the animals – contributes to the unique character of the place.

I visited Holker Farm in late summer with my partner Lilly. We were fortunate enough to sample the very first trials of Holbrook cheese, named after the pioneering cheesemaker Mary Holbrook.

This recipe is Martin's, who loves to have St James for lunch – spread on toast with a good chunk of damson cheese and toasted hazelnuts sprinkled on top.

SERVES 2-3

70g shelled hazelnuts
1 rustic loaf, such as *pain de campagne* (or the sourdough loaf on page 59), sliced
250g St James, cut into slices
100g damson cheese, cut into slices (see below)

You can buy damson cheese or, if you prefer, make it as follows:

DAMSON CHEESE/ PASTE (MAKES AROUND 500G)

900g damsons
150ml water
220g preserving or granulated sugar

Preheat the oven to 180°C/350°F/gas mark 4.

Place the hazelnuts on a baking tray and bake for 5–8 minutes or until the nuts are lightly singed. Keep an eye on them and toss halfway through the cooking, then set aside to cool. Once the hazelnuts have cooled, place in a clean tea towel and gently rub to remove the skins, then finely chop the toasted nuts and place in a small serving bowl.

Lightly toast each slice of bread, then serve with the cheese, toasted hazelnuts and damson cheese, allowing everyone to help themselves.

DAMSON CHEESE

Wash and stone the damsons. Put the water and damsons in a large saucepan over a high heat. Bring to the boil, then reduce the heat and simmer for 15–25 minutes, or until the damsons are soft. Using a sieve, drain the liquid into a separate bowl (you can keep this and add into crumble mixes), then leave the damsons to drain for 10 minutes. In to the same large saucepan, press the damsons through a sieve with a wooden spoon. I ended up with around 300g of smooth damson sauce in the saucepan – make sure to scrape the bottom of the sieve as there will be pulp clinging to the bottom.

On a low heat, add the sugar to the smooth damson sauce and stir constantly for the first 5 minutes until the sugar has dissolved. On the same low temperature, heat for a further 25–35 minutes until the mixture turns into a very thick paste, stirring frequently to avoid burning the paste on the bottom of the pan.

Next you can either fill a sterilised jar (see page 183) with the paste and leave to cool before refrigerating for 24 hours before serving, or you can pour the mixture into a loaf tin lined with baking parchment and leave to cool. Once cool, lift the paste out of the tin, using the baking parchment, and roll the paste into a sausage shape, twisting the parchment at both ends to close. Then refrigerate for 24 hours before serving. The paste keeps for around 3–4 weeks.

ST JUDE

Left: St Jude is a soft lactic-style cheese, made using raw milk from Fen Farm just outside Bungay in Suffolk.

Right: The raw milk used for St Jude is from the farm's herd of Montbéliarde cows, producing milk that is wonderfully creamy and rich in protein.

St Jude Cheese, Bungay, Suffolk

St Jude, a soft lactic cheese with a mould-ripened rind, is made by Julie Cheyney using raw milk from a herd of Montbéliarde cows at Fen Farm in the picturesque Waveney Valley. Julie chose to make her cheese at Fen Farm as her values align with those of the Crickmore family who run the farm, working with nature to produce the distinctive Montbéliarde milk that is made into the cheese. Montbéliarde cows do not produce as much milk as the more common Holstein-Friesian breed, but the milk they do produce is protein-rich and sumptuously creamy in taste – perfect for making cheese.

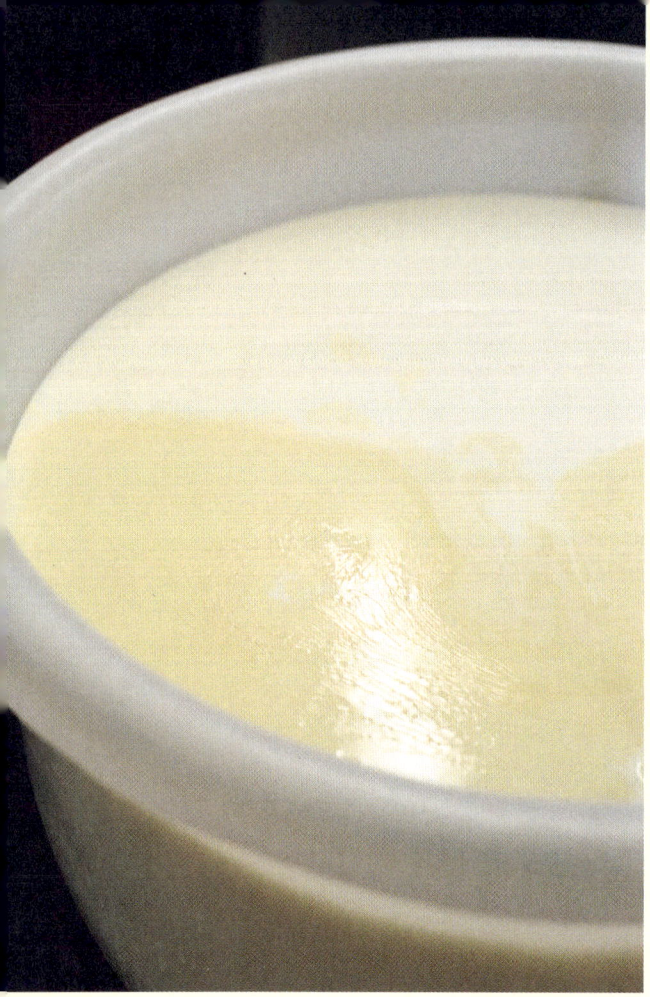
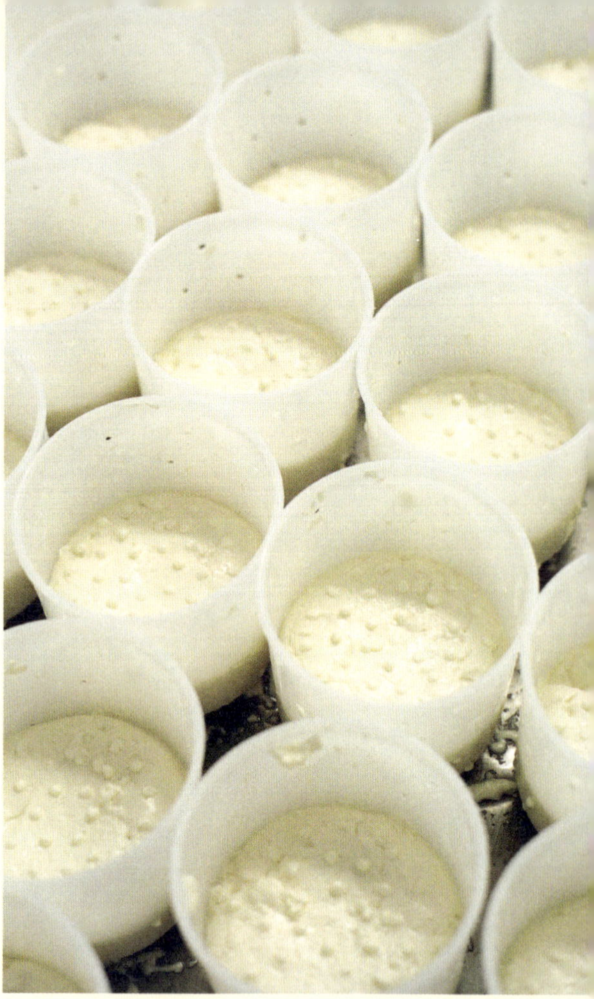
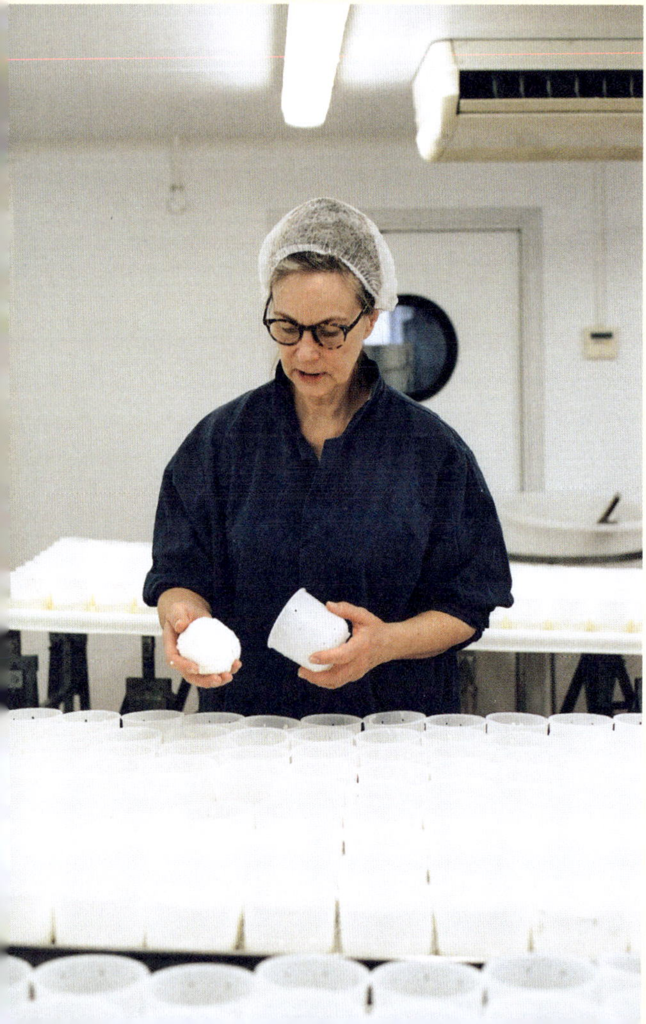
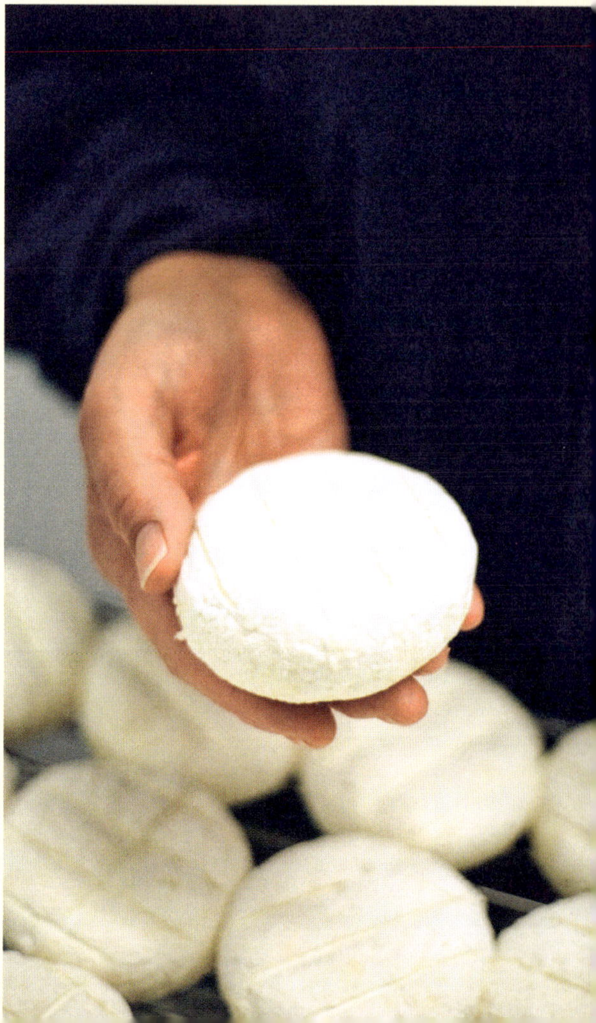

The making of a soft lactic cheese is a slow and gentle process, with minimal intervention. In the early hours of the morning, Julie starts by carefully pouring the warm milk, straight from the cow, into the cheese vats. Starter culture is added to the milk to begin the acidification process, along with yeasts and the *Geotrichum* fungus. The milk is left until the early afternoon when the rennet is added to coagulate the milk, which is left to ripen overnight.

The following morning, the curds are cut and ladled into moulds. The moulds, now filled with the curds, are turned three times at spaced intervals and left to rest in a warm room for twenty-four hours to drain the whey and for the curds to naturally compress into young cheeses. These are then placed on wire racks and taken to the hastener room, where they are left for three days. This room is warm and very humid to encourage the *Geotrichum* to grow. On the third day, the cheeses are salted by hand and then transferred to a cool maturing room to slow down the ageing process. If the maturing room is too hot, the rind of a soft-style cheese like St Jude may 'slip' and break up.

St Jude can be eaten from ten days onwards. Julie recommends eating it at 2–3 weeks old, when the paste starts to develop a gentle acidity but retains its milky flavour. As the cheese matures, it begins to break down around the rind, resulting in a softer, more oozing texture and a stronger flavour. The taste of the cheese differs throughout the year. During the winter months, the cheese tends to develop more buttery flavours, while in summer the taste becomes more vegetal and savoury.

Other cheeses made by Julie and her cheesemakers, Blake Bowden and Nic Hordern, include St Cera (a soft lactic cheese with a washed rind) and St Jude Curd (fresh curd), along with St Helena (a semi-soft cheese with a washed rind), created by Blake.

St Jude characteristics
Milk: Raw milk from the farm's herd of Montbéliarde cows
Rennet: Animal
Appearance: Soft ivory paste with an edible, wrinkled, mould-ripened white rind
Tasting notes: Fresh, milky flavour with savoury and acidic notes. Varies according to the season and length of maturation

Clockwise from top left: The variety of colours in the vat at the start of the cheesemaking process, from deep yellow to pale ivory.
Once the curds and the whey have been separated, the curds are placed in small moulds to drain and compress.
St Jude stacked on wire racks in the hastening room, a warm room in which the young cheeses are dried before being transferred to the maturing room.
When the time is right, Julie turns the young cheeses in the moulds to maintain an even structure.

Roasted tomatoes with St Jude and fresh basil

My visit to Julie at Fen Farm was on a typically cold, fresh day early in the year, the time when the snowdrops are in full flush and the sparrows are feeding profusely for the upcoming breeding season. After a tour of the cheesemaking, hastener and maturing rooms, Julie suggested this recipe, which she loves to make for lunch after a long morning making St Jude from 3 a.m. onwards, which must make it seem more like supper to her!

Suffolk is perhaps one of my favourite counties in the whole of the British Isles, home to my favourite landscape painter, John Constable, and the buried treasures of Sutton Hoo – a county steeped in history and rural magic. This was where the notoriously inedible Suffolk Bang was produced only a couple of centuries ago – a far cry from the award-winning cheeses now on offer in the region.

SERVES 2

4 tomatoes, halved
olive oil, for drizzling
4 slices of sourdough bread (see pages 59–61)
100g St Jude, thinly sliced
a few fresh basil leaves, roughly torn
sea salt and freshly ground black pepper

Preheat the oven to 200°C/400°F/gas mark 6.

Place the tomatoes, cut side up, on a baking try. Drizzle over a layer of olive oil, add a pinch of salt and a few grinds of black pepper and bake in the oven for 10–15 minutes.

While the tomatoes are cooking, toast the slices of sourdough. These are perfect for mopping up any surplus tomato juice or runny cheese.

Once the tomatoes are nicely sizzling and sticky, transfer to a serving plate and top with the thin slices of St Jude and freshly torn basil leaves. Dribble over a little more olive oil, add an extra grind or two of black pepper and serve with the toasted sourdough.

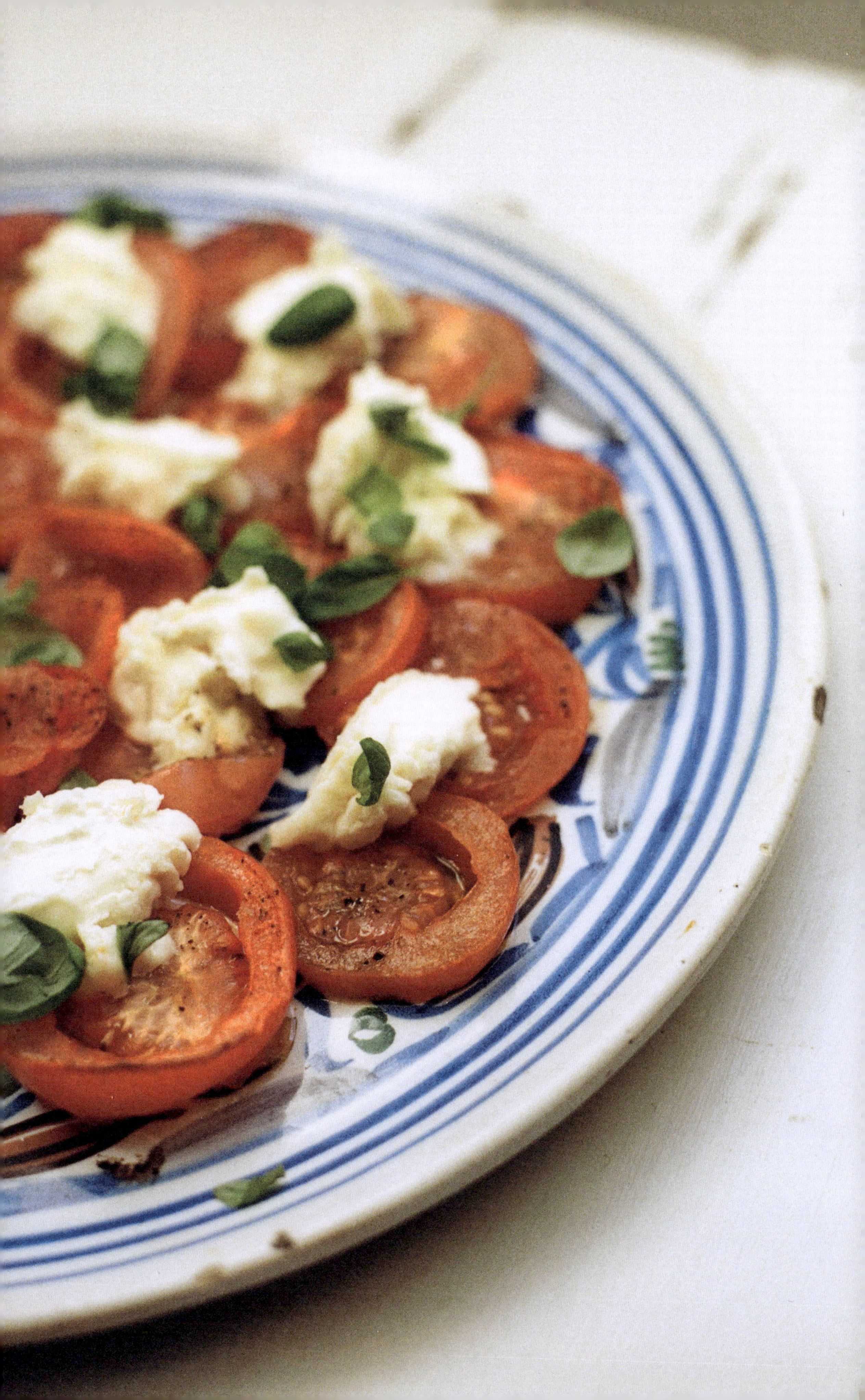

SHROPSHIRE BLUE

From left to right: The attractive rumpled texture of a matured Shropshire Blue in the maturing rooms at Sparkenhoe Farm. Each batch of Shropshire Blue is small, and checked regularly during maturation.

The Clarke family who run Sparkenhoe Farm, making delicious cheeses using raw milk. From left to right: Dottie the terrier, Annie, Jo, David, Fizz the sheepdog and Will.

A fine example of a Holstein-Friesian. When the weather is fine, the cows are out all night grazing on diverse herbal leys planted by the Clarkes to improve soil health and the diet of their livestock.

Will using his trusty cheesemaker's iron to monitor the progress of his Shropshire Blue. The fine fissures of blue veining start to develop when the cheeses are pierced in weeks five and seven.

Sparkenhoe Farm, Upton, Warwickshire

Along the main street of Upton village, bordered by thick hawthorn hedges and towering horse chestnuts, you'll find Sparkenhoe Farm. The farm, which sits just over the border in Leicestershire but with a Warwickshire address, makes Shropshire Blue, as well as Sparkenhoe Red Leicester and Sparkenhoe Blue. David and Jo Clarke run the farm along with their son, Will. David and Jo started making cheese in 2005 as a way to diversify, a move triggered especially by the low milk prices at the time. They soon found that their loamy, marl clay soil was perfect for producing good-quality milk to make their renowned Sparkenhoe Red Leicester.

At the farm, the Clarke family focus on a low-input farming system that aims to work in harmony with the environment, rather than against it. They use no artificial fertilisers or pesticides on their grazing pasture, and direct drill instead of ploughing, so as not to disturb the soil structure or microbial activity. The Clarkes also split their pasture into smaller paddocks, so that not all the land is grazed simultaneously, and plant diverse herbal leys to improve soil fertility. The herbal leys

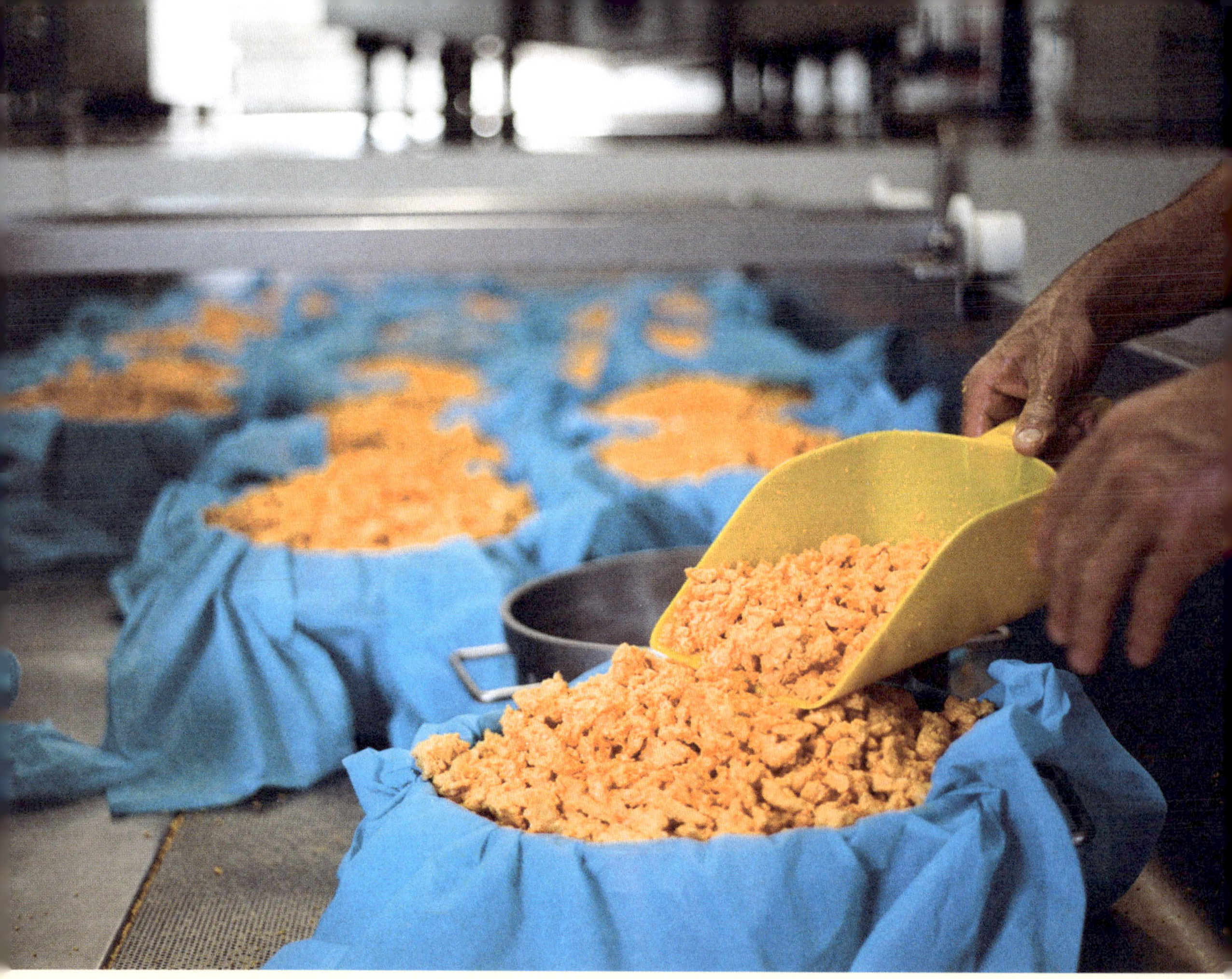
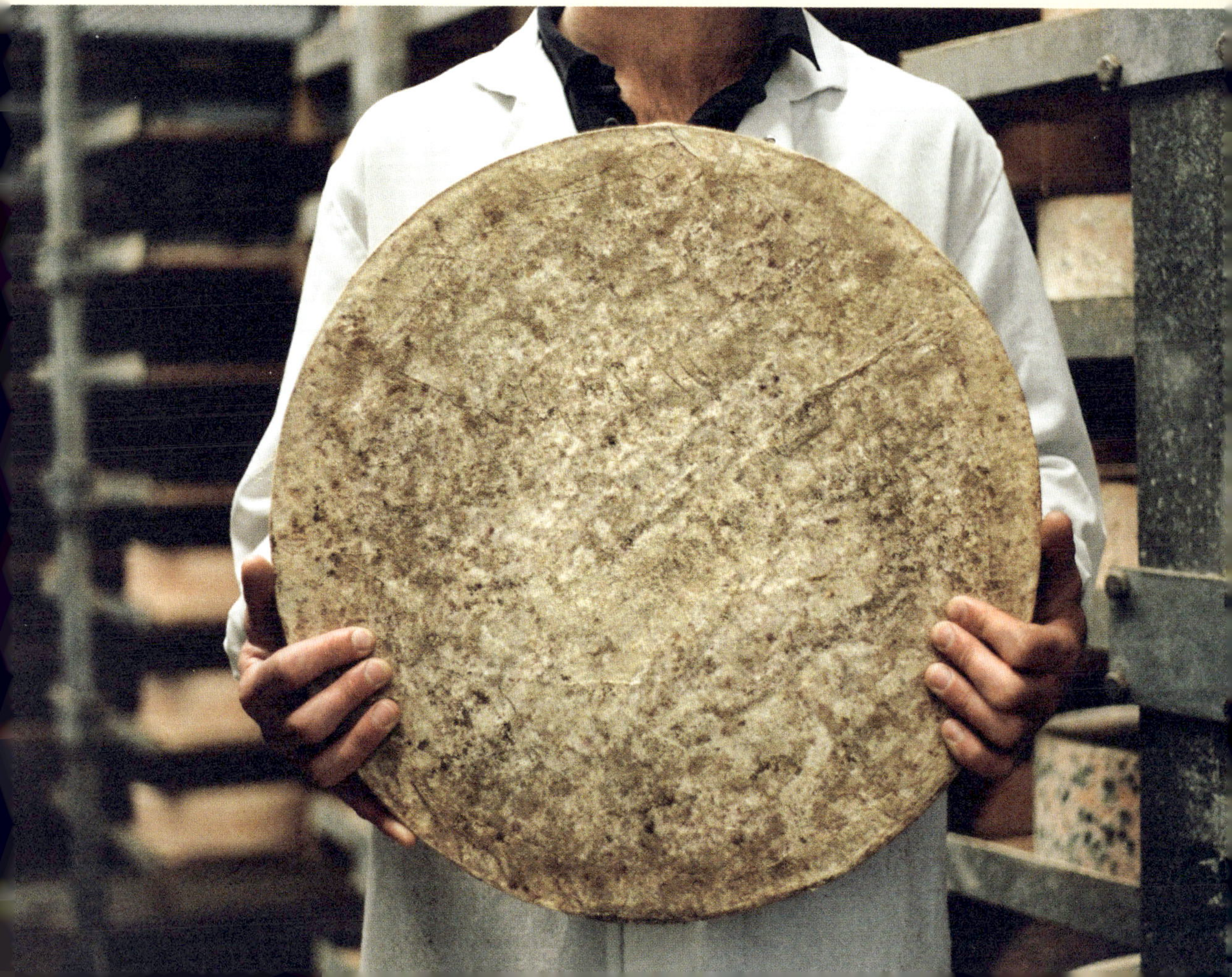

attract a wider range of wildlife to the fields too, including pied and yellow wagtails and multiple varieties of insect. The family's aim is to grow as much feed on the farm as possible, working towards producing the best possible quality of milk from happy cows on healthy soil.

Shropshire Blue is a crumbly blue cheese made using raw milk from the farm's herd of Holstein-Friesian cows. The unique feature of Shropshire Blue is that it is the only blue cheese to which annatto is added in the making, giving the cheese its characteristic pale orange colour speckled with blue mould. Using only the morning's milk, the method is slow and gentle, carried out over two days. The cheeses are aged for 3–5 months, depending on the time of year, during which time they are pierced with spikes at weeks five and seven to encourage the *Penicillium roqueforti* mould to proliferate and produce the cheese's distinctive blue fissures.

Another cheese made at the farm is Sparkenhoe Red Leicester, a hard cheese made to a traditional Red Leicester recipe, the main difference being that the Sparkenhoe Red Leicester is made using raw milk from the farm's herd of Holstein-Friesian cows, making it the only raw-milk farmhouse Red Leicester in the British Isles. The cheese is made over a 24-hour period using the evening and morning's milk. Once the young cheeses have been moulded and pressed, they are bound with cheesecloth and coated in lard to help the cheese form a naturally marbled rind during maturation. The best time to eat Sparkenhoe Red Leicester is at 8–9 months, though it can be left to age for 16–18 months, when it is referred to as 'Sparkenhoe Vintage'.

Other cheeses Sparkenhoe Farm makes are Battlefield Blue and Bosworth Field.

Shropshire Blue characteristics

Milk: Raw milk from the farm's herd of Holstein-Friesian cows

Rennet: Animal

Appearance: Smooth, firm orange paste with light blue veins and an edible, rough terracotta rind capped with white mould

Tasting notes: Rich, sweet caramel flavour with hints of apple. Varies according to the season and length of maturation

Top: The vivid orange curds in a vat during the make of Sparkenhoe Red Leicester. Here, David is filling various moulds with the curds to be pressed overnight to form young cheeses.

Bottom: A Sparkenhoe Red Leicester weighing in at 20kg, the traditional size, though they tend to be smaller now, at 10kg in weight. These big wheels of cheese are taken to farmers' markets and shows, where they are sliced up for sale.

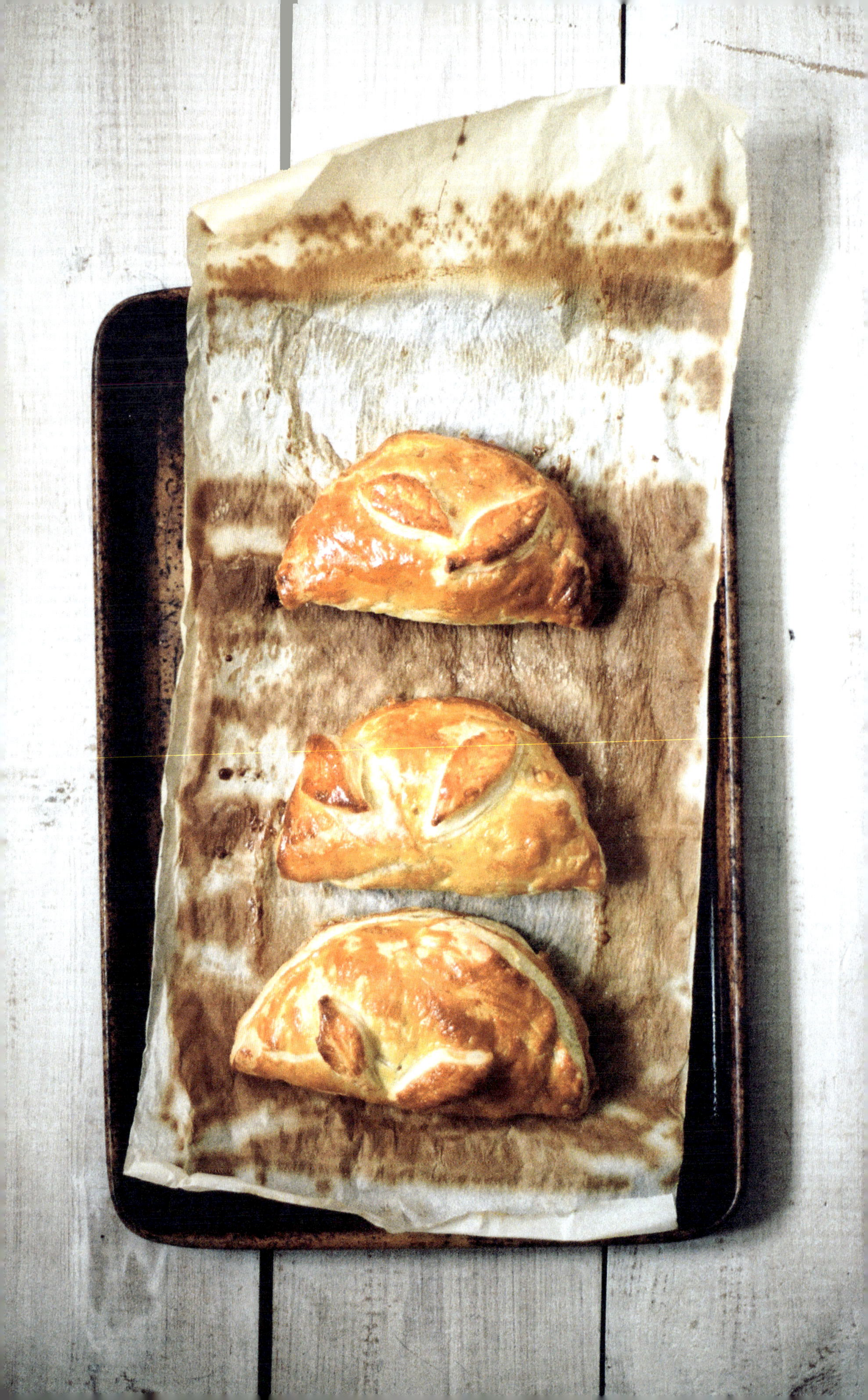

Leek and Shropshire Blue pasties

Sparkenhoe Farm is home to the Clarke family, not to mention all the animals – dogs, cats, horses, chickens, sheep and cows – that populate the farm, either running circles around your feet or, far out towards the horizon, grazing the nearby pastures. Lying just over the border in Leicestershire, the farm has wonderful long views across the county and towards Warwickshire. It is a lovely set-up, with the milking parlour and cheesemaking rooms in close proximity, and with an on-site shop, which was once the old pig house, now selling dairy goodies made on the farm and other local produce.

I visited the Clarkes on a fantastic sunny day in late spring, marvellous for taking sunlit photographs but perhaps not so good for farming – well, at that particular time of year, anyway. I believe that on the day I visited Sparkenhoe Farm, it had been nearly a whole month since it had last rained in the area, with the cracks in the ground showing the earth's thirst.

This recipe is perfect if you know you're going to be out all day and need a quick, portable lunch. I often make these pasties early in the morning and have them cold come lunchtime. You'll most certainly find one stuffed in my rucksack when I'm going for a long walk or if I'm travelling in the car from one side of the country to the other.

MAKES 3 PASTIES

15g butter
1 small leek, finely sliced
1 small potato, peeled and finely diced into small cubes
1 x 320g sheet of ready-rolled all-butter puff pastry (about 35cm x 23cm)
flour, for dusting
100g Shropshire Blue, cut into 6 slices
1 large egg
sea salt and freshly ground black pepper

Preheat the oven to 200°C/400°F/gas mark 6.

In a non-stick pan on a medium heat, melt the butter and sauté the leek and potato for about 10 minutes until softened. Add a small pinch of salt and a few turns of black pepper, and set aside to cool.

Unroll the puff pastry and cut it in half widthways. Place a small plate (about 15cm in diameter) on the pastry to use as a template, and cut around it. You should have enough room for two circles – one on each pastry half. Gather up the remaining pastry and, on a floured worktop, roll it out with a rolling pin before cutting out a third circle the same size as the first two. There will still be a little pastry left over, which you could cut into leaf shapes to add to the top of the pasties.

Place a tablespoon of the cooled potato-leek mixture on to one half of one pastry circle, and top with two slices of cheese. Next, beat the egg and, using a pastry brush, brush the edge of the pastry circle with the egg before folding over to cover the filling and pressing down the edges well to seal. Repeat with the other two pasties. Once you have completed all three, brush the pasties with the remaining egg and attach the leaf shapes, if using. Pierce a little hole in the top of each pasty to let the air out, then place on a baking tray lined with baking parchment and bake for 15 minutes at the top of the oven until golden brown.

SINGLE GLOUCESTER

Left: Jonathan and Annabelle Crump at Standish Park Farm with one of their dogs. The three are standing outside the cheesemaking rooms in the Gloucestershire sunshine.

Right: A wheel of Single Gloucester, cut in two, alongside the rustic Longney Russet, a local Gloucestershire variety of apple that goes perfectly with the cheese.

Standish Park Farm, Oxlynch, Gloucestershire

On the edge of the Cotswolds escarpment with stunning views over the Severn Vale is the charming Standish Park Farm, where Single Gloucester is made using raw milk from the farm's native herd of Gloucester cows. Jonathan and Annabelle Crump run the 300-acre mixed farm. As well as making farmhouse cheese, the Crumps also specialise in raising rare breeds. Jonathan is the cheesemaker at Standish Park Farm, having made cheese for nearly thirty years.

There are several cheesemakers in Gloucestershire who make Single Gloucester – awarded a Protected Designation of Origin (PDO) mark in 1997 – a hard cheese made using milk from mixed breeds. A unique feature of the Crumps' Single Gloucester is that they use only the milk of Gloucester cows to make their cheese. Like many of the best farmhouse cheesemakers, the Crumps focus on producing the best possible quality of milk for their cheesemaking. To do this, they ensure the permanent pasture is treated with no artificial fertilisers or chemicals, and during the winter months they feed their animals only hay, which is produced on the farm. Feeding them hay reduces the quantity of milk being produced but the milk that is produced is far superior in quality. Growing hay also encourages biodiversity, as the meadows – before they are cut late in the season – are vital habitats for wildlife, providing food and grounds for breeding late into the summer months. Stored appropriately, hay also omits the need for plastic wrapping.

The method of making Single Gloucester is similar to that of many territorial hard-style cheeses. Once the milk is heated, the starter culture and rennet are added. The curds and whey are separated, after which 'Cheddaring' takes place, the curds are cut by hand into small cubes and pressed together into slabs, which helps expel any excess whey and enables the bacterial culture in the curds to become active. The curds are then milled, salted and pressed for two days. The maturing takes two months before it is ready to eat, during which time the cheeses are turned regularly. In winter, the cheese forms an incredible grey-brown, moleskin-like rind that is truly unique to the Crumps' cheese.

The Crump family also make Double Gloucester, the method being similar to that of Single Gloucester, except that the milk is heated to a higher temperature, annatto is added for colouring and the maturation period is twice as long as for Single Gloucester, which explains where the name 'Double' came from. Single Gloucester was traditionally sold locally and used as part payment to farm workers, whereas Double Gloucester – originally dyed with carrot juice – was more attractive and sold at market stalls in the major British cities and 'the new colonies'.

Single Gloucester characteristics

Milk: Raw milk from the farm's herd of Gloucester cows

Rennet: Vegetarian

Appearance: Light milky paste with a soft, moleskin-like edible rind

Tasting notes: Moist, buttery flavour with a light lactic, citrusy finish. Varies according to the season and length of maturation

Clockwise from top left: The Crumps know each of their animals by name. Here Jonathan leads Rebecca and her new calf down the hill to fresh pastures.

Stainless-steel blades cutting into the curd that has just set. Cutting the curds into fine particles can be a therapeutic process.

As the Crumps' Single Gloucester ages, the cheese develops a moleskin-like rind the colour of the local sandstone.

The intricate pressed patterns on the surface of a young Single Gloucester are fascinating to see. The young cheeses are taken to the maturing rooms to be aged for two months.

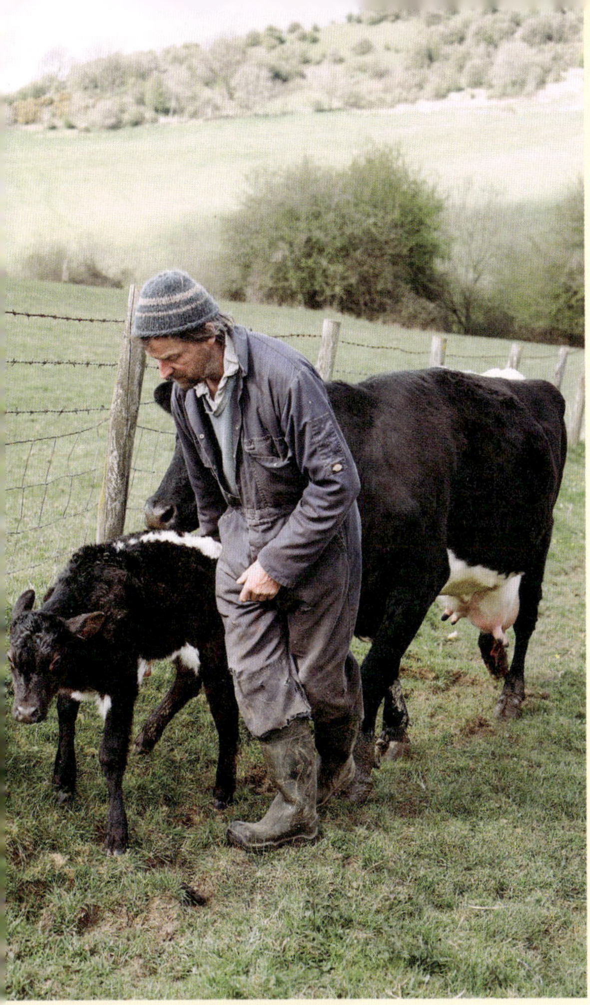
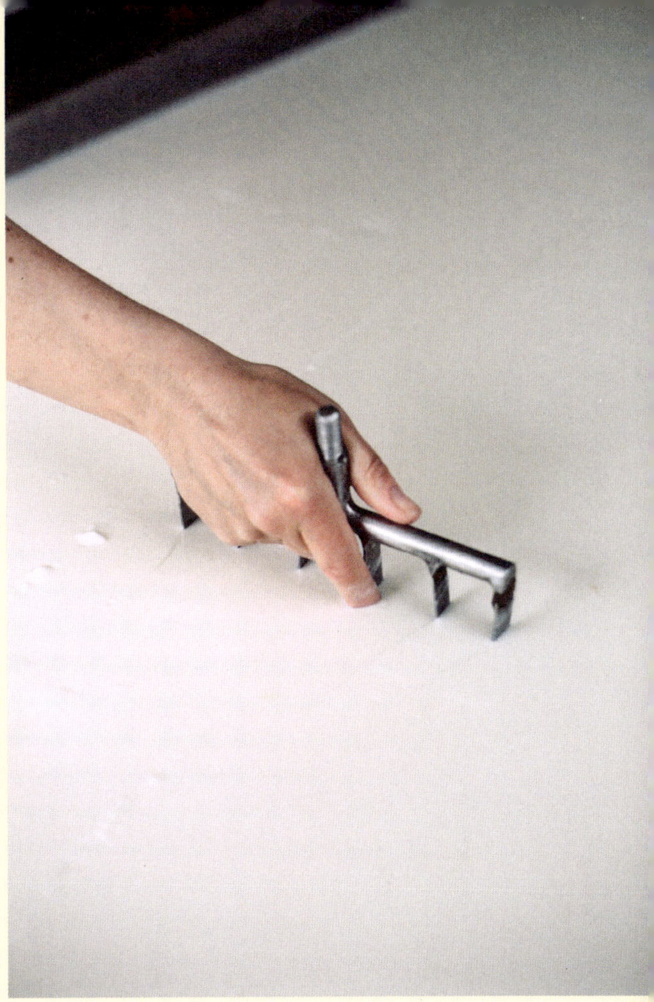
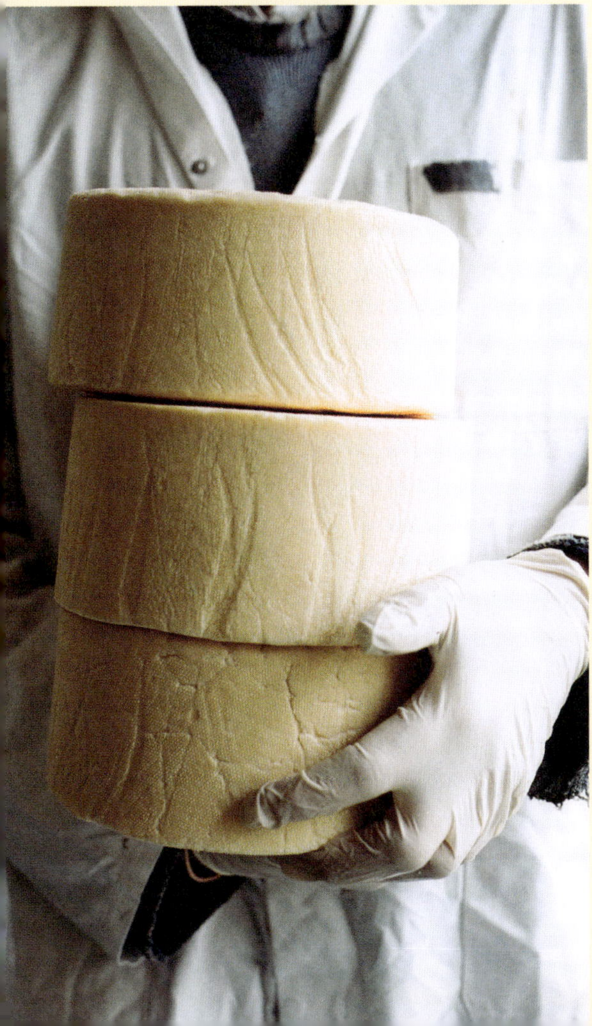
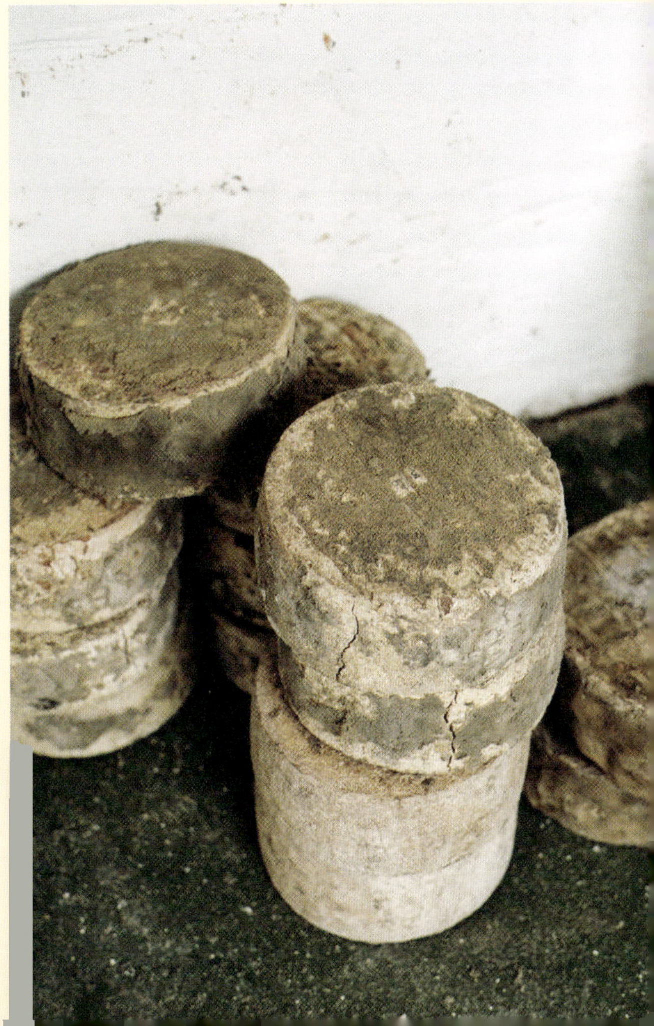

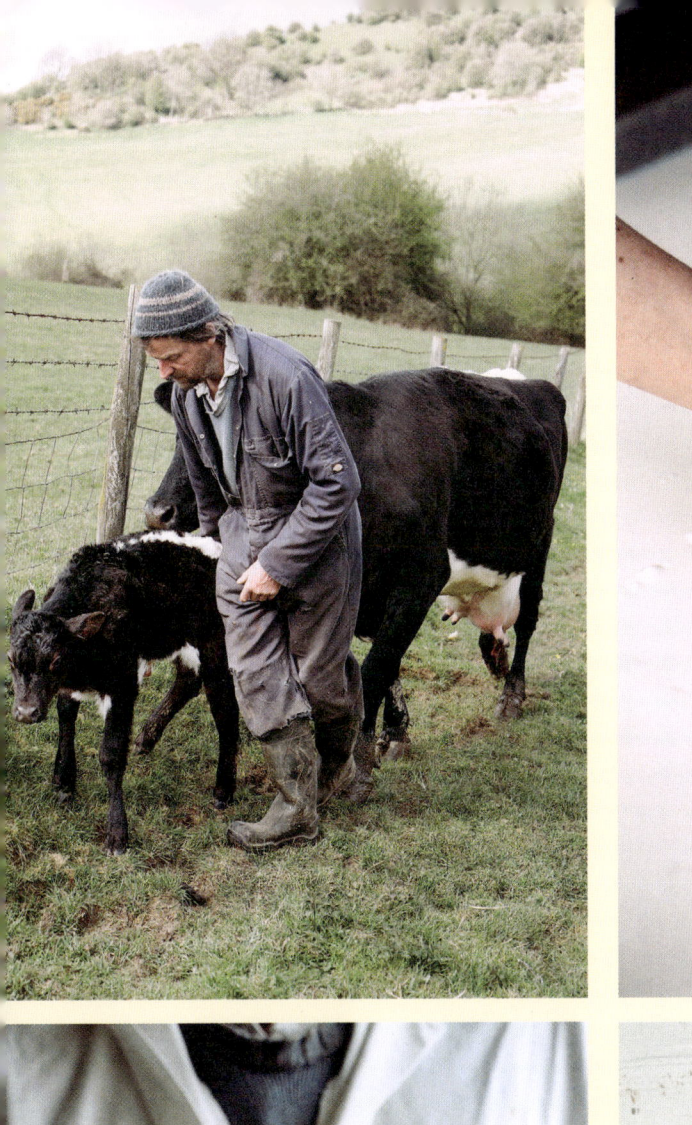

Crumps' spiced apple and custard cake

The Crump family are the embodiment of a farmhouse cheesemaker, with all types of animals running around happily, cider and cheese being made in small batches, hens laying copious quantities of eggs, and the whole family – Jonathan, Annabelle and children Hettie and Olla – being involved on the farm.

When Lilly and I arrived, the Crumps alongside their very friendly goat, Pip, greeted us like old friends. As well as Pip, the farm is populated by Gloucester cows, Gloucestershire Old Spots (and their piglets), sheep of various kinds (Cotswold, Jacob, Lleyn, Llanwenog, Shetland and Herdwick), chickens (Sussex, Silver Dorking and Hamburg), guinea fowl, ducks and Brecon Buff geese, to name but a few.

This recipe is a celebration of Gloucestershire provenance. We had a variation of this cake at the Crumps after a ploughman's lunch of Single Gloucester, homemade chutney, salad and freshly baked bread. The cake is normally served with homemade custard and a hot cup of tea. Any eating apples will work in this recipe, but I use Longney Russet – a local variety dating back to 1796. The Longney Russet is traditionally picked in late autumn and stored for winter, looking and feeling more like a rock than an apple. Over the ensuing months, the apple naturally softens, and is perfect to eat in late winter or early spring with a good chunk of Single Gloucester (but of course!).

SERVES 6–8

CAKE TOPPING
60g butter, plus extra for greasing
60g soft brown sugar
400g eating apples, peeled and cored
2 tsp ground cinnamon

SPONGE
180g butter, softened
220g soft brown sugar
4 large eggs
1 tsp vanilla extract
220g self-raising flour
small pinch of sea salt
2 tsp baking powder

Preheat the oven to 180°C/350°F/gas mark 4. Grease a 23cm-diameter, deep-sided cake tin (with a removable base) with a little butter and line the base with baking parchment.

First make the topping. Place the butter and sugar in a large saucepan and allow to melt and dissolve over a medium heat. Dice the apple and add it the pan with the cinnamon. Stir and cook the apple for 4–5 minutes until glazed and softened, then set aside to cool.

Next make the sponge. Whisk the butter and sugar together in a large bowl until nice and fluffy. Add the eggs, one at a time, and whisk constantly, then add the vanilla extract.

In a separate bowl, mix together the flour, salt and baking powder, and gradually sift this dry mixture into the egg mixture. Add half of the cooked apple pieces, including the syrup, to the batter, combine well and then pour evenly into the lined cake tin.

Ingredients and method continued overleaf

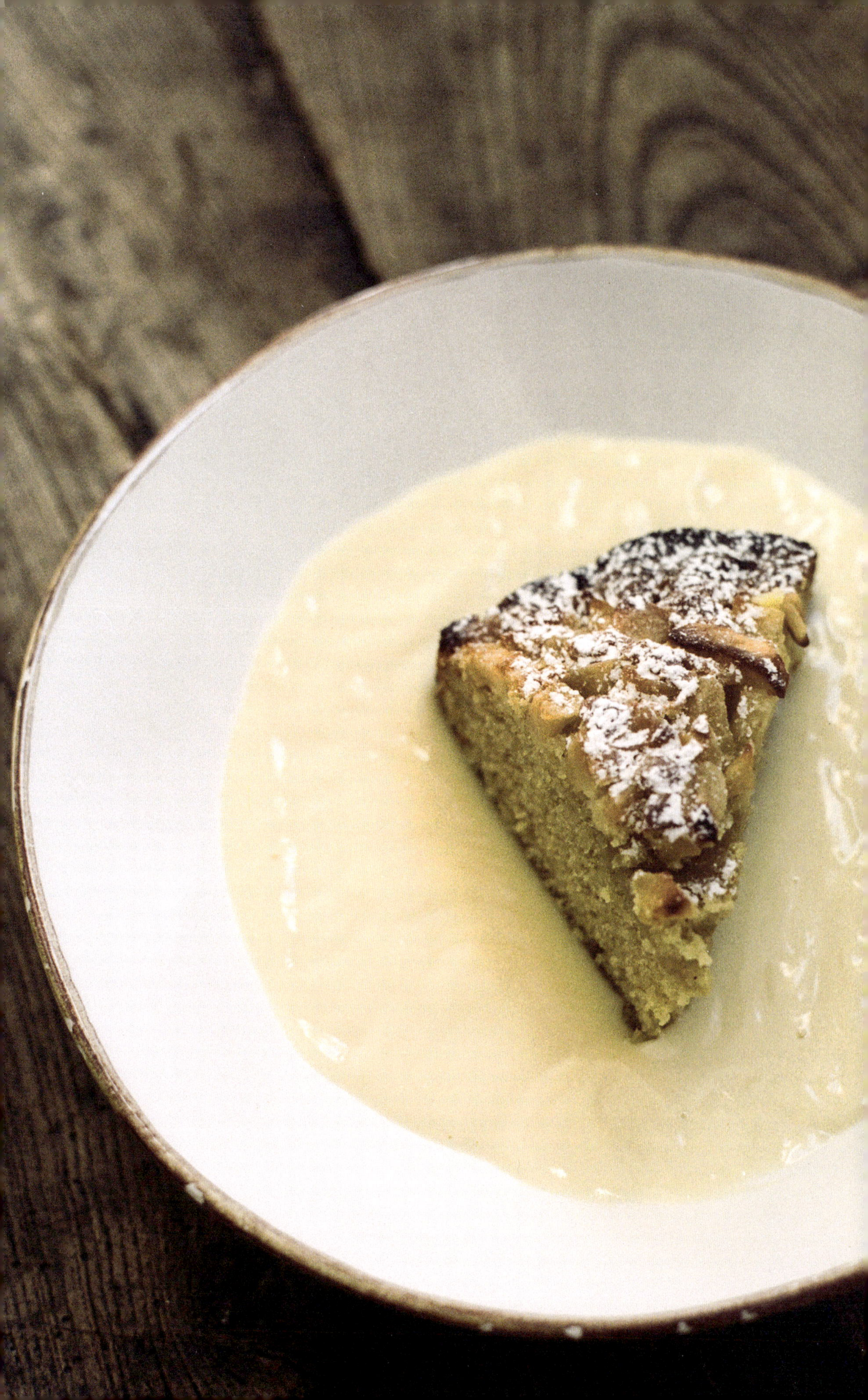

A hefty slice of Double Gloucester, which the Crumps also make. The scored line is where Jonathan used his cheesemaker's iron to sample the cheese as it matured to check its flavour and texture.

CUSTARD
1 large egg and
 1 egg yolk
80g caster sugar
25g cornflour
600ml whole milk
½ tsp vanilla bean
 paste
10g butter
small pinch of
 sea salt

Evenly sprinkle with another quarter of the cooked apple and syrup – half of what you have left – then bake in the oven for 40–50 minutes, or until well risen and a skewer inserted into the centre of the cake comes out clean. Allow the cake to cool in the tin for a few minutes, then remove from the tin and transfer to a wire rack to finish cooling.

To make the custard, I like to use two large saucepans. Add the egg, extra yolk, sugar and cornflour to the first saucepan and combine well. Place the second saucepan on a medium heat and add the milk and vanilla bean paste. When the milk begins to boil, remove the pan from the heat. Pour a little of the milk into the first saucepan with the egg mixture and whisk until it thickens. Now place this saucepan on a low heat and gradually pour in the hot milk, whisking constantly. Once all the milk has been incorporated, take the pan off the heat and add the butter and a very small pinch of salt. Pour into a jug for serving straight away.

To serve, pour the rest of the cooked apples and syrup over the cake, cut into slices and serve with lots of thick fresh custard.

STICHELTON

Left: The Sheffield knives used by the cheesemakers at Stichelton Dairy to rub down the cheeses – perfect for the job.

Right: The handsome ruddy profile of a wheel of Stichelton ageing on a wooden shelf in the maturing rooms at Stichelton Dairy.

Stichelton Dairy, Collingthwaite Farm, Cuckney, Nottinghamshire

Situated in the ancient arboreal landscape of Sherwood Forest in north Nottinghamshire is Stichelton Dairy. The dairy was set up on Collingthwaite Farm in the Welbeck Estate by Joe Schneider and Randolph Hodgson in 2006 to revive the making of Stilton using raw milk. Run by Joe and his team of cheesemakers, the dairy produces Stichelton, a blue cheese made using raw milk from the farm's herd of Holstein-Friesian cows, which graze on the land surrounding the dairy. Stichelton is made to virtually the same traditional recipe as Stilton, yet, as it's produced with raw milk, it cannot officially be labelled 'Stilton Cheese', as Stilton must be made using pasteurised milk.

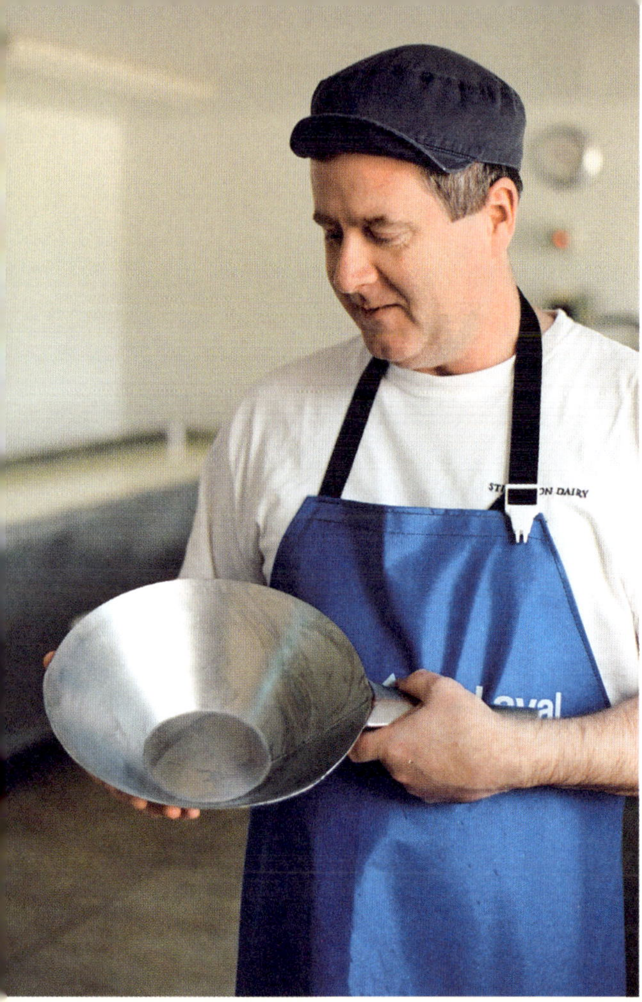

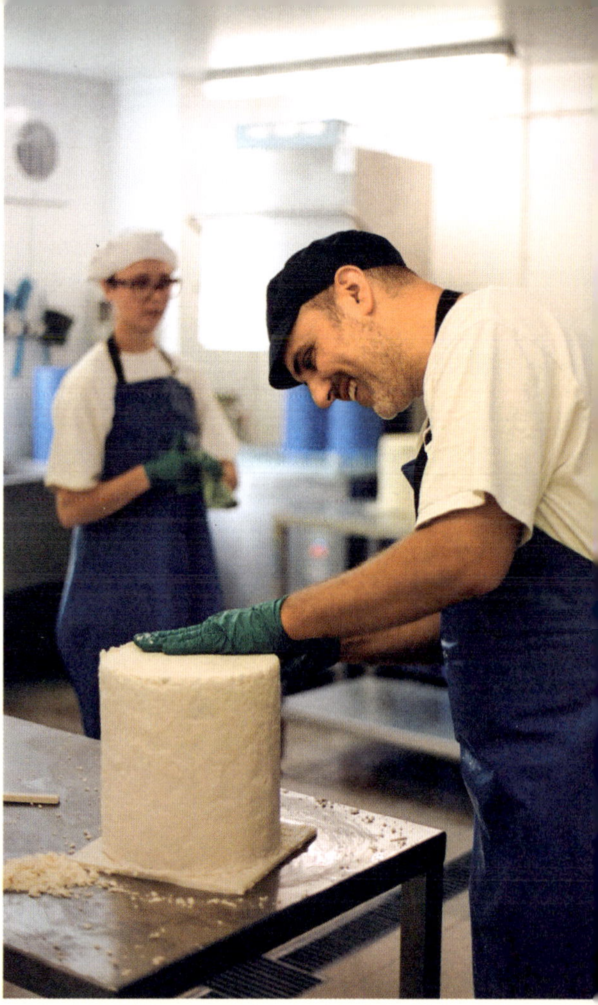

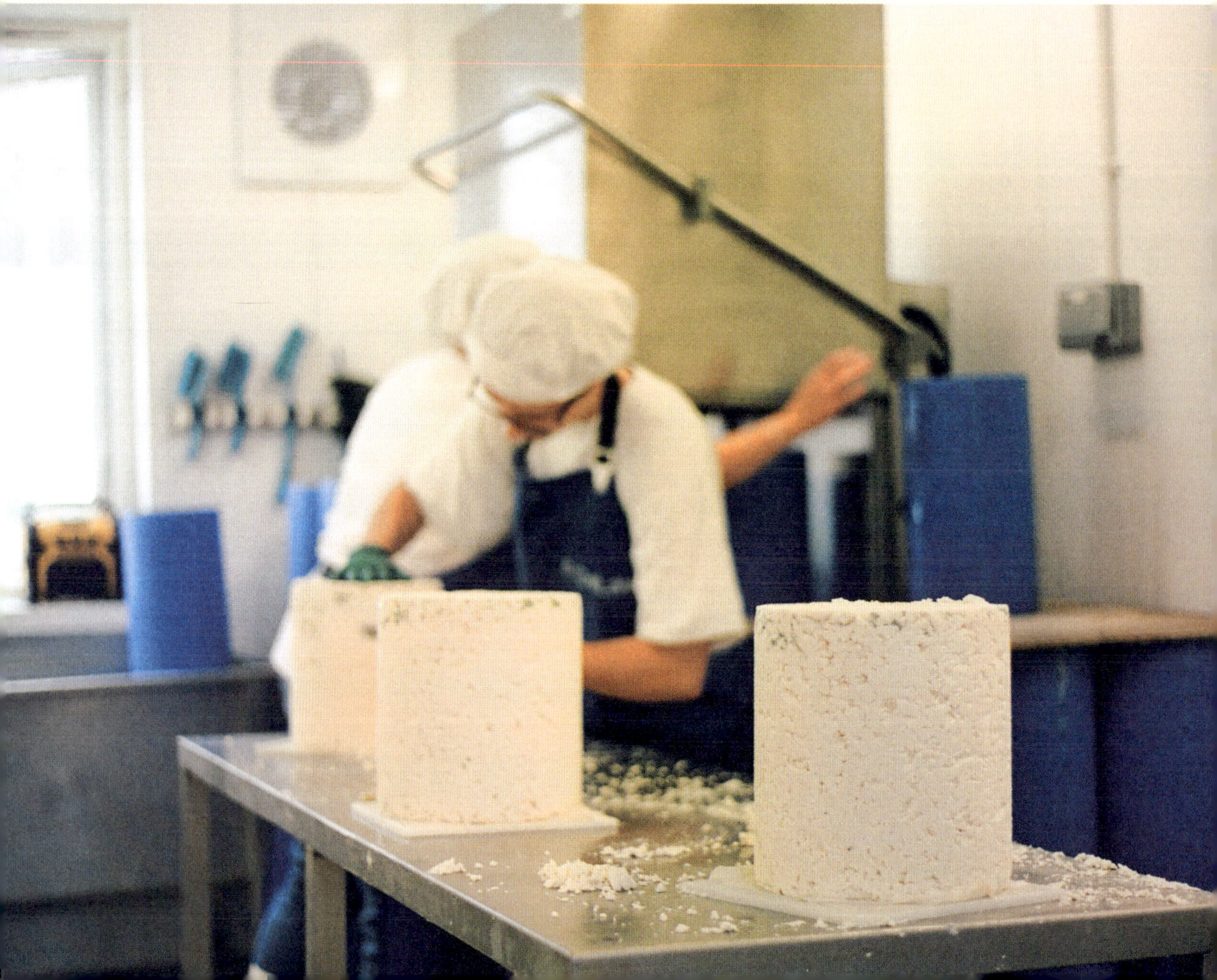

The entire make of a Stichelton cheese takes twenty-four hours. It starts with the morning's warm milk being channelled into the vats and then heated to around 29°C, straight from the cows. During the heating of the milk, blue *Penicillium* is added, lying dormant in the milk until maturation when the famous blue veins develop in the cheese. At the appropriate times, small amounts of both starter culture and rennet are added, after which the mixture is then left for several hours to set into soft, delicate curds. The cheesemakers assess when the curds are ready to be cut, which will remove much of the whey. One of the unique aspects of the process for making Stichelton is the way in which the curds are treated. Using a specially made wide ladle, the cheesemakers carefully spoon out the curds from the vats and place them gently on a drainage table to drain overnight.

The next morning, the drained curds on the table are cut into blocks and milled. The milled curds are then salted before being ladled into individual moulds, which are then taken to the hastening room to dry for a week, during which time they are turned every day. The next stage involves 'rubbing' the young cheeses to close any gaps on the surface – a flat butter knife is perfect for the job. Once rubbed, they are placed in the drying room for three weeks before being moved into the maturing room. At week six, and again at week seven, they are pierced with metal spikes to let in oxygen to encourage the mould to develop into blue veins. Depending on the time of year, Stichelton is aged for 20–22 weeks in winter, and around sixteen weeks in summer and autumn, when the milk has a higher fat content.

Stichelton characteristics

Milk: Raw milk from the farm's herd of Holstein-Friesian cows

Rennet: Animal

Appearance: Ivory paste with fine fissures of blue mould and an edible, rough natural rind with a ruddy-brown hue and a white bloom

Tasting notes: Sweet cream, syrupy flavour with notes of biscuit and Bovril. Varies according to the season and length of maturation

Top left: Joe brandishing his hand-crafted ladle, specially designed for making Stichelton and used for transferring curds from the vat on to the drainage table.

Top right: The 'rubbing' stage in the making of Stichelton, a process performed to close any gaps in the cheese and produce an even rind.

Bottom: Each day at the dairy is full-on, from the make, the 'rubbing' stage and the maturation, to the washing down of everything to start the process again.

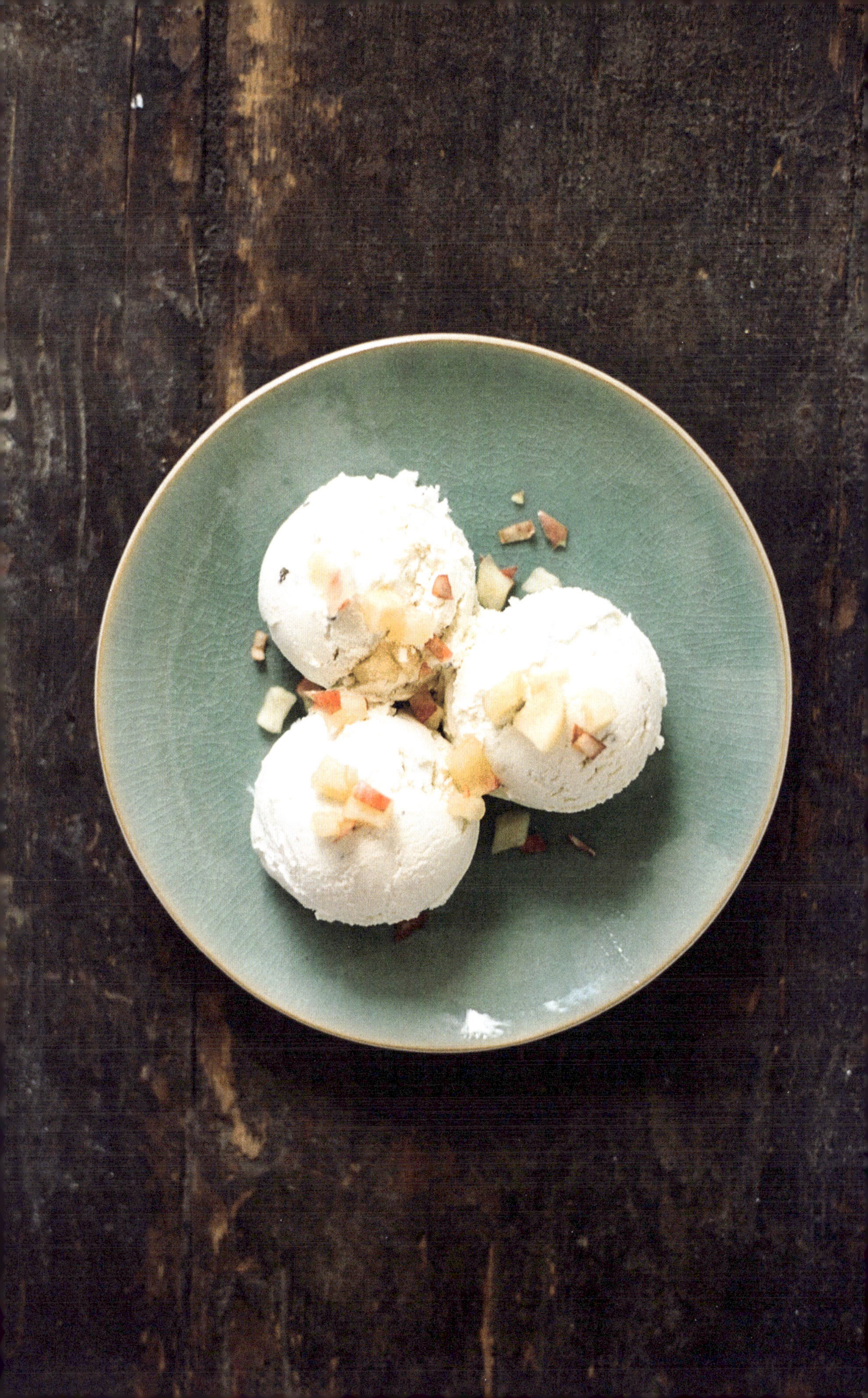

Stichelton ice cream with candied apple

This is a love or hate recipe, and one I personally love. It was inspired by a trip to the Red Boat, an ice cream parlour in the heart of Beaumaris in Anglesey. Like the ice cream parlour, Beaumaris itself is small and exceedingly charming, and with its seaside setting and mountain views, you cannot help but fall for the place.

Anglesey is somewhere I now visit regularly, and a trip to the Red Boat is a must when I am in the area. It does your standard flavours, as well as some very quirky ones, including sea buckthorn, which is deliciously sweet, and Stilton and apple. The latter was a flavour combination that has stuck with me ever since, and having substituted Stilton with Joe's raw-milk Stichelton and one of my very own Discovery varieties of apple from the garden, it was a real winner. You can use any type of eating apple, of course. The brilliance of using Stichelton in this recipe is that it is already mouth-wateringly sweet and milky, so you don't need to go overboard with the condensed milk.

SERVES 6

ICE CREAM
600ml double cream
180g condensed milk
100g Stichelton

CANDIED APPLE
1 large eating apple, peeled, cored and finely diced
juice of ½ lemon
100ml water
100g caster sugar

First make the ice cream. Pour the cream into a large bowl, then add the condensed milk and crumble in 80g of the cheese, leaving the rest to crumble on top when serving. Using a handheld electric whisk, combine all the ingredients in the bowl into thick, frothy peaks. Tip the mixture into an airtight container and freeze overnight.

To make the candied apple, preheat the oven to 165°C/325°F/gas mark 3 and line a baking tray with baking parchment, allowing enough to hang over the sides to enable you to remove the paper and cooked apple easily from the tin.

Place the diced apple in a small bowl and add the lemon juice. Toss the apple in the juice, then drain in a sieve to remove any excess liquid.

Pour the 100ml of water into a small saucepan, add the sugar and bring to the boil. Add the diced apple and simmer over a medium heat, stirring constantly, for 6–7 minutes until the apple is glazed and the water vapour smells sweetly of apple. Using a sieve, drain the remaining liquid then place the diced apple on the lined baking tray in an even layer. Bake in the oven for 30 minutes, then transfer the apple, still on the baking parchment, to a wire rack and leave the apple pieces to cool completely.

Take the ice cream out of the freezer 5–10 minutes before serving. Scoop the ice cream into bowls and crumble over the candied apple and the rest of the cheese to serve.

Overleaf: The wonderful team of cheesemakers at Stichelton standing with their 'rubbed' young cheeses that will later be pierced and left to mature.

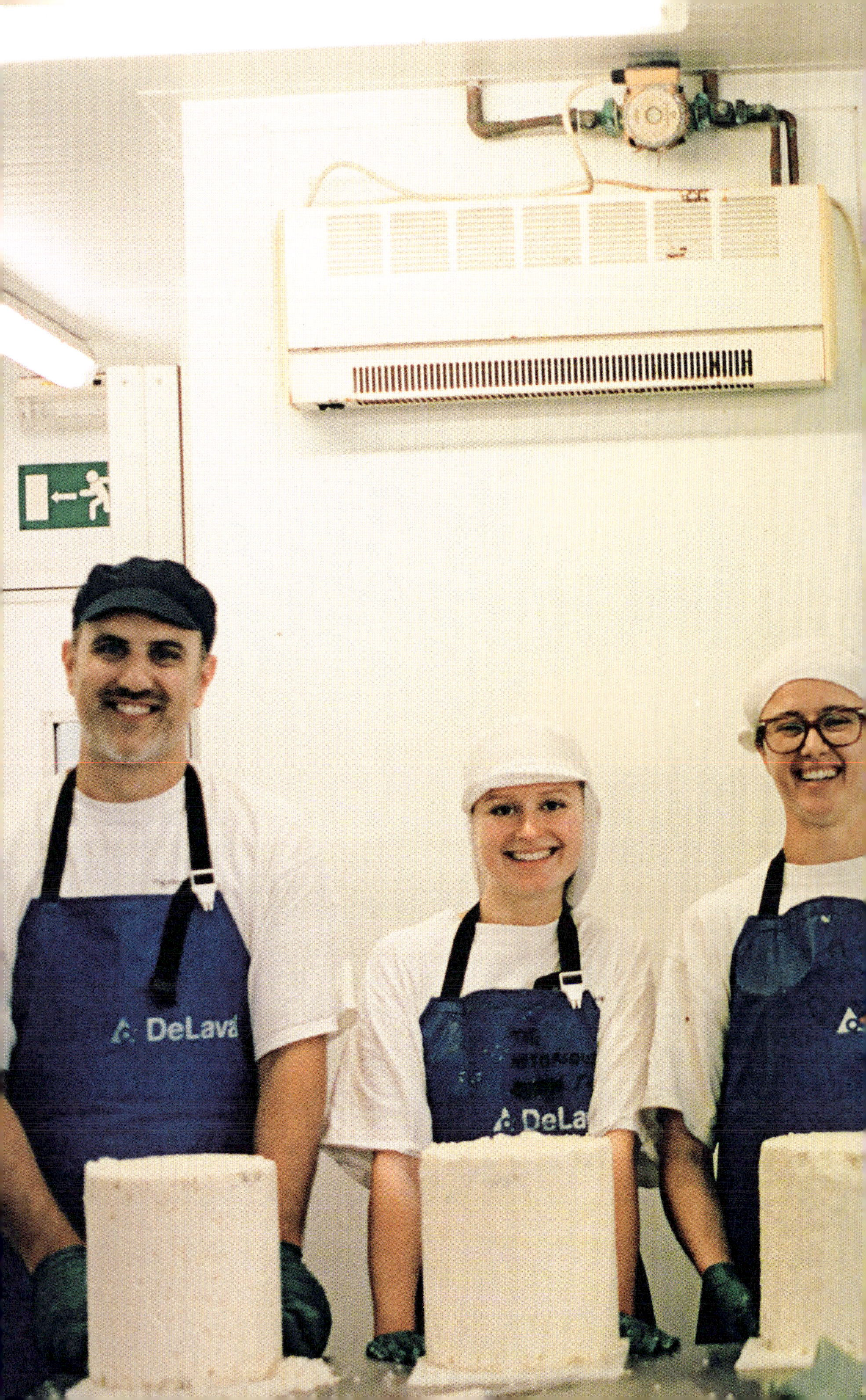
DeLaval

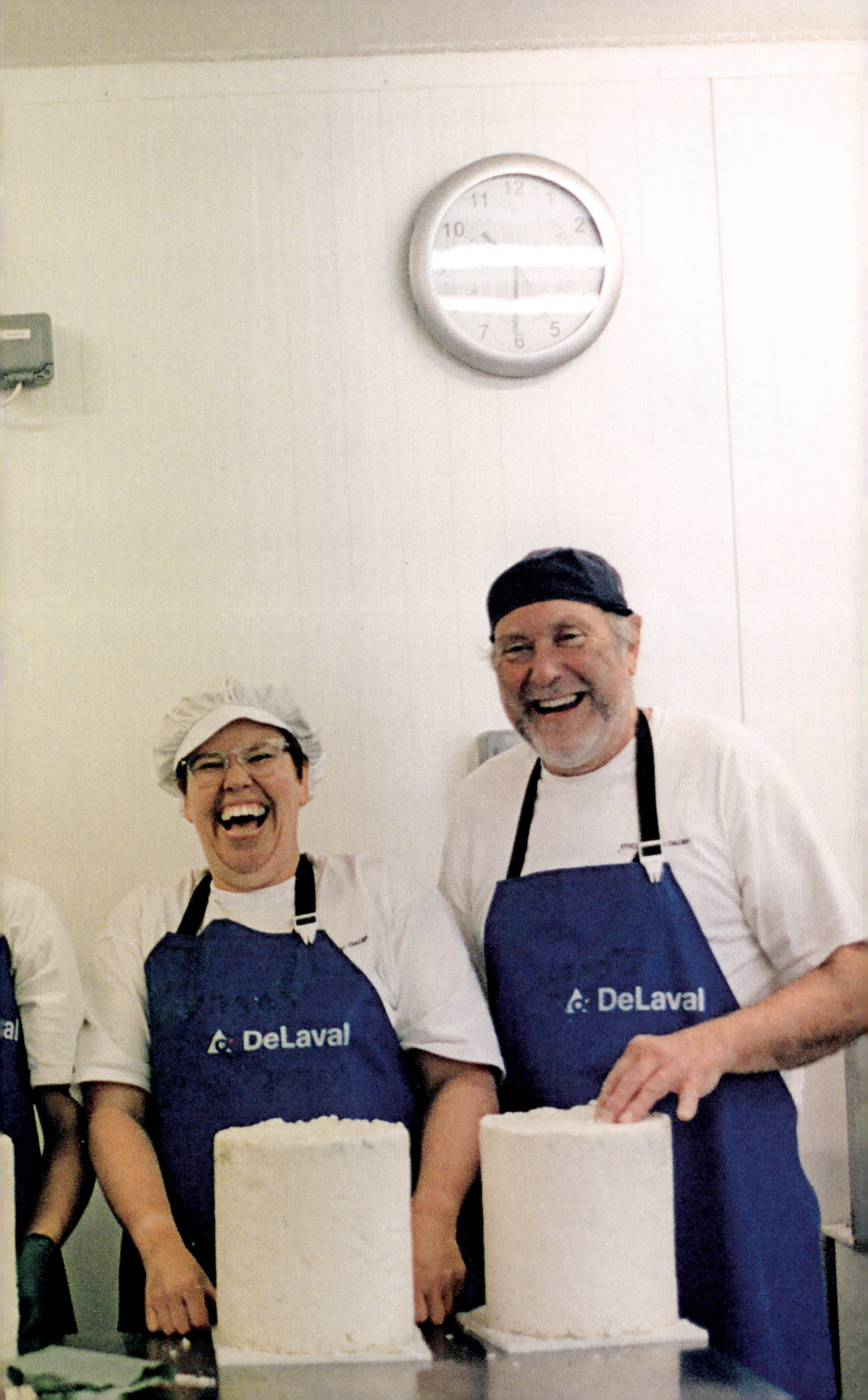
DeLaval
DeLaval

STINKING BISHOP

Left: The Gloucester breed of cow has a distinctive white tail and dark mahogany body. Here is Lillia, who, at twelve years old, is the oldest cow in the herd.

Right: A round of Stinking Bishop, named after a local variety of perry pear and made by Charles Martell in the Forest of Dean.

Charles Martell & Son, Dymock, Gloucestershire

In the ancient Forest of Dean, sandwiched between the Malvern Hills and the Wye Valley, and a stone's throw away from where the Dymock Poets once lived and worked, is Hunts Court, where Stinking Bishop is made. A soft cheese with a washed rind, Stinking Bishop is made using milk from the farm's herd of Gloucester cows and from other local Holstein-Friesian herds. Produced by Charles Martell using an old recipe originally made by Cistercian monks, the name Stinking Bishop is not so much a reference to the smell of the cheese, pungent though it is, but to a variety of pear, which itself is thought to be named after a rogue local farmer, Frederick Bishop, who lived during the 1800s. Perry made from these pears is used to wash the rind. Hunts Court specialises in making cheese and growing pears, with the dairy producing cheese and the adjoining distillery creating pear spirits made from fruit growing in the surrounding orchards. Just as cider and cheese make a good combination, the strong savoury notes of Stinking Bishop go exceedingly well with the sweet, moreish flavours of pear.

The method of making Stinking Bishop is gentle and slow, and at a low temperature and low level of acidification, the milk heated gently using a boiler that runs on wood sustainably sourced from the local area. What gives the cheese its famous aroma and flavour is the perry in which the rind is washed, along with a little extra brine to treat the rind. The monks used this technique as a way of preventing mould from growing on the cheese, and found that it enhanced the flavour in the process. At the early stages of maturation, the young cheeses are wrapped in a band of beechwood for structural integrity. Stinking Bishop is matured for around 4–6 weeks, by which time it is ready to eat.

The other cheeses made at Hunts Court include Hereford Hop, a hard-style cheese made using animal rennet and covered in toasted hops, along with May Hill Green, Double Berkeley, Single Gloucester, Double Gloucester and Slack-ma-Girdle.

Stinking Bishop characteristics

Milk: Pasteurised milk from the farm's herd of Gloucester cows and other local herds of Holstein-Friesian cows

Rennet: Vegetarian

Appearance: Soft light paste with an edible, rusty-red rind wrapped in (inedible) beechwood

Tasting notes: Robust, creamy flavour with sharp, fresh notes of perry. Varies according to the season and length of maturation

Charles Martell standing outside his distillery with a round of Stinking Bishop and an ox yoke, which Charles made for his oxen from a mixture of Wych elm and elm.

Stinking Bishop and Poireau

If you visit Herefordshire and certain parts of Gloucestershire in the autumn, you will notice that the air is laced with the sweet smell of apples from trees lining the roads in their thousands – nay, millions, probably. I visited Charles's home near Dymock in late spring when the magnolias were in bloom and the new leaves of the hawthorn were a fresh green.

Hunts Court – the farmstead, the cheesemaking rooms and the distillery – celebrates everything that is to do with rural Gloucestershire, from farmhouse foods, such as small-batch cheeses, and rare varieties of pear, to traditional carriages and farming memorabilia. Charles has devoted much of his life to saving and supporting Gloucestershire's rural heritage, having written books on local varieties of apple and perry pear and helping to save the traditional Gloucester breed of cow by setting up the Gloucester Cattle Society.

This recipe is not so much a recipe but a celebration of Gloucestershire, pairing Stinking Bishop with the sweet hit of Poireau, the pear spirit that Charles also produces, using pears grown in his orchards. The distilled spirit is 'cut' with fresh pear juice and aged for a year. The flavour is similar to a sweet sherry – a complex, fruity drink.

SERVES 2–3

1 x 500g round of Stinking Bishop
100–150ml Poireau

Cut the cheese into slices and enjoy with a glass of Poireau, allowing 50ml per person.

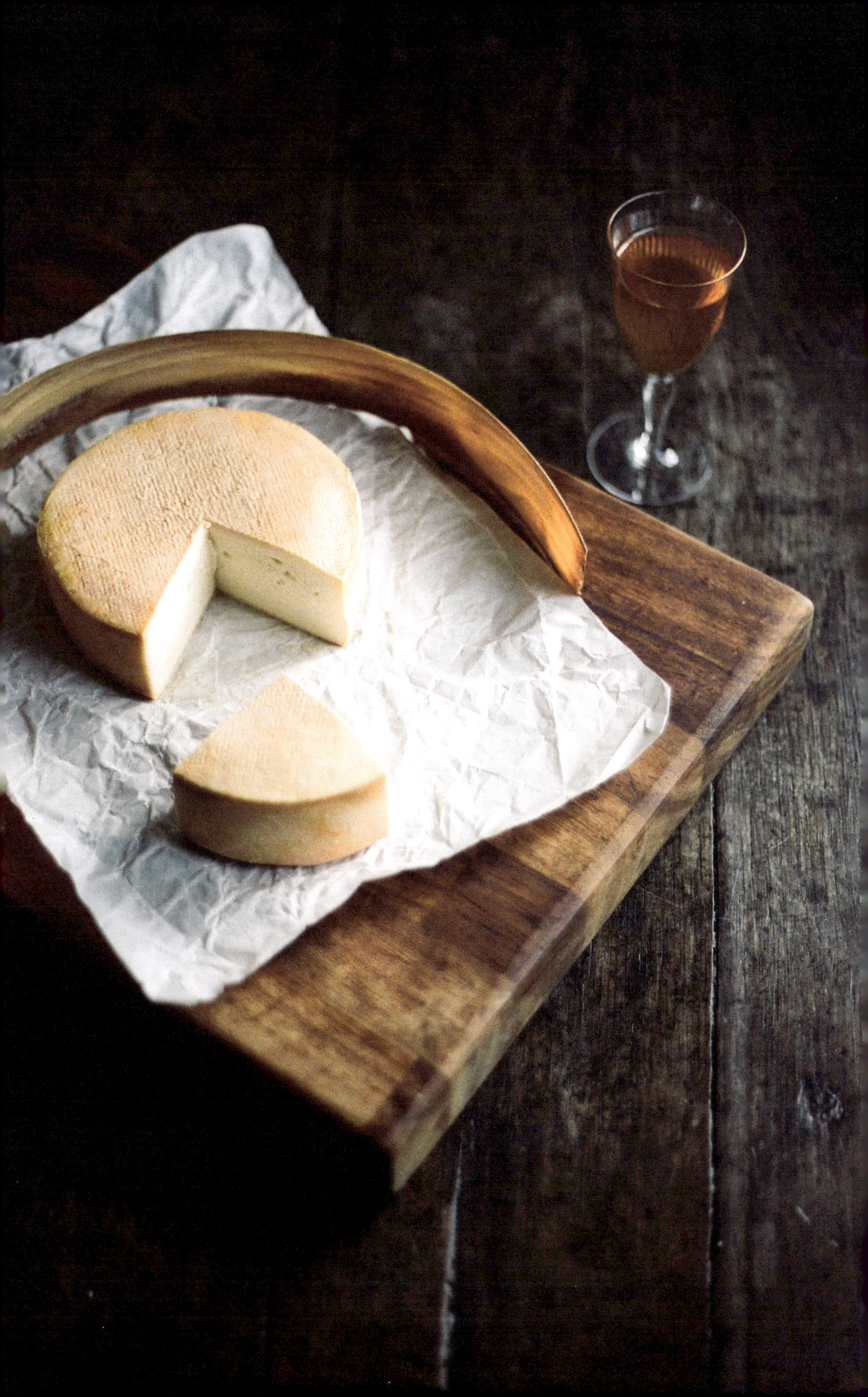

STONEBECK

Left to right: A young Stonebeck just taken out of its mould and soon to be wrapped in cheesecloth. The young cheeses will then be placed in the maturing rooms and aged for a minimum of six weeks.

Cameron Abery is a cheesemaker at Stonebeck who learned his trade at Neal's Yard Dairy and Mons Cheesemongers. Here he checks young Stonebeck cheeses.

Each wheel of Stonebeck is wrapped in cloth and hand-sewn by Sally Hattan. Sally got the idea from talking to a local lady called Mrs Mable Peacock, aged 101, who used to make farmhouse Wensleydale in the twentieth century.

Deep within the maturing room at Low Riggs Farm, you can see Sally's handy needlework on a mature Stonebeck. Binding the cheese in cloth is an unusual feature of the way the Hattans make their cheese.

Low Riggs Farm, Nidderdale, North Yorkshire

Nestled within the stunning Nidderdale landscape of North Yorkshire, high up in the vast unpopulated moorlands, is the isolated farmstead of Low Riggs, home to Andrew and Sally Hattan, who make Stonebeck. The 460-acre farm lies on the banks of the Stean Beck (local dialect for 'Stone Beck'), a tributary of the River Nidd, at around 890 feet above sea level, with some of its surrounding farmland rising to 2,000 feet. The farm is mostly made up of rough grazing, including 100 acres of heather moorland, 75 acres of pastureland and 50 acres of hay meadows. The land is a haven for birds – ground-nesting types, such as the redshank, lapwing, curlew, golden plover, snipe and woodcock, and other rare species including the wheatear and pied flycatcher.

Andrew and Sally are true stewards of the land, farming holistically and focusing on the quality of husbandry, which will be expressed in the cows' milk, and restoring the original wildflower meadows, an area of 35 acres in total, in the hope of encouraging greater biodiversity.

Andrew Hattan with Dairymaid, a crossbreed of Shorthorn and Northern Dairy Shorthorn. Andrew is slowly but surely reviving the Northern Dairy Shorthorn from near extinction.

Named after the local parish, which itself is named after the local stream, Stonebeck is made using raw milk from the farm's rare-breed collection of Northern Dairy Shorthorns, native to Yorkshire and the surrounding counties. The Northern Dairy Shorthorn is a hardy, small animal with a thick woolly coat – perfect for grazing on the steep terrain. The cows are milked once a day and graze for much of the year outside on species-rich pasture. During the winter months, the cows are fed on hay made from grass grown in the summer. The vast majority of the feed is grown on the farm, a necessity, you might say, as delivering to the farm is not easy owing to its impressive isolation down a three-mile track from the main road and inaccessible to anything but a 4x4.

Described as a raw-milk farmhouse Wensleydale, Stonebeck has its own distinctive character. The cheese is based on a marriage of three Wensleydale recipes: the first from the 1930s by Kit Calvert, who helped save the Wensleydale Creamery; the second based on an illustrated book from 1997 by Mary Hartley and Joan Ingilby called *Making Cheese and Butter*; and the third from a book called *Factory and Farming Cheese-making*, published in 1938. Helped by local cheesemonger Andy Swinscoe at The Courtyard Dairy and Bronwen Percival of Neal's Yard Dairy, Andrew and Sally now make a truly unique cheese. As with so many artisan cheeses, what makes Stonebeck so wonderfully distinctive is determined by everything that goes into producing it – from the local climate and grazing seasons to the working day of the farmer – in a tradition that goes back to how cheese was made a hundred years ago.

Made only around mid-April to mid-October, when the grass is at its best and the cattle can happily graze outside, Andrew starts the cheesemaking process in the early hours of the morning. Making the cheese for three days in every week, Andrew tends to it between his other jobs on the farm. The length of time Andrew spends out on the farm reflects the length of each stage of the cheesemaking, a process that is thus inextricably interwoven with the daily routine of the farm and the Hattans' way of life – an increasingly rare phenomenon these days. Taking inspiration from historical records and interviews with local centenarians who made Wensleydale way back in the early twentieth century, the Hattan family carries out the age-old tradition of hand-sewing the cheesecloth on to the young cheeses before they are aged. Stonebeck can be eaten fresh from six weeks, or matured up to three months, when the cheese develops a richer, more complex flavour.

Stonebeck characteristics
Milk: Raw milk from the farm's collection of Northern Dairy Shorthorn cows
Rennet: Animal
Appearance: Crumbly, pale yellow paste with a heavily mottled edible rind
Tasting notes: Rich buttery flavour with bright zingy notes that lasts long in the mouth. Varies according to the season and length of maturation

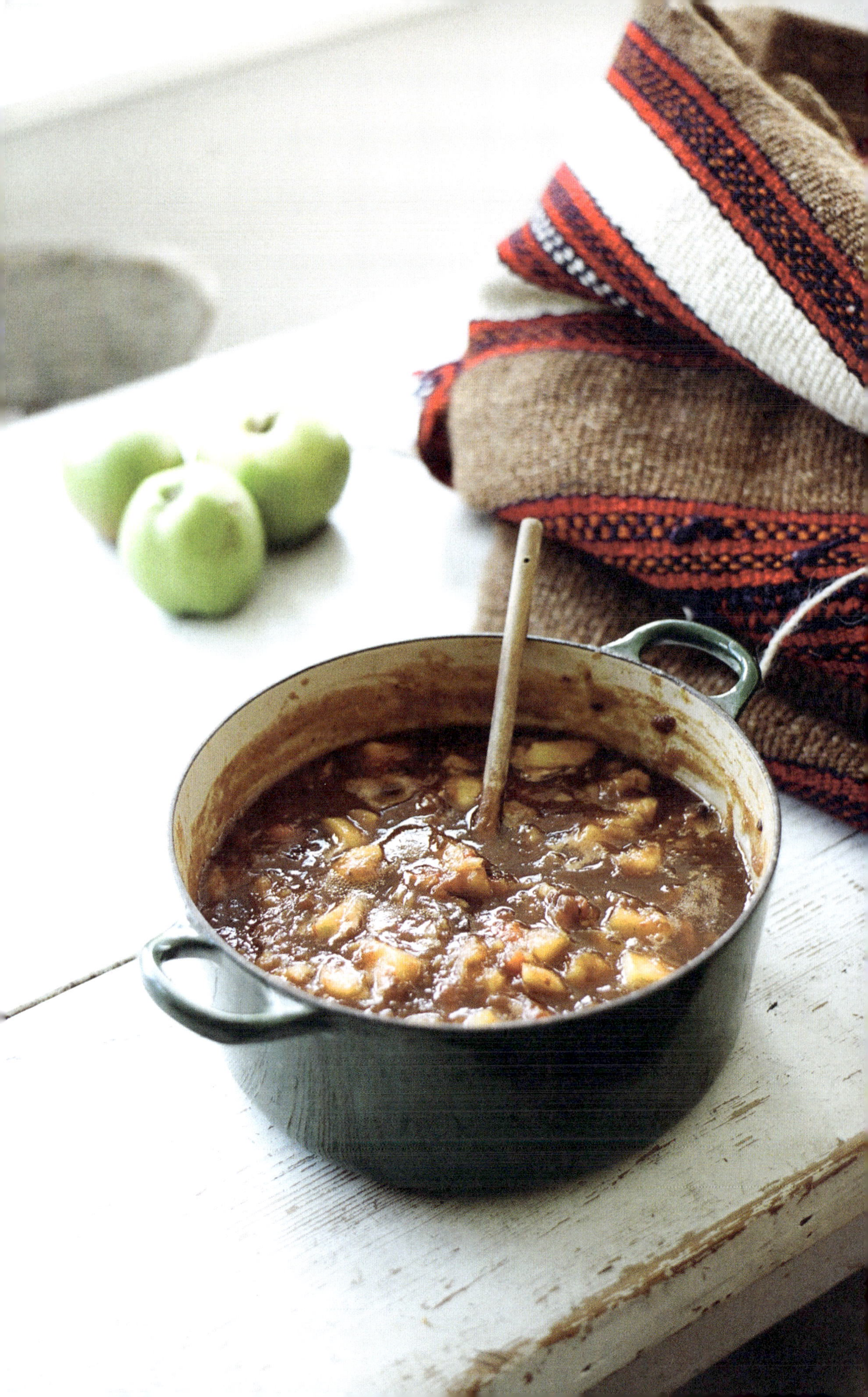

The Hattan family chutney with Stonebeck

In order to make my visits to cheesemakers more manageable, I divided them into specific regions, visiting a cluster of cheesemakers in the South West, Scotland, Wales, the East of England, and so on. Perhaps because it was high summer, when the sky was blue and there were birds in every direction singing their hearts out, my visit to Yorkshire, and to Stonebeck in particular, was one of the most memorable.

The day Lilly and I visited the Hattan family at Low Riggs Farm was unbelievably beautiful: the weather was roasting hot, swifts were screaming overhead and the scenery was 'postcard perfect', with wildflower meadows bordered by miles of dry stonewalls climbing the steep sides of the valley. Andrew and his daughter, Rachael, showed Lilly and I around the farm, meeting their lovely collection – not herd! – of Northern Dairy Shorthorns. Most striking was that the farm not only makes outstanding cheese and is saving a rare species of cow, but it is also a paradise for birds. I saw my first wheatear and pied flycatcher, alongside plenty of curlews, lapwings and oystercatchers that were calling among the long grasses.

Lunch came around quickly, and Andrew and Rachael served up a veritable banquet of cheese, crackers, tomatoes, salads and different types of bread – a ploughman's lunch on a grand scale. The meal included a delicious chutney that was made to an old family recipe, and was so yummy, in fact, that I had to ask whether I could share the recipe. And generous as they are, here it is!

MAKES 4–5 X 300G JARS

1kg cooking apples, peeled, cored and roughly sliced
450g tomatoes
½ tsp mustard
½ tbsp sea salt
¼ tsp freshly ground black pepper
½ tsp curry powder
½ tsp ground ginger
300ml cider vinegar
450g pitted dates, chopped
225g onions, peeled and finely sliced
225g soft brown sugar
Stonebeck, oatcakes and butter, to serve

In a large saucepan on a medium heat, lightly cook the apples for 10–15 minutes until soft, then set aside.

Meanwhile, skin the tomatoes by placing in a bowl of boiling water, then transferring after 30 seconds to a bowl of iced water and leaving for 5 minutes before peeling off and discarding the skins. Chop up the tomato flesh.

In a small bowl, combine the mustard, salt, pepper and spices with a light splosh of the vinegar and set aside.

Place the tomatoes, dates and onions in a separate large saucepan on a medium heat, add the sugar, vinegar and spice mixture and bring to the boil. Add the softened apples and bring back up to the boil, then reduce the heat and simmer for 30–45 minutes until thickened and glossy. Divide the hot chutney between sterilised screw-top jars (see note below), then seal with the lids and leave to cool before storing in a dark place for 3–4 months. Once opened, store in the fridge for up to 2 weeks.

Serve the chutney with traditional Yorkshire oatcakes spread with plenty of butter and topped with large slivers of Stonebeck. A true Yorkshire lunch!

STERILISING JARS AND LIDS
Wash in warm soapy water and place upside down on a parchment-lined baking tray to dry in the oven for 20 minutes on a low heat.

WESTCOMBE CHEDDAR

From left to right: The team of cheesemakers at Westcombe Dairy in the midst of milling the 'Cheddared' curds to make their Westcombe Cheddar. Robert Howard, on the left at the back, feeds the mill with layers of curd.

A close-up of the 'Cheddared' curds at Westcombe Dairy, which have been left a while to gradually increase in acidity.

The stacked wheels of Westcombe Cheddar in the concrete maturing cave at Westcombe Dairy. These cheeses are ready to be delivered to wholesalers across the British Isles.

Westcombe Dairy, Lower Westcombe Farm, Somerset

Deep within the undulating hills of Batcombe Vale is Westcombe Dairy, which spans a number of farms – Westcombe Hill Farm, Lower Westcombe Farm, Milton Farm and Manor Farm – that all back on to each other in the valley. Westcombe Dairy makes Westcombe Cheddar, Duckett's Aged Caerphilly and ricotta using raw milk from their mixed herd of Holstein-Friesian, Ayrshire and British Shorthorn cows. Tom Calver co-runs Westcombe Dairy with his father, Richard, and works alongside his team of cheesemakers, headed by Robert Howard, and herdsmen Raymond Stone and Nicholas Millard.

The ethos at Westcombe Dairy, specifically in its farming set-up, is to gain a proper understanding of regenerative farming and how it would affect the flavour and texture of the finished cheese. Over the coming years, the Westcombe Dairy farming team are moving more towards employing methods that aim to mimic nature, such as planting diverse grazing leys with numerous species of grass, legumes and herbs to improve soil health and cattle nutrition, while also using techniques such as controlled paddock grazing that are better for both the land, allowing it to recover over longer periods, and the health of the grazing animals. What they are hoping to do over time is to revive the soil and its seed bank to be as close as possible to its natural state and for that quality to be reflected in the cows' milk. In terms of the cheese, the Westcombe team hope that these more regenerative farming methods will reduce the need for chemical intervention and create a healthier environment that will produce a better, more complex cheese.

Nicholas and Raymond have noticed how many different wildflowers have already reappeared in the pasture following their change in farming practice. The farms under the Westcombe Dairy umbrella also grow heritage grains for Tom's other venture, Landrace Bakery in Bath, and make charcuterie on site using local pasture-fed pigs.

Westcombe Cheddar is the dairy's most renowned cheese, its distinctive character determined by how the curds are treated. Once the whey is expelled, the curds are formed into slabs, each wrapped in a scrim cloth and stacked to expel more moisture and stretch the proteins out – a process known as 'Cheddaring'. The curds, at this point, have the stringy texture of mozzarella. They are then milled and salted to hasten the process of acidification before being ladled into moulds and pressed. On the third day, the young cheeses are covered in muslin and coated in lard before being transferred to the maturing rooms. Each batch of Westcombe Cheddar is different, and to assess when a particular batch will be ready, the cheesemaker tastes it quarterly. The cheese is ready to eat at 11–18 months, even up to two years for a more mature cheese. The cheesemakers at Westcombe Dairy like to reproduce historical recipes for small batches of Cheddar, such as a recipe by Dora Saker from 1917 and one by Joseph Harding from 1860.

During the production of Westcombe Cheddar and Duckett's Aged Caerphilly, another cheese made by the dairy, the surplus whey is placed in vats to make ricotta. The whey, which at this stage is around 30–40°C, is quickly heated to around 90°C – hence the name 'ricotta', meaning 'recooked' in Italian. This swift rise in temperature flocculates the whey, helping any proteins and fats that remain from the initial cheesemaking to rise to top of the vat. These hot proteins and fats are then left for 10 minutes or so to firm up a little before being ladled into basket moulds and placed in the fridge. The following day the ricotta is sold fresh. It is Jan Orenic at Westcombe Dairy who normally makes the ricotta cheese.

Westcombe Cheddar characteristics
Milk: Raw milk from the farm's mixed herd of Holstein-Friesian, Ayrshire and British Shorthorn cows
Rennet: Animal
Appearance: A warm yellow paste with an inedible, clothbound, brown-grey rind with touches of silvery mould
Tasting notes: Deep savoury flavour with grassy tones, and a hint of the natural sweetness of butterscotch towards the end. Varies according to the season and length of maturation

Tom Calver co-runs Westcombe Dairy with his father, Richard. Tom's back garden opens on to the farm and dairy, where the family's chickens can be seen roaming freely.

Westcombe Ricotta cheesecake

It was early in the year when we travelled down to see Tom and Mel Calver and Tom's father Richard, along with the cheesemakers and the farming team at Westcombe Dairy. I was with my mother Serena, who was house hunting at the time. Whizzing along the high-hedged country lanes in my mother's Fiat 500, we passed some of the most stunning villages and parishes on the way to Lower Westcombe Farm, including Bruton and Pitcombe – 'combe' meaning a steep, narrow valley, of which there are many in the area.

We also made the most of what Westcombe Dairy had to offer. Cheeses wedges, charcuterie sausages (also made at the dairy) and a bottle of local cider were all bought from the charming little shop on site – which I would urge anyone to visit. Add beers from the Wild Beer Company Brewery, next to the dairy, and you have the makings of a proper party.

For this recipe, I thought I'd use Westcombe Ricotta, which is so soft and smooth, making it ideal for a fluffy cheesecake that isn't too heavy and just perfect for a light pudding. The ricotta is also delicious served warm with crackers and a fresh salad, which Tom and Mel generously provided for us on our visit, using salad leaves straight from Mel's kitchen garden.

SERVES 8

butter, for greasing
6 amaretti biscuits
750g Westcombe Ricotta (at room temperature)
150g caster sugar
grated zest of 4 unwaxed lemons
30g white spelt flour
2 tsp vanilla extract
pinch of sea salt
6 large eggs

Preheat the oven to 180°C/350F/gas mark 4 and butter a 20cm-diameter springform cake tin.

Start by blending the amaretti biscuits into a fine crumb in a food processor, or by crushing them with a rolling pin, then tip the crumbs into the buttered tin and give it a shake so that they coat the sides and base of the tin in a thin layer.

Place the ricotta and half the sugar in a large bowl with the lemon zest, flour, vanilla extract and salt, and mix until well combined.

Separate the eggs, adding the yolks to the ricotta mix and placing the whites in a separate, clean bowl. Using a handheld electric whisk, beat the egg whites on a slow speed for a minute, then increase the speed while gradually adding the rest of the sugar. Continue beating until the egg whites form soft peaks.

With a large metal spoon, gently fold the egg whites into the ricotta mix. Pour the whole mixture into the crumb-dusted cake tin and bake for 50 minutes in the oven, until the cheesecake is firm to the touch and the top is lightly golden. Remove the cheesecake from the oven and place on a wire rack to cool completely before carefully removing the tin and transferring the cheesecake to a serving plate. Chill in the fridge for a few hours before serving.

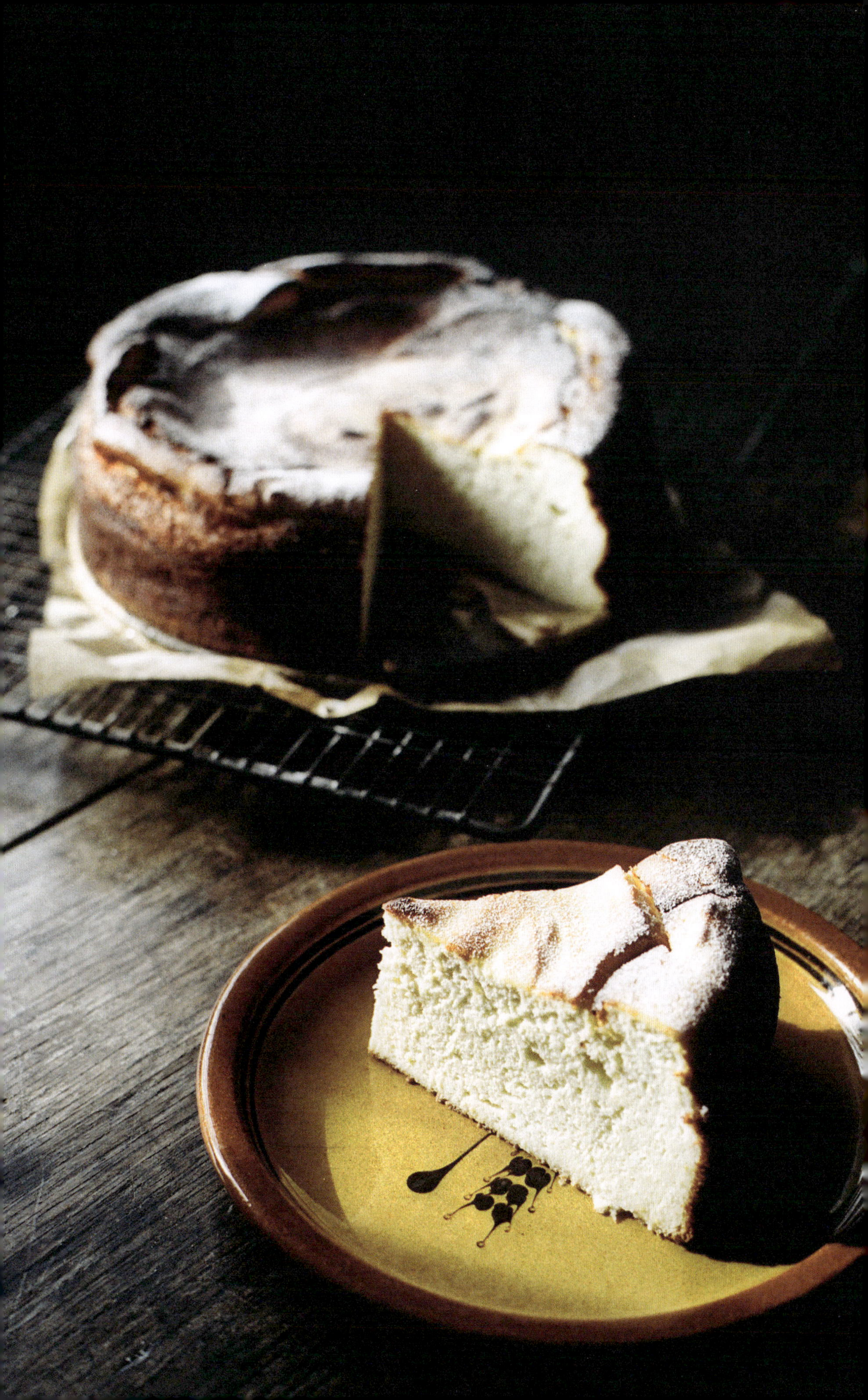

WITHERIDGE

Left: A beautiful round of Witheridge that has been maturing for about six months, during which time it will have been wrapped in fresh hay from the farm.

Right: Rose and Sylvia look on as Gideon, the farm's herdsman, herds his cattle across a series of country lanes. Gideon knows the name and individual character of each cow.

Nettlebed Creamery, Henley-on-Thames, Oxfordshire

At the southern end of the Chilterns in Oxfordshire, an area famed for its far-ranging hills dotted with beech woods and criss-crossed by chalk streams, lies Nettlebed Creamery, where Witheridge is made. Named after a local hill, which the cheesemakers can see from the creamery, Witheridge is a semi-hard cheese made using organic, unhomogenised milk from the nearby farm's mixed herd of Swedish Red, Montbéliarde and Holstein-Friesian cows.

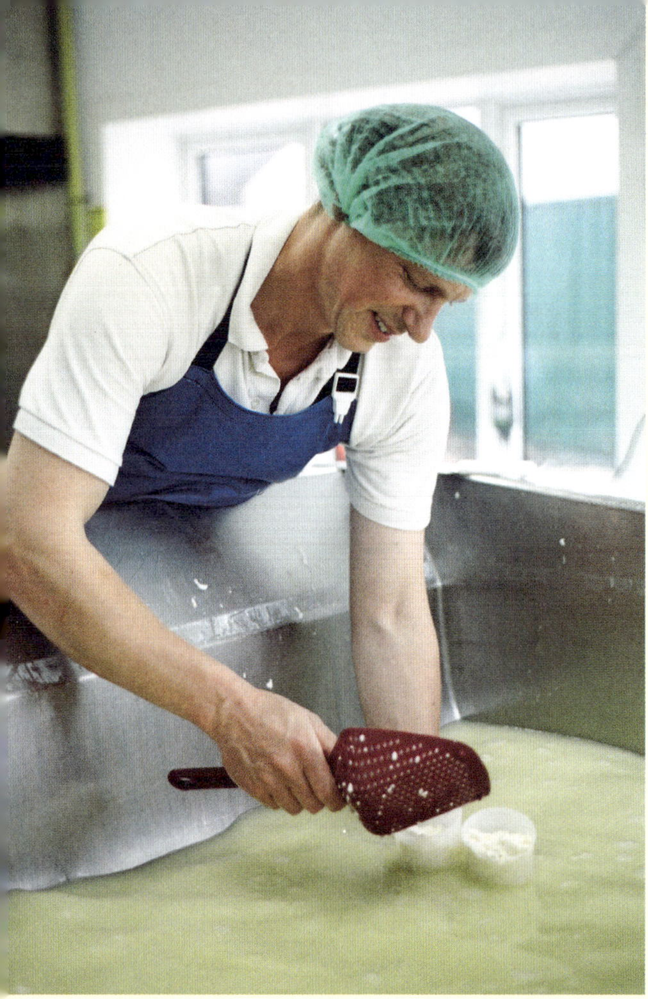

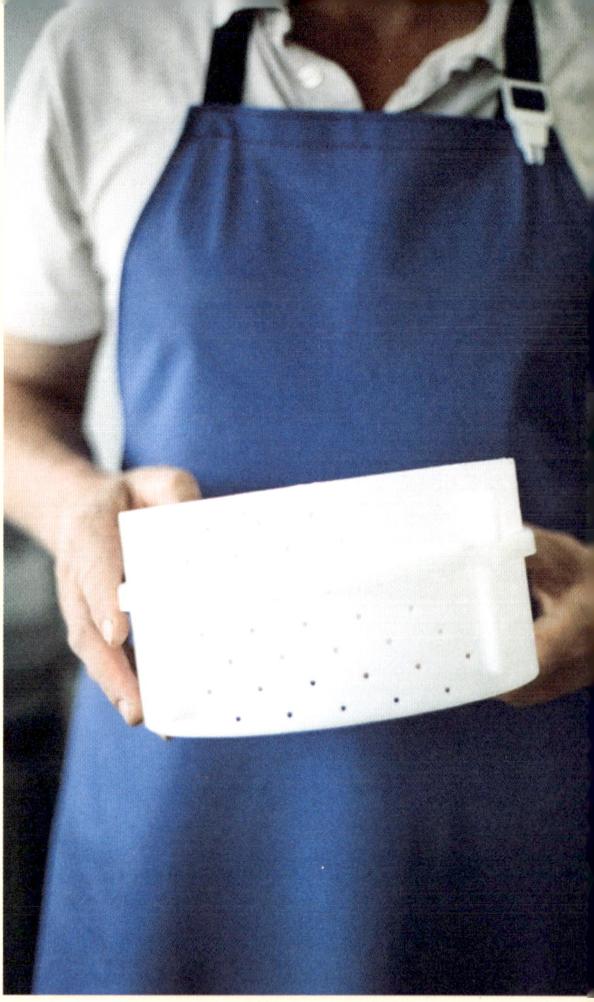

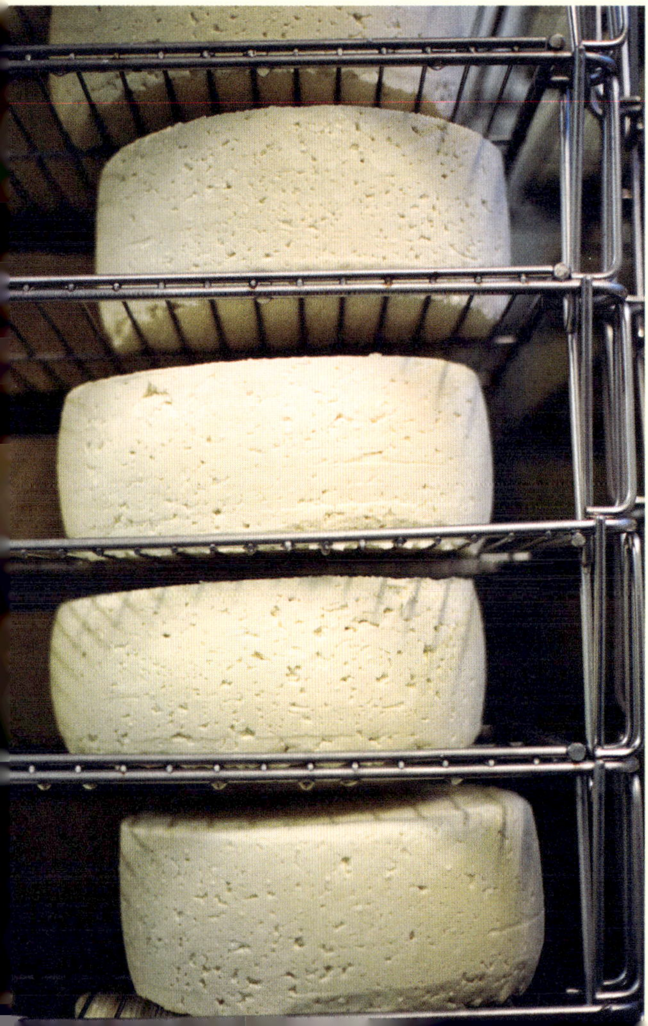

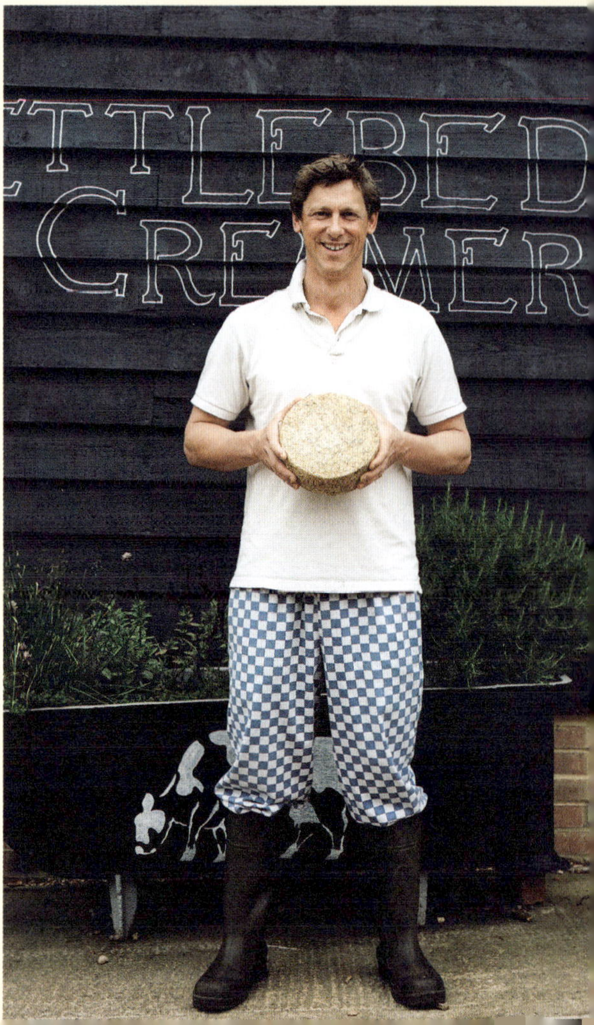

Founded by Rose Grimond, Nettlebed Creamery is less than two miles from Merrimoles Farm, where it sources its milk from the mixed herd of cows that graze in the surrounding fields. Merrimoles Farm, which has been in Rose's family since 1903, became organic in 2001. In 2015, Rose began to make cheese, starting with Bix, a soft variety, before moving on to Highmoor, a semi-soft, washed-rind cheese.

Patrick Heathcoat Amory is the head cheesemaker at Nettlebed Creamery, and he and Rose work closely with Philip Day, the manager at Merrimoles Farm. As milk is a natural product that changes from day to day, a close relationship with the farm manager and herdsman is vital for knowing exactly how the animals are faring and if there are any significant changes in the farming system that may affect the quality of the milk. Being organic, there are huge benefits to both the ecosystem and animal welfare. The farm is on an organic crop rotation, so can feed the livestock with a nutrient-rich diet while simultaneously improving soil fertility. The system also encourages huge numbers of insects to pollinate the hedgerows and wildflowers. The farm has a few acres of permanent pasture.

The making of Witheridge is what's known as a 'hot fast make', using a thermophilic starter culture, based on bacteria that work better at hotter temperatures. After the starter culture and rennet have been added to the milk, the curd is set and cut quite finely. The curds are then scalded to around 42°C and ladled into moulds to drain. From milk to mould, it usually takes around six hours, give or take. The young cheeses are then placed in brine baths to soak for twenty-four hours, during which time they slowly cool and become salted from the brine.

The next day, the cheeses are taken to the maturing rooms and aged for at least six months. The maturing cheeses are wrapped in hay, adding flavour and helping to preserve them. Before each 2.5kg wheel of Witheridge is ready to sell, the cheesemakers strip off the original hay and wrap the cheese in fresh hay.

Witheridge characteristics

Milk: Organic, unhomogenised milk from the nearby farm's mixed herd of Swedish Red, Montbéliarde and Holstein-Friesian cows

Rennet: Animal

Appearance: Soft yellow, smooth and firm paste with a hay-aged edible rind

Tasting notes: Complex, savoury flavour with grassy notes from the hay. Varies according to the season and length of maturation

Clockwise from top left: Patrick and the cheesemaking team fill moulds with soft curds from a vat of whey. The curds will then be left in the moulds to naturally compress into young cheeses.

An essential part of making Witheridge is the mould, which keeps the curds in place so that they compress naturally while allowing whey to drain.

Patrick Heathcoat Amory is the head cheesemaker at Nettlebed Creamery in Oxfordshire. Patrick has also been a consultant environmental scientist for fourteen years.

A few young Witheridge cheeses ageing in the maturing rooms at Nettlebed Creamery. Each batch is small and changes with the seasons.

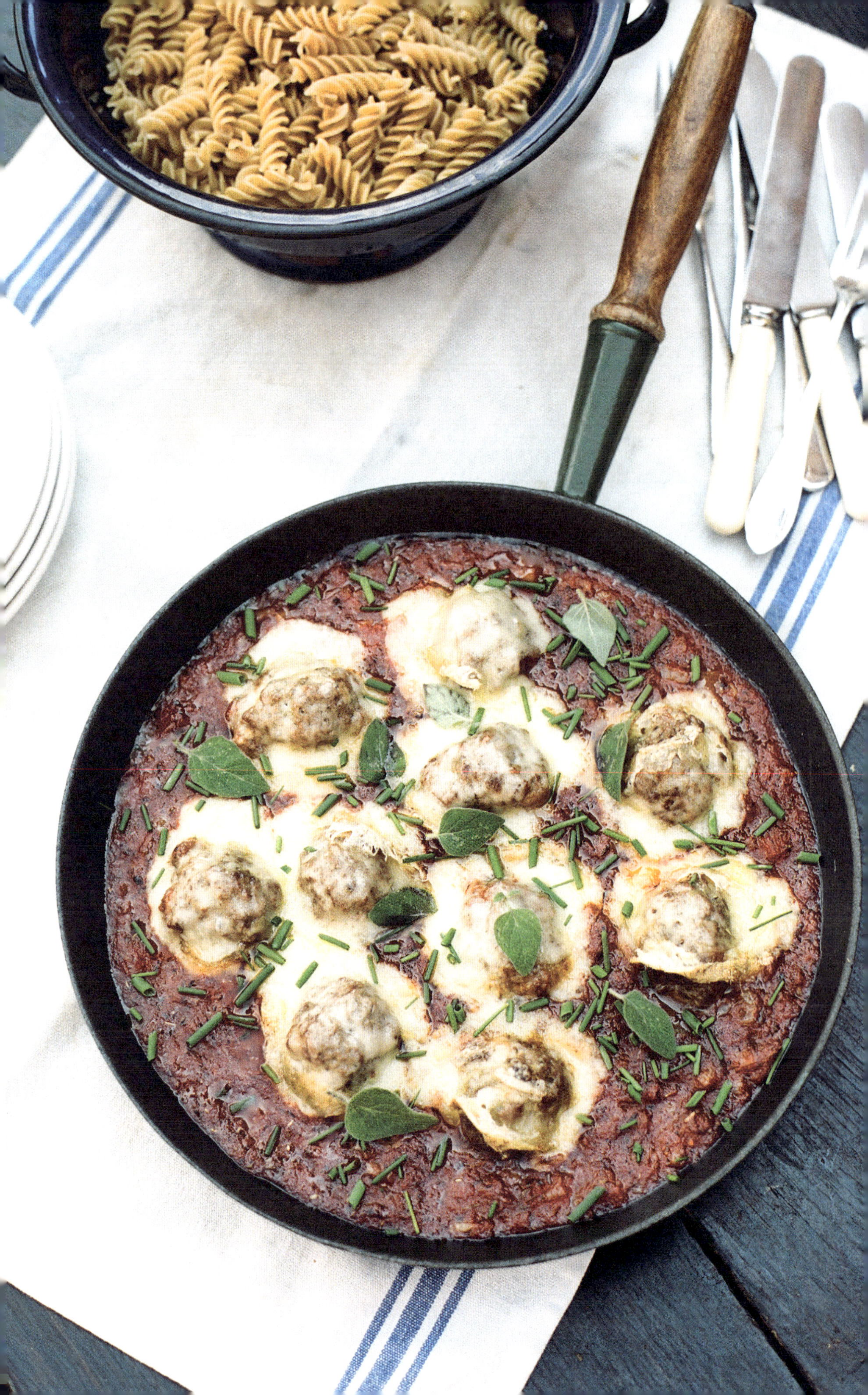

Meatballs in tomato sauce with melted Witheridge

I've said it before and I'll say it again, but artisan cheesemakers certainly know how to find the best spot – always, it seems, with a splendid view! Though it's perhaps no surprise that the view should be so good, especially in the case of farmhouse cheesemakers, where the dairy overlooks the surrounding fields with the cows peacefully grazing. The dairy at Nettlebed Creamery has perhaps one of the best views, with huge windows looking out on the rolling hills of the southern Chilterns.

My visit to the dairy and farm was on a particularly muggy summer's day, but beautiful nonetheless. The beech trees were in full leaf and the blackbirds, dry again after the recent rainfall, were singing happily. At the dairy, Patrick, the head cheesemaker, took me around the main cheesemaking room and the dairy's series of maturing rooms that were full of Bix, Highmoor and Witheridge, plus rows of cartons of organic milk and kefir.

The farm is only a short drive or long walk from the dairy, through avenues of tall trees and dense mixed hedges. At the farm I met Rose, who, along with her delightful daughter, Sylvia, gave me a tour of the farm and milking parlour, where we met Philip, the farm manager, and Gideon, the herdsman, who was in the process of herding the cows from the parlour to the fields. We walked with Gideon and the cows, crossing a number of country lanes to reach the fields and discussing the general condition and grazing habits of the herd, Gideon knowing the name and individual character of each cow.

This recipe was something I thought would celebrate Witheridge and pasture-fed beef. The meat I used was certified 'Pasture for Life' (see pages 30 and 196) and bought from a farm local to Nettlebed Creamery. With the creamery's Witheridge melted on top, it was super.

MAKES 8–9 MEATBALLS / SERVES 2–4

500g minced beef (see overleaf)
2 tsp dried oregano or chilli flakes (optional)
1 tbsp olive oil
250g Witheridge, sliced

First make the tomato sauce. In a large saucepan, on a medium heat, fry the onions in the olive oil for 5–7 minutes until soft, then add the garlic and stir-fry for a further minute or two. Now add the tinned tomatoes (I used a tin of cherry tomatoes as they have a sweet, dense flavour), passata, oregano, sugar, two good pinches of sea salt and a few turns of black pepper. Bring to the boil, then reduce to a simmer and cook for 10 minutes until the mixture starts to thicken slightly, then reduce the heat to keep the sauce warm while you make the meatballs.

Preheat the grill to 150°C/300°F.

Ingredients and method continued overleaf

handful of fresh chives, wild marjoram (or oregano) and thyme leaves, to serve

TOMATO SAUCE
2 medium onions, peeled and finely chopped
1 tbsp olive oil
3 large garlic cloves, peeled and finely chopped
1 x 400g tin of cherry tomatoes
300ml passata
1 tbsp dried oregano
2 tsp caster sugar
sea salt and freshly ground black pepper

Place the minced beef in a large bowl along with two good pinches of sea salt and a few turns of black pepper and mix thoroughly with your hands. (You may think I've used an excessive amount of salt, but the meat really does need it!) If you want to, you could add some dried oregano or chilli flakes for a little heat. Break off pieces of the meatball mixture and form them into 8–9 walnut-sized meatballs.

Pour the olive oil into an ovenproof frying pan over a medium heat and gently fry the meatballs until they are nicely browned on all sides. Remove the meatballs from the pan and pour in the tomato sauce, then return the meatballs to the pan, nestling them down on top of the sauce (like eggs in a nest), and top the meatballs with slices of Witheridge. Pop the frying pan under the grill for 10 minutes or longer until the cheese is gooey and has melted over the meatballs and the tomato sauce is hot. To finish, roughly tear the chives and marjoram and sprinkle on top with the thyme leaves.

These meatballs are fantastic served with fresh crusty bread or pasta.

PASTURE FOR LIFE
Look out for meat certified 'Pasture for Life' by the Pasture-Fed Livestock Association, which supports farmers who work towards the highest food and farming standards, using regenerative farming methods to produce 100 per cent grass-fed meat.

The lovely hay pattern on slices of Witheridge, ready to be wrapped in paper and sent out to cheesemongers across the UK.

WREKIN WHITE

Left: A slice of Wrekin White on a marble slab, showing the characteristic ivory-white paste, the breakdown of the rind and a series of eyelets or small holes.

Right: Martin holding a Wrekin White in the maturing rooms, where he turns the cheeses every couple of days and brushes them with local rapeseed oil.

Moyden's Handmade Cheese, Market Drayton, Shropshire

In the vast rural county of Shropshire just outside the town of Market Drayton is the small village of Wistanswick, where Wrekin White is produced by cheesemakers Martin and Beth Moyden. Martin and Beth's cheeses typify everything about Shropshire, from cheeses named after Salopian events like the Great Fire of Newport in 1665 to creating a specific 'Shropshire mould' to capture the essence of their Shropshire location and express it in their cheeses. Wrekin White, named after the Wrekin, a well-known hill rising steeply above the Shropshire Plain, is a hard-style cheese made using raw milk from a local mixed herd of British Friesian, Ayrshire, Montbéliarde and Danish Red cows.

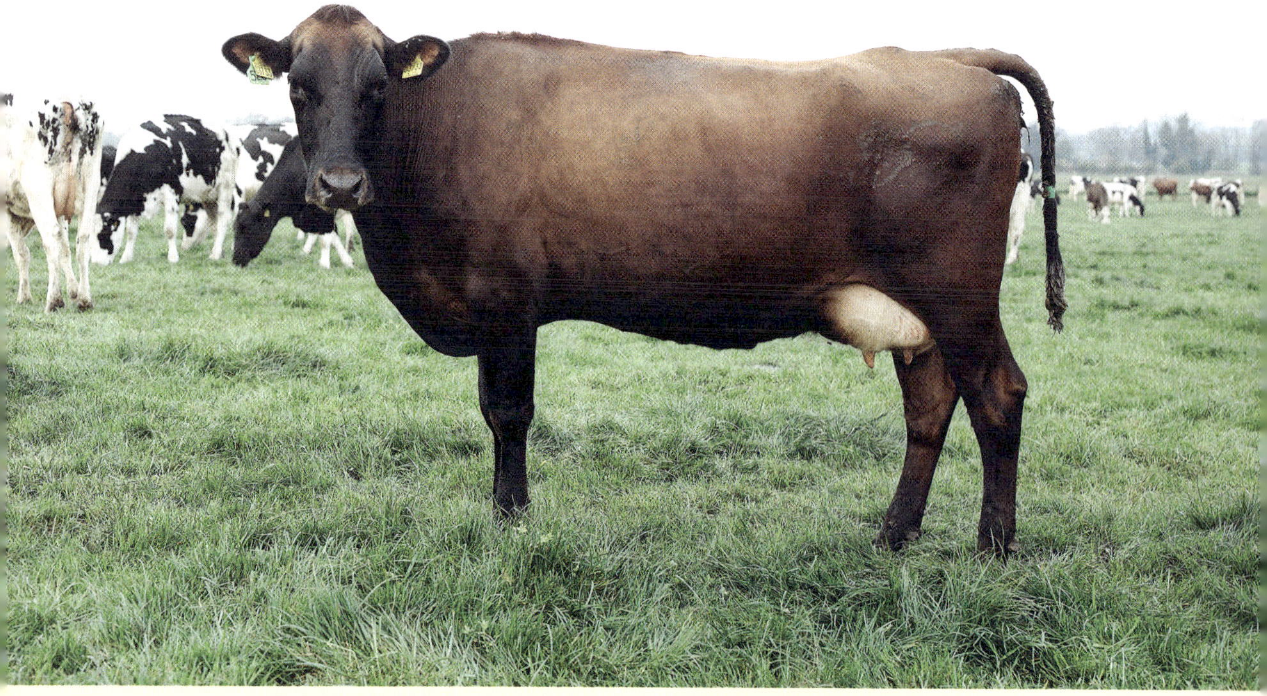
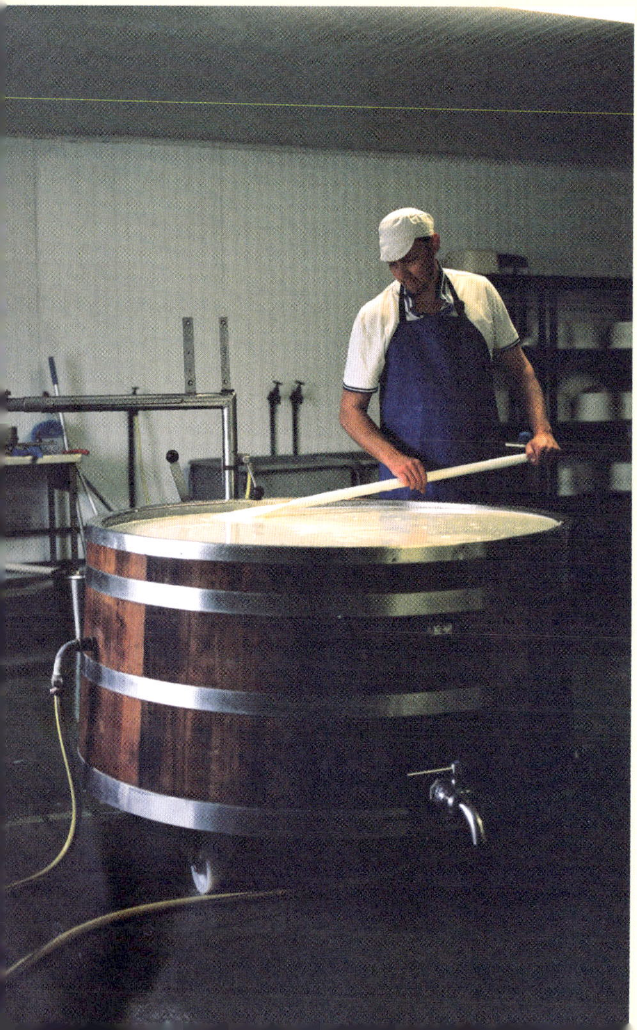
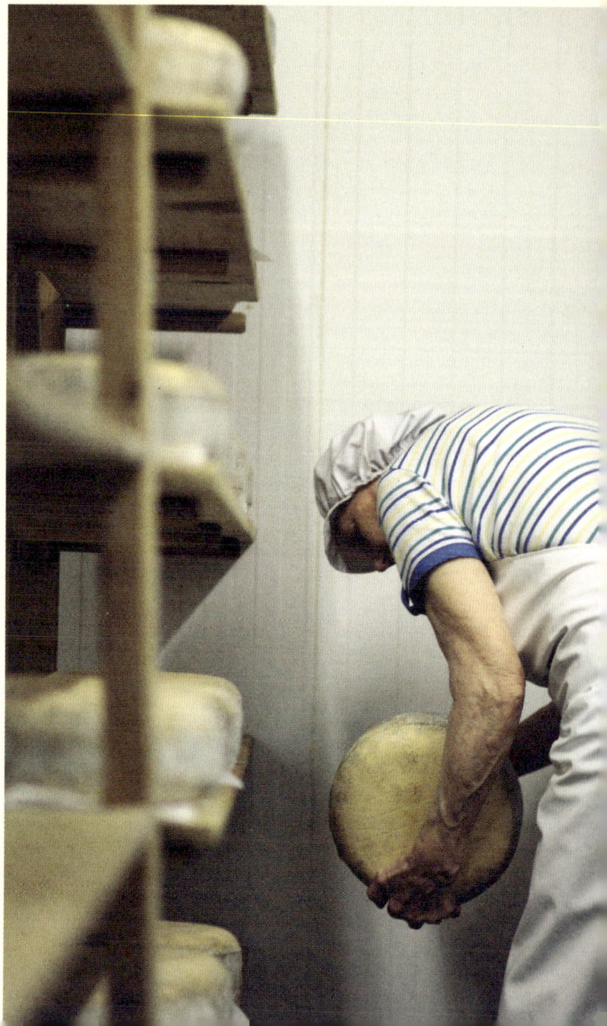

Brought up on a small dairy farm just down the road from the current creamery, Martin became interested in milk and cheese from an early age. Inspired by his grandparents' tales of how they would deliver their milk locally every day, telling their customers exactly how each cow was faring, Martin wanted to do the same with farmhouse cheese, producing cheese made with milk whose quality and provenance he knew intimately and could assess daily. Wrekin White was the first cheese he produced.

Wrekin White is made using raw milk collected every day from the local farm, Hawkstone Abbey Farm (see also 'Appleby's Cheshire', page 54), where the cows graze on diverse herbal leys that include chicory, plantain and three types of clover. Wrekin White is brushed with local rapeseed oil during the maturing phase – similar to the maturing of Manchego, which is brushed with olive oil. This brushing technique, performed every week for 4–6 weeks, slowly softens the rind and helps the cheese to develop its distinctive flavour and aroma. Depending on the season and conditions of the make, the cheeses are matured for 2–3 months, even up to six months for a particularly strong, hard Wrekin White.

The Moyden family also make Caer Caradoc, Newport, Newport 1665, Wrekin Blue, Shrewsbury Fretta and Ironbridge.

Wrekin White characteristics

Milk: Raw milk from a local mixed herd of British Friesian, Ayrshire, Montbéliarde and Danish Red cows

Rennet: Vegetarian

Appearance: Slightly soft, pale paste dotted with eyelets (small holes) and an edible rind

Tasting notes: Light creamy, nutty flavour with hints of meat and milk and fruity aromas. Varies according to the season and length of maturation

Top: The cows' milk that Martin uses is from a local farm in Shropshire. Here is a Danish Red from the herd grazing on the early-spring pastures.
Bottom left: Cheesemaker Martin Moyden in his creamery in the heart of Shropshire. Martin stirs milk as it heats up to temperature in a traditional Dutch vat.
Bottom right: Martin's mother, Ann, who helps Martin make cheese, checks the cheeses in the maturing rooms, turning each cheese regularly to maintain an even structure.

Wild garlic pesto spaghetti

This recipe is a spring staple of mine, inspired by living in the Dee Valley of North Wales just after leaving university. As the River Dee itself forms the border between Wales and Shropshire in some places, I thought that pairing wild garlic that grows on its banks with Martin's Wrekin White would be an appropriate way of celebrating the wonderful produce of both regions.

Every spring, the valley is flush with the rich green of wild garlic. Most mornings, I would be out there, next to the rushing waters of the river, picking leaves to blend into a fresh pesto or roast in the oven to make wild garlic crisps. Wild garlic grows in a cluster of bulbs that produces a lovely bouquet of leaves and spikes of star-like white flowers in April or May, depending on the weather earlier in the year. The key is to pick sustainably, so a couple of leaves from each clump should do it. Be careful not to over-pick as this will stunt their growth the following spring. The honey-scented flowers make a fantastic addition to any savoury dish.

SERVES 4

400g spaghetti
sea salt and freshly ground black pepper

WILD GARLIC PESTO

50g wild garlic leaves (or 2–3 garlic cloves, peeled, and a good handful of chives)
60ml olive oil, plus extra if needed
80g Wrekin White, grated, plus extra to serve
20g pine nuts
pinch of sea salt

Start by blending all the ingredients for the pesto in a food processor, then set aside. If the mixture needs thinning a little, add a bit more olive oil.

Fill a large saucepan with water, add a pinch of salt and bring to the boil, then add the spaghetti and cook for 2 minutes less than the time specified on the packet so that the pasta is still al dente. Drain the pasta in a colander, tip back into the empty saucepan and stir in the wild garlic pesto before dividing between plates to serve. I like to grate plenty of Wrekin White on top and add a few grinds of black pepper to finish.

Overleaf: Another cheese that Martin makes is Wrekin Blue. Made in a similar way to Wrekin White, it incorporates a blue mould to create these striking blue veins.

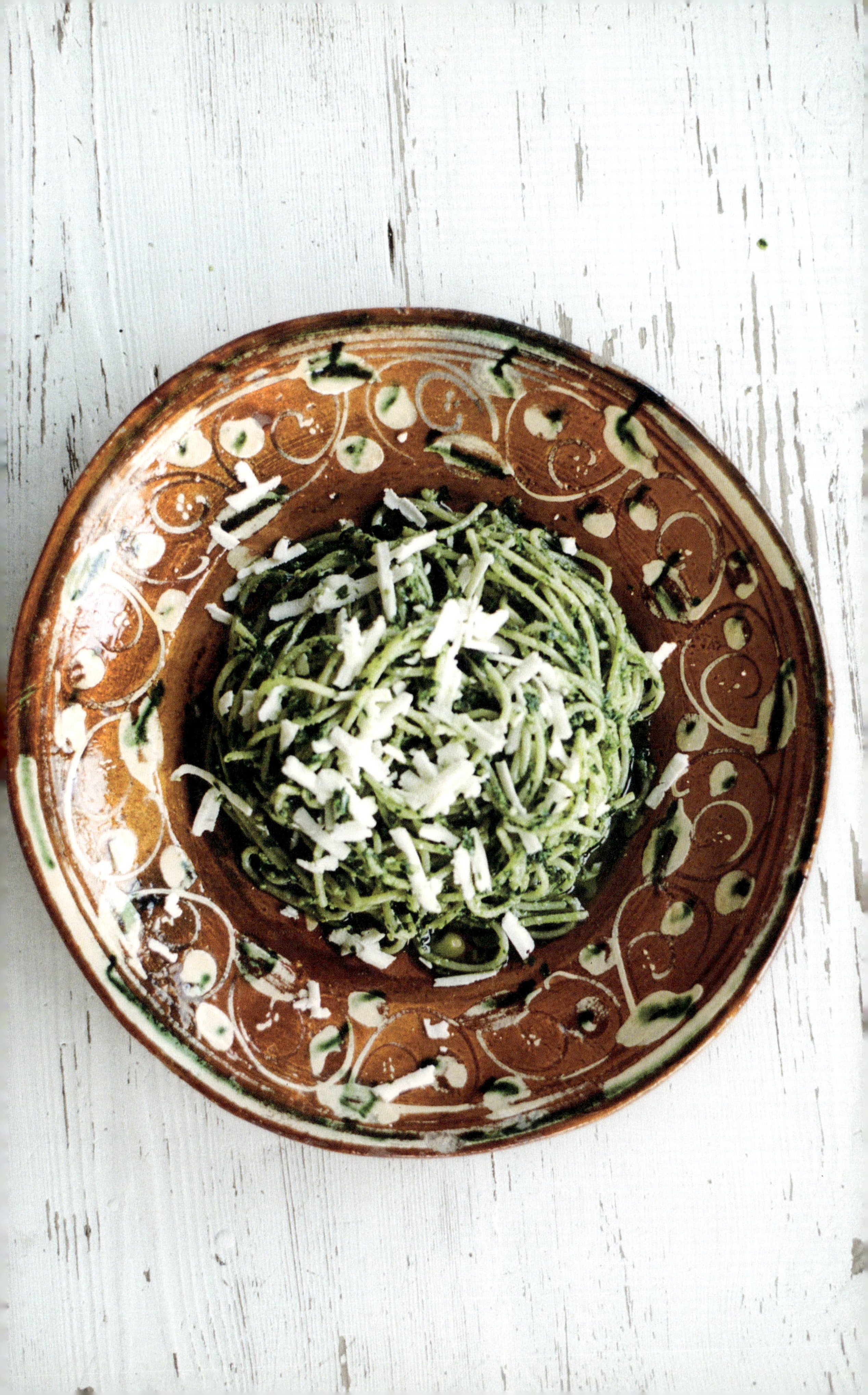

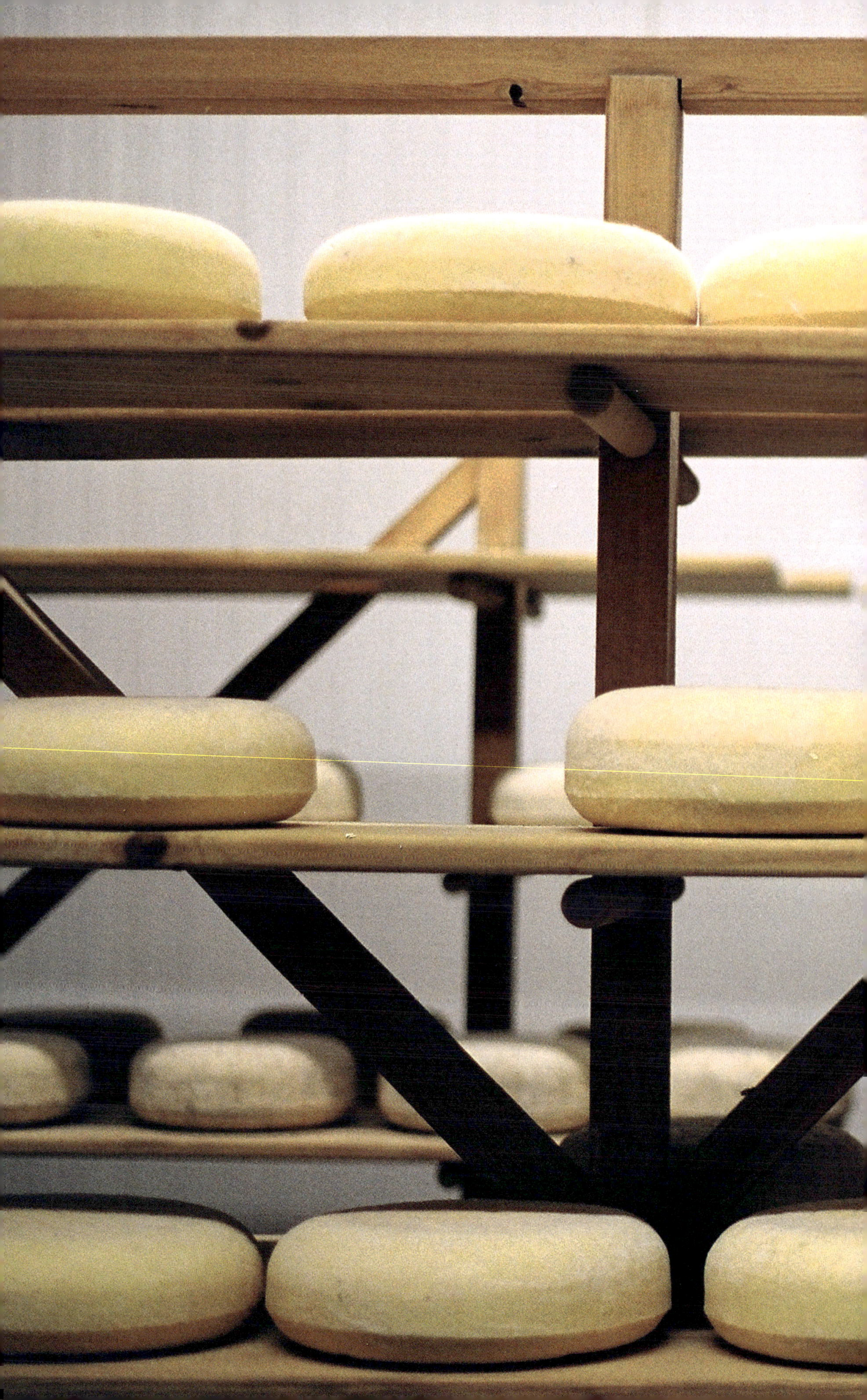

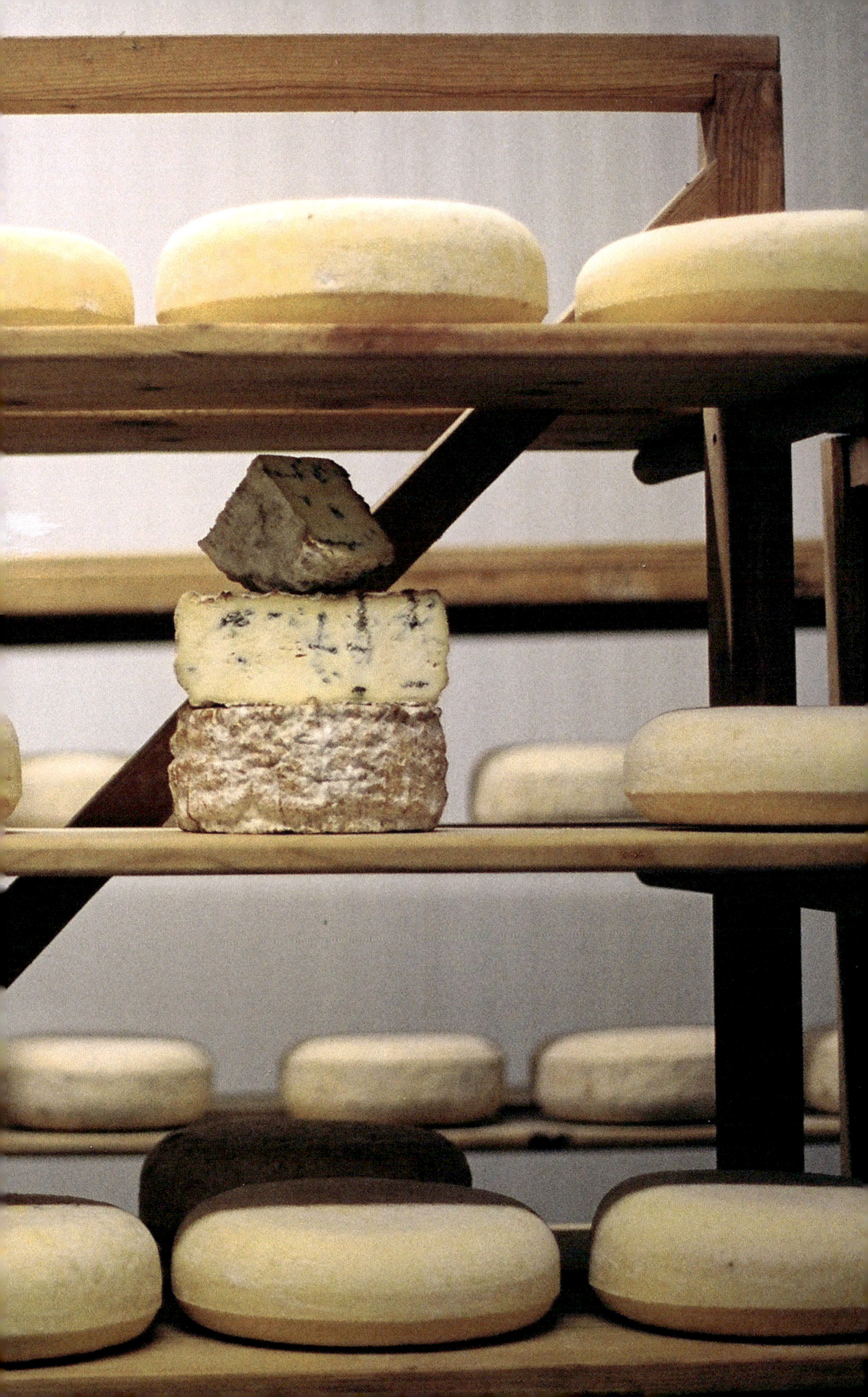

YORKSHIRE SQUEAKY

From left to right: Razan and Raghid on the farm in Yorkshire where they source the milk for their cheeses. The cows are predominately Holstein-Friesian.

A stunning view of the lovely Yorkshire countryside.

Made by Razan Alsous and her husband, Raghid Sandouk, the halloumi-style Yorkshire Squeaky comes in a range of flavours, including this version with onion seeds.

Yorkshire Dama Cheese, Halifax, West Yorkshire

In the borough of Calderdale, West Yorkshire, Razan Alsous and her husband, Raghid Sandouk, make Yorkshire Squeaky, a halloumi-style cheese inspired by their Syrian heritage. Going back thousands of years, halloumi-style cheese was originally made with a mixture of goat's and ewe's milk, and traditionally washed in brine to help preserve it in the hot climate of the Mediterranean and Middle East.

When Razan and Raghid first came to the British Isles in 2012, they found that there wasn't much in the way of great-tasting 'squeaky' cheese in supermarkets. With that in mind – and helped by Razan's background in microbiology and Raghid's in food engineering – the couple started to make their own halloumi-style cheese using locally sourced milk.

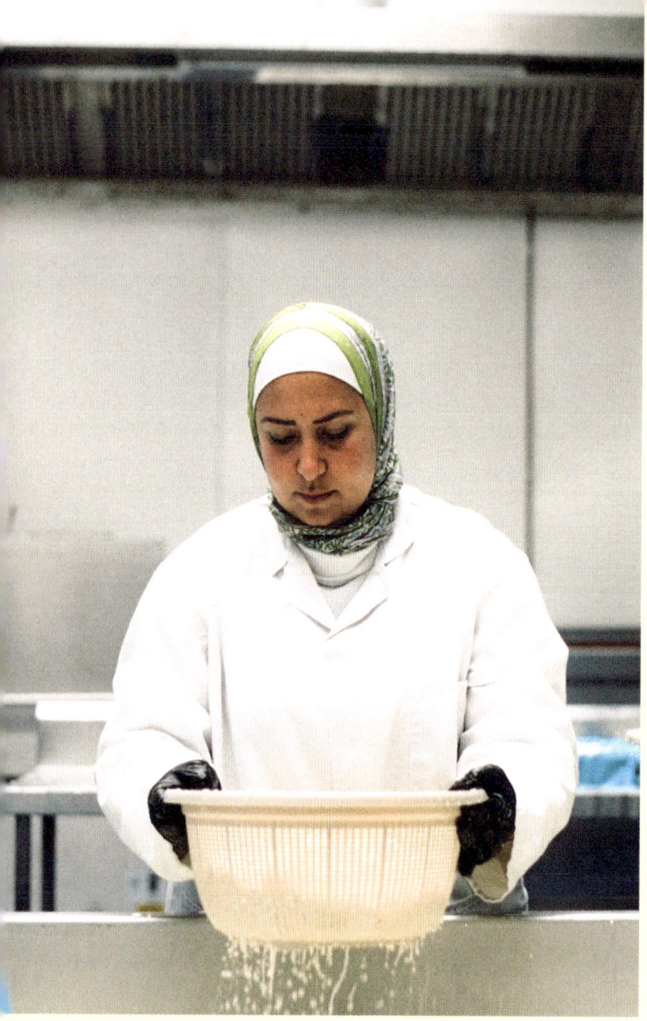
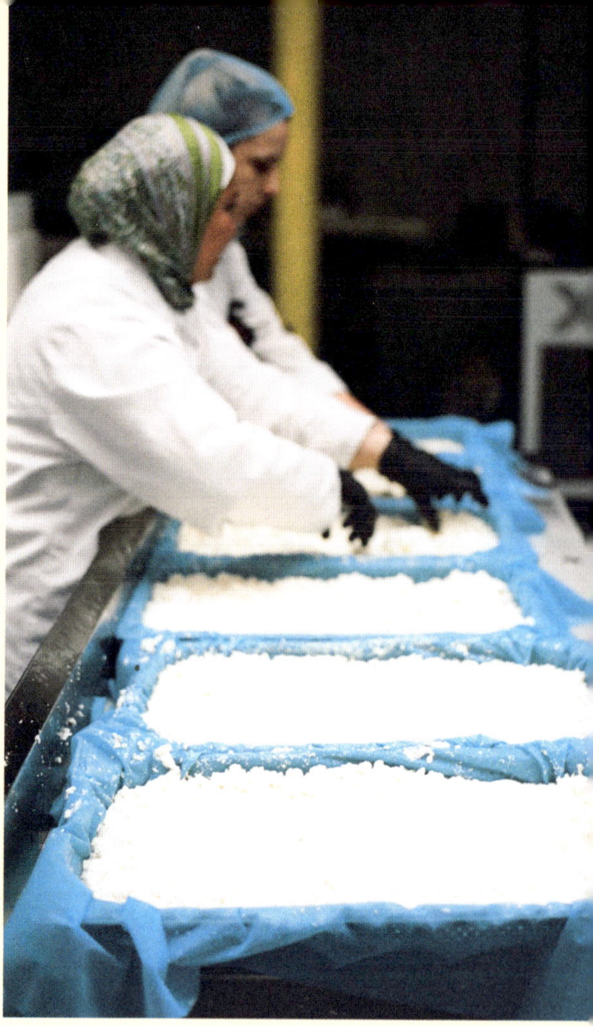
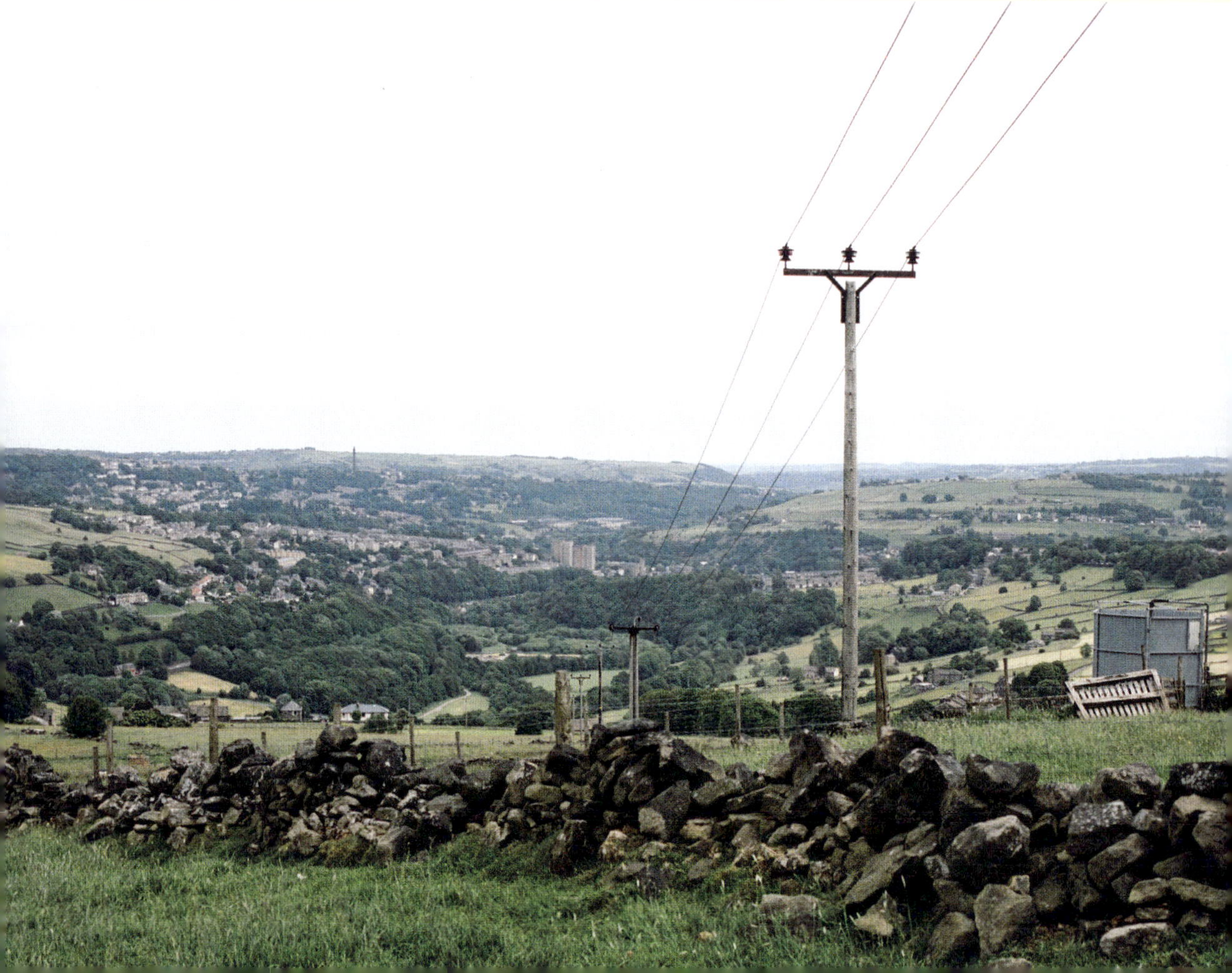

Yorkshire Squeaky is made using milk from a local herd of Holstein-Friesian cows. The milk is delivered to their creamery every day from a nearby farm in the surrounding Upper Calder Valley. Razan's cheese uses only rennet, and no starter culture, to set the milk. This is because halloumi-style cheese is a fresh cheese with low acidity that enables it to retain its shape and become crispy on the outside while being grilled or fried over high heat. After the milk has been coagulated with rennet, the curds are removed and moulded in flat, rectangular shallow trays and left for an hour to naturally compress. Some of the whey is removed to make ricotta, but the majority is kept and heated again in a large vat, in which the young compressed cheeses are then cooked. It is this stage, of cooking the cheese, that creates its renowned squeaky, meaty texture.

Once the cheeses have been cooked, they are salted, folded in half by hand and placed in a brine solution to mature for a further eight hours. The cheeses are then packaged and sold fresh. Named Yorkshire Squeaky, Razan's cheese is a true fusion of the produce and traditions of two countries – Yorkshire cow's milk and Syrian know-how.

The other cheeses Razan makes are different versions of Yorkshire Squeaky – flavoured or made with raw goat's milk or raw ewe's milk – labneh and matured yoghurt balls.

Yorkshire Squeaky characteristics
Milk: Pasteurised milk from a local herd of Holstein-Friesian cows
Rennet: Vegetarian
Appearance: Firm cream paste with a squeaky, meaty texture
Tasting notes: Creamy, salty and nutty flavour

Top left: Razan in the cheesemaking rooms at Yorkshire Dama Cheese. Here Razan sieves the curds from the whey before placing the curds in regimented trays.

Top right: Once the trays are full of curds, Razan and her team of cheesemakers level out the curds in each tray in an even layer before dividing them into sections that will become the finished blocks of cheese.

Bottom: The pleasing view towards Sowerby Bridge and Halifax from the farm where Razan and Raghid source their milk to make their award-winning cheeses.

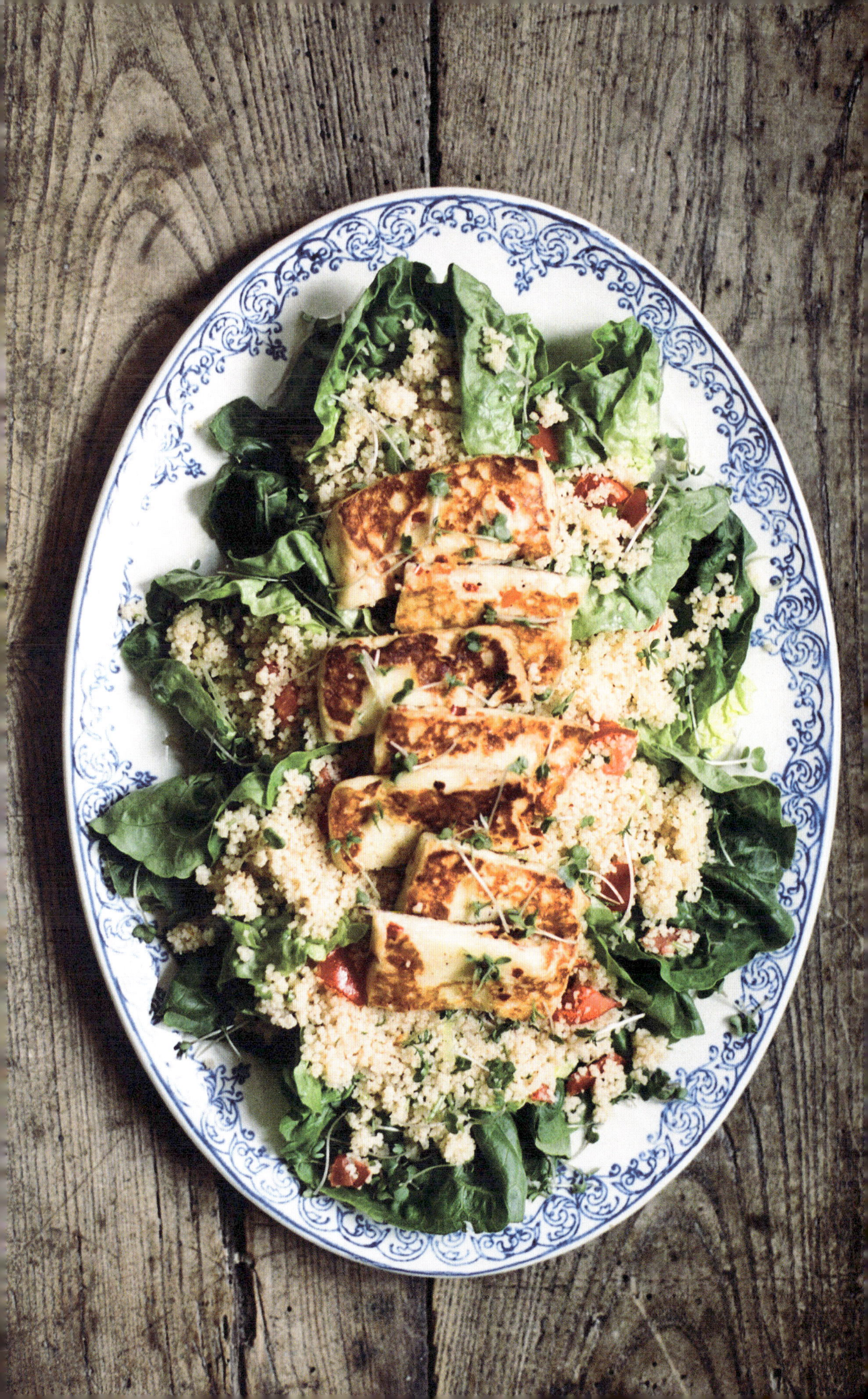

Couscous tabbouleh with Yorkshire Squeaky

Razan and Raghid make their cheese in a charming, historic area of Calderdale in West Yorkshire. I got to the creamery just in time to see the curds being sieved from the whey and ladled into regimented shallow trays to be pressed into large bars of Yorkshire Squeaky. The whole room smelled of warm souring milk, reminiscent of the mug of hot milk I used to drink before bed as a child. Throughout the whole time I was there, including a short trip to the local farm where they source their milk, Razan and Raghid were so hospitable and generous with their time, and I thank them dearly for it.

Using milk delivered from a local farm in the Upper Calder Valley, Razan and Raghid make their cheese in a truly individual way, showing the benefits of blending two cultures together – Syrian knowledge and British produce – to create a unique product.

This is a favourite recipe of Razan's that she likes to cook for her family, generally using mint-flavoured Yorkshire Squeaky, though you could use the plain version and add fresh mint to the tabbouleh. I've enjoyed this with the chilli-flavoured cheese, to give the dish a little heat. The recipe is perfect for a light and refreshing lunch on a hot day in spring or summer.

SERVES 2–3

180g couscous
1 tsp ground cumin
pinch of sea salt
420ml boiling water
olive oil, for dressing the couscous
handful of fresh parsley, finely chopped
2 large tomatoes, finely diced
3 spring onions, finely chopped
juice of 1 lemon
1 x 220g pack of Yorkshire Squeaky, sliced
1 romaine or Little Gem lettuce
pomegranate molasses or fresh pomegranate seeds, to serve (optional)

Place the couscous in a large bowl, add the cumin and a pinch of salt and mix together well. Pour the boiling water over the couscous, then cover the bowl with a tea towel and leave until all the water has been absorbed – this should take around 5 minutes. Stir in a generous slosh of olive oil to enrich the couscous.

Add the parsley, tomatoes and spring onions to the couscous, followed by the lemon juice, and combine everything together well.

Place a cast-iron or heavy-based frying pan on a high heat, and once hot, add the slices of Yorkshire Squeaky to the pan and fry the cheese on each side for 1–2 minutes or until golden.

Separate the lettuce leaves and place in a large serving dish. Spoon the couscous and vegetable mixture on to the leaves and arrange the fried cheese on top. Razan suggests serving the dish with a drizzle of pomegranate molasses or a sprinkling of pomegranate seeds to finish.

BREFU BACH

From left to right: A close-up of the irresistible-looking set curds that Carrie will be scooping into small moulds to be shaped into young cheeses.

The most recent batch of Brefu Bach in their moulds (on the right), next to an earlier batch that has been left to age on wire racks (on the left).

Once the curds have been left to naturally compress in their moulds, they form into a young cheese like this one.

Translated as 'Little Bleat', Brefu Bach is made using raw milk from a local flock of Lleyn sheep, a traditional Welsh breed.

Cosyn Cymru, Bethesda, Gwynedd

Nestled within the mountains of Snowdonia is the Cosyn Cymru dairy, where Brefu Bach is made by Carrie Rimes. Loosely translated as 'Little Bleat', Brefu Bach is a soft lactic cheese made using raw milk from Lleyn sheep. The milk comes from a local farm on the Llŷn (or 'Lleyn') Peninsula, where the sheep graze year-round on the patchwork of tree-lined pastures and marshy grasslands. As the weather is often wet and windy on the peninsula, a hardy, robust breed like the Lleyn is perfect. The milk is of a high quality, forming soft, silky curds in the make and a flavoursome cheese.

Carrie originally learned the art of cheesemaking in several regions of France, from the Pyrenees to the northern Auvergne, where she found that the majority of cheesemakers she learned from sold different cheeses at various times of year. Returning to Wales, Carrie applied the same principles, making both soft and hard cheeses during the summer months, then selling the fresher, soft cheeses in the summer while allowing the hard cheeses to mature further to then be sold in the winter. Carrie developed her soft lactic cheese from a traditional French recipe, and living in Wales, famous for its sheep farming, decided to use ewe's milk in place of cow's. The Lleyn ewes produce milk from spring through to autumn, reaching a peak in early summer when the pasture they graze on is particularly rich. The fresh, grassy taste of the milk in May and June turns to creamy, buttery flavours in September and October as the milk season draws to a close.

The making of Brefu Bach is a slow and gentle process taking place over a couple of days. Carrie collects the milk from her local farmer on the Llŷn Peninsula, and on each trip, before she leaves the farm to go back to her cheesemaking rooms, she adds just a little starter culture to the fresh milk that she has collected. This gives a boost of 'friendly' bacteria, so that during the journey back to the dairy, the milk begins to gently acidify, thus beginning the cheesemaking process.

In the cheesemaking rooms, the fresh, warm milk is poured into a vat and filtered for a second time, having already been filtered at the farm. The milk is then warmed again to around room temperature, and then tipped into large plastic buckets, where it continues to slowly acidify for a few hours. When the correct pH level has been reached, a very small amount of rennet is added to the buckets to encourage the coagulation of the curds, and the mixture is left overnight. The following day, the curds now resemble a thick-set yoghurt – the right level of firmness is essential for making this cheese, and only experience can tell when the curds are ready. They are then ladled into moulds and left to firm up further before being turned and salted. Brefu Bach can be eaten fresh from several days after the make, to up to six weeks, and as the cheese matures, a soft, silky breakdown often develops just beneath the rind.

Other cheeses from Cosyn Cymru include ewe's milk set yoghurt, fresh lactic curd (Brefu Wen), and over the summer when lots of milk is coming in, Carrie makes three types of hard cheese: Caws Chwaral (Quarry Cheese), Olwyn Fawr (Big Wheel) and Caws Calan (Calan Cheese).

Brefu Bach characteristics

Milk: Raw milk from a local flock of Lleyn sheep

Rennet: Vegetarian

Appearance: White paste, a firm centre and often oozing sides, with an edible, wrinkled, ivory-coloured rind

Tasting notes: Creamy and silky flavours with hints of fresh grass and lemon. Varies according to the season and length of maturation

Carrie Rimes, who makes Brefu Bach, acquired her cheesemaking skills in several regions of France, from the Pyrenees to the northern Auvergne.

Brefu Bach on bara brith with a glass of mead

North Wales is a special place for me, and I like to visit the mountains and Anglesey as much as I can. When I do travel up the A5, it is always nice to drop in on Carrie in Bethesda to talk about cheese and what's going on locally.

Each time I cross the old Britannia Bridge over to the island of Anglesey, I look back over the Menai Strait to the mainland, and take in one of the finest views in all of Wales – the spectacular vista of the Snowdonia National Park. It is so often the case that you arrive on the island in the dark only to wake up to this view on a fine morning, full of promise for the day ahead, and a calm sea with mussel trawlers ploughing the surface in gentle furrows as they pass.

Wales is home to a wealth of food producers, and this recipe, a traditional Welsh tea bread (bara brith meaning 'speckled bread'), made here without sugar, is a celebration of the region's culinary heritage, as well as a favourite of Carrie's to have on a weekend. The fruity loaf is beautifully complemented by the tangy cheese and a glass of mead. Carrie loves Mountain Mead, in particular, made by a company based in Snowdonia.

SERVES 4

TEA LOAF
- 280g raisins
- 380ml chai (or other) tea, freshly made
- 250g dark rye flour
- 2 tsp baking powder
- 1 tsp ground cinnamon
- 1 tsp ground ginger
- 2 large eggs
- 2 tsp olive oil, plus extra for greasing

TO SERVE
- 1 x 120g round of Brefu Bach
- 4 glasses of mead

Preheat the oven to 200°C/400°F/gas mark 6. Grease a 900g loaf tin with olive oil and line with baking parchment.

Place the raisins in a bowl, pour in the freshly made chai tea and leave to soak for 30 minutes.

Place the flour, baking powder, ground cinnamon and ginger in a separate, large bowl and add the soaked raisins and their liquid. Add the eggs and olive oil, and combine well with a wooden spoon.

Pour the mixture into the prepared loaf tin and bake in the oven for 45 minutes. I normally check after around 30 minutes, inserting a skewer into the centre of the loaf to see if it comes out clean. Once it does come out clean, and is well risen and firm to the touch, it is ready. Leave to cool in the tin for a few minutes before removing from the tin and transferring to a wire rack to finish cooling.

Cut the loaf into slices, spread a generous layer of Brefu Bach on to each slice, and serve with a glass of mead.

Overleaf: One of the finest views in all of Wales: the Snowdonia National Park where, nestled within the mountains, lies the dairy where Carrie makes her Brefu Bach.

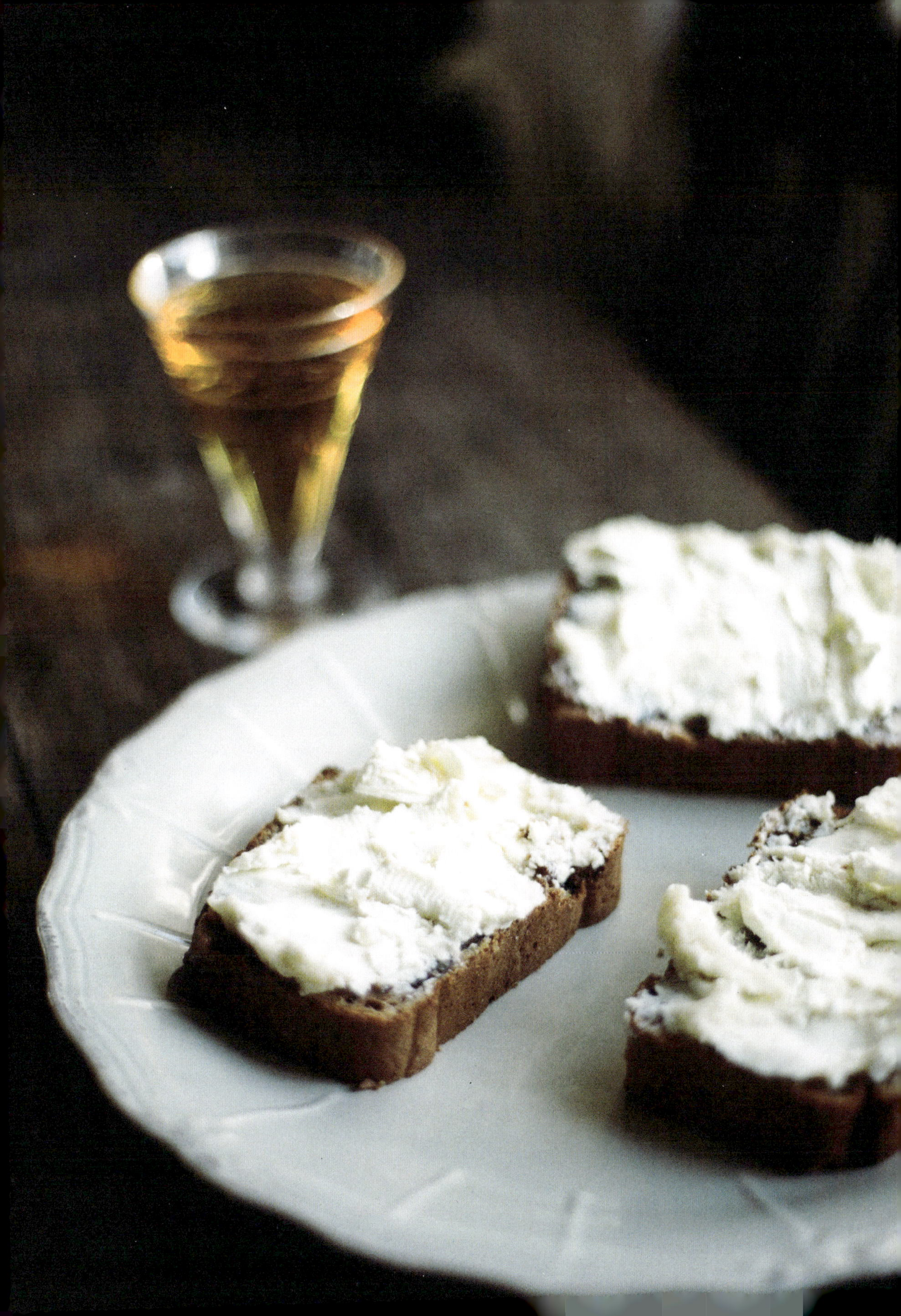

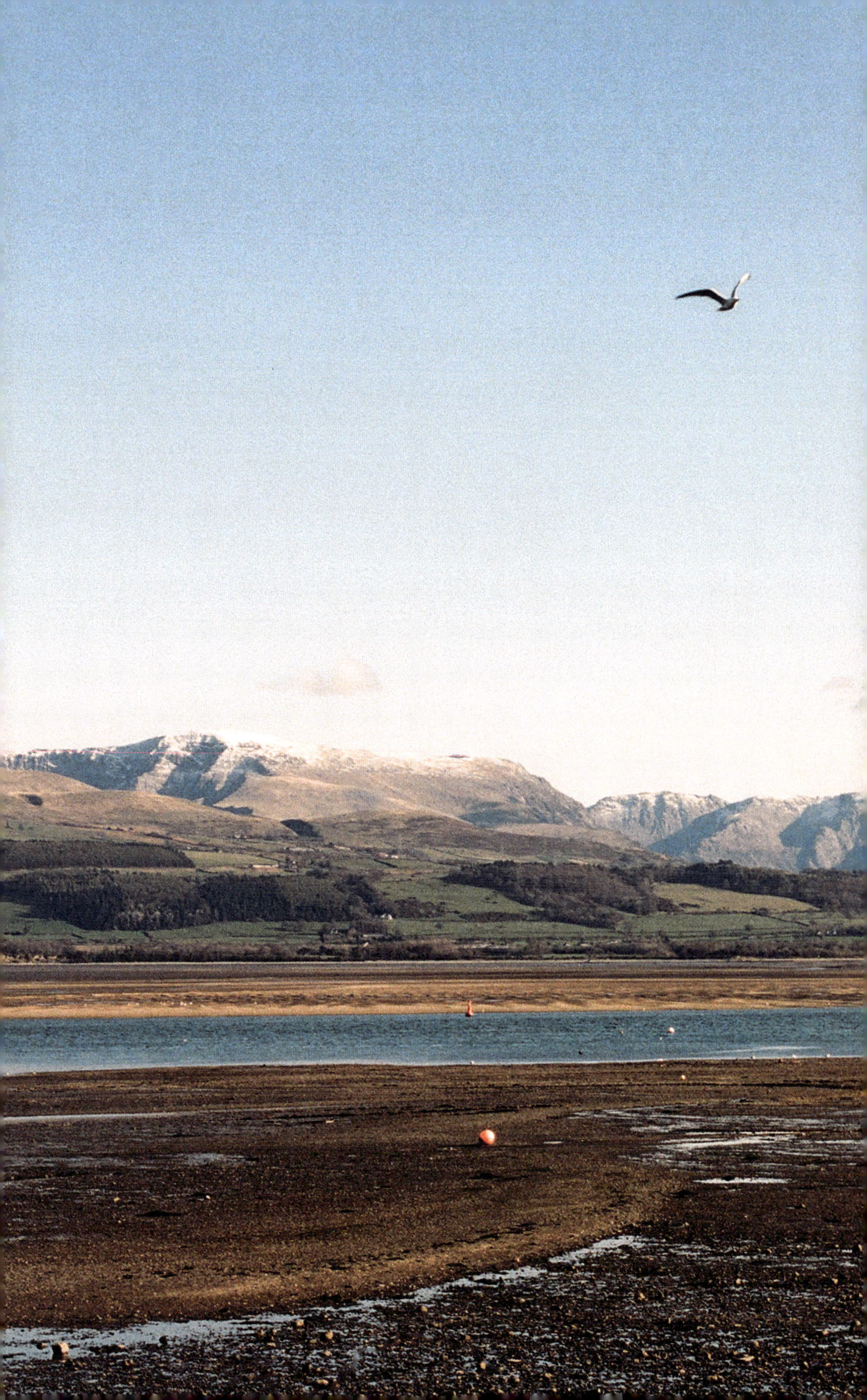

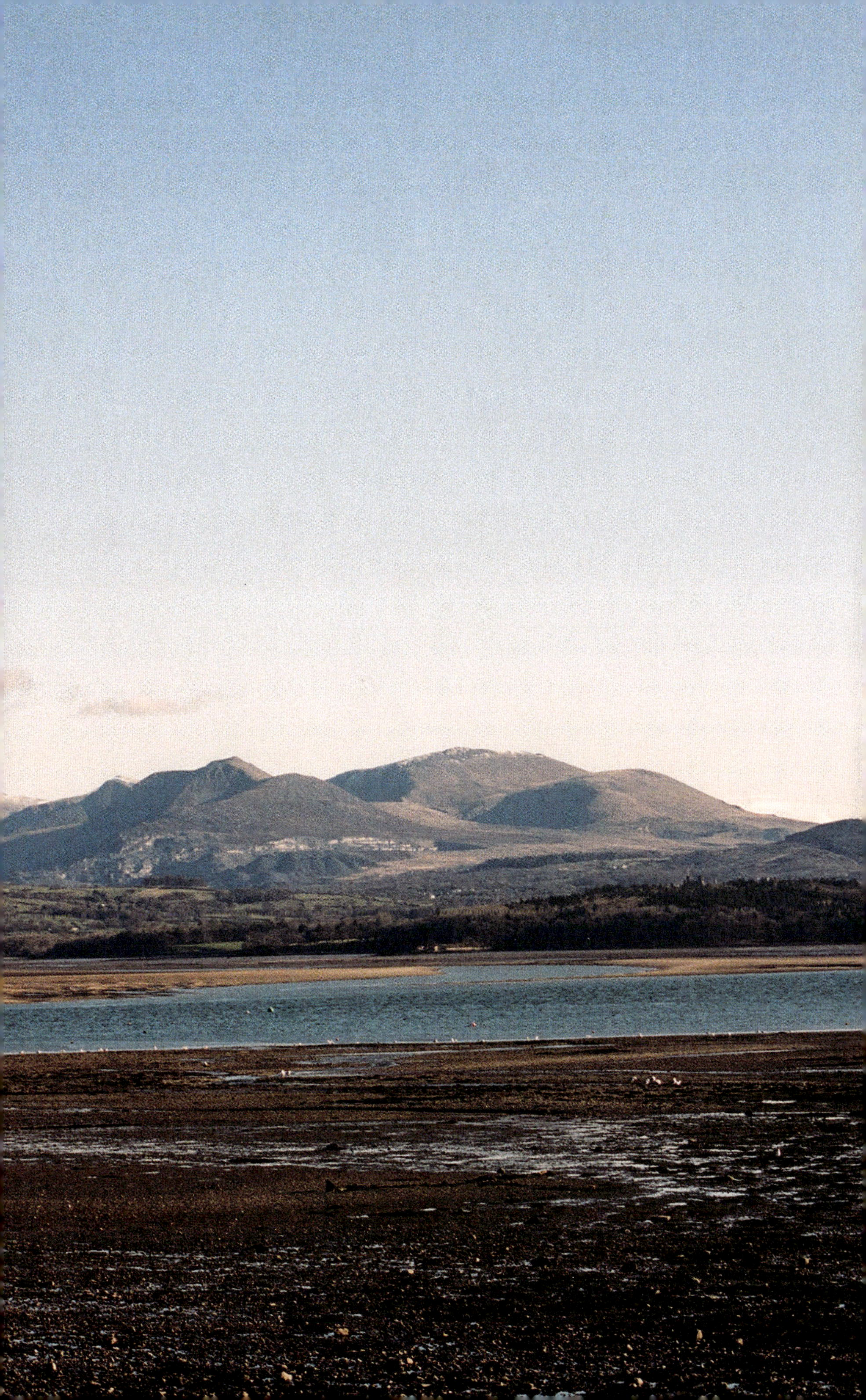

CELTIC PROMISE

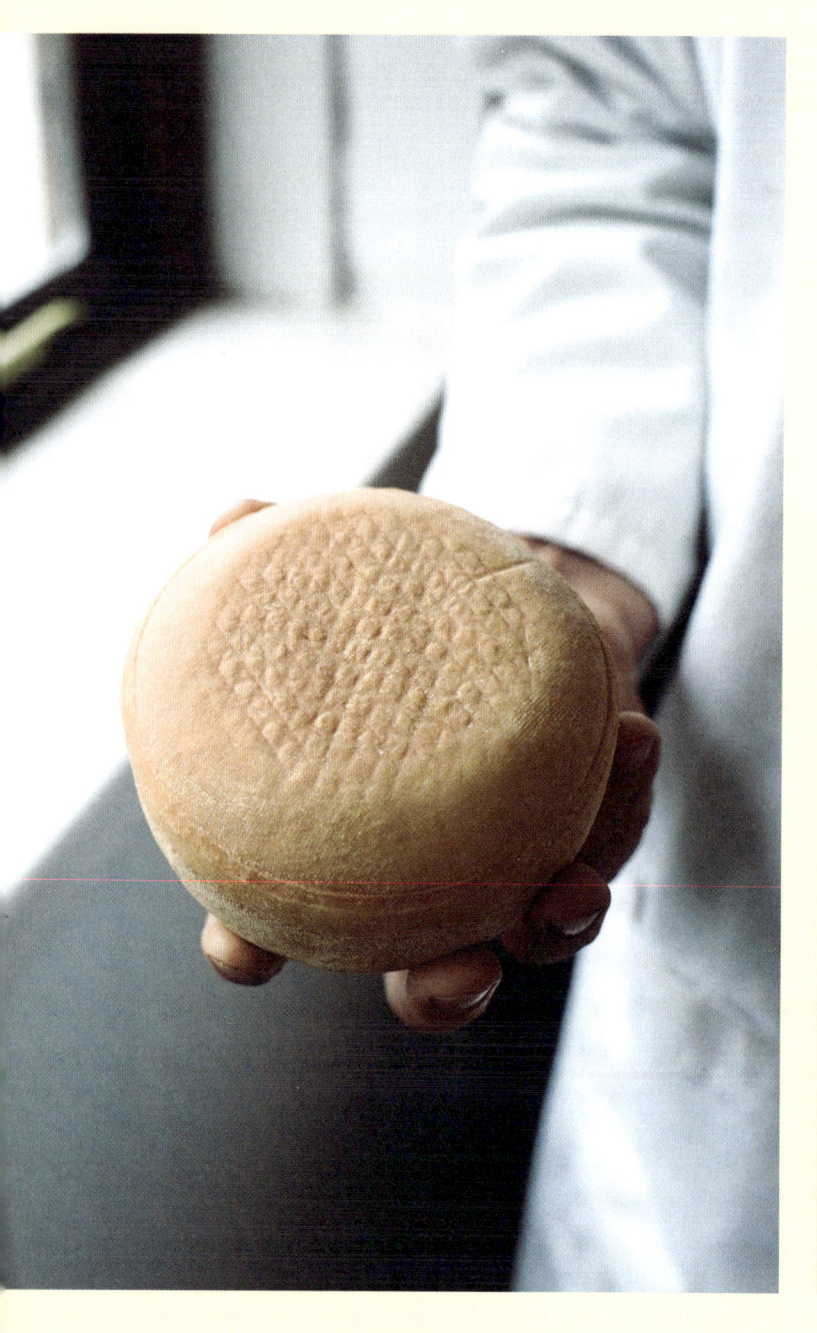

Left: A wheel of Celtic Promise at seven weeks, when it will have been washed twenty-one times in a solution of *Brevibacterium linens*. The cheese will be left to mature for a further week and washed another three times.

Right: The beautiful scenic view towards the Preseli Hills in South Wales. In the foreground is Glynhynod Farm, which sits upon a headland intersecting two valleys.

Caws Teifi Cheese, Glynhynod Farm, Ceredigion

Glynhynod Farm sits snug within the steep hills of the Glynhynod Valley in Ceredigion. The farm is home to the Savage-Onstwedder family, who make Celtic Promise, a semi-hard washed-rind cheese, using organic raw milk from a local herd of Jersey and New Zealand Friesian cows.

Established by Patrice and John Savage-Onstwedder in 1982, Caws Teifi Cheese is now run by their son Robert with head cheesemaker Tim Mitchell. Their other son, John-James, manages the farm's organic distillery, Dà Mhìle, which is next to the dairy and produces organic gin, rum, apple brandy and whisky.

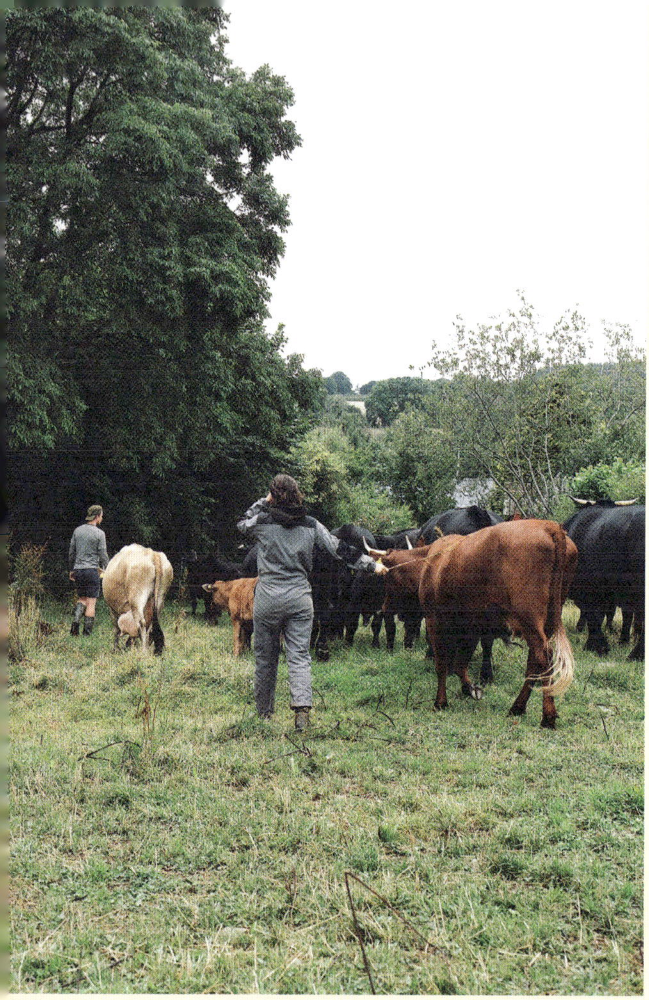

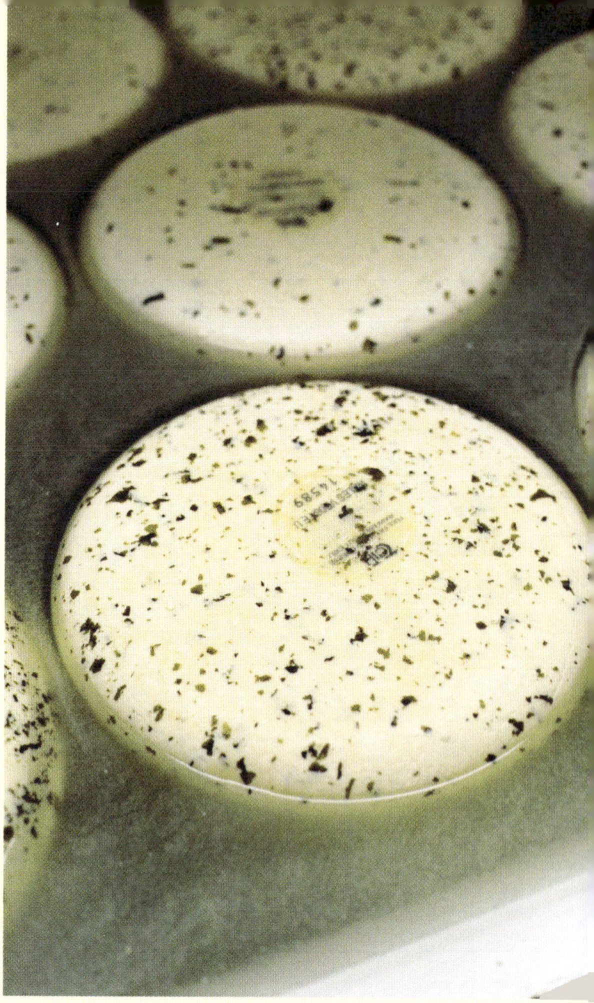

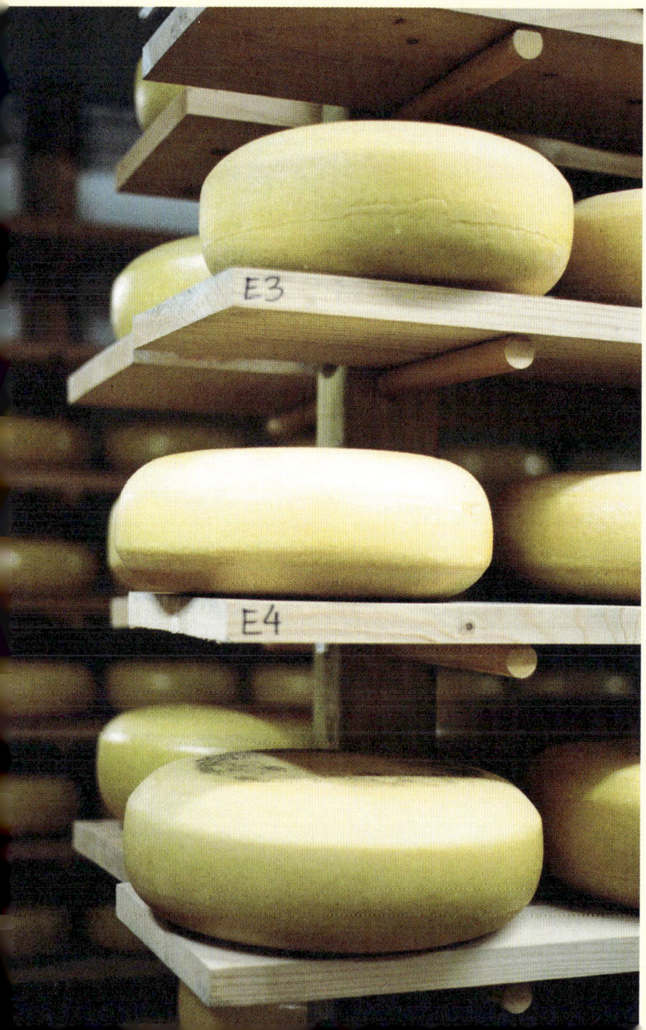
E3
E4

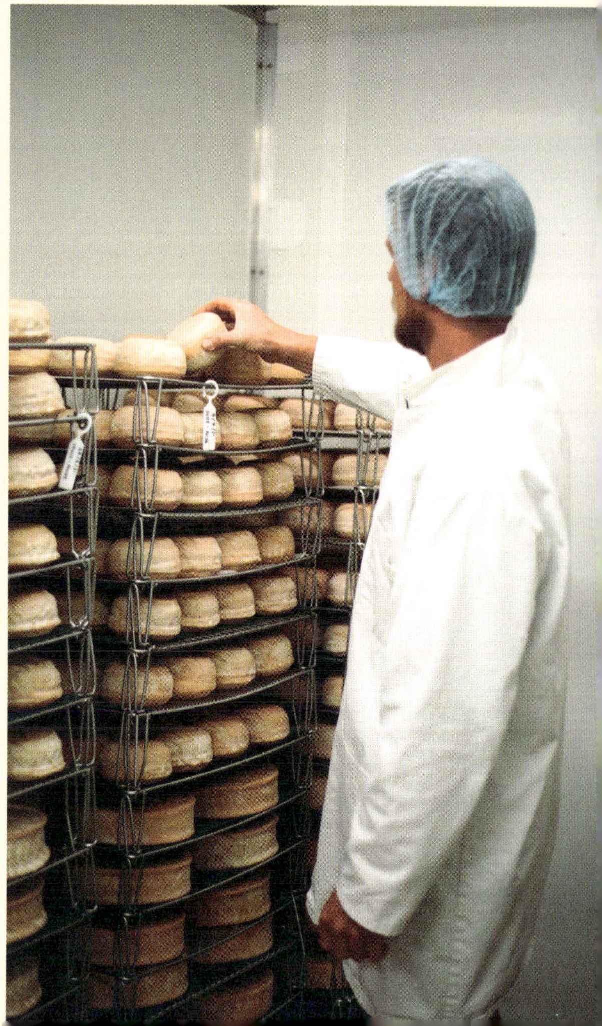

The Savage-Onstwedder family's history of cheesemaking goes back to when Patrice and John lived in their native Holland, where Patrice made Gouda from the 1970s onwards. Guided by John Seymour's *Complete Book of Self-Sufficiency*, Patrice, John and their business partner, Paula van Werkhoven, relocated to Wales in 1981 to set up a self-sufficient farm that would take on students from the local area to teach them rural skills. For the past twenty years, Glynhynod Farm has been working with French universities to support interns who want to come to Wales to learn about dairy farming and food production at the farm.

John created Celtic Promise in 1995 with his great friend the late James Aldridge, a renowned advocate of washed-rind cheeses made with raw milk. Together, they developed the cheese, making it to a Caerphilly recipe – very unusual for a washed-rind cheese. For the past eighteen years, Tim Mitchell has been making the farm's cheeses, having learned how to make cheese from Patrice.

The raw milk used to make Celtic Promise is now sourced from Pantglas Farm, run by Sally Wood, Garry Ehms and their business partner, Dafydd. Organic, and certified with the Pasture-Fed Livestock Association (see pages 30 and 196), the farm operates to the highest food and farming standards.

One of the unique aspects of Celtic Promise is how it is treated during maturation. Once the young cheeses have been pressed, they are soaked in brine and then immediately transferred to a room with a high level of humidity. Over the next eight weeks, the cheeses are washed three times a week in a solution of *Brevibacterium linens*, diluted with spring water from the farm. At the end of each week, the cheeses are wiped with a damp cloth to add moisture to the rind. Over time, this process creates the pinky orange colour that is so characteristic of *B. linens*. Celtic Promise is aged for a minimum of eight weeks before it is eaten.

Caws Teifi Cheese also make Traditional Welsh Caerphilly, an organic halloumi-style cheese, and various flavours of Teifi, a Gouda-style cheese.

Celtic Promise characteristics

Milk: Organic raw milk from a local herd of Jersey and New Zealand Friesian cows

Rennet: Animal

Appearance: Light creamy paste with an edible, pink washed rind

Tasting notes: Soft, buttery flavours with farmyard and gamey notes and a slightly pungent aroma. In the summer it has a bolder flavour and aroma

Clockwise from top left: Herding the farm's Jersey cows and small collection of Welsh Black cattle, reared for their meat, from one side of the valley to the next, reflecting the intimate bond between herdsman and beast.

A Gouda-style cheese based on a 500-year-old recipe, Teifi is made in a range of flavours, including this nettle one, shown soaking in a brine bath.

Robert in the maturing room for Celtic Promise. Getting the right conditions for maturation is a real balancing act between temperature, humidity and level of treatment.

The maturing rooms at Caws Teifi, full of different flavours of Teifi: Natural, Seaweed, Oak Smoked, Mature and even Extra Mature.

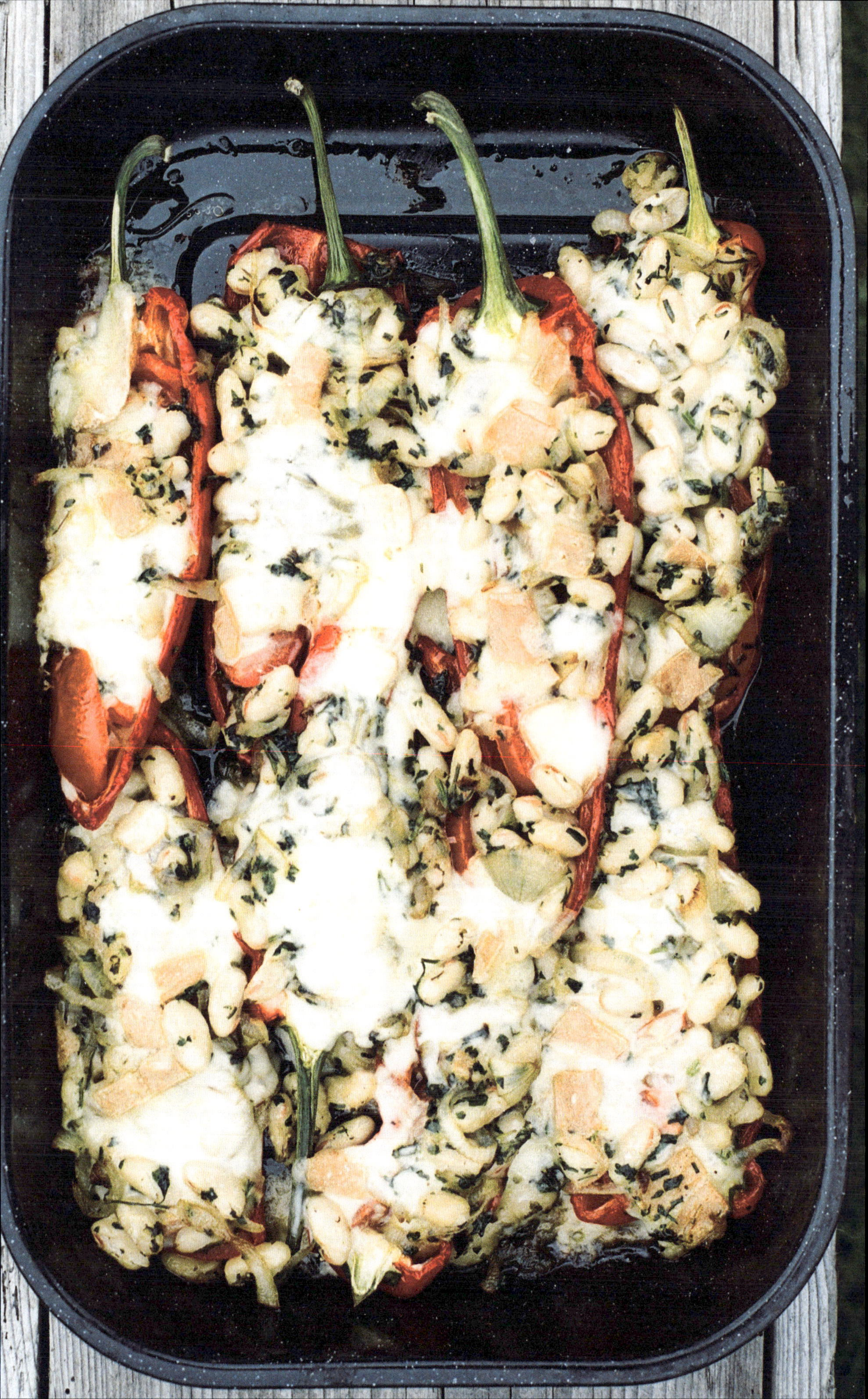

Celtic Promise stuffed red peppers

One of the first things that enticed me into the world of cheese was how different cheesemaking traditions can determine the flavour and appearance of a cheese. And that's exactly what drew me to meeting the Savage-Onstwedder family, including, among other things, their drive to be self-sufficient and use nature-friendly farming methods. Their fusion of Welsh and Dutch cheesemaking practices has resulted in the most delightful cheeses. You only need to visit their farm shop or look online to see that their cheeses have been awarded the top prizes in Wales, the UK and beyond.

When I visited the Savage-Onstwedder family in South Wales, it was a typically rainy day but still stunningly lush and, at the height of the summer, quite muggy. Robert was the perfect host, showing me around the entire farm, dairy and maturing rooms, and inundating me throughout the day with dairy-related delights, from cheese on toast and cheese tastings to several glasses of raw milk, so rich that it was more like double cream. Perhaps the best part of the day was helping to guide the farm's Jersey cows and small collection of Welsh Black cattle, reared for their meat, down the valley to fresh pasture. The whole experience felt so deep-rooted, a time-honoured practice, one of vanishingly few in our modern world that still link us directly to what our ancestors did thousands of years ago.

This recipe seemed like something that would complement the tanginess of the cheese. Using fresh parsley and thyme from my garden and a handy tin of beans, it makes a wonderfully fresh dish to have for lunch or supper.

SERVES 3–4

4 pointed red peppers
olive oil, for drizzling and frying
2 medium onions, peeled and thinly sliced
1 x 400g tin of cannellini beans, drained and rinsed
good handful of fresh parsley, finely chopped, and thyme leaves
280g Celtic Promise, cut into small cubes
4 tomatoes, halved and thinly sliced
sea salt and freshly ground black pepper

Preheat the oven to 200°C/400°F/gas mark 6.

Cut the peppers in half lengthways and remove the seeds, then place in a deep-sided baking tray. Drizzle over a glug of olive oil, sprinkle with 1 teaspoon of salt and roast in the oven for 10 minutes to soften.

Meanwhile, on a medium heat, pan-fry the onions in 1 tablespoon of olive oil for about 10 minutes until soft. Add the beans, fresh herbs, 1 teaspoon of salt and a few grinds of black pepper, and mix well for a further minute.

Add half of the cheese to the pan and stir for another minute to combine before taking the pan off the heat.

Next, take the peppers out of the oven and fill each roasted half-pepper, starting with the tomatoes and then the herb and bean mixture, before topping with the rest of the cubed cheese. Place back in the oven, on the top shelf, to bake for 15 minutes until the stuffed peppers are cooked through and the cheese is bubbling and golden on top.

Overleaf: The farming team at Glynhynod Farm. From left to right: Robert, Louane, Naomi, John, Petra, Justine and Isabelle.

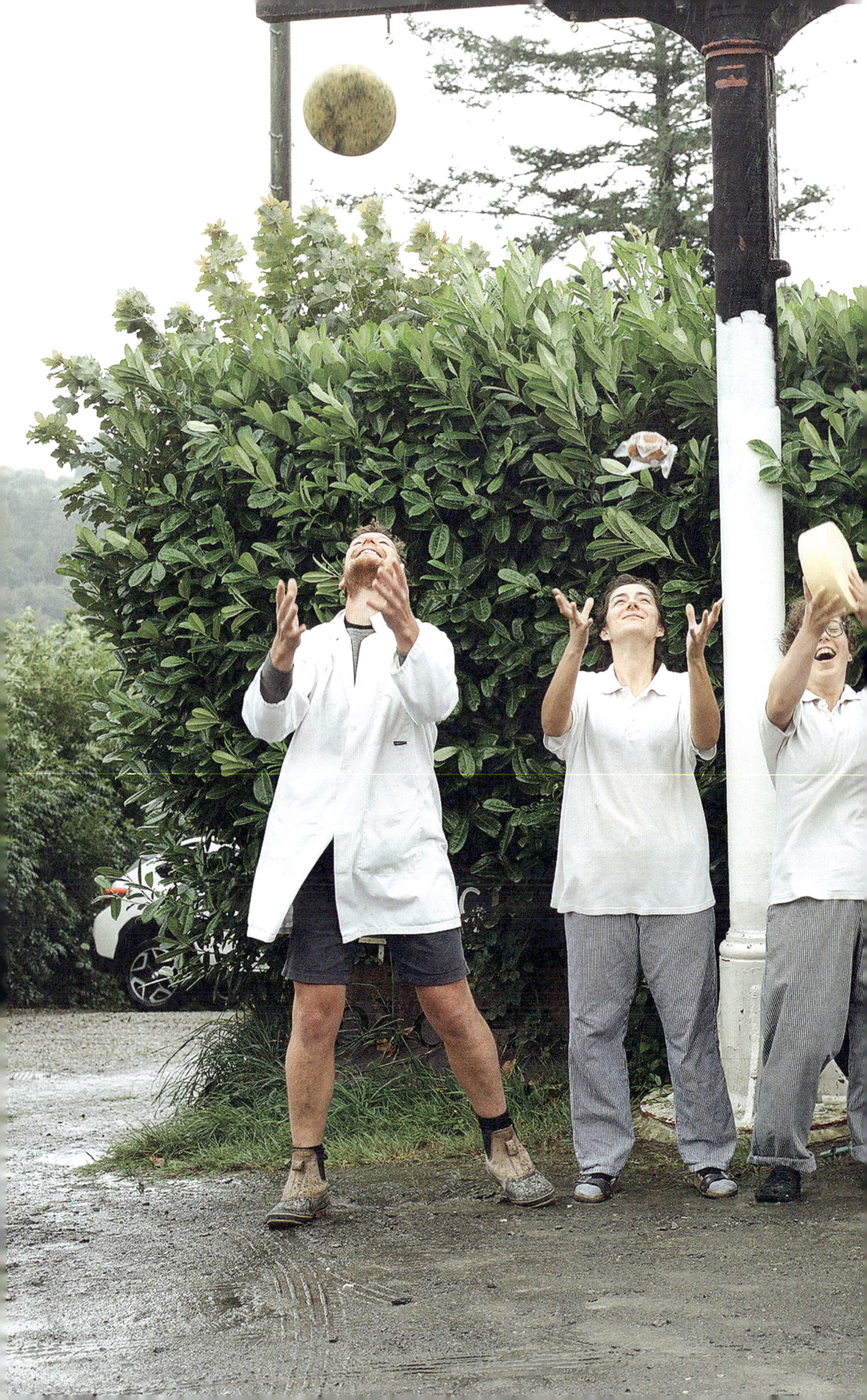

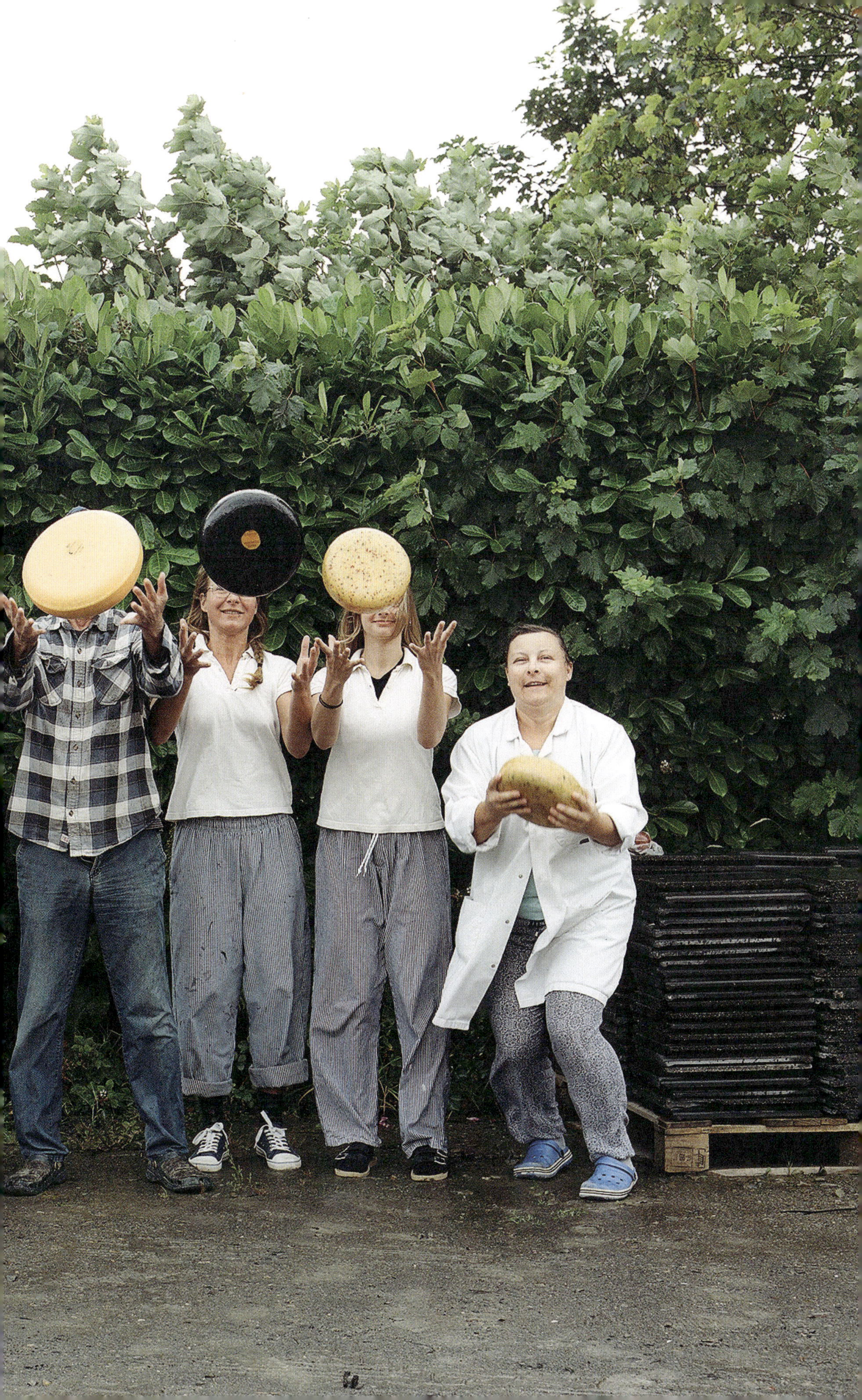

HAFOD

Left: Becky and Patrick at Holden Farm Dairy are keen to farm in harmony with nature as much as possible, which includes leaving areas wild to increase biodiversity.

Right: Hafod cheeses in the maturing rooms at Holden Farm Dairy, where they are left to mature for several months to age and develop.

Holden Farm Dairy, Bwlchwernen Fawr, Lampeter, Ceredigion

Located in the hills of West Wales, where small grassland fields meet hedgerows of gnarled oak and beech trees, Hafod is made at Holden Farm Dairy on the 300-acre Bwlchwernen Fawr run by Patrick and Becky Holden. Managed organically since 1973 and certified in 1985, it is now the longest standing organic dairy farm in Wales. Hafod is made to a Cheddar recipe using raw milk from the farm's herd of 80 Ayrshire cows. Hafod, pronounced 'Havod', translates as 'summer place' or 'pasture', reflecting how Welsh farmers used to graze their animals on distant pastures in the summer, after releasing them from the hendre, or farmhouse, where they were kept in adjoining barns over the winter.

The Holdens chose the Ayrshire breed for a variety of reasons, including their hardiness and ability to convert the grasses and clovers from pastureland into high-quality milk containing the right balance of protein and butterfat for cheese-making. In the spring and summer months, the cows graze on lush organic pasture made up of a variety of grasses, legumes and herbs, including three types of clover (alsike, red and white), bird's-foot trefoil, chicory and plantain. The cows are also fed a mixture of hay and silage, which is made on the farm from the same diverse mixture of grasses and other plants. It is this species-rich pasture and cattle feed that, via the milk, gives Hafod its unique flavour. The ethos of the farm is based on core principles: of the circular economy, of biologically based farming, using no artificial fertilisers or pesticides, and the production of vital healthy milk in harmony with nature.

Made using the 'Cheddaring' technique – in which the curds are cut finely, left to form into long wedges and then layered on top of each other to further acidify and expel whey – Hafod is normally left to mature for 9–12 months before eating, sometimes even up to eighteen months. The cheeses are initially turned twice a week when they are younger, and only once a week as they get older. During this ageing period, the cheese forms a mottled rind, produced by moulds that add to its distinctive nutty flavour and heady aroma. Everything that goes into the production of Hafod – from the Welsh climate and species-rich pasture to the quality of the Ayrshire milk – combines to give the cheese its own unique taste and provenance.

Hafod characteristics

Milk: Raw milk from the farm's herd of Ayrshire cows

Rennet: Animal

Appearance: Smooth, firm golden paste with an unclothed natural rind

Tasting notes: Warm buttery, earthy flavours that live long in the mouth. Varies according to the season and length of maturation

Top: Cheesemaker Jos feeds the peg mill with layers of 'Cheddared' curds. After milling, the curds are then salted and placed in moulds.
Bottom left: Patrick and Becky Holden, farmers and cheesemakers, with their herd of Ayrshire cows deep within the rolling Welsh countryside.
Bottom right: The beautiful herd of Ayrshire cows at Holden Farm Dairy grazing on species-rich pasture, which contributes to the flavour of their delicious milk and the cheese made from it.

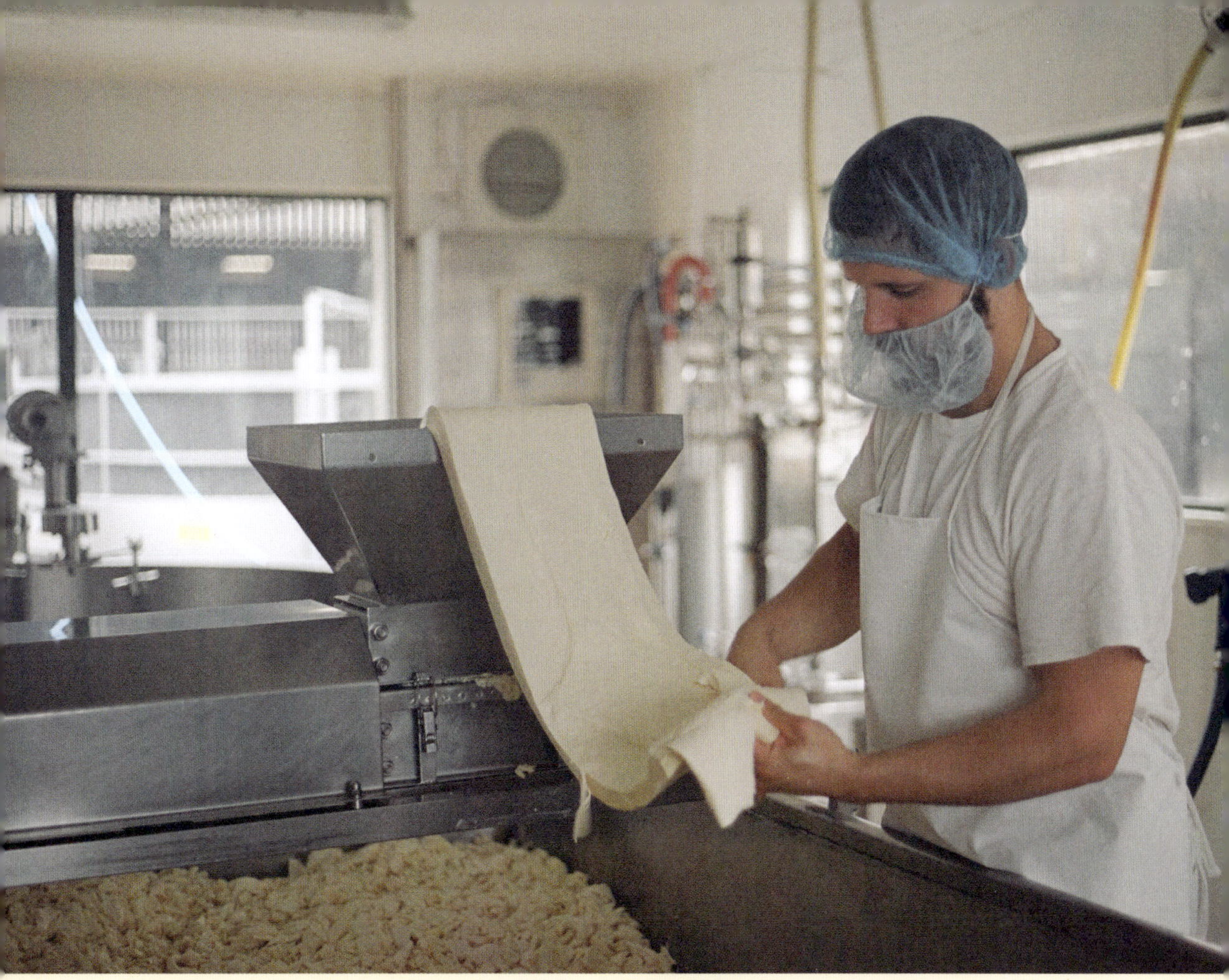
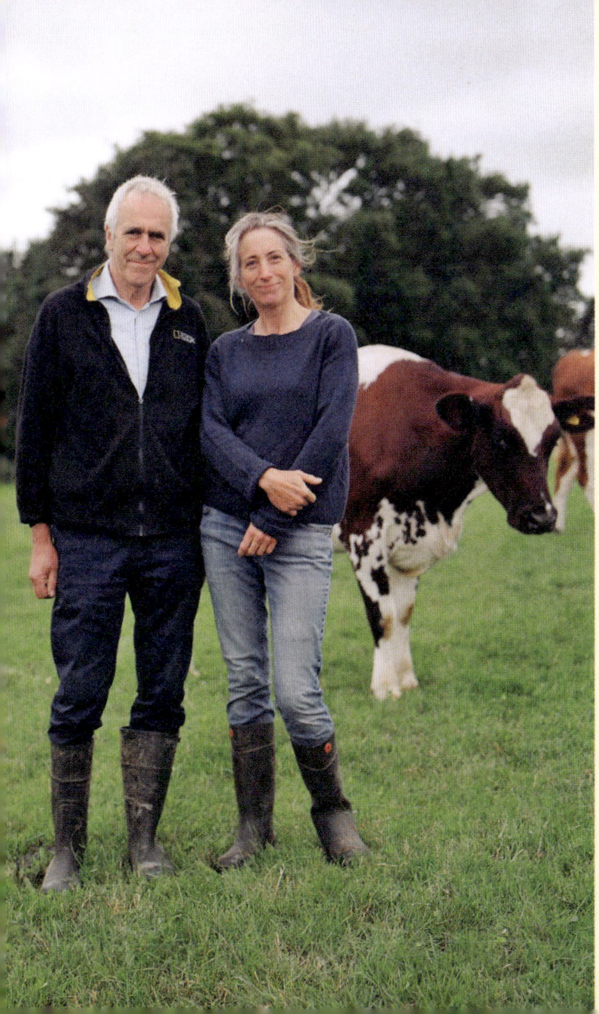
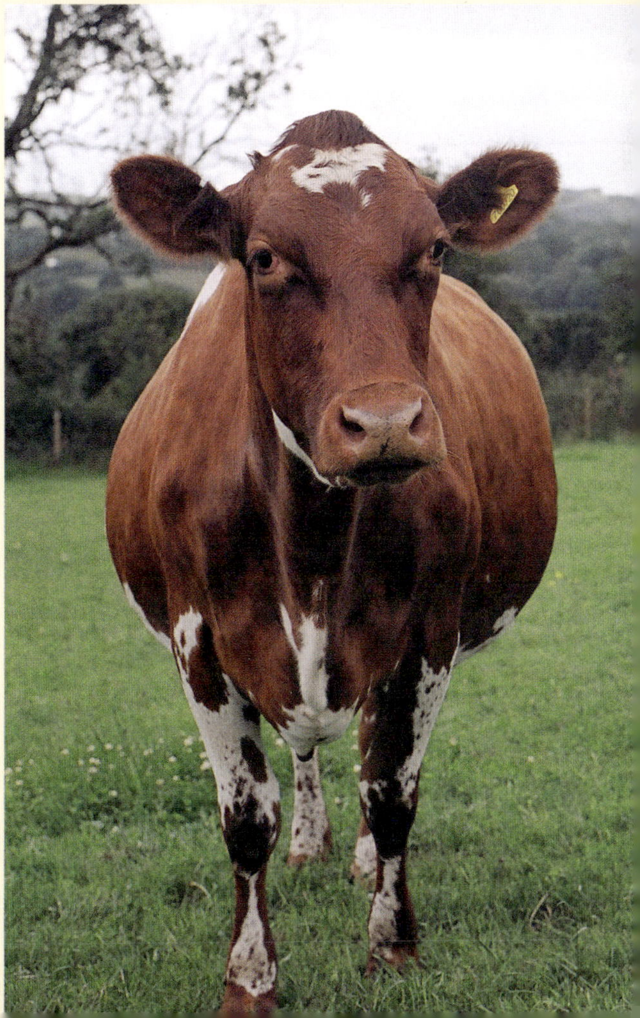

Roasted vegetable quiche with Hafod

This quiche was devoured on a visit to Holden Farm Dairy when my partner Lilly and I were welcomed into the Holden farmhouse to share lunch with Patrick and Becky and their four sons. Baked by Becky, the quiche was served with a mixture of fresh salad leaves, radishes and edible flower petals, all grown on the farm, reflecting how they like to be as self-sufficient as possible.

Over a fruitful discussion about their cheese, the quality of milk, the history of the British landscape and the importance of working in harmony with nature, the quiche was then washed down with plenty of fresh coffee. It was a lunch that, with every delicious mouthful, you could tell was doing you good.

SERVES 6

PASTRY
225g wholemeal flour
100g butter, chilled and cut into cubes
pinch of sea salt
3 tbsp cold water

FILLING
3 red onions, peeled and sliced
1 large courgette, diced
2 garlic cloves, peeled and finely chopped
leaves from a handful of fresh thyme sprigs
1 tbsp olive oil
100g spinach
4 large eggs, lightly beaten
225g Hafod, grated
200ml double cream
pinch of sea salt

First make the pastry. Place the flour, butter and salt in a food processor, and blend until the mixture looks like breadcrumbs. Then add the water and briefly blend until it resembles damp breadcrumbs. For this recipe, there is no need to make a dough: simply tip the pastry mixture into a 25cm-diameter fluted tart tin with a removable base and, with your fingertips, press and flatten it out to cover the base and sides of the tin. Refrigerate the pastry for 30 minutes; this will prevent it from shrinking during cooking.

Meanwhile, preheat the oven to 200°C/400°F/gas mark 6.

In a frying pan on a medium heat, fry the red onions, courgette, garlic and thyme in the olive oil for about 10 minutes, stirring regularly, until the mixture is soft. Set aside to cool.

In a separate saucepan, quickly cook the spinach until wilted, then squeeze out as much water as possible. Add the cooked spinach to the vegetable mixture.

In a large bowl, combine the eggs, grated cheese, double cream and salt.

After the 30 minutes is up, take the pastry out of the fridge and cover the base with a circle of baking parchment and a handful of baking beans, then blind bake for 15 minutes in the oven until lightly golden. Once cooked, set aside to cool.

Once the vegetable mixture is cool, tip into the cheese mixture in the bowl and combine. Tip the combined mixture into the cooled pastry case and bake in the oven for 30–40 minutes until the filling is cooked and golden on top. A slice of this quiche is super with a fresh salad, coleslaw or even a baked potato.

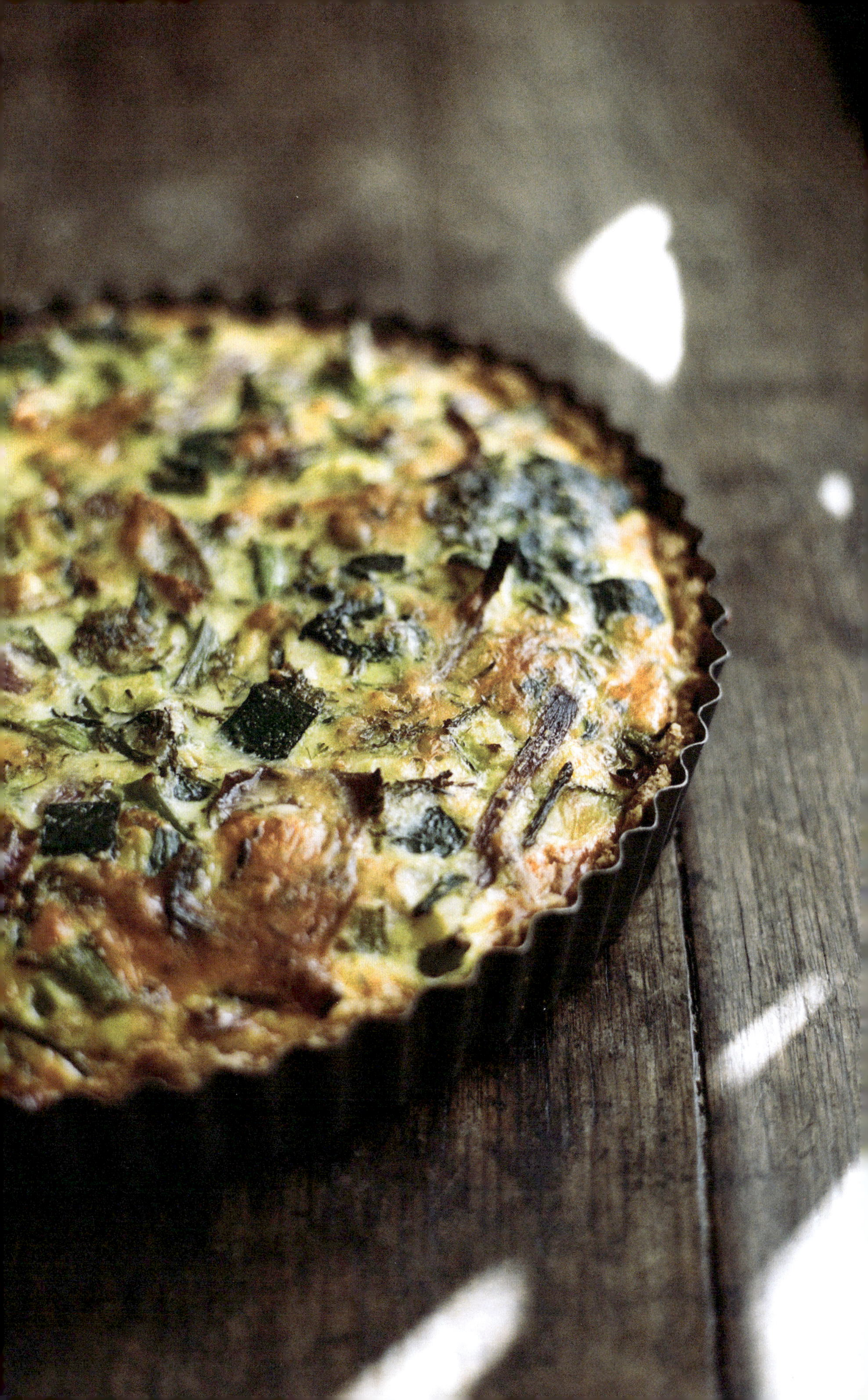

ELRICK LOG

Left: The farm's Tamworth pigs that are fed on the whey, a by-product of the cheesemaking process. The pigs are slaughtered and sold locally.

Right: An ash-coated Elrick Log, made with raw milk from the farm's mixed herd of Saanen, Toggenburg, British Alpine and Anglo-Nubian goats.

Errington Cheese, Walston Braehead Farm, South Lanarkshire

A thousand feet above sea level, between the Pentland Hills to the north east and the River Clyde a few miles to the west, is Walston Braehead Farm, where Selina Cairns, née Errington, makes the ash-coated fresh lactic cheese called Elrick Log using raw milk from the farm's mixed herd of Saanen, Toggenburg and British Alpine goats.

Taking the reins from her father, Humphrey Errington – who started the farm and cheesemaking business in the early 1980s with a small flock of sheep – Selina now works alongside her husband Andrew, who runs the farm. Walston Braehead Farm

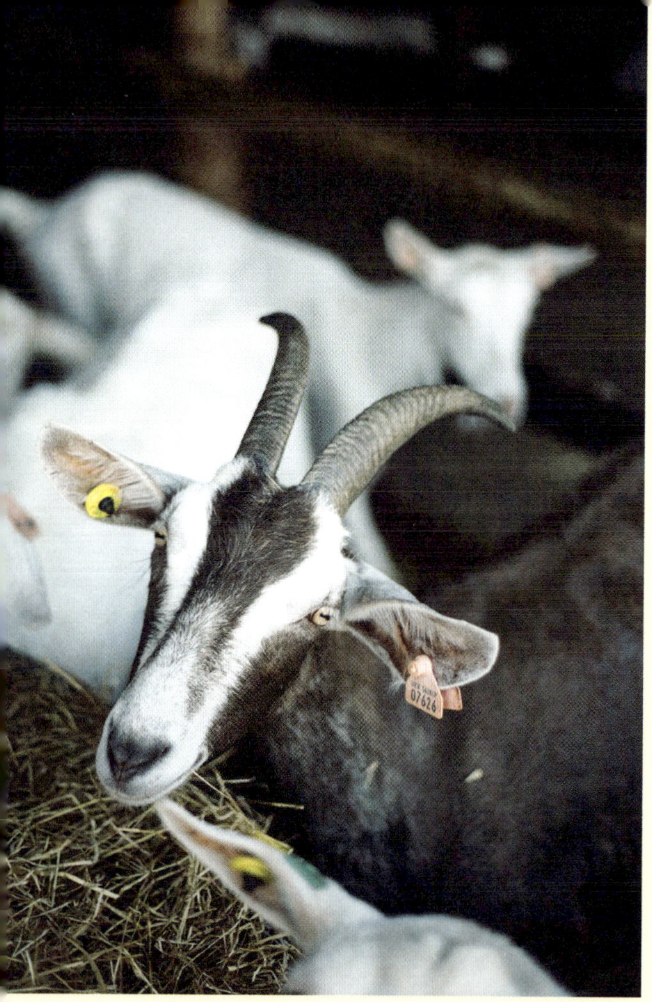

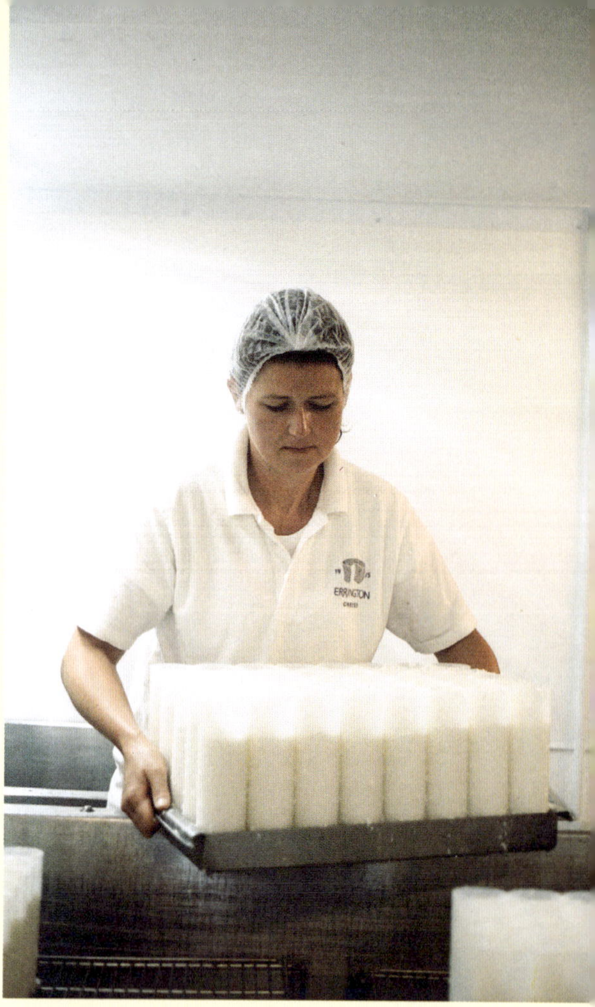
ERRINGTON

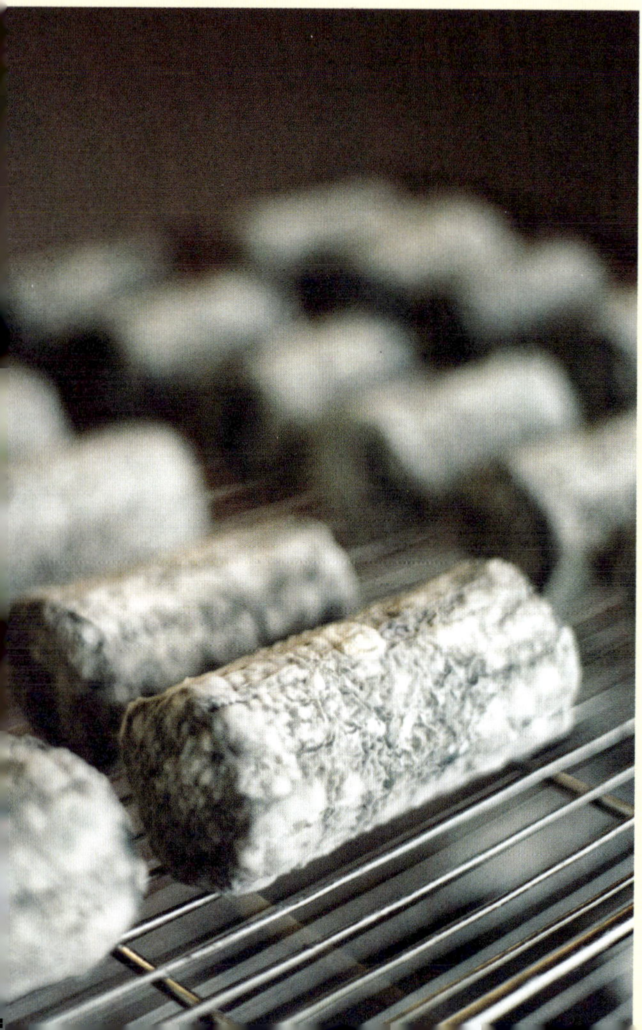

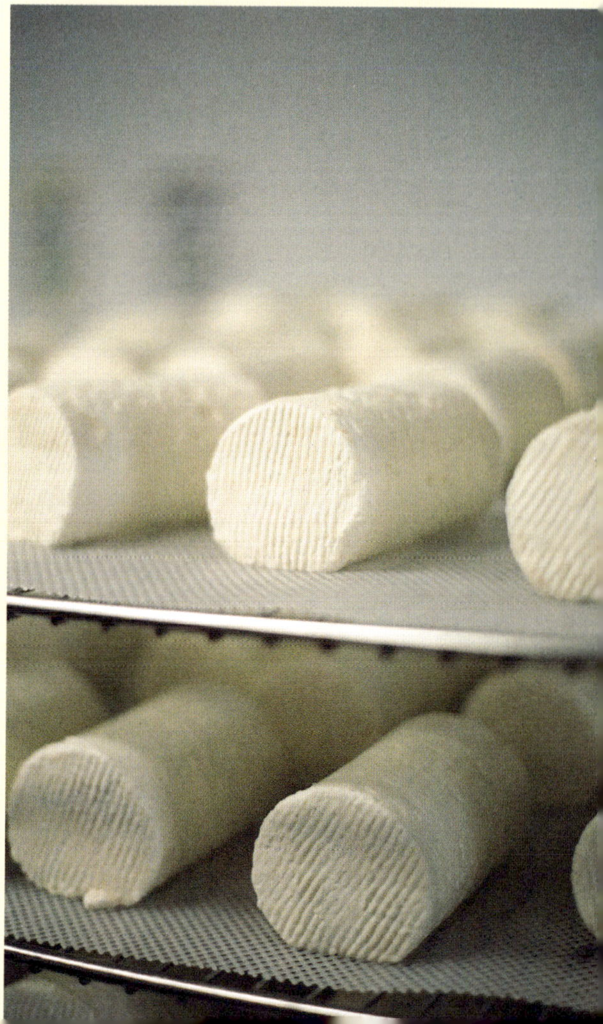

comprises just under 300 acres of mixed grazing and arable land, on which the Cairns grow enough barley, hay and grass for silage to feed their livestock. It was in 2019 when Selina and Andrew decided to diversify into rearing goats, alongside their flock of Lacaune sheep, to produce milk to make cheese. The goats consist of breeds that are well suited to the area's high altitude and specific microclimate. Selina and Andrew are also developing their herd by interbreeding them with Anglo-Nubian goats, whose milk has a high content of butterfat and protein.

Like many farmhouse cheesemakers, Selina makes cheese according to what she likes eating, which is supremely logical. Working alongside Selina is Angela, head cheesemaker at Errington Cheese. Angela also happens to be Andrew's sister, making Walston Braehead Farm and Errington Cheese a truly family affair.

Named after the historic village of Elsrickle nearby, Elrick Log is made in a slow process, in which the curds are left to set overnight. The next day, Selina or Angela ladles the curds by hand into thin cylindrical moulds, leaving them to naturally compress into young cheeses. After a couple of hours, the young cheeses are removed from their moulds and rubbed all over in a dry mixture of salt and ash. Once they have been evenly coated, the young cheeses are left in a hastening room for a few days to dry a little and to encourage mould to grow. The young cheeses are then taken to the maturing rooms to age for at least two weeks. Elrick Log can be eaten from 2–4 weeks – the longer the maturation, the greater the breakdown of the rind, which produces a rich creamy flavour with spicy notes.

Other cheeses made at the farm include Lanark Blue, Lanark White, Corra Linn, Tinto, Sir Lancelot, Blackmount, Bonnington Linn, Biggar Blue and Goats Curd.

Elrick Log characteristics
Milk: Raw milk from the farm's mixed herd of Saanen, Toggenburg, British Alpine and, more recently, Anglo-Nubian goats
Rennet: Animal
Appearance: White-paste log with an ash-covered, mould-ripened edible rind
Tasting notes: Fresh, creamy flavour with hints of citrus, and spicy notes when aged. Varies according to the season and length of maturation

Clockwise from top left: Goats are wonderful, mischievous creatures that will roam to their hearts' content. Here's a British Alpine crossed with a Saanen munching on hay at Walston Braehead Farm.

In the morning of the second day of making Elrick Log, Selina fills a series of cylindrical moulds with the curds that have set over the previous night.

After the curds have naturally compressed in their moulds, the adolescent cheeses are turned out and left to dry a little on wire racks lined with mesh.

The fresh batch of ash-coated cheese logs are then left in a hastening room for a few days to dry further and encourage mould to grow.

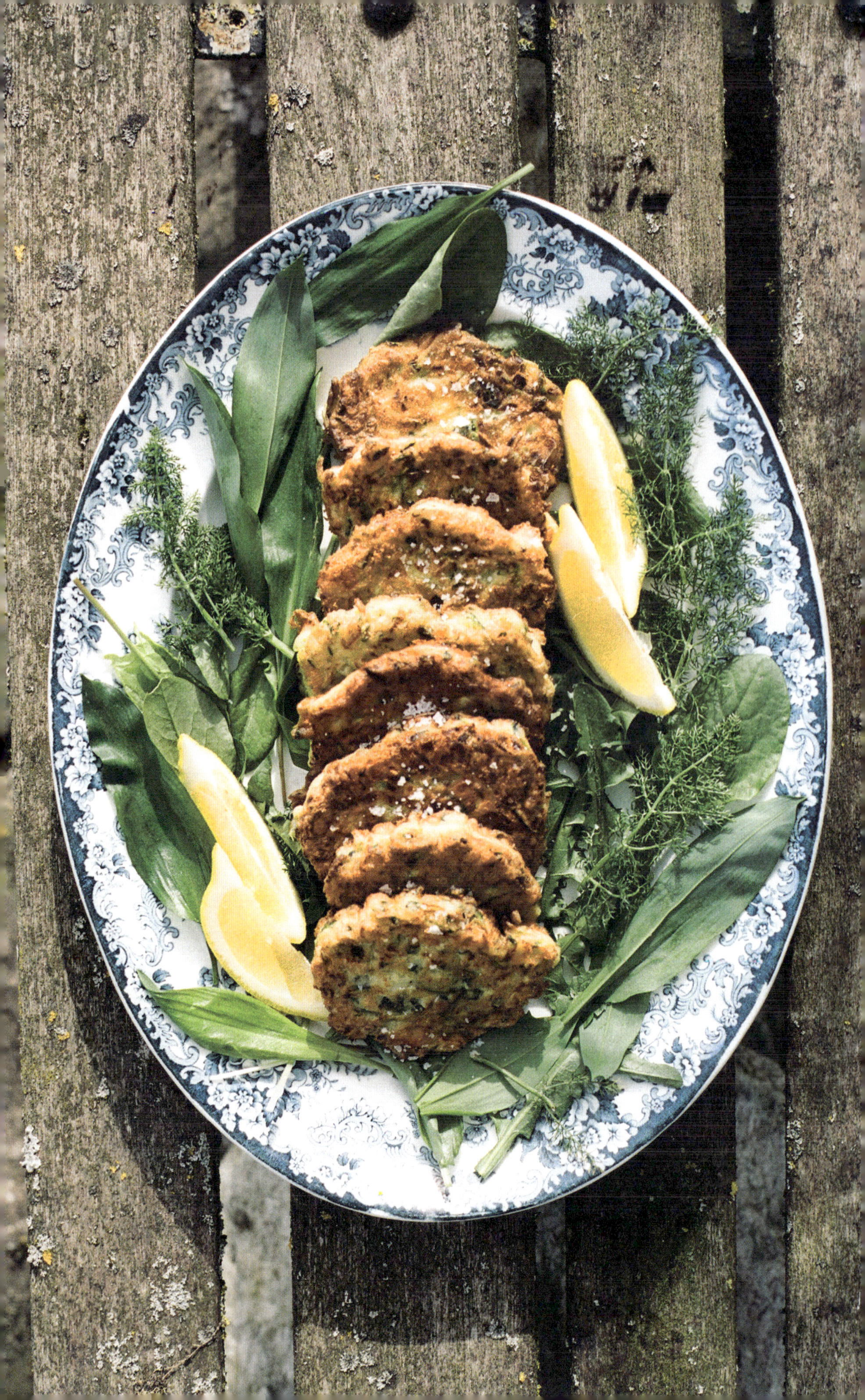

Courgette, Elrick Log and wild garlic fritters

I visited Selina and Andrew at Walston Braehead Farm on a particularly hot day in midsummer, when the land was parched and the skies were completely cloudless and thronging with screaming swifts. Driving up towards the farm, we passed a sizeable row of beech trees on the left and sloping fields to the right that stretch towards the horizon and beyond, on to Edinburgh.

On arrival I met Truffle, Selina and Andrew's border terrier, who greeted me like every good terrier should, full of bristling protectiveness for its kingdom and rulers! The day seemed to fly past. I was given a tour of the dairy, seeing how all the Errington cheeses were made, from Corra Linn to Elrick Log, and shown around by Angela, Andrew's sister, who has been making cheese for well over a decade.

Elrick Log is a fresh lactic cheese, so I thought it would work well mixed with grated courgettes and shallow-fried as fritters – a really easy but impressive recipe to do for supper parties. I love to cook these fritters in spring and early summer when the wild garlic is in season. To serve with the fritters, I've also used fresh foraged spring leaves, something I urge you to do when the leaves are at their best, though always double-check what you are foraging and pick sustainably, taking only a couple of leaves from each plant. I used sorrel, fennel fronds and dandelion leaves, but you could use any fresh salad leaves you like instead.

MAKES 6-8 FRITTERS / SERVES 3-4 AS A STARTER OR 2-3 FOR A LIGHT LUNCH

2 large courgettes (300g after grating and squeezing)
1 large egg
50g wild garlic leaves (or 2-3 garlic cloves, peeled, and a handful of chives), finely chopped
1 large spring onion, finely chopped
1 x 190g whole Elrick Log, chilled
40g plain flour
¼ tsp baking powder
sunflower oil, for frying
sea salt and black pepper

Preheat the oven to 140°C/275°F/gas mark 1 and line a baking tray with baking parchment.

Grate both courgettes and then wrap the grated courgette in a clean tea towel and wring out over the sink to remove as much liquid as you can. Alternatively, place the gratings in a sieve and press the moisture out using a wooden spoon. Weigh the gratings after squeezing them, and once you have 300g, set aside.

In a separate large bowl, beat the egg and add the wild garlic and spring onion. Crumble in the cheese – I normally keep the cheese in the fridge right up until using it to make it easier to crumble. Sift in the flour, baking powder and a good pinch of salt and add several turns of black pepper.

Add the grated courgette to the cheese mixture and combine well.

Ingredients and method continued overleaf

TO SERVE
1 lemon, cut into wedges
young dandelion, fennel and sorrel leaves (or mixed salad leaves)

Place a deep-sided non-stick frying pan on a medium heat and pour in enough oil to fill the pan to a depth of about 1cm. Once the oil is hot, place 2 tablespoons of the mixture in the pan and pat down with the back of the spoon to make a flat round patty shape 6–8cm in diameter, taking care not to splash the hot oil. Repeat, adding as many patties as will fit in the pan without crowding. (You'll need to do this in batches adding more oil as needed.) Cook the courgette patties for 3–5 minutes on one side until golden, then flip over and cook on the other side for the same amount of time. Once a batch of patties is cooked, place on kitchen paper to absorb the excess oil, then transfer to the prepared baking tray and pop in the oven to keep warm.

Once you have fried the last fritters, remove the other fritters from the oven and divide between plates, serving with lots of lemon juice squeezed over and a pile of fresh leaves on the side.

Andrew and Selina graze their Lacaune sheep in small paddocks on clover-rich pasture. The ewe's milk is used to make their renowned Corra Linn, a Cheddar-like cheese.

ISLE OF MULL

Left: Isle of Mull cheese is made only a stone's throw from the island's coast and the quaint town of Tobermory, with its harbourside houses in vivid colours.

Right: Every wheel of Isle of Mull cheese ages in the farm's cellars, a labyrinth of underground rooms that are naturally cool and hence perfect for maturation.

Isle of Mull Cheese, Tobermory, Isle of Mull

Looking out over the Sound of Mull towards the neighbouring islands of the Inner Hebrides, Sgriob-ruadh Farm lies just half a mile from Tobermory on the Isle of Mull off the west coast of Scotland. The farm is home to the Reade family, who make Isle of Mull, a Cheddar-style hard cheese. Chris and Jeff Reade initially farmed in Somerset before relocating their whole farm in 1979 to the current location at Sgriob-ruadh Farm in multiple trips. Alongside Chris, her eldest son, Brendan, his wife Shelagh and Brendan's brother Garth now run the farm and make the cheese.

The Reade family pride themselves on using renewable energy sources to generate all of the electricity and heating needed each day on the farm. Everything is as sustainable as possible, from the wind and water turbines, to burning wood-chip biomass sourced from local wood to heat the milk in the cheesemaking process. The island, the mixed farm and the cheese production are all interlinked in a circular system in which each element sustains another. The island's spring water feeds the farm to grow pasture for the cows, which in turn produce milk to make cheese and the by-product, whey, that feeds the pigs. The whey is also used to make a selection of spirits produced in the farm's distillery. The manure produced by the animals is used to feed the land and enrich the soil. Much of it is used to make compost, which feeds the fruit and vegetables that Chris grows in her greenhouse.

Isle of Mull is made using raw milk from the farm's mixed herd of British Friesian, Norwegian Red and Ayrshire cows. The farming methods employed are aimed at producing high-quality milk in a way that is in harmony with the environment.

Although the rocky, boggy terrain has its own challenges, the family are able to graze the cows outside for most of the year and grow grass to make silage for feed in the winter months. The cows are also fed on draff (protein-rich malted barley), a by-product of whisky making obtained from the local Tobermory Distillery. They calve year-round to ensure a consistent supply of milk.

The method of making Isle of Mull follows a traditional Cheddar-style recipe. The quality and handling of the raw milk, the farm's particular terrain and climate, and the maturation process, all contribute to the uniqueness of the cheese. Aged for 12–16 months, Isle of Mull frequently develops the odd sharp line of blue mould running through the paste, seen by many as a natural bonus in terms of flavour.

The Reade family also make Hebridean Blue and Smoked Isle of Mull.

Isle of Mull characteristics

Milk: Raw milk from the farm's mixed herd of British Friesian, Norwegian Red and Ayrshire cows

Rennet: Animal

Appearance: Pale yellow paste with a mottled, inedible clothbound rind

Tasting notes: Punchy savoury flavour with bright fruity notes. Varies according to the season and length of maturation

Clockwise from top left: The view over to Sgriob-ruadh Farm – whose name means 'Red Furrow' in Gaelic, referring to the region's reddish soil – and the Glass Barn, the vine-covered farm shop and café.
Isle of Mull is made to a traditional Cheddar-style recipe. Here Molly, Chris's granddaughter and assistant cheesemaker, stirs the curds and whey.
Ro Beale, dairy manager at the farm, starts the process of pitching, allowing the curds to settle in the drainage table, before removing the whey.
Each pressed wheel of Isle of Mull is wrapped in muslin and coated in lard. While Ro Beale and Molly do it effortlessly, it's much harder than it looks, I can tell you!

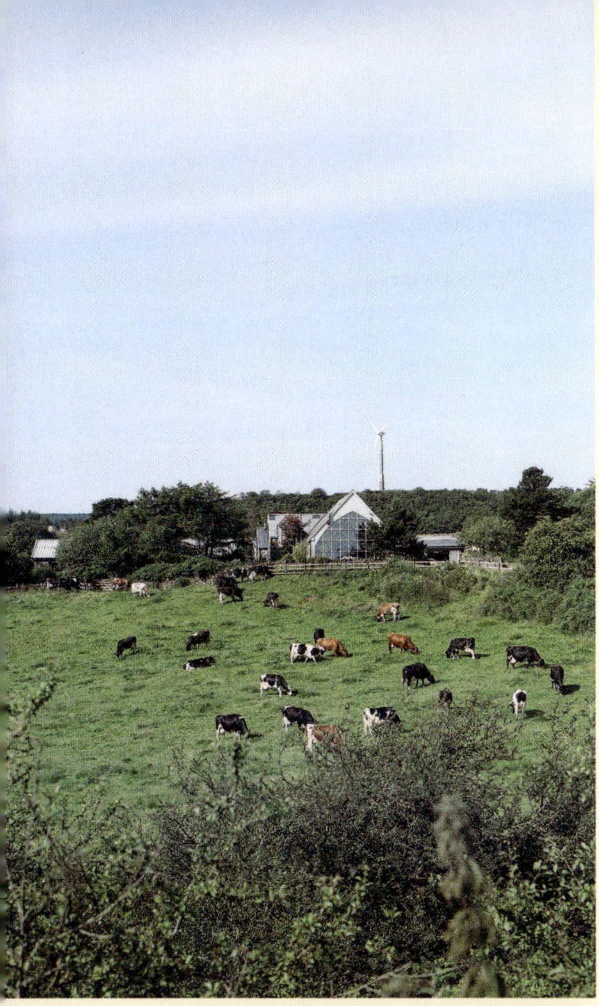
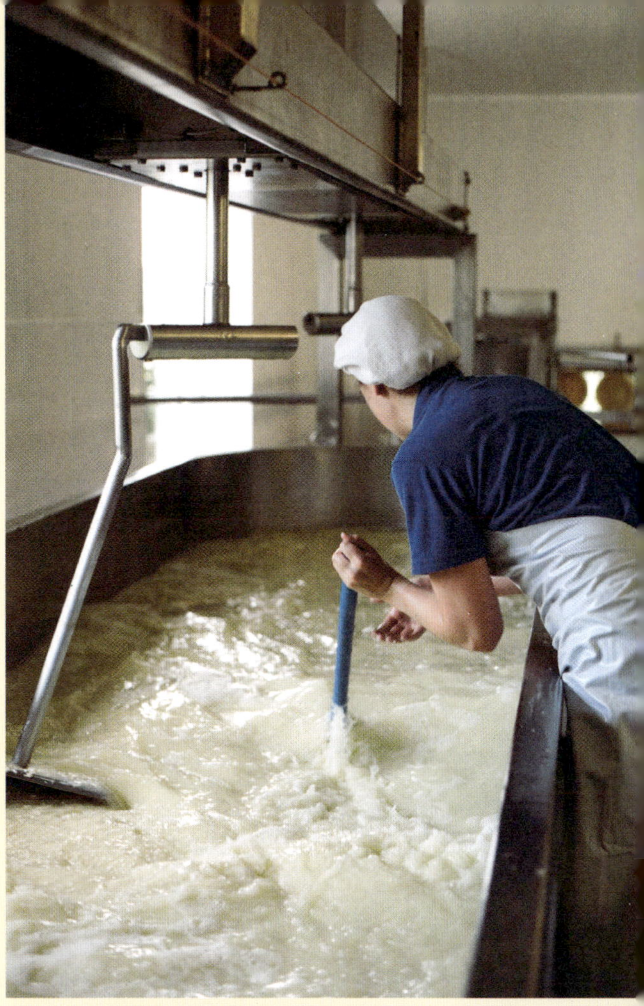
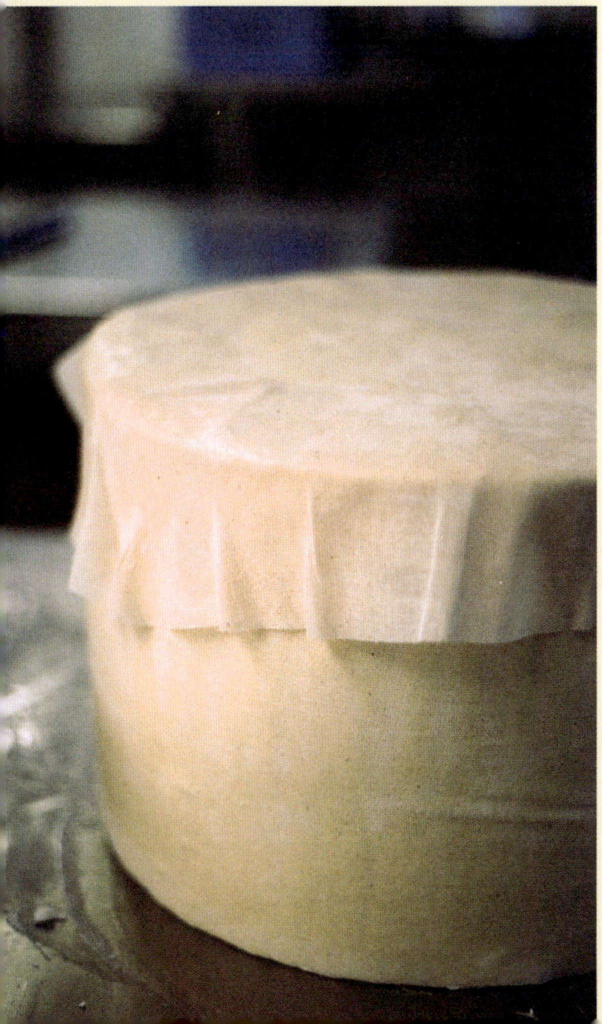
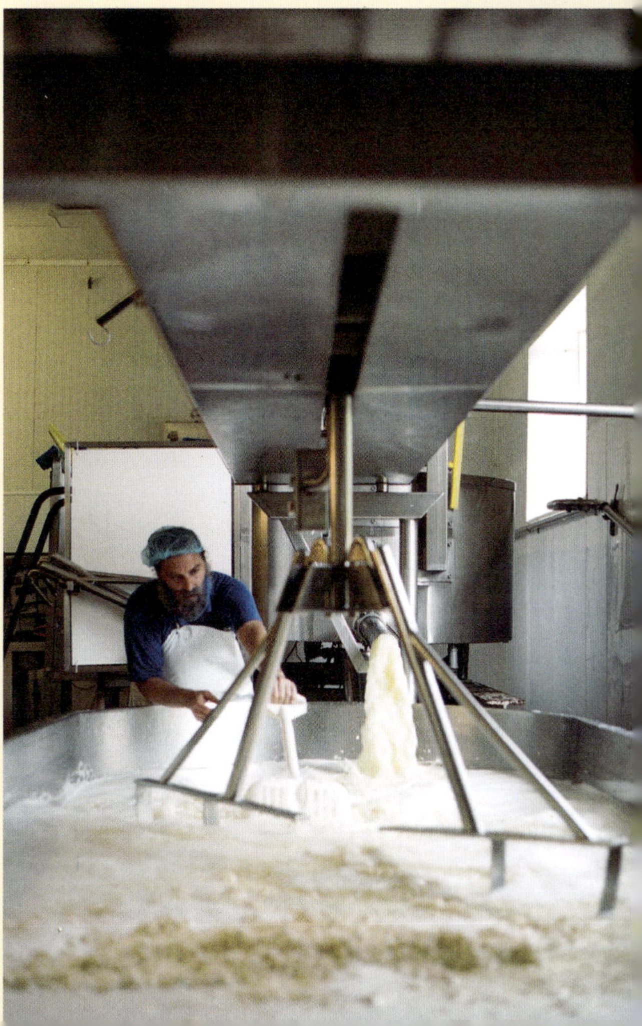

Isle of Mull macaroni cheese

Before I had even decided on which cheesemakers to visit for this book, I knew that the Reade family had to be included, because of their wonderful cheese, inspiring story and sustainable ways of working – plus, what a brilliant excuse to visit one of the most beautiful regions of the British Isles, where you can swim in crystal-clear waters and sample delicious local seafood.

The trip to the Isle of Mull was one leg of my British cheese journey that I was particularly looking forward to, and as you can imagine, it didn't disappoint! The whole trip was simply breathtaking, from taking the ferry from Oban and seeing the spectacular array of islands in every direction, to driving along the very narrow coastal lanes to Tobermory and walking the scenic route to Sgriob-ruadh Farm. It was thoroughly enjoyable, not least because the whole time I was there, the island was bathed in what the locals referred to as 'a strong spell of Scottish sunshine, unheard of here on the Isle!'

This macaroni cheese recipe was something I had to include in the book, using the best local ingredients, plenty of Isle of Mull cheese and a red onion from Chris's greenhouse. A good heap of this cheesy pasta followed by a dram of single malt whisky distilled on the island at the Tobermory Distillery is utterly scrumptious.

SERVES 3-4

1 medium red onion, diced
1 tbsp olive oil
1 tbsp balsamic vinegar
1 tbsp soft light brown sugar
30g butter, plus extra for greasing
30g flour
350ml whole milk
50ml double cream
250g Isle of Mull cheese, grated
300g macaroni
sea salt and freshly ground black pepper

Preheat the oven to 200°C/400°F/gas mark 6 and butter a deep-sided, medium (30cm x 20cm) ovenproof dish.

On a medium heat, pan-fry the onion in the olive oil for 5–6 minutes until softened and translucent. Turn the temperature down a little and add the balsamic vinegar and brown sugar. Keep stirring for 3–4 minutes until the onions are coated and sticky, then remove from the heat and set aside.

In a large saucepan, melt the butter and add the flour, whisking constantly to make a roux. Then add the milk in stages, continuing to whisk to prevent lumps from forming. Keep whisking until the sauce thickens, then add the double cream, 1 teaspoon of salt and 150g of the grated cheese, and stir until the cheese is melted. Add the glazed onions to the cheese sauce and combine well.

Meanwhile, bring a large pan of salted water to the boil, add the macaroni and cook until al dente – usually a minute or two less than the cooking time given in the packet instructions. Drain the pasta, then tip into the pan with the cheese and onion sauce, and mix well.

Pour the cheese and onion pasta into the prepared ovenproof dish, sprinkle over the rest of the cheese and bake in the oven for 30–35 minutes until bubbling and browned on top. Serve with plenty of black pepper ground on top.

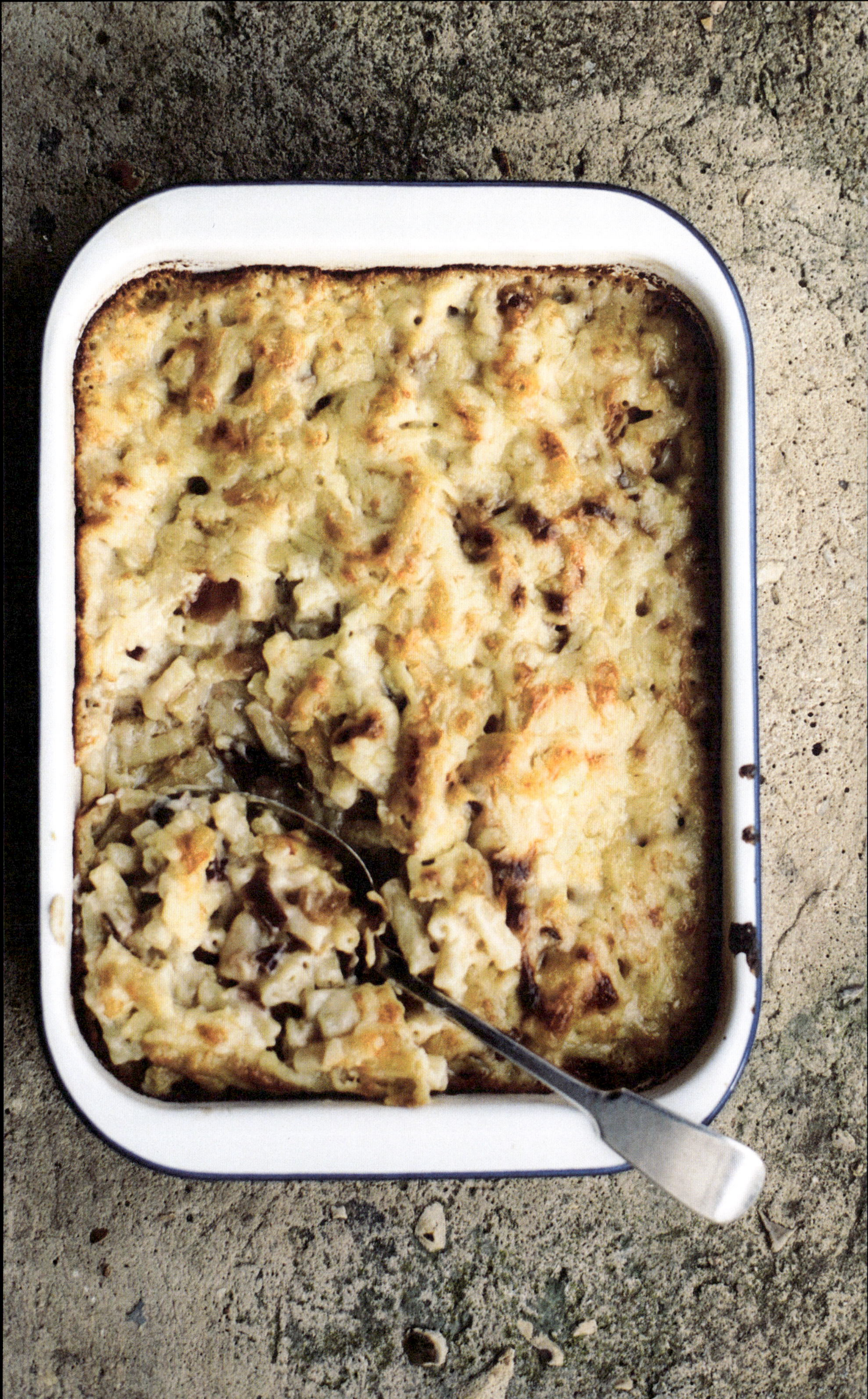

YOUNG BUCK

From left to right: Back at the creamery, the tank full of raw milk is connected up to a pipe, which channels the milk gently through to the cheesemaking rooms.

Not a crop circle, but a curd circle! Here in the cheesemaking rooms, cheesemaker Jonathan is quickly but carefully ladling the curds on to the drainage table in one smooth motion to keep the curds intact.

Each make creates between ten and twelve 8kg wheels. Here is Mike in the hastening room, checking over the previous day's batch sitting nicely in their hoops (moulds). The room is kept hot and humid to encourage mould to grow in the cheese.

According to Mike, the most satisfying feeling for a cheesemaker is to have a room full of cheese that is maturing nicely and tasting fantastic.

Mike's Fancy Cheese, Newtownards, County Down

On the northern shores of Strangford Lough, on the Ards Peninsula in County Down, lies the creamery where Young Buck is made by Mike Thomson. Young Buck is a blue cheese produced using raw milk from a local herd of Holstein-Friesian cows. Working closely with the farmer, Smyth McCann, Mike collects milk from the farm 3–4 times a week. The creamery where Mike makes his Young Buck has a view towards Scrabo Hill and Scrabo Tower, a nineteenth-century lookout tower on top of the hill with stunning views of Strangford Lough.

Mike started out working in a deli in Belfast, before completing a cheesemaking course at the School of Artisan Food in Nottinghamshire, where fellow students included Andy Swinscoe, who now runs The Courtyard Dairy, and David Jowett, head cheesemaker at King Stone Dairy (see page 132). The cheesemaking course took Mike all around the British Isles, including placements with Martin Gott, who makes St James (see page 138), Joe Schneider, who produces Stichelton (see page 164), and Stacey Hedges, who makes Tunworth. Mike also spent a year with David

Mike Thomson makes Young Buck, a blue cheese made using raw milk from a local herd of Holstein-Friesian cows.

and Jo Clarke in Leicestershire, making Sparkenhoe Red Leicester and their blue cheeses (see page 150). Mike moved back to Northern Ireland in 2013 to make his own cheese and after an inspiring discussion with Andy Swinscoe, decided to create a raw-milk blue cheese.

Young Buck is made to a traditional Stilton-type recipe, characterised by the gentle handling of the raw milk and slow acidification of the curds. When the starter culture and rennet have been added, and the cheesemaker feels the curds have set enough, they are cut into small pieces using a cheese knife and left to settle on the bottom of the vat. After a couple of hours, most of the whey is drained but enough is kept back to help the next stage, when the curds are ladled by hand on to a drainage table and left overnight to acidify.

The following day, the curds are cut into blocks, turned and broken up by hand into small pieces. Once they have been salted, the curds are ladled into moulds and taken to the hastening room for a week, where they are turned every day. At the end of the week, the young cheeses are rubbed with a knife to close any gaps in the surface and placed in the drying room for a month to reduce the level of moisture in them. In the maturing rooms, the cheeses are pierced twice with metal spikes, in weeks five and seven, to encourage the blue mould to develop. Young Buck is aged for a minimum of twelve weeks. As Mike says of the process for making Young Buck: 'I try to allow the cheese to do its own thing as much as possible, because at the end of the day, milk really wants to turn into cheese!'

Young Buck characteristics

Milk: Raw milk from a local herd of Holstein-Friesian cows

Rennet: Animal

Appearance: Light and creamy, blue-veined crumbly paste with an edible red and white mould-ripened rind

Tasting notes: Three flavours in one cheese: sweet pear in the white paste; sharp crunchy notes in and around the blue veins; and rich biscuit beneath the rind. Varies according to the season and length of maturation

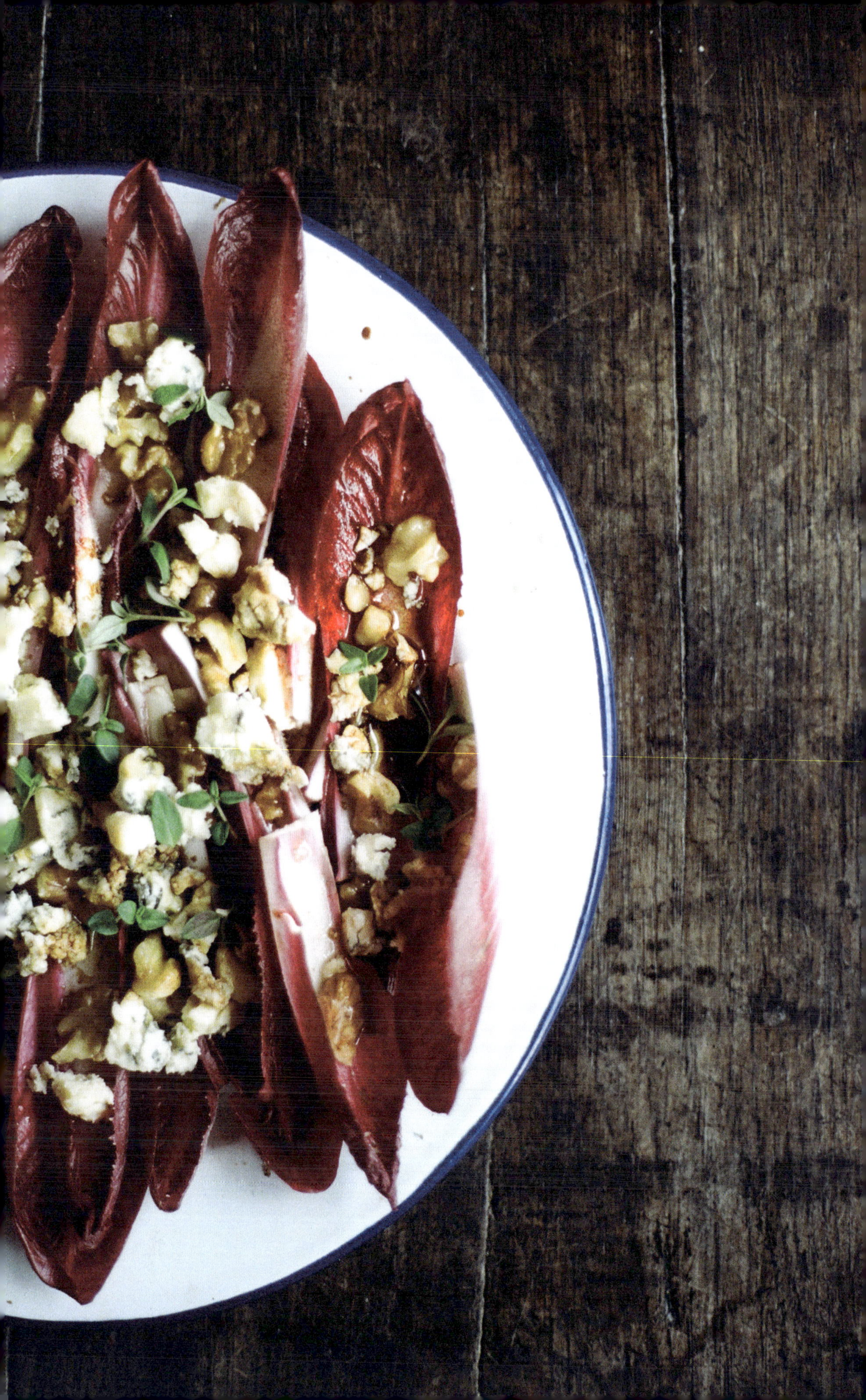

Chicory, walnut and Young Buck salad

The late-summer sun was with me for the entire journey as I drove to meet Mike in Northern Ireland, from Wales, where I started, through Scotland and on the ferry across to Belfast. The drive went relatively smoothly and the sea on the crossing was teeming with wildlife – I spotted grey seals, dolphins, gannets, guillemots and puffins diving in and out of the waves that rose and fell across the vast metallic surface of the Irish Sea.

Having reached Belfast, I packed in as much as I could in the short time I was there. Mike makes Young Buck on the outskirts of Newtownards, a pleasant half-an-hour's drive north-east of the city. I visited the farm where Mike sources his milk and the cheesemaking rooms at the creamery, where I watched cheesemaker Jonathan ladle the curds on to the drainage table – incredibly satisfying to watch but, as Mike wryly observed, 'Not so satisfying to do,' owing to the back-breaking, back-twisting nature of the work!

After seeing Young Buck in the making, it was back to Belfast to visit 'Mike's Fancy Cheese', Mike's shop in the Cathedral Quarter of the city. If you want to sample the finest British and Irish cheeses, Mike's shop is the place to go as it has an incredible selection. One of the most important aspects of the job for Mike is knowing each cheesemaker personally so that, when selling their cheese in his shop, he can tell the customer everything about it. And that's what's so impressive: Mike is both a cheesemaker and a cheesemonger. At the end of my visit – a day packed with cheesemaking and scrumptious sampling – we took ourselves off to Mike's local to enjoy a strong pint of Irish craft beer.

This recipe is a favourite of mine, something really fresh and light to have on a baking-hot day, served with an ice-cold pint or glass of wine. It would be delicious served as a side with a tomato-based pasta or on its own with some crusty bread.

SERVES 2–3 AS A SIDE

leaves from 3 small or 2 large chicory heads
2 tbsp extra-virgin olive oil
1 tbsp balsamic vinegar
50g walnuts, finely chopped
50g Young Buck
freshly ground black pepper
sprigs of fresh thyme, to serve

Really easy recipe, this! Just arrange the chicory leaves on a serving plate and mix the oil and vinegar in a small jug. Scatter the chopped walnuts over the leaves and crumble over the cheese, then pour over the dressing and add several grinds of black pepper. Top with the sprigs of fresh thyme. Toss everything together to serve.

Overleaf: The ferry across the Irish Sea passes multiple lighthouses and small islands with a great variety of seabirds, from gannets and guillemots, to cormorants and razorbills.

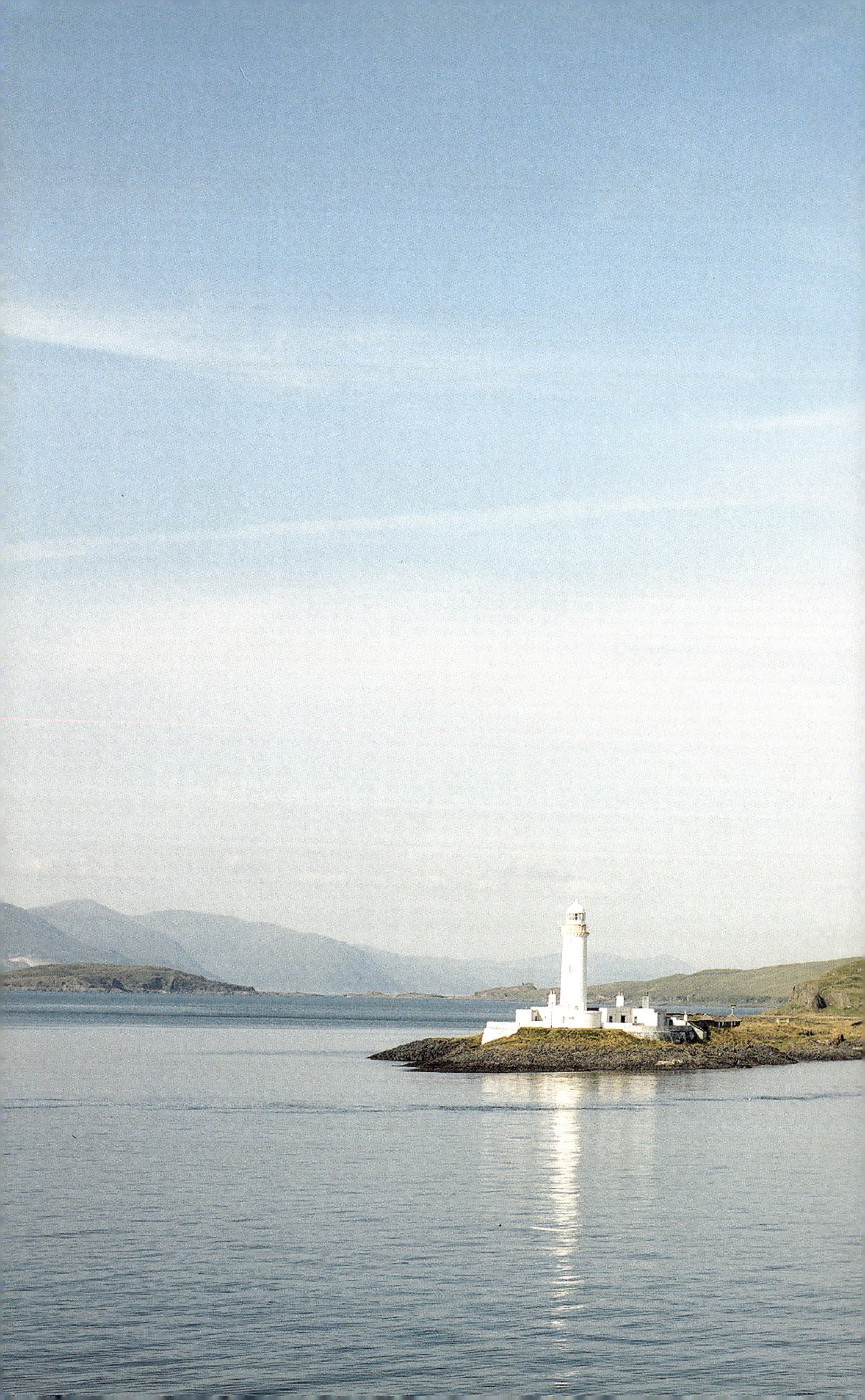

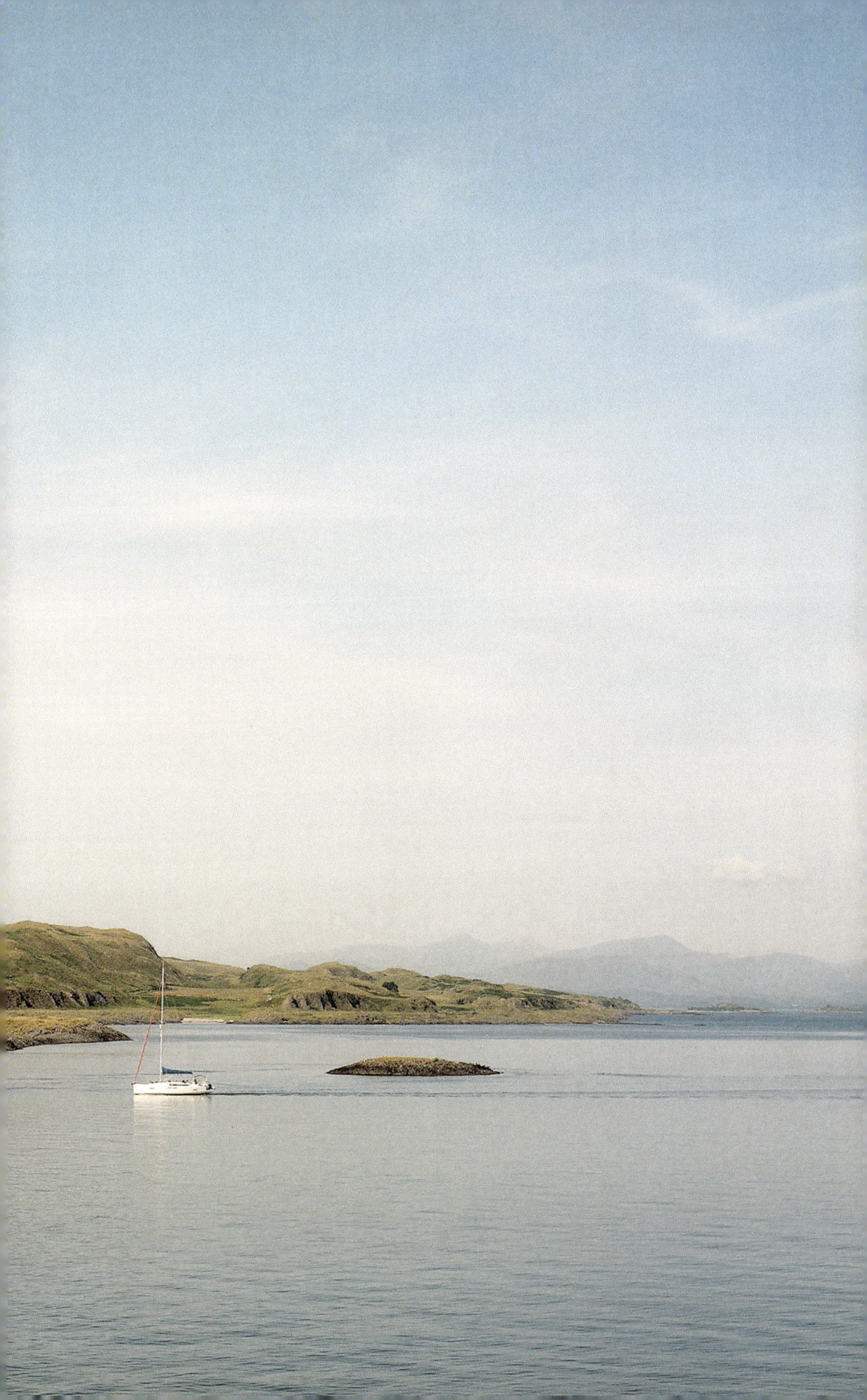

The last view

My love of the rural environment took hold of me at a very young age. I can still remember springtime in a field of rapeseed like a yellow sea, chasing one of my brothers along the tractor lines, following the deep herringbone imprint of massive tyres, stick (imagined sword) thrust out in front of me, not close enough to strike my brother's bouncing laces or his floppy hair, but near enough to behead several unsuspecting yellow flowerheads in our breakneck rush through the floral sea.

It was freedom. Freedom to run, shout and play, in as much space as you dared to venture. Growing up beneath the enormous skies in rural Cambridgeshire, my two brothers and I were spoilt in that regard, with a garden that looked out on to a long sloping field that ran into mixed woodland and then out the other side, stretching away for another mile or two. 'The view', as my mother would lovingly call it, was our world. Whenever my brothers and I weren't playing with toy cars we would head out into 'the view' – bags packed with a squashed sandwich, a plastic compass and trusty stick to see off any imagined fantasy creatures. The view marked the beginning of a new adventure – the starting point to who knows where.

As we grew older, the sticks were swapped for books, though the love of cars remained. The heedless running around was changed for long walks, and instead of chopping the heads off life-threatening plants, we stopped and identified them. We soon discovered a whole host of different varieties in the field or back garden – all quite literally on our doorstep. That bloody painful plant was called a nettle; it had much friendlier lookalikes called white and red dead-nettles. Those sweet-smelling, chandelier-like flowers growing in the hedgerows belonged to the honeysuckle family, those tacky buds that covered our socks were cleaver seeds and the sticky darts that we threw at one another and often chewed on our way back home were the heads of barley. With each changing season we were encouraged by our mother to look out for birds – swallows marking the beginning and end of summer with their happy arrival and sad departure, rogue kites and keening buzzards soaring overhead, and the resident gang of sparrows swooping joyously in and out of the privet hedge.

With the coming and going of each season, my appreciation for the natural environment grew apace. 'The view' changed every few months: flooded in the spring by the sea of vibrant rapeseed; covered in the summer by a tawny expanse of wheat or hay; or completely shorn at other times by roving horses that would sometimes jump the fence and begin munching on our lawn. I started to notice that the field margins and banks of trees were in constant flux, continually changing in colour and amount of vegetation, sometimes smelling of soap or delicate perfume and always teeming with wildlife, from roving bugs to shrieking shrews. I would often get to see the latter at close quarters on our doorstep most afternoons in summer – a gift from the wild, courtesy of our part-feral cat, Lillie. 'Well done!' we always said, albeit tinged with dismay at the sight of yet another small corpse. 'Thank you!'

Each spring I now look forward to the land being lit up by May blossom and wildflowers, vivid spots of colour that dot the fields and hedgerows like runway lights, guiding the swifts and swallows as they touch down for summer after their winter migration. It is the time of year when I rejoice in the sight of new green shoots splitting through the soil beneath a chorus of sweet skylark song, and new spring lambs that roam and play in joyful gaggles. Though it is not until I smell the gloriously pungent scent of wild garlic drifting through the woodland that I feel that spring has well and truly arrived.

In summer, it is invigorating to see the land at its liveliest, drenched in lush green and bright colour. Now is the time for long walks with the family, clocking up the miles, passing verges with their frothy firework displays of cow parsley, and scented with fragrant wild roses and meadowsweet. The fields of summer are at their richest, dotted with peacefully grazing cows or straying ewes, and the skies above a deep blue, alive with butterflies and busy bees – like me, savouring the warm weather.

When autumn arrives, the land slips into warm, rusty hues, leaves curl and fall and branches laden with apples and plums sweep the ground. This is the time of year I try to make the most of any warm evenings, foraging for the flurry of mushrooms that pop up, such as the chicken of the woods that bulge from oak trees, and picking as much fruit as my jumper can hold. Such nights normally end with me stuffed to the brim with any fruit crumble going, falling asleep to the grating lullaby of tractors at work in distant fields, the farmers harvesting until the wee hours in their brightly lit cabins.

Winter brings the sharp, bitter days and long, dark nights. For someone who doesn't best cope with the long, cold, relentless days of winter, I look for things to cheer me up, finding delight in the season's hedgerows, decorated with frozen baubles of sloes and haw berries, perfect fodder for hardy migrants like the redwing and fieldfare to line their stomachs for the next stage of their journey. Like us, each and every one of them is a traveller, passing through life.

Now, looking back at those years of growing up in the countryside, chasing my brothers through fields and woodlands, trying to catch anything that moved and chewing on god knows what plant but miraculously surviving, I didn't realise it then, but they have shaped my whole outlook on life and how the bounty of nature is to be valued and never taken for granted.

Glossary

See also the Introduction (pages 4–9) for further details about some of the cheesemaking and farming terms below.

acidification: The part of the cheesemaking process during which the milk acidifies, most often accelerated with a starter culture, and the lactose in the milk is converted into lactic acid, beginning the process by which the milk is changed from a liquid into a solid.

artisan cheese: There are differing definitions for what constitutes an 'artisan' cheese, but I would describe it as one produced with natural ingredients, predominantly made by hand and using traditional methods.

Cheddaring: A technique used in the cheesemaking process for hard-style cheeses such as Cheddar in which the curds are cut into large blocks and repeatedly stacked over the next few hours. This process increases the acidity of the curds, while it also encourages the proteins to come together, slowly pressing out moisture and transforming the large blocks into wide, flat sheets.

cheese knife: A single-bladed long knife used to cut the curds during cheesemaking.

coagulation: Also known as clotting, this is when the milk is converted to curds (solid) and whey (liquid) during the cheesemaking process.

curd cutter: A single-handled instrument with blades/wires used to cut the curds.

curds: The solids produced after coagulation of the milk during the cheesemaking process, mainly made up of milk proteins and fat.

cutting the curds: A stage in the cheesemaking process that helps to expel whey.

direct drilling: Planting seeds directly into the ground to avoid disturbing the soil and hence maintain a good soil structure.

farmhouse cheese: Cheese that has been produced on the same farm where the milk is sourced.

flocculation test: A way to find out the point of flocculation, or coagulation, during cheesemaking. The cheesemaker measures the time it takes from when the rennet is added to the milk to when coagulation occurs. To help find out the exact point of coagulation, the cheesemaker repeatedly places a light object on top of the acidifying milk until the object is supported by the curds forming in the milk. A soft-style cheese has a longer flocculation time than a hard-style cheese.

fluffing: An informal term for breaking up the curds before placing them into moulds.

hastening room or 'hastener': A room with the right conditions for drying the cheeses and lowering their moisture content. Such a room can be seen at dairies that make blue cheese, for example.

herbal ley, diverse/mixed: A mixture of plant species grown to improve biodiversity and soil health in a particular field or pasture. Many farmers use different plant species in varying quantities in their herbal leys to suit the specific geology, ecology and topography of their farms.

iron, cheesemaker's: An instrument used in the maturing process to assess the structure and flavour, mainly in the case of semi-hard and hard cheeses.

lactic cheese: Otherwise known as a 'soft lactic cheese', this refers to a cheese that has undergone a slow coagulation (normally overnight) during the cheesemaking process.

maturing room: A room with the right conditions for leaving adolescent cheeses to age and develop flavour, texture and aroma.

milling: The stage in the cheesemaking process when the curds (often in large blocks that are broken up by hand) are fed through a mill to become fine particles.

mould-ripened cheese: Cheese to which one or more moulds have been added to the milk during the cheesemaking process, as in the case of blue cheeses such as Stichelton (see page 164) and/or sprayed on the surface of the cheese during the maturing phase.

natural-rind cheese: Cheese that is encouraged to grow a natural rind, often clothbound to prevent mould from infiltrating the cheese and to increase shelf life.

peg (or curd) mill: Essentially an open box with a series of rotating pegs or rods inside, powdered by hand or via electricity. The mill reduces the size of the curds and is normally positioned over the vat during the cheesemaking process.

permaculture: A farming system that aims to work in harmony with nature, not against it, using no artificial fertilisers or pesticides. See also regenerative agriculture.

permanent pasture/grassland: An area of land, mainly used for grazing livestock, that has been used to grow herbaceous forage, including grasses, and that has not been in a crop rotation for at least five years.

piercing: The stage during maturation (for many blue cheeses) when the cheese is pierced with metal spikes to allow more oxygen to infiltrate the cheese and thereby encourage the familiar veins of blue mould to develop.

'pint' starter culture: A pint of frozen milk, used as a starter culture, that includes strains of bacteria that have been captured at a particular place and time.

pitching: When the curds are allowed to sink to the bottom of the vat after cutting and before the whey is drained.

provenance, food: Like artisan cheese, another term whose definition is contested but, as I see it, relates to the very essence of something, going beyond a simple definition of 'place of origin'. Applied to food, provenance identifies something as the product of a specific environment, embodying its qualities and, at a wider level, connecting the consumer to the land and soil, where it all begins.

raw milk: Straight from the animal, milk that has not been pasteurised and is known to contain an abundance of natural microbes that arguably makes for a more complex cheese.

regenerative agriculture: Farming in a way that mimics nature as much as possible, implementing practices that actively seek to improve the health of the land (soil) and its wider environment, including rotational/mob or paddock grazing, silvopasture (a management system that integrates livestock, pasture and trees, to provide shelter and food for the livestock while improving biodiversity), minimum or no tillage, direct drilling and planting native trees or cover crops. See also permaculture.

rennet: An enzyme, either animal-based or vegetarian, added to the milk in the cheesemaking process that triggers the separation of the curds from the whey.

rind breakdown: Mostly occurring during the maturation process, when microbes secrete enzymes that break down the proteins and the fats in the cheese from larger molecules into smaller ones associated with enhanced flavour.

rotational/mob or paddock grazing: The opposite of 'set stocking', in which the livestock is allowed to graze without restriction, this is a practice by which the farmer divides a larger piece of land into a series of small 'paddocks', grazed on a rotational basis, with the aim of allowing most of the land to rest. Plants thus have time to grow, developing longer roots that help to improve soil structure and health in the process. A diverse/mixed herbal ley is often planted as part of this, with the idea of improving biodiversity.

starter culture: 'Friendly' bacteria, otherwise known as 'cultures', added to the milk at the beginning of the cheesemaking process to trigger the acidification process.

strap: A wooden band that is wrapped around a cheese, usually a soft one, to give structure and impart flavour. A spruce strap is used on Rollright cheese made by David Jowett at King Stone Dairy (see page 132), for example.

territorial cheese: A cheese taking the name of the county or area in the British Isles in which it was made, e.g. Cheshire or Cheddar.

washed-rind cheese: A treatment used in the maturing process, in which the rind of the cheese may be washed with a brine solution and/or with an alcoholic drink such as beer, perry or cider, or in the case of some Scottish cheeses, with single malt whisky.

whey: The watery liquid produced after coagulation during the cheesemaking process.

Where to buy artisan cheese

To help you find where to buy artisan cheese, such as the cheeses included in this book, and the many, many more scrumptious artisan cheeses that come in all shapes, sizes and flavours from all over the British Isles, I have listed a whole load of reputable cheesemongers, shops and delis. From Orkney to Hackney, Manchester to the Midlands, each entry includes the business's name and their website, where you can find full addresses and details. Any entry marked with a '*' is featured within the pages of this book.

East England

Alder Carr Farm Shop, Suffolk
aldercarrfarm.co.uk

Bevistan Dairy, Bedfordshire
bevistandairy.co.uk

Bury Lane Farm Shop, Herfordshire
burylanefarmshop.co.uk

Ben & Ella's Farm Shop, Essex
benandellasfarmshop.co.uk

Blackwells Farm Shop, Essex
blackwellsfarmproduce.co.uk

Deersbrook Farm & Farm Shop, Essex *deersbrookfarm.com*

* Fen Farm Dairy, Suffolk
fenfarmdairy.co.uk

Liquorice, Essex
liquoricewine.co.uk

Little Pig Bakery, Suffolk
littlepigbakery.co.uk

Meadows, Cambridgeshire
meadowscambridge.com

Mini Miss Bread, Essex
minimiss.co.uk

Rennet & Rind, Cambridgeshire
rennetandrind.co.uk

Shelford Deli, Cambridgeshire
shelforddeli.co.uk

Slate Cheese, Suffolk
slatecheese.co.uk

Sparrows End Farm Shop & Deli, Essex
sparrowsendfarmshop.co.uk

The Goat Shed Farm Shop, Norfolk *fieldingcottage.co.uk/the-goat-shed-farm-shop*

The Gog Farm Shop, Cambridgeshire *thegog.com*

Walsingham Farms Shop, Norfolk *walsingham.co*

East and West Midlands

Bridge 67 Butchers, Leicestershire
bridge67.co.uk

Croots Farm Shop & Café, Derbyshire *croots.co.uk*

Dalton's Dairy Honesty Shop, Derbyshire *daltonsdairy.co.uk*

Farndon Fields Farm Shop, Leicestershire
farndonfields.co.uk

* Leicestershire Handmade Cheese Company, Sparkenhoe Farm, Upton, Warwickshire
leicestershirecheese.co.uk

* Lincolnshire Poacher Cheese, Ulceby Grange Farm, Lincolnshire
lincolnshirepoachercheese.com

Riverside Kitchen, Peak District *riversidekitchen.uk*

* Stichelton Dairy, Collingthwaite Farm, Nottinghamshire
stichelton.co.uk

The Cheese Society, Lincolnshire
thecheesesociety.co.uk

The Hartington Cheese Shop, Derbyshire
hartingtoncheeseshop.co.uk

Welbeck Farm Shop, Nottinghamshire
welbeckfarmshop.co.uk

Clockwise from top left: Head cheesemaker Joe Schneider outside the Stichelton Dairy on Collingthwaite Farm in the Welbeck Estate, proudly holding a wheel of the cheese he created.

Julie Cheyney is the cheesemaker of St Jude. Originally from a farming family, she works with Fen Farm to source her raw milk.

Chris Reade with Garth, one of her four sons. Chris and her husband Jeff came to the Isle of Mull in 1979 to keep cows to make cheese with their milk.

Robert outside the cheesemaking rooms at Glynhynod Farm with a two-year-old Teifi.

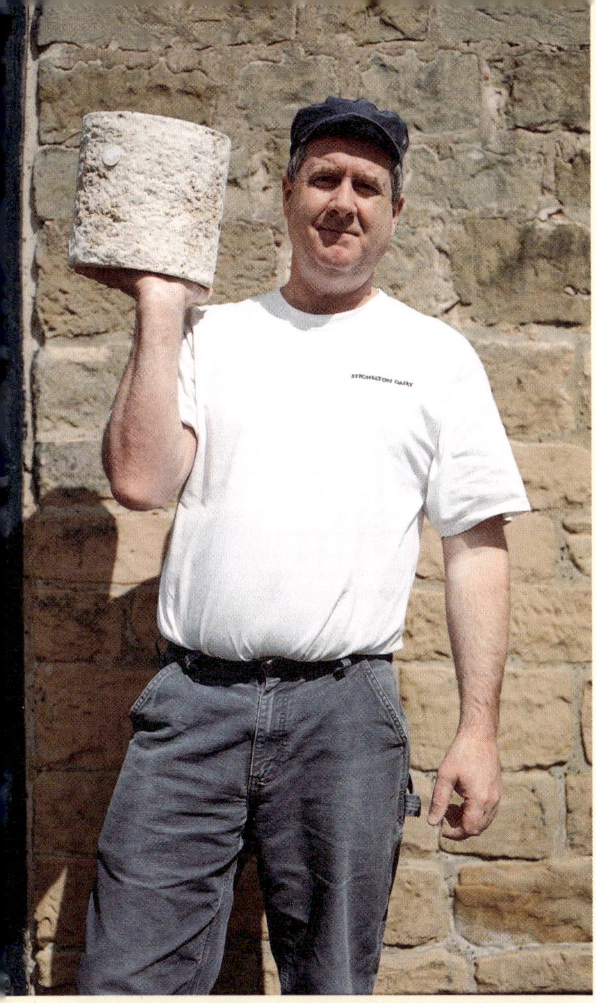
STICHELTON DAIRY

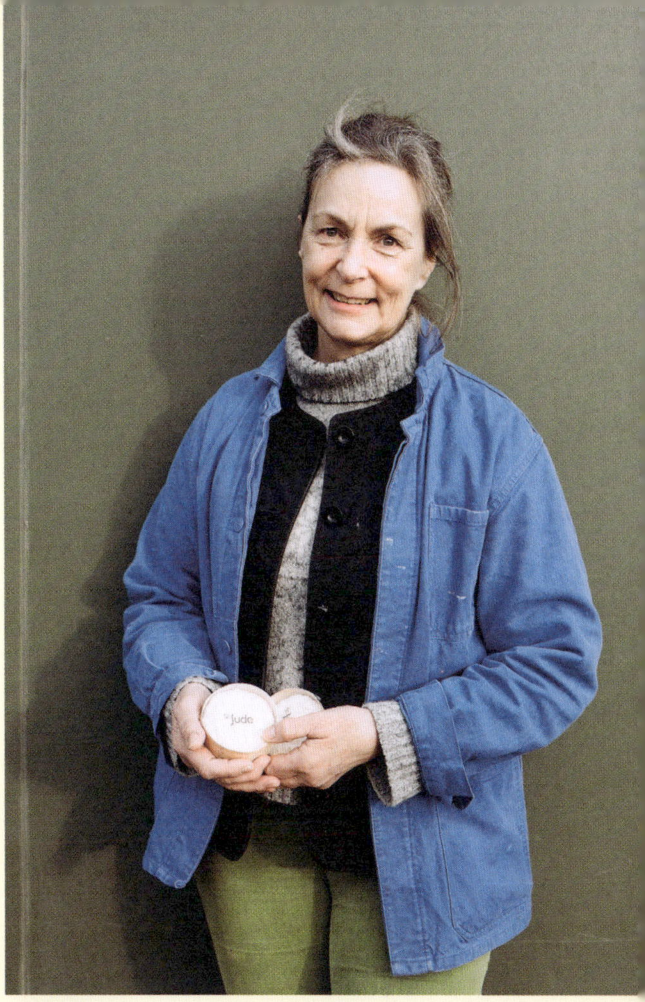
Jude

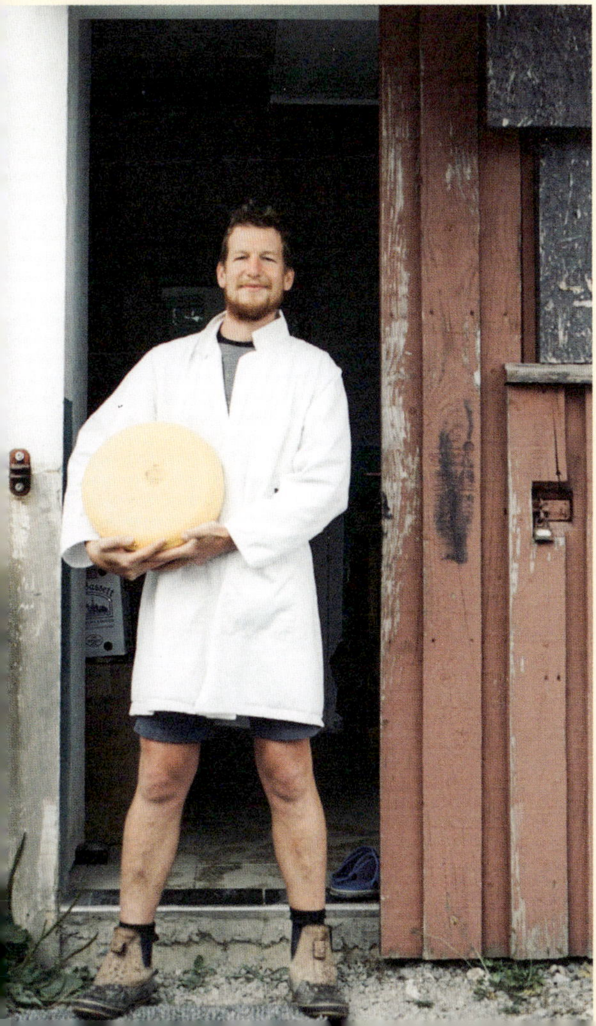

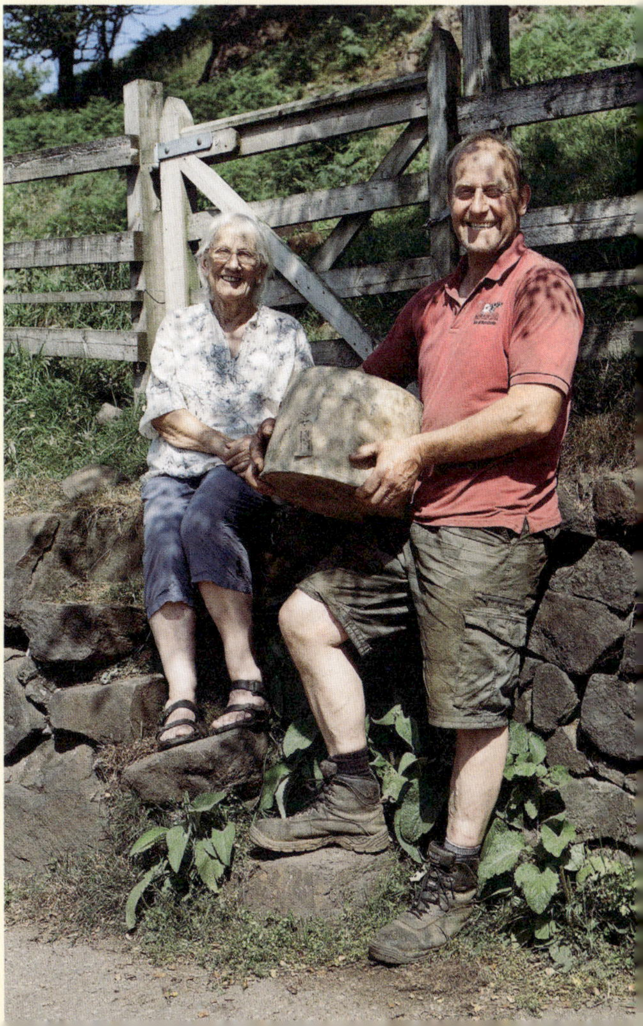

South East

Brogdale Farm, Kent
brogdalefarm.co.uk

Cowdray Farm Shop, West Sussex *cowdray.co.uk*

Crossroads Stores, Surrey
crossroadsstores.com

Eggs to Apples Farm Shop, East Sussex
eggstoapples.co.uk

Flint & Oak Farm Shop, Kent
flintandoak.shop

Macknade Food Hall, Kent
macknade.com

No2 Pound Street, Buckinghamshire
2poundstreet.com

Penbuckles Delicatessen, East Sussex
facebook.com/penbuckles

Plaw Hatch Farm, West Sussex
plawhatchfarm.co.uk

Rye Deli, East Sussex
ryedeli.co.uk

The Cheese Hut, East Sussex
thecheesehut.co.uk

The Cheese Shop, Kent
thecheeseshopcanterbury.co.uk

The Cheese Stall, Hampshire
thecheesestall.com

The Goods Shed Food Hall, Kent *thegoodsshed.co.uk*

*Village Maid Cheese, Berkshire
villagemaidcheese.co.uk

Wellington Farm Shop, Hampshire
wellingtonfarmshop.co.uk

London

Big Wheel Cheese, Hackney
bigwheelcheese.co.uk

Blackwoods Cheese Company, Borough Market
blackwoodscheesecompany.co.uk

Borough Market,
boroughmarket.org.uk

Buchanans Cheesemonger, Connaught Village
buchananscheesemonger.com

Cheddar Deli, Ealing
cheddardeli.co.uk

Funk, Columbia Road
thecheesebar.com/funk

Heritage Cheese, Dulwich Village
heritagecheese.uk

Jones of Brockley, Crofton Park and East Dulwich
jonesofbrockley.com

La Fromagerie, Bloomsbury, Highbury and Marylebone
lafromagerie.co.uk

Little Mouse, South Norwood
littlemousecheese.com

London Cheesemongers, Chelsea
londoncheesemongers.co.uk

Meat London Butcher & Delicatessen, Stoke Newington and Tufnell Park
meatlondon.co.uk

Mons Cheesemongers, Bermondsey, Borough Market, Brockley Market, East Dulwich
mons-cheese.co.uk

Neal's Yard Dairy, Borough Market, Covent Garden, Islington
nealsyarddairy.co.uk

Paxton & Whitfield, Cale Street and Jermyn Street
paxtonandwhitfield.co.uk

Pick & Cheese, Seven Dials
thecheesebar.com/seven-dials

Provisions Wine & Cheese, Holloway Road
provisionslondon.co.uk

The Cheese Bar, Camden
thecheesebar.com/camden

The Cheese Barge, Paddington
thecheesebar.com/paddington

The Cheeseboard, Greenwich
cheese-board.co.uk

The Ealing Grocer, Ealing
theealinggrocer.com

The Fine Cheese Co., Belgravia
finecheese.co.uk

The Teddington Cheese, Teddington
teddingtoncheese.co.uk

Wood Street Deli, Walthamstow
woodstreetdeli.co.uk

West England

*Berkswell Cheese, Ram Hall Farm, West Midlands
berkswell-cheese.myshopify.com

*Charles Martell & Son, Gloucestershire
charlesmartell.com

Daylesford Organic, Gloucestershire
daylesford.com

Denstone Hall Farm Shop & Café, Staffordshire
denstonehall.co.uk

Diddly Squat Farm Shop, Oxfordshire
diddlysquatfarmshop.com

Gloucester Services Farm Shop & Kitchen, Gloucestershire
gloucesterservices.com

*Hawkstone Abbey Farm, Shropshire
applebysdairy.com

WHERE TO BUY ARTISAN CHEESE

Hilltop Farm Shop & Cafe, Warwickshire *hilltopfarmshop.com*

Jericho Cheese Company, Oxfordshire *jerichocheese.co.uk*

Jolly Nice Farm Shop, Gloucestershire *jollynicefarmshop.com*

Jonathan Crump's Gloucester Cheeses, Gloucestershire *jonathancrumpsgloucestercheeses.co.uk*

*King Stone Dairy, Gloucestershire *kingstonedairy.com*

L'Affinage du Fromage, Gloucestershire *laffinage.co.uk*

Ludlow Farm Shop, Shropshire *ludlowfarmshop.co.uk*

*Moyden's Handmade Cheese, Shropshire *moydenscheese.co.uk*

*Nettlebed Creamery, Oxfordshire *nettlebedcreamery.com*

Paxton & Whitfield, Warwickshire *paxtonandwhitfield.co.uk*

The Cotswold Cheese Co., Oxfordshire, Gloucestershire *cotswoldcheese.com*

The Mousetrap Cheese Shop, Herefordshire *mousetrapcheese.co.uk*

Wells Farm Shop & Cafe, Oxfordshire *wellsfarmshop.com*

South West

Ben's Farm Shop, Devon *bensfarmshop.co.uk*

Bird & Carter, Wiltshire *birdandcarter.co.uk*

Brassica Mercantile, Dorset *brassicamercantile.co.uk*

Chelsea Road Deli, Somerset *facebook.com/Chelsearoaddeli8*

Country Cheeses, Devon *countrycheeses.co.uk*

Darts Farm, Devon *dartsfarm.co.uk*

Durslade Farm Shop, Somerset *dursladefarmshop.co.uk*

Fat Mouse Dairy, Devon *facebook.com/fatmousedairy*

Fee's Food, Cornwall *feesfood.co.uk*

Fowey Farm Shop, Cornwall *facebook.com/foweyfarmshop*

Gullivers Farm, Shop & Kitchen, Dorset *gulliversfarmshop.co.uk*

Hartley Farm, Wiltshire *hartley-farm.co.uk*

*Lynher Dairies, Cornwall *lynherdairies.co.uk*

Magdalen Cheese, Devon *magdalencheese.co.uk*

Paxton & Whitfield, Somerset *paxtonandwhitfield.co.uk*

Quicke's Cheese, Devon *quickes.co.uk*

Soulshine, Dorset *wearesoulshine.co.uk*

St Kew Farm Shop & Cafe, Cornwall *facebook.com/St-Kew-Farm-Shop-Cafe-1638076656244037*

The Bath Soft Cheese Company, Somerset *parkfarm.co.uk*

The Bristol Cheesemonger, Bristol *bristol-cheese.co.uk*

The Cheese Shed, Devon *thecheeseshed.com*

The Fine Cheese Co., Bath *finecheese.co.uk*

The Frome Independent, Somerset *thefromeindependent.org.uk*

*The Old Cheese Room, Neston Park Home Farm, Wiltshire *theoldcheeseroom.com*

The Truckle Truck, Dorset *thetruckletruck.com*

*Ticklemore Cheese Dairy, Devon *ticklemorecheesedairy.wordpress.com*

*Trethowan Brothers, Somerset *trethowanbrothers.com*

Two Belly, Bristol *twobelly.co.uk*

*Westcombe Dairy, Somerset *westcombedairy.com*

North West

Albion Farm Shop & Cafe, Greater Manchester *albionfarmshop.co.uk*

Aldred's Fine Cheese, North Yorkshire *aldredsfinecheese.co.uk*

Chopping Block Penrith, Cumbria *thechoppingblockpenrith.com*

Chorlton Cheesemongers, Greater Manchester, *chorltoncheesemongers.co.uk*

George & Joseph Cheesemongers, West Yorkshire *georgeandjoseph.co.uk*

Hill Farm Real Food, Cheshire *hillfarmrealfood.co.uk*

Isca Wines, Levenshulme, Manchester *iscawines.com*

Keelham Farm Shop, North Yorkshire *keelhamfarmshop.co.uk*

*Kirkham's Lancashire, Lancashire
mrskirkhamscheese.co.uk

Littlewoods Butchers, Greater Manchester
littlewoodsbutchers.co.uk

*St James Cheese, Holker Farm, Cumbria
stjamescheese.co.uk

*Stonebeck Cheese, Low Riggs, North Yorkshire
stonebeckcheese.co.uk

Tebay Services Farm Shop & Kitchen, Cumbria
tebayservices.com

The Cheese Hamlet, Greater Manchester
thecheesehamlet.co.uk

The Cheese Shop, Chester, Cheshire
chestercheeseshop.co.uk

The Cheese Wheel, Merseyside
facebook.com/cheesewheelliverpool

The Courtyard Dairy, North Yorkshire
thecourtyarddairy.co.uk

The Deli at 40A, Merseyside
facebook.com/thedeliat40a

The New Market Dairy, Greater Manchester
newmarketdairy.com

Thornby Moor Dairy, Cumbria
thornbymoordairy.co.uk

Town End Farm Shop, North Yorkshire
townendfarmshop.co.uk

Winter Tarn, Cumbria
wintertarndairy.com

*Yorkshire Dama Cheese, West Yorkshire
yorkshiredamacheese.co.uk

*Yorkshire Pecorino, West Yorkshire
yorkshirepecorino.co.uk

North East

Broom House Farm Shop, Durham
broomhousedurham.co.uk

Blacks Corner, South Tyneside
blackscorner.co.uk

*Doddington Cheese, North Doddington Farm, Wooler, Northumberland
doddingtoncheese.co.uk

Grate Newcastle, Newcastle
gratenewcastle.co.uk

Minskip Farm Shop, York
minskipfarmshop.com

Wales

Caffi Moelyci, Gwynedd
moelyci.org

Canna Deli, Cardiff
cannadeli.co.uk

Caws Cenarth Cheese, Carmarthenshire
cawscenarth.co.uk

*Caws Teifi, Ceredigion
teificheese.co.uk

*Cosyn Cymru, Gwynedd
cosyn.cymru

FarmCo, Swansea
farmco.wales

Fauvette, Glamorgan
fauvette.co.uk

Forage Farm Shop & Kitchen, Vale of Glamorgan
foragefarmshop.co.uk

Happy Planet Green Store, Ceredigion and Pembrokeshire
happyplanetgreenstore.co.uk

Hawarden Estate Farm Shop, Flintshire hawardenestate.co.uk

*Holden Farm Dairy, Ceredigion
holdenfarmdairy.co.uk

Hooton's Farm Shop, Anglesey and Gwynedd
hootonshomegrown.co.uk

Pant Mawr Farmhouse Cheeses, Pembrokeshire
pantmawrcheeses.co.uk

Porter's Delicatessen, Denbighshire portersdeli.co.uk

The Cheese Room Conwy, Conwy facebook.com/cheeseroomconwy

The Grate Cheese Deli, Conwy
thegratecheesedeli.co.uk

The Little Cheesemonger, Denbighshire
thelittlecheesemonger.co.uk

Tŷ Caws, Markets (Pontcanna, Rhiwbina, Roath, Riverside), Cardiff tycaws.com

Scotland

Ardross Farm & Farm Shop, Fife ardrossfarm.co.uk

Arran Cheese Shop, Isle of Arran
arrancheeseshop.co.uk

Balgove Larder, Fife balgove.com

Ballintaggart, Perthshire
ballintaggart.com

Cairn Lodge Farm Shop & Kitchen, Lanarkshire
cairnlodgeservices.com

Cambus O'May Cheese & Milk Hoose Café, Aberdeenshire
cambusomay.com

Connage Highland Dairy and Cheese Pantry, Inverness
connage.co.uk

Craigies Farm Shop & Café, Edinburgh craigies.co.uk

*Errington Cheese, South Lanarkshire erringtoncheese.com

Finzean Farm Shop, Aberdeenshire finzean.com

Forest Farm, Aberdeenshire
forestfarmdairy.co.uk

George Mewes Cheese, Edinburgh and Glasgow
georgemewescheese.co.uk

Gourmet Cheese Co., Aberdeenshire
gourmetcheeseco.com

I. J. Mellis, Glasgow, Edinburgh and Fife
mellischeese.net

*Isle of Mull Cheese, Isle of Mull
sgriobruadh.co.uk

JK Fine Foods, Aberdeenshire
facebook.com/jkfinefoods

Kirkness & Gorie, Orkney
kirknessandgorie.com

Nature's Larder, Aberdeenshire
natureslarderaberdeen.co.uk

Park Shop, Aberdeenshire
facebook.com/parkshopdrum

Rosemount Market, Aberdeenshire
facebook.com/rosemountmarket

Starter Culture, Glasgow,
wearestarterculture.com

The Cheese Lady, East Lothian
thecheeselady.co.uk

The Cheesery, Dundee
thecheesery.co.uk

The Mainstreet Trading Company Deli, Roxburghshire
mainstreetbooks.co.uk

Northern Ireland & Ireland

Broughgammon Farm, County Antrim
broughgammon.com

Indie Fude, Belfast and County Down
indiefude.com

*Mike's Fancy Cheese, Belfast
mfcheese.com

Sheridans Cheesemongers, Cork, Dublin, Galway, Meath, Limerick, Kerry, Kildare, Waterford
sheridanscheesemongers.com

Online

The Cheese Geek
thecheesegeek.com

The Crafty Cheeseman
facebook.com/thecraftycheeseman

Pipers Farm, *pipersfarm.com*

Farmers and producers

There are some brilliant databases that you can use to source farmers and producers that work to the highest levels of food, farming and environmental standards and resources to learn more about what's happening in the food and farming industries. Here are just a handful of databases and organisations that will point you in the right direction:

Agricology (*agricology.co.uk*)
Biodynamic Association (*biodynamic.org.uk*)
Biodynamic Land Trust (*biodynamiclandtrust.org.uk*)
Compassion in World Farming (*ciwf.org.uk*)
Eating Better (*eating-better.org*)
FarmED (*farm-ed.co.uk*)
Farmerama Radio (*farmerama.co*)
Farms Not Factories (*farmsnotfactories.org*)
Farms to Feed Us (*farmstofeedus.org*)
Food Ethics Council (*foodethicscouncil.org*)
Food, Farming & Countryside Commission (*thersa.org*)
Friends of the Earth (*friendsoftheearth.uk*)
LEAF (*leaf.eco*)
Nature Friendly Farming Network (*nffn.org.uk*)
Organic Research Centre (*organicresearchcentre.com*)
Our Isles (*ourisles.co.uk*)
Pasture-Fed Livestock Association (*pastureforlife.org*)
Real Farming Trust (*feanetwork.org*)
Soil Association (*soilassociation.org*)
Sustain (*sustainweb.org*)
Sustainable Food Trust (*sustainablefoodtrust.org*)
Sustainable Soils Alliance (*sustainablesoils.org*)
The Farming and Wildlife Advisory Group (*fwag.org.uk*)
The Landworkers' Alliance (*landworkersalliance.org.uk*)

There are also annual events like Groundswell (*groundswellag.com*), the Oxford Real Farming Conference (*orfc.org.uk*) and the Northern Real Farming Conference (*northernrealfarming.org*) and the Cheese festival organised by Slow Food (*slowfood.com*).

There are also plenty of awards to keep your eye on throughout the year. Ones to look out for include: the Guild of Fine Food's (*gff.co.uk*) World Cheese Awards that judges nearly 4,000 cheeses from more than 40 countries, The International Cheese & Dairy Awards (*internationalcheeseawards.co.uk*) and The British Cheese Awards (*britishcheeseawards.com*).

If you are interested in how we can define or regulate what 'sustainability' really means, the Sustainable Food Trust are trying with their new Global Farm Metric (GFM), a global framework for measuring sustainability. Developed by farmers, experts and stakeholders in the food and farming world, the GFM measures the social, economic and environmental impacts in food and farming systems. The GFM will be useful for governments to deliver public goods, food companies to help with their transparency in the supply chain, and the financial sector to inform more sustainable investments.

The Specialist Cheesemakers Association (SCA) was established to encourage excellence in cheesemaking and it is a great place to search for cheesemakers, retailers, wholesalers and others involved with artisan cheese. Anyone interested in cheese can join and support the SCA, and by doing so, receive quarterly newsletters, invitations to events, seminars and offers. (*specialistcheesemakers.co.uk*)

References

BOOKS

Gabe Brown, *Dirt to Soil: One Family's Journey into Regenerative Agriculture* (Chelsea, VT, and London: Chelsea Green Publishing, 2018)

Kit Calvert, *Kit Calvert of Wensleydale, The Complete Dalesman* (Skipton: Dalesman Publishing, 1981)

Giana and Clovisse Ferguson, *Gubbeen, The Story of a Working Farm* (London: Kyle Books, 2014)

Marie Hartley and Joan Ingilby, *Making Cheese and Butter* (Skipton: Dalesman Publishing, 1997)

W. G. Hoskins, *The Making of the English Landscape* (Beaminster: Little Toller Books, 2013)

Steven Lamb, *Cheese and Dairy: River Cottage Handbook No.16* (London: Bloomsbury Publishing, 2018)

Richard Mabey, *Food for Free* (London: Collins, 1972)

William Marshall, *The Rural Economy of Gloucestershire* (London: G. Nicol, 1796)

A. T. R. Mattick, *The Handling of Milk and Milk Products* (London: His Majesty's Stationery Office, 1937)

Ned Palmer, *A Cheesemonger's History* (London: Profile Books, 2019)

'Ministry of Agriculture and Fisheries, Farm and Factory Cheese-making' (London: His Majesty's Stationery Office, 1938)

Bronwen and Francis Percival, *Reinventing the Wheel: Milk, Microbes and the Fight for Real Cheese* (London: Bloomsbury, 2017; quotation taken from page 135)

Patrick Rance, *The French Cheese Book* (London: Macmillan, 1989)

Patrick Rance, *The Great British Cheese Book*, new edition (London: Macmillan, 1988; quotations taken from pages 24, 53 and 17)

Dora G. Saker, *Practical Cheddar Cheese-making* (Harpenden: D. G. Saker, 1917)

WEBSITES

Cheshire Basin, salt beds: *lionsaltworks. westcheshiremuseums.co.uk/whatissalt/*

Geographical indications: *ec.europa.eu/info/food farming-fisheries/food-safety-and-quality/certification/ quality-labels/quality-schemes-explained_en*

New post-Brexit geographical indications: *worldtrademarkreview.com/brand-management/ close-look-the-united-kingdoms-post-brexit-gi-regime*

Pastures for profit: *nrcs.usda.gov/Internet/FSE_ DOCUMENTS/stelprdb1097378.pdf*

Tufts University research on the microbiome: C. M. Cosetta, N. Kfoury, A. Robbat and B. E. Wolfe, 'Fungal volatiles mediate cheese rind microbiome assembly', Environmental Microbiology, 9 September 2020 (*now.tufts.edu/news-releases/those-funky-cheese-smells-allow-microbes-talk-and-feed-each-other*)

If you wish to learn more about artisan cheese, the Academy of Cheese offers a series of fantastic courses and certifications; Level One, Level Two, Level Three, and even a 'Master of Cheese' certification for those cheese aficionados. Each level includes plenty of learning, talking, and of course, smelling and tasting cheese, taught by some of the industry's best cheese experts in the business. (*academyofcheese.org*)

Index

A
Alsous, Razan 13, 206–11
Appleby family 24, 33, 36, 54–61
Appleby's Cheshire 18, 46, 54–61
apples: candied apple 169
  Hattan family chutney 183
  spiced apple and custard cake 160–3

B
bacon: Berkswell and streaky bacon straws 75
baked Rollright 136
bara brith 216
Baron Bigod 40, 44, 49, 62–9
beef: Harbourne Blue burgers 101
  meatballs in tomato sauce 195–6
Beesley Farm 108–13
Berkswell 49, 70–5
biodiversity 30–1, 34–5
bread: Kirkham's Lancashire loaf 113
  sourdough loaf 59–61
Brefu Bach 13, 36, 212–17
broccoli with creamy Gorwydd Caerphilly 94
buffalo milk 14
burgers, Harbourne Blue 101

C
Caerphilly 47, 90–5
Cairns, Selina and Andrew 235–41
cake, spiced apple and custard 160–3
Calver, Tom 185–8
Campbell, Dougal 13, 24, 121
cauliflower cheese 130
Caws Teifi Cheese 221–7
Celtic Promise 46, 49, 220–7
cheesecake 188
cheesemaking 15, 26, 33–47
Cheshire cheese 18, 20, 23, 54–61
Cheyney, Julie 66, 145–8
chicory, walnut and Young Buck salad 253
chutney, Hattan family 183
Clarke family 150–5, 249–51
Congdon, Robin 24, 97
Connolly, Ruth 76, 80
Cornish Yarg 46, 76–81
Cosyn Cymru 213–14
courgette, Elrick Log and wild garlic fritters 239–40
Courtyard Dairy 43, 49, 181, 249
couscous tabbouleh 211
cows 14
Crickmore, Jonny 63–6
Crump, Jonathan and Annabelle 156–60
curds 36–7

D
Doddington 82–9

E
Elrick Log 234–41
Errington Cheese 24, 235–41

F
farming 26–33
Fen Farm 44, 63–5, 145–8
fish pie 86–9
Fletcher family 70–5
food provenance 16–19
fritters: courgette, Elrick Log and wild garlic 239–40

G
Gadles Farm 76, 77–9
GI designations 18
goats' milk 14
Gorwydd Caerphilly 47, 90–5
Gott, Martin 25, 36, 139–43, 249
Grimond, Rose 193–5

H
Hafod 28, 31, 46, 228–32
Harbourne Blue 96–101
Harris, Ben 97, 99, 101
Hattan, Sally and Andrew 14, 178–83
Hawkstone Abbey Farm 18, 33, 54–8, 201
Hay, Julie 73
Heathcoat Amory, Patrick 193–5
Heckfield Home Farm 127–9
herbal leys 28–30
history of British cheese 20–5
Hodgson, Randolph 24–5
Holbrook, Mary 24, 25, 103, 143
Holden, Patrick and Becky 19, 28, 30, 31, 228–32
Holden Farm Dairy 28, 30, 31, 228–32
Holker Farm 25, 36, 47, 139–43
Hosken, Jonathan 76, 77–9
Howard, Robert 37
Hunts Court 173–4, 176

I
ice cream, Stichelton 169
Isle of Mull 49, 242–7

J
Jersey Curd 102–7
Jones, Simon and Tim 13, 121–5
Jowett, David 25, 44, 132–6, 249

K
King Stone Dairy 25, 37, 46, 132–6, 249
Kirkham's Lancashire 13, 108–13

L
Leeds Blue 115–19
leek and Shropshire Blue pasties 155
Lincolnshire Poacher 13, 42, 120–5
Low Riggs Farm 178–83
Lynher Dairies 37, 76, 77–80

M
macaroni cheese 246
Maida Vale 46, 49, 126–31
Martell, Charles 24, 46, 172–6
maturation 42–4
Maxwell family 83–6
Mead, Catherine 76, 77, 80
meatballs in tomato sauce 195–6
microbiome 40, 42
Mike's Fancy Cheese 248–53
milk 26–8, 35, 40
mould-ripened cheeses 44

Moyden's Handmade Cheese 44, 199–205
mushrooms, stuffed portobello 80

N
natural-rind cheeses 46
Neal's Yard Dairy 24, 40, 43, 181
Neston Park Home Farm 25, 102–6
Nettlebed Creamery 191–5
Niazy, Karim 102–6
North Doddington Farm 82–9
Norton, Fraser 36

O
Old Cheese Room 25, 103–5
Olianas, Mario 13, 115–18
ovens 51

P
pancakes with Jersey Curd 106
pasties, leek and Shropshire Blue 155
Pasture-Fed Livestock Association 30, 51, 196
Paxton & Whitfield 24
peppers, stuffed 225
Percival, Bronwen 40, 43, 181
pesto, wild garlic 202
Poireau 176
potatoes: fish pie 86–9
    potato pie 66
Puxton Court Farm 90–1, 94

Q
quiche, roasted vegetable 232

R
Ram Hall Farm 70–5
Rance, Patrick 23–4
raw milk 24
Reade family 243–6
regenerative agriculture 28–30
rennet 36
Rennet & Rind 43
Ricotta, Westcombe 186, 188
Rimes, Carrie 13, 213–16
rinds, edible 49
risotto, mantecatura 118
Robinson, Nicola 139–43
Rollright 25, 44, 46, 132–7
rotational grazing 29, 30

S
St James 47, 138–43, 249
St Jude 49, 66, 144–9
Sandouk, Raghid 206–11
sandwich, toasted Cheshire cheese 59–61
Savage-Onstwedder family 221–7
Schneider, Joe 44, 47, 165, 249
Sedli, Julianna 13, 25, 102–6
sheep's milk 14
Shropshire Blue 150–5
Single Gloucester 156–63
soufflé, Lincolnshire Poacher 125
sourdough loaf 59–61
spaghetti, wild garlic pesto 202
Sparkenhoe Farm 150–5, 251
Specialist Cheesemakers' Association 25
Standish Park Farm 156–60
starter cultures 35–6
Stichelton 36–7, 42, 44, 47, 164–71, 249
Stinking Bishop 46, 172–7
Stonebeck 14, 178–83
storing cheese 49
straws, Berkswell and streaky bacon 75
Swinscoe, Andy 43, 49, 181, 249, 251

T
tabbouleh, couscous 211
tasting the cheese 46–7
tea bread: bara brith 216
Thomson, Mike 42, 248–53
Ticklemore Cheese Dairy 97–101
tomatoes: meatballs in tomato sauce 195–6
    roasted tomatoes 148
Trethowan Brothers 35–6, 40, 46, 47, 90–4

U
Ulceby Grange Farm 121–5

V
Village Maid Cheese 127–30

W
Wakeman, Perry 43
washed-rind cheeses 44–6

Westcombe Dairy 30, 37, 42, 46, 49, 184–9
Westhead, Charlie 43
whey 36–7
Wigmore, Anne and Jake 126–30
Witheridge 190–7
Wrekin White 198–205

Y
Yarrow, Rachel 36
Yorkshire Dama Cheese 207–11
Yorkshire Pecorino 115–18
Yorkshire Squeaky 206–11
Young Buck 42, 44, 248–53

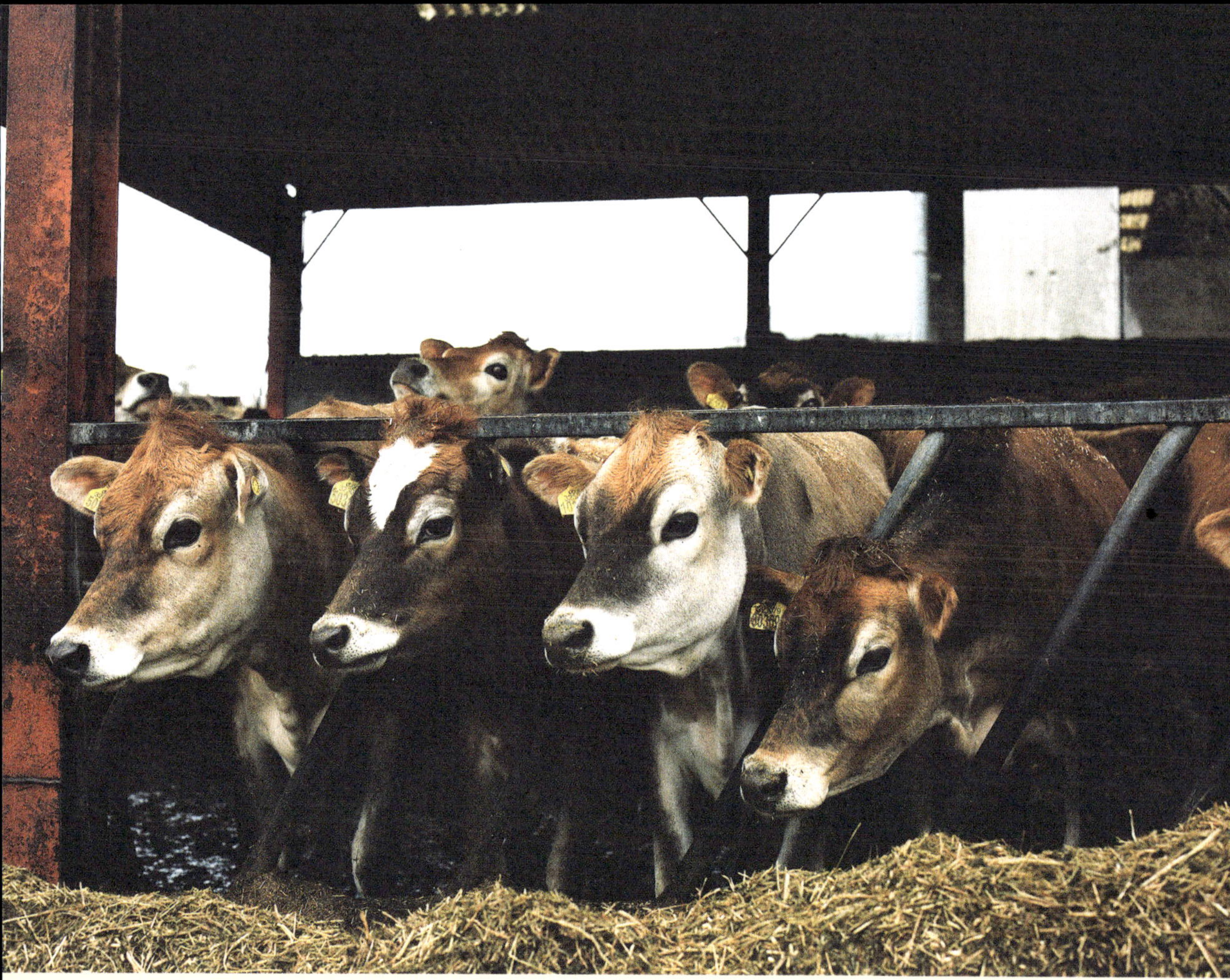

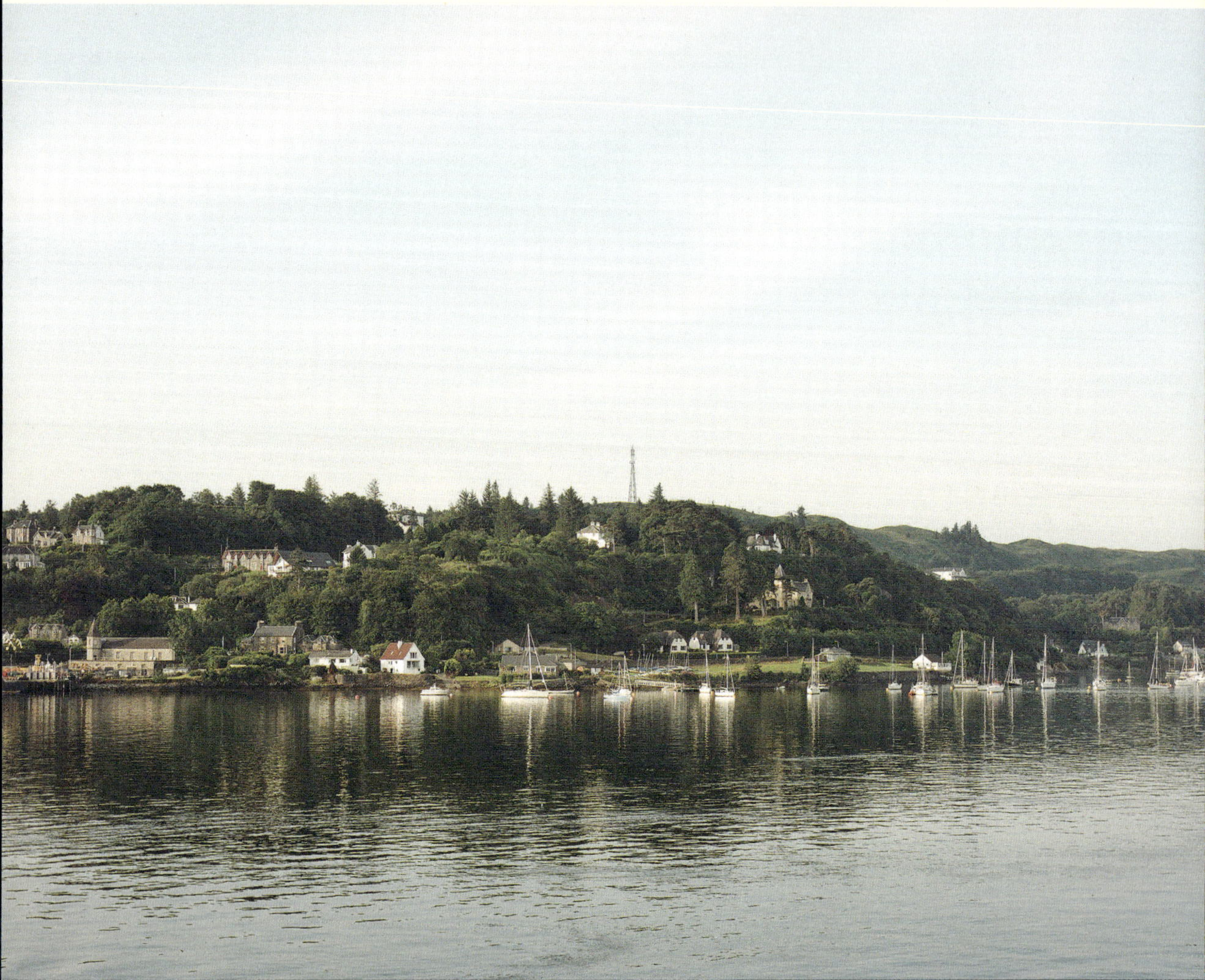

Acknowledgements

First of all, I'd like to thank a thousand times the cheesemakers and associated rural food and farming folk who have been involved with this book. This book wouldn't have happened if it weren't for your incredible hospitality and generosity in giving up your valuable time to invite me into your homes, farms, cheesemongers and dairies to capture your photos and try your wonderful cheeses – I think I have gained several stone since meeting all of you, which I'm not going to thank you for!

A belated apology to many of you who had to put up with my questions and nagging phone calls. A special thanks goes to Bronwen Percival and Patrick Holden, both figureheads of the dairy and farming industries respectively – two people I happily call my friends. The whole concept of making cheese is rather tricky, so I am unbelievably grateful to have Bronwen as a guiding star, reading my initial introduction and giving me expert advice. The same goes to Patrick. Over the last year, I have called him numerous times, most often when he was in his tractor or just before he was tucking into his supper! Our phone calls were frequently filled with laughter thanks to Patrick's mischievous sense of humour, and the chance to pick his enormous brain was thoroughly appreciated and always fascinating.

And thank you to David Lockwood from Neal's Yard Dairy, who is always encouraging and appreciating the finer detail in all things.

Top: Jersey cows munching at Neston Park Farm.
Bottom: A beautiful view of Oban in the sunshine.

An unfathomable thank you goes to my darling family for supporting me through the process of creating this book. A special thanks goes to Serena, my mother, and Lilly, my partner – and the illustrator of this book – who both, on several occasions, came with me all over the British Isles to meet cheesemakers. Thank you for your invaluable help and patience. I enjoyed every minute – I hope the consistent payment in cheese parcels was enough to suffice for the hours of waiting for me to finish.

A massive thanks goes to Quadrille and to their incredible team. Thank you to Sarah Lavelle who saw the potential in this book. Sarah contacted me in deepest darkest lockdown and her offer to publish this book could not have come at a better time. She gave me the opportunity to write a book on something I am truly passionate about so I cannot thank her enough. Thank you to Stacey Cleworth, Alicia House, Claire Rochford and Sofie Shearman for overseeing and designing such a fabulous book and being so patient with me bombarding them with thousands of words and photographs from every direction during the last year or so. Thank you to Kate Parker who copyedited the book. Kate was terrifically patient and accepting of my constant changes here and there, so, thank you!

And last, but in no way least, are my wonderful friends who have let me stay for long weekends or even weekly stays at their houses and flats during the couple of years making this book; Jude in the beautiful Yorkshire Dales, Ollie and Zoë in the South West of England, Cathy and Catherine in Cornwall, James and Alice in Anglesey, just to name a few places. Thank you to all of you!

Left: Pasture glowing in the summer sunshine.
Right: Cheese maturing to perfection at Neal's Yard Dairy.

Managing Director Sarah Lavelle
Commissioning Editor Stacey Cleworth
Copy Editor Kate Parker
Assistant Editor Sofie Shearman
Proofreader Susan Low
Designer Alicia House
Photographer Angus D. Birditt
Illustrator Lilly Hedley
Head of Production Stephen Lang
Production Controller Sabeena Atchia

Published in 2022 by Quadrille,
an imprint of Hardie Grant Publishing

Quadrille
52–54 Southwark Street
London SE1 1UN
quadrille.com

Reprinted in 2022
10 9 8 7 6 5 4 3 2

All rights reserved. No part of this publication may be reproduced, stored in a retrieval system or transmitted in any form by any means, electronic, mechanical, photocopying, recording or otherwise, without the prior written permission of the publishers and copyright holders. The moral rights of the author have been asserted.

Cataloguing in Publication Data: a catalogue record for this book is available from the British Library.

Text © Angus D. Birditt 2022
Design © Quadrille 2022
Illustrations © Lilly Hedley 2022
Photography © Angus D. Birditt 2022

ISBN 978 1 78713 798 1

Printed in China

Westcombe Cheddar

Elrick Log

Yorkshire Squeaky

Brefu Bach

Young Buck

St James

Berkswell

Cornish Yarg

Lincolnshire Poacher

Isle of Mull Cheddar

Gorwydd Caerphilly

Stonebeck

Single Gloucester

Harbourne Blue

Wrekin White

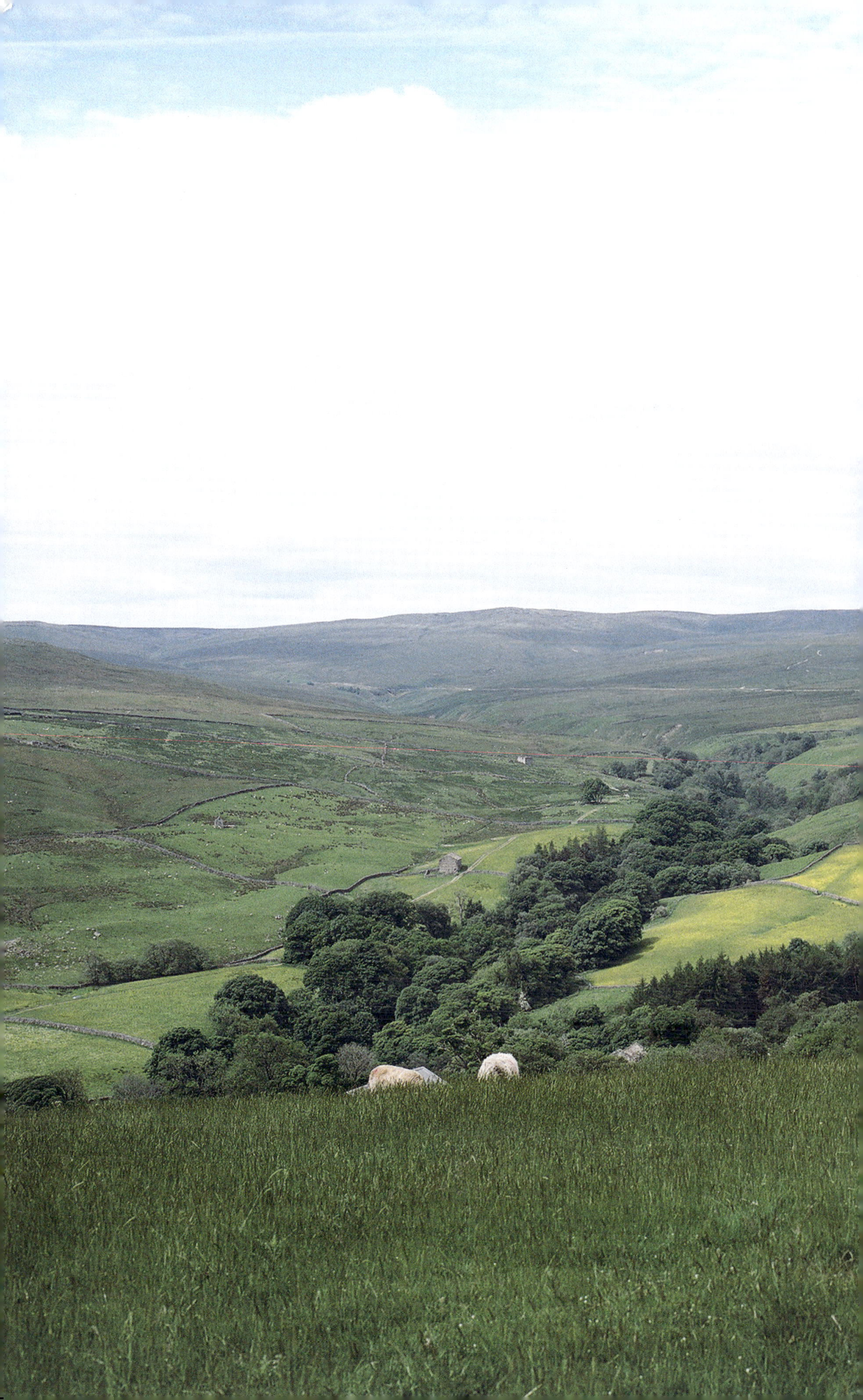